CliffsTestPrep™

ACT™

6th Edition

by

Jerry Bobrow, Ph.D.

William A. Covino, Ph.D.

David A. Kay, M.S.

Harold Nathan, Ph.D.

Contributing Authors

Allan Casson, Ph.D.

Jean Eggenschwiler, M.A.

Karen Saenz, Ph.D.

Consultants

Peter Z Orton, Ph.D.

Don Gallaher, M.S.

Dale W. Johnson, M.A.

Wiley Publishing, Inc.

About the Author

Dr. Jerry Bobrow, Ph.D., is a national authority in the field of test preparation. As executive director of Bobrow Test Preparation Services, he has been administering the test preparation programs at over 25 California institutions for the past 27 years. Dr. Bobrow has authored over 30 national best-selling test preparation books, and his books and programs have assisted over two million test-takers. Each year, Dr. Bobrow personally lectures to thousands of students on preparing for graduate, college, and teacher credentialing exams.

Publisher's Acknowledgments

Editorial

Project Editor: Kathleen A. Dobie

Acquisition Editor: Gregory W. Tubach

Copy Editor: Corey Dalton

Technical Editor: Michele Spence

Editorial Assistants: Melissa Bluhm, Laura Jefferson, Carol Strickland

Production

Proofreader: Vickie Broyles, Christine Pingleton

Wiley Publishing, Inc. Indianapolis Composition Services

CliffsTestPrep™ ACT™ 6th Edition

Published by:
Wiley Publishing, Inc.
909 Third Avenue
New York, NY 10022
www.wiley.com

Published by Wiley Publishing, Inc., New York, NY
Published simultaneously in Canada

Library of Congress Control Number: 00-102514

ISBN: 0-7645-8613-0

Printed in the United States of America

10 9 8 7 6 5 4 3 2

6X/QR/QW/QS/IN

For general information on our other products and services or to obtain technical support, please contact our Customer Care Department within the U.S. at 800-762-2974, outside the U.S. at 317-572-3993, or fax 317-572-4002.

Wiley also published its books in a variety of electronic formats. Some content that appears in print may not be available in electronic books.

Author's Acknowledgments

I would like to thank Michele Spence and Linnea Fredrickson, for their many hours of editing the original manuscript, and Christy Beck, of Wiley, for her assistance and careful attention to the production process. I would also like to thank my office staff of Joy Mondragon, Cindy Hadash, Allison Drucker, and Deena Mondragon for their assistance. Finally, I would like to thank my wife, Susan; daughter, Jennifer (22); and sons, Adam (19) and Jonathan (15), for their patience, moral support, and comic relief.

Table of Contents

PART II: FOUR FULL-LENGTH PRACTICE TESTS

Preface

Your ACT Assessment Program: ACT Tests, Interest Inventory, and Student Profile are important to your future! They can help you (1) assess your interests and skills, (2) plan your career, (3) get a scholarship, and (4) get into a college of your choice. Because of this, you must use your study time effectively. You need the most comprehensive test preparation guide that you can realistically complete in a reasonable time. It must be concise, direct, easy to use, and thorough, giving you all the assistance you need to do your best on the ACT Tests.

In keeping with the fine tradition of CliffsNotes, this guide was developed by leading experts in the field of test preparation as part of a series to specifically meet these standards. The testing strategies, techniques, and materials have been researched, tested, and evaluated and are presently used at test preparation programs at many leading colleges and universities. This guide emphasizes the *Bobrow Test Preparation Services* approach, which focuses on the six major areas:

- Ability Tested
- Basic Skills Necessary
- Understanding Directions
- Analysis of Directions
- Suggested Approaches with Samples
- Practice-Review-Analyze-Practice

Four complete simulation ACT exams are included with answers and in-depth explanations. Each exam is followed by analysis charts to help you analyze your results and evaluate your strengths and weaknesses.

This guide was written to give you the edge in doing your best by maximizing your effort in a reasonable amount of time. It is meant to augment, not substitute for, formal or informal learning throughout junior high and high school. If you follow the Study Guide Checklist in this book and study regularly, you will get the best preparation possible.

Study Guide Checklist

❑ 1. Read the ACT Information Bulletin.

❑ 2. Become familiar with the Test Format, page 1.

❑ 3. Familiarize yourself with the answers to Questions Commonly Asked about the ACT, page 2.

❑ 4. Learn the techniques of Four Successful Overall Approaches, page 4.

❑ 5. Carefully read Part I, Analysis of Exam Areas, beginning on page 9.

❑ 6. Strictly observing time allotments, take Practice Test 1, section by section, beginning on page 71.

❑ 7. Check your answers, page 119, and analyze your Practice Test 1 results, page 119.

❑ 8. Fill out the Tally Sheet for Problems Missed, page 123.

❑ 9. While referring to each item of Practice Test 1, study ALL the Answers and Explanations that begin on page 125.

❑ 10. Review as necessary basic skills and techniques discussed in Part I.

❑ 11. Strictly observing time allotments, take Practice Test 2, section by section, beginning on page 157.

❑ 12. Check your answers, page 205, and analyze your Practice Test 2 results, page 208.

❑ 13. Fill out the Tally Sheet for Problems Missed, page 209.

❑ 14. While referring to each item of Practice Test 2, study ALL the Answers and Explanations that begin on page 211.

❑ 15. Strictly observing time allotments, take Practice Test 3, section by section, beginning on page 241.

❑ 16. Check your answers, page 305, and analyze your Practice Test 3 results, page 308.

❑ 17. Fill out the Tally Sheet for Problems Missed, page 309.

❑ 18. While referring to each item of Practice Test 3, study ALL the Answers and Explanations that begin on page 311.

❑ 19. Strictly observing time allotments, take Practice Test 4, section by section, beginning on page 345.

❑ 20. Check your answers, page 403, and analyze your Practice Test 4 results, page 406.

❑ 21. Fill out the Tally Sheet for Problems Missed, page 407.

❑ 22. While referring to each item of Practice Test 4, study ALL the Answers and Explanations that begin on page 409.

❑ 23. Again, review as needed Part I, Analysis of Exam Areas.

❑ 24. Carefully Read "Final Preparation" on page 435.

Using a Calculator on the Mathematics Test

The ACT now allows the use of calculators on the Mathematics Test only. Even though no question will require the use of a calculator, in some instances using one will save you valuable time. If you regularly use a calculator, you may feel more comfortable using one on the test.

If you decide to use a calculator, you should

- Bring your own, because you can't borrow or share one.

- Make sure you are familiar with the use of your calculator.

- Make sure it has new, fresh batteries and is in good working order.

- Bring extra batteries or a spare in case your primary calculator fails.

- Practice using it on sample problems to see when and where it will be helpful.

- Check for a shortcut to any problem that seems to involve much computation. If there appears to be too much computation or the problem seems impossible without a calculator, you're probably doing something wrong.

- Quickly and carefully check the numbers you key in on the display to make sure they're the right numbers.

- Set up the problem and/or steps on paper. Write down the numbers as you perform each step on your calculator. (It is generally safer not to use the memory function on your calculator.)

- Be sure to clear it before beginning a new calculation.

- Keep in mind that a calculator will not solve a problem for you by itself; you must understand the problem first.

Be careful that you

- Don't rush out and buy a sophisticated calculator.

- Don't bring a calculator that you're unfamiliar with.

- Don't bring a pocket organizer, handheld minicomputer, laptop computer, electronic writing pad, pen-input device, or a calculator with a typewriter-type keypad or paper tape.

- Don't bring a calculator that requires an outlet or any other external power source.

- Don't bring a calculator with wireless communication capability.

- Don't bring a calculator that makes noise.

- Don't use your calculator's memory to store test materials.

Format of the ACT		
Englist Test	45 minutes	75 questions
Mathematics Test	60 minutes	60 questions
Reading Test	35 minutes	40 questions
Science Reasoning Test	35 minutes	40 questions
Total Testing Time	175 minutes (or 2 hours, 55 minutes)	215 questions

General Description

The Act Assessment Program helps you make important decisions about your future. It does so in many ways. First, the ACT Interest Inventory and the ACT Student Profile section collect information about your past experiences, your interests, and your goals. You'll fill out these sections when you register for the ACT Assessment.

The ACT Assessment is the second phase of the program; it's a battery of tests that you take at an ACT test center on a designated national test date. The tests cover four subject areas: English, mathematics, reading, and science reasoning.

These four tests generate twelve scaled scores—four test scores, a composite score, and seven subscores:

English Score 1-36

Subscores

> Usage/mechanics 1-18
>
> Rhetorical skills 1-18

Mathematics Score 1-36

Subscores

> Pre-algebra/elementary algebra 1-18
>
> Intermediate algebra/coordinate geometry 1-18
>
> Plane geometry/trigonometry 1-18

Reading Score 1-36

Subscores

Social sciences/sciences 1-18

Arts/literature 1-18

Science Reasoning Score 1-36

Composite Score 1-36

Questions Commonly Asked about the ACT

Q: Who administers the ACT?

A: The ACT is administered by the American College Testing Program. For further information about the ACT Assessment Program, write to ACTP, P.O. Box 168, Iowa City, Iowa 52243-0168, call (319) 337-1000, or check the ACT World Wide Web site at www.act.org.

Q: What is the structure of the ACT Assessment?

A: The ACT Assessment consists of four tests. The English Test contains 75 questions and lasts 45 minutes. The Mathematics Test contains 60 questions and lasts 60 minutes. The Reading Test contains 40 questions and lasts 35 minutes. The Science Reasoning Test contains 40 questions and lasts 35 minutes. All four tests consist exclusively of multiple-choice questions.

Q: How is the ACT Assessment scored?

A: Each of the tests is scored from 1 to 36, with a mean score of 18. The subscores within sections are scored from 1 to 18, with a mean score of 9. The composite score is from 1 to 36.

Q: How do colleges use the information on my SPR?

A: Most colleges use the information on your Student Profile Report in two ways: (1) as part of the admission process, to assess your ability to do college-level work and (2) to help you plan your program of study.

Q: May I take the ACT Assessment more than once?

A: Yes, you may, but you should try to take it only once and do your best. If you do need to take the test a second time, check the registration/information bulletin for *re*registration procedures.

Q: How often is the test given?

A: The test is given five or six times a year, depending on your location. The test is usually given in October, December, February, April, and June. At some locations it is also given in September. Regular administrations are on Saturday morning.

Q: How and when should I register?

A: The registration period opens about ten weeks before the test date and closes about four weeks before the test date. To register within this period, obtain an ACT registration/information booklet from your high school counselor and follow the registration instructions it includes.

If you're registering for the first time, you can register in one of two ways: (1) by paper folder included in the registration bulletin or (2) by using ACT's home page on the World Wide Web (www.act.org). For the latter method of registration, payment must be made by VISA or MasterCard.

If you're reregistering, that is, if you're in high school and have taken the ACT within the last two years on a national test date, you don't have to complete the entire folder, since your record should already be on file. There are three ways you can *re*register: (1) by telephone (the toll-free number is 1-800-525-6926; payment must be made by VISA or MasterCard, and there is a $10 additional fee for phone *re*registration), (2) by using ACT's home page on the World Wide Web (www.act.org; payment must be made by VISA or MasterCard), or (3) by paper folder included in the registration bulletin (pay special attention to *re*registration tips given throughout the bulletin).

Regardless of how you register, pay special attention to the registration deadlines.

Q: What if I miss the registration deadlines?

A: You're encouraged to register *before* the deadlines, but there is a late registration period. If you register during the late registration period, there is an additional fee. If you miss the late registration deadline, you could try to take the test as a "standby." To do so, you must arrive early (before 8:00 a.m.) and realize that you will be admitted after the registered students have been admitted, but only if space and materials are available. *There is no guarantee that you'll be admitted as a "standby."* "Standby" test takers should check the information bulletin for materials to bring, method of payment, and additional fee required.

Q: What if I can't take the regular Saturday administration because of religious beliefs?

A: Most states have non-Saturday test centers. Check your registration bulletin for a listing of states and the dates on which non-Saturday testing is given. For additional information, call ACT at 319-337-1270 or write to ACT Registration, P.O. Box 414, Iowa City, IA 52243-0404. (If a non-Saturday testing center is more than 50 miles from your home, call 319-337-1332 or write to ACT Universal Testing, P.O. Box 4028, Iowa City, IA 52243-4028).

Q: What if I have a diagnosed disability or am confined to a hospital? Can special arrangements be made?

A: ACT attempts to make special arrangements whenever possible. For more information call 319-337-1332 or write to ACT Universal Testing, P.O. Box 4028, Iowa City, IA 52243-4028.

Q: **What materials should I bring to the ACT?**

A: You should bring:

- your test center admission ticket

- acceptable identification (your admission ticket is *not* identification)

- three or four sharpened number 2 pencils

- a good eraser

- a watch (alarms must be turned off on watches)

- a calculator (to assist you on the Mathematics Test)

NO books, notes, highlighters, or scratch paper are permitted. Room for your figuring will be provided in the test booklet itself. Phones, pagers, food or drink, or other reading materials are also NOT permitted.

Q: **May I cancel my score?**

A: Yes. You may do so by notifying your test supervisor before you leave the examination, or you may cancel your test scores by calling 319-337-1270 no *later* than 12 noon, central time, on the *Thursday* immediately following your test date.

Q: **Should I guess on the test?**

A: Yes, you should guess if you don't know the answer. There's no penalty for guessing, so it's to your advantage to answer every question.

Q: **How should I prepare for the ACT Assessment?**

A: Understanding and practicing test-taking strategies can help a great deal. Subject-matter review is particularly useful for the Mathematics Test and the English Test. Both subject matter and strategies are reviewed in this book.

Four Successful Overall Approaches to Taking the ACT

I. The "Plus-Minus" System

Many who take the ACT don't get their best possible score because they spend too much time on difficult questions, leaving insufficient time to answer the easy questions. *Don't let this happen to you.* Because every question within a section is worth the same amount, use the following system.

1. Answer easy questions immediately.

2. When you come to a question that seems "impossible" to answer, mark a large – (minus sign) next to it on your test booklet. Then mark a "guess" answer on your answer sheet and move on to the next question.

3. When you come to a question that seems solvable but appears too time-consuming, mark a large + (plus sign) next to that question in your test booklet and mark a guess answer on your answer sheet. Then move on to the next question.

   Because your time allotment is usually less than a minute per question, a "time-consuming" question is one that you estimate will take you more than a minute or two to answer. But don't waste time deciding whether a question is a plus or a minus. Act quickly, as the intent of this strategy is, in fact, to save you valuable time.

   After you work all your easy questions, your booklet should look something like this.

      1.
    +2.
      3.
    −4.
    +5.
   and so on

4. After you complete all the questions in one section that you can answer immediately, go back through the section and locate the questions you marked a "+" next to. Work these questions as quickly as you can. Change the "guess" on your answer sheet to the answer you arrive at for those questions you're able to work.

5. If you finish working the "+" questions and still have time left, you can do one of two things.

   a. You can attempt those "−" questions—the ones that you considered "impossible." Sometimes a question later in the section you're working on will "trigger" your memory, and you'll be able to go back and answer one of the earlier "impossible" questions.

      or

   b. You can decide not to bother with those "impossible" questions. Rather, spend your time reviewing your work to be sure you didn't make any careless mistakes on the questions you thought were easy to answer.

Remember: You *don't* have to erase the pluses and minuses you make on your *question booklet.* This would waste valuable time. And be sure to fill in all your answer spaces—if necessary, with a guess. Because there's no penalty for wrong answers, it makes no sense to leave an answer space blank. And, of course, remember that you may work only in one section of the test at a time.

II. The Elimination Strategy

Take advantage of being allowed to mark in your testing booklet. As you eliminate an answer choice from consideration, make sure to *mark it out in your question booklet* as follows:

(A̶)
?(B)
(C̶)
(D̶)
?(E)

Notice that some choices are marked with question marks, signifying that they may be possible answers. This technique will help you avoid reconsidering those choices you've already eliminated. It will also help you narrow down your possible answers. Again, these marks you make on your testing booklet don't have to be erased.

III. The "Avoiding Misreads" Method

Sometimes a question may have different answers depending upon what is asked. For example,

If $6y + 3x = 14$, what is the value of y?

The question may instead have asked, "What is the value of x?"

Or   If $3x + x = 20$, what is the value of $x + 2$?

Notice that this question doesn't ask for the value of x, but rather the value of $x + 2$.

Or   All of the following statements are true EXCEPT . . .

Or   Which of the expressions used in the first paragraph does NOT help develop the main idea?

Notice that the words EXCEPT and NOT change the above question significantly.

To avoid "misreading" a question (and therefore answering it incorrectly), simply circle what you must answer in the question. For example, do you have to find x or $x + 2$? Are you looking for what is true or the exception to what is true? To help you avoid misreads, mark the questions in your test booklet in this way:

If $6y + 3x = 14$, what is the value of y?
If $3x + x = 20 + 4$, what is the value of $x + 2$?
All of the following statements are true EXCEPT . . .

Which of the expressions used in the first paragraph does (*NOT* help develop) (the main idea?)

And, once again, these circles in your question booklet do not have to be erased.

IV. The Multiple-Multiple-Choice Technique

Some math and verbal questions use a "multiple-multiple-choice" format. At first glance, these questions appear more confusing and more difficult than normal five-choice (A, B, C, D, E) multiple-choice problems. Actually, once you understand "multiple-multiple-choice" problem types and technique, they are often easier than a comparable standard multiple-choice question. For example,

If x is a positive integer, then which of the following must be true?

I. $x > 0$

II. $x = 0$

III. $x < I$

A. I only

B. II only

C. III only

D. I and II only

E. I and III only

Because x is a positive integer, it must be a counting number. Note that possible values of x could be 1, or 2, or 3, or 4, and so on. Therefore, statement 1, $x > 0$, is always true. So next to I on your question booklet, place a T for true.

T   I. $x > 0$

    II. $x = 0$

    III. $x < 1$

Now realize that the correct final answer choice (A, B, C, D, or E) must contain true statement I. This eliminates **B.** and **C.** as possible correct answer choices, because they do not contain true statement 1. You should cross out **B.** and **C.** on your question booklet.

Statement II is incorrect. If x is positive, x cannot equal zero. Thus, next to II, you should place an F for false.

T   I. $x > 0$

F   II. $x = 0$

    III. $x < 1$

Knowing that II is false allows you to eliminate any answer choices that contain false statement II. Therefore, you should cross out **D.**, because it contains false statement II. Only **A.** and **E.** are left as possible correct answers. Finally, you realize that statement III is also false, as x must be 1 or greater. So you place an F next to III, thus eliminating choice **E.** and leaving **A.**, I only. This technique often saves some precious time and allows you to take a better educated guess should you not be able to complete all parts (I, II, III) of a multiple-multiple-choice question.

PART I

Analysis of Exam Areas

This section is designed to introduce you to each ACT area by carefully reviewing the

- Ability tested
- Basic Skills necessary
- Directions
- Analysis of directions
- Suggested approaches with samples

This section emphasizes important test-taking techniques and strategies and how to apply them to a variety of problem types.

INTRODUCTION TO THE ENGLISH TEST

The English Test is 45 minutes long and contains 75 multiple-choice questions.

Ability Tested

The English Test tests your ability to recognize and correct errors in standard written English. It tests your knowledge of grammar, punctuation, sentence structure, and rhetoric. It is *not* a test of spelling, vocabulary, or recall of grammar rules.

The test covers five or six prose passages of differing styles and content, upon which the multiple-choice questions are based.

Basic Skills Necessary

The basic skills necessary to perform well on the English Test include the six elements of effective writing.

Usage/Mechanics

- **punctuation,** with an emphasis on punctuation that influences meaning, such as that which avoids ambiguity or identifies an appositive

- **basic grammar and usage,** such as agreement, case, verb form, and idiomatic usage

- **sentence structure,** including correct subordination, parallelism, and placement of modifiers

Rhetorical Skills

- **strategy,** including questions about the audience, purpose, and effectiveness of prose

- **organization,** including questions about the order, unity, and coherence of a passage

- **style,** including questions about diction, imagery, freedom from ambiguity, and economy in writing

Directions

In the left-hand column, you will find passages in a "spread-out" format with various words and phrases underlined and numbered. In the right-hand column, you will find a set of responses corresponding to each underlined portion. If the underlined portion is correct standard written English, is most appropriate to the style and feeling of the passage, or best makes the intended statement, mark the letter indicating "NO CHANGE." If the underlined portion is not the best choice given, choose the one that is. For these questions, consider only the underlined portions; assume that the rest of the passage is correct as written. You will also see questions concerning parts of the passage or the whole passage. Choose the response you feel is best for these questions.

For some passages, you may also be given a box of additional directions similar to the following.

The following paragraphs are given a number in parentheses above each one. The paragraphs may be in the most logical order, or they may not. Item ___ asks you to choose the paragraph sequence that is the most logical.

Analysis of Directions

1. Make sure you understand the passage as a whole; a correct choice must be appropriate to the meaning of the passage, the author's purpose, the audience, and so forth. Read through the entire passage quickly and make sure you understand it before dealing with the underlined portions.

2. You're looking for errors in standard written English, the kind of English used in most textbooks. Don't evaluate a sentence in terms of the spoken English we all use.

3. When deciding whether an underlined portion is correct or not, *assume that all parts that aren't underlined are correct.*

4. Several alternatives to an underlined portion may be partially correct. You are to pick the one that *fits the meaning of the sentence and is grammatically and structurally sound.*

5. You may also be given some general questions about the rhetoric (organization, style, purpose) of the passage.

Suggested Approach with Samples

Some of the types of errors you'll encounter are errors in

- punctuation
- grammar
- sentence structure
- logic and organization
- idiom

A short discussion of each of these types of errors using simple questions will give you a basic understanding of the structure of the English Test. Remember, though, that there are many other types of errors, which are discussed in the explanations for the practice test questions.

Punctuation errors. Suspect a punctuation error when a period, comma, semicolon, colon, or dash is part of the underlined portion. Note, however, that simply because a punctuation mark is underlined doesn't mean that it is *necessarily* part of the error. (If the underlined portion is, for example, at the end of a sentence, the test regularly underlines the period, whether it is involved in the error or not.)

---

1. At sunrise, we assembled <u>the climbing, gear that we had hidden</u> the night before.

                                                1

  A. NO CHANGE

  B. the climbing gear that we had hidden

  C. the climbing; gear that we had hidden

  D. the climbing—gear that we had hidden

The comma following *climbing* makes the sentence unintelligible; you can't assemble a *climbing,* but you can assemble *climbing gear.* So removing the comma altogether, choice **B.**, restores meaning to the sentence.

Grammar errors. A grammar error requires that the *form* of the work be changed. Common grammar errors involve incorrect pronouns or disagreement between subject and verb.

Pronoun error.

> **2.** The computer <u>corrected oneself</u> and continued to run the program.
> ₂
>
> **F.** NO CHANGE
>
> **G.** corrects itself
>
> **H.** corrected itself
>
> **J.** corrects oneself

Oneself may correctly refer to a person, but not to a thing. Since a computer is a thing, the correct pronoun is *itself,* so **H.** is the best choice because it supplies *itself* without unnecessarily changing *corrected.*

Subject-Verb Agreement error.

> **3.** The carton of roses and carnations <u>were</u> beautifully displayed in the window.
> ₃
>
> **A.** NO CHANGE
>
> **B.** was
>
> **C.** weren't
>
> **D.** OMIT the underlined portion.

The subject is singular, *carton,* so the verb must be singular, *was* instead of *were.* Choice **B.** is correct.

Sentence Structure errors. A sentence structure error occurs when the parts of a sentence are not arranged in a logical order or when an essential part or parts have been omitted. Common sentence structure errors are faulty parallelism and dangling modifiers.

Faulty Parallelism.

> **4.** He drank, smoked, and <u>watching TV</u> too much.
> ₄
>
> **F.** NO CHANGE
>
> **G.** to watch TV
>
> **H.** watched TV
>
> **J.** will watch TV

Watching TV isn't parallel to (doesn't have the same form as) the other verbs with which it's listed; the correct parallel phrase is *drank, smoked, and watched TV,* in which each element is a verb in the past tense.

Dangling Modifier.

> **5.** A <u>piano is for sale by a woman with walnut legs.</u>
> ₅
>
> **A.** NO CHANGE
>
> **B.** piano with walnut legs is for sale by a woman.
>
> **C.** piano is for sale with walnut legs by a woman.
>
> **D.** with walnut legs a piano is for sale.

The sentence seems to say that the woman has walnut legs! This confusion is corrected by placing *walnut legs* after the word that it's meant to describe, *piano,* as in choice **B.**

Logic and Organization errors. These errors can occur when sentences aren't arranged in logical order or when paragraphing isn't done properly.

Incorrect Paragraphing.

> **6.** The requirements for graduation are a 2.5 minimum grade-point average and two semesters of science.
>
> <u>In addition to the above, a written</u> thesis is also required.
> ₆
>
> **F.** NO CHANGE
>
> **G.** (Begin new paragraph) Also a written
>
> **H.** (Begin new paragraph) However, a written
>
> **J.** (Do NOT begin new paragraph) A written

No new paragraph is needed. The final sentence continues the main idea expressed in the initial sentence. Choice **J.** is correct.

Idiom errors. Idioms are the usual way in which phrases or expressions are put together in a language. Most problems in idiom come from the improper use of prepositions (*on, of, to, by, than, from,* etc.).

> **7.** His problems began <u>prior of</u> his first day at work.
> ₇
>
> **A.** NO CHANGE
>
> **B.** prior to
>
> **C.** prior than
>
> **D.** on an occasion previous to

Prior to, choice **B.,** is the correct idiomatic usage, not *prior of.*

Sample Passage

The following is a shorter passage than appears on the exam, but it gives examples of the kinds of questions the English Test asks. Most of the questions offer alternative versions or "NO CHANGE" to underlined portions of the text. Remember, you must assume that only the underlined section can be changed and that the rest of the sentence that isn't underlined is correct.

The ancestor of our modern microscopes <u>are nearly</u> four hundred years old. The early
8

microscopes <u>were worked and operated by</u> lenses that, by forcing light to bend, could fo-
9
cus and enlarge the image of whatever object

<u>reflecting</u> the light. <u>By improving lensmaking,</u>
10   11
microscopes could be made to enlarge an object as much as one thousand times its original size. The word "telescope" derives from the Greek meaning "to view" and "far off"; "microscope" comes from the Greek meaning "to

view" and "small." 12

8. **F.** NO CHANGE
   G. are near
   H. is near
   J. is nearly

9. **A.** NO CHANGE
   B. were worked and were
   C. worked and operated by
   D. worked by

10. **F.** NO CHANGE
   G. was reflecting
   H. reflected
   J. will reflect

11. **A.** NO CHANGE
   B. By having improved lensmaking,
   C. Lensmaking having improved,
   D. With the improvement of lensmaking,

12. **F.** NO CHANGE
   G. OMIT the preceding sentence.
   H. OMIT the semicolon and the part of the sentence preceding the semicolon only.
   J. OMIT the semicolon and the part of the sentence following the semicolon only.

<u>But—for a time</u> microscopes could not be
improved beyond that point. When the objects
to be studied were smaller than the light waves
that were used to see them, the objects could
not be seen. $\boxed{14}$ The first attempt to solve this

problem, <u>in the 1920s,</u> <u>will use</u> shorter light

waves, such as ultraviolet. <u>And</u> the improvement was negligible. Waves any shorter than
these could not be focused properly. The

<u>problem was unlocked and set free</u> by using

13. A. NO CHANGE
   B. But for a time:
   C. But, for a time,
   D. But, for a time;

14. What might most logically be added to
the paragraph at this point?

   F. A quotation from a famous scientist
   G. A comparison of microscopes and
telescopes
   H. Examples of objects too small to be
seen by these instruments
   J. The names of the scientists who
worked on microscopes

15. A. NO CHANGE
   B. (Delete the commas around "in the
1920s.")
   C. (Move "in the 1920s" to the
beginning of the sentence.)
   D. (Move "in the 1920s" to after
"attempt to.")

16. F. NO CHANGE
   G. will have used
   H. used
   J. did use

17. A. NO CHANGE
   B. Therefore,
   C. But
   D. Thus,

18. F. NO CHANGE
   G. problem was unlocked and opened
   H. difficulty was unlocked
   J. problem was solved

the much shorter electron waves, <u>which</u> can be [19]

focused by magnetic fields. [20]

19. A. NO CHANGE

    B. and these

    C. and the waves

    D. who

20. The probable audience for this passage is:

    F. elementary-school children.

    G. general readers with some science.

    H. advanced students of the history of science.

    J. advanced students of mathematics.

Answers

8. **J.** The subject of the sentence is the singular noun *ancestor,* so the singular verb, *is,* is correct. The adverb *nearly* is the correct modifier of the adjectives *four hundred.*

9. **D.** Although all four choices are grammatically correct, three of them are wordy. Since *worked* and *operated* mean the same, one of the verbs is all that's needed. The active verb *worked* is briefer than the passive *were worked.*

10. **H.** So far, this sentence has used the past tense in *worked* and *could focus.* There's no reason to change to another tense here.

11. **D.** Choices **A.** and **B.** are gerund phrases. A gerund (a verbal noun; for example, *improving*), like a participle, dangles if it isn't placed close to a noun or pronoun, or the performer of the action it describes. In this sentence, there's no word like *scientists.* To correct the sentence, remove the dangling gerund, as in choice **D.**

12. **G.** The telescope half of this sentence has no relation to the rest of this paragraph. The explanation of the roots of the word *microscope,* although more related than the telescope, still isn't appropriate here, and the paragraph is improved if the entire sentence is omitted.

13. **C.** The correct punctuation here is commas setting off the phrase *for a time.*

14. **H.** At this point, specific references to what still could not be seen (for example, viruses or atomic particles) would make clear the need for continued improvements.

15. **C.** The best place for the prepositional phrase is at the beginning of the sentence.

16. **H.** The past tense is the basic verb tense in this paragraph.

17. **C.** The sense of the sentence suggests that the necessary conjunction is *But.*

18. **J.** As it stands, the phrase is verbose, and the metaphors are confusing. Choice **J.** is the conventional phrasing with no mixed metaphor or wordiness.

19. A. The *which* has a specific antecedent (*waves*) and says in one word what takes two or three in choices **B.** and **C.**

20. G. The level of the passage is evidently above elementary-school children but below what could be expected of advanced students of the history of science.

In the passage and questions above, you have examples of the grammar/usage questions in numbers 8, 10, and 16. Question 13 is a punctuation question, and questions 11 and 15 are questions about sentence structure. Questions 12, 14, 18, and 19 are examples of the sort of question the rhetorical skills portion of the test uses.

Content Area Breakdown

The English Test contains approximately the following number of items and percentages of questions in each category.

CONTENT AREA BREAKDOWN
(Approximate Percentages)

Content/Skills	Number of Items	Percentages
Usage/Mechanics	40	53%
Punctuation	10	13%
Grammar and Usage	12	16%
Sentence Structure	18	24%
Rhetorical Skills	35	47%
Strategy	12	16%
Organization	11	15%
Style	12	16%
Total	75	

In addition to the total English Test score, two subscores are reported in the following areas.

Usage/mechanics (40 items)

Rhetorical skills (35 items)

The total English Test is scored from 1 to 36, with a mean score of 18. The subscores range from 1 to 18, with a mean of 9.

INTRODUCTION TO THE MATHEMATICS TEST

The Mathematics Test is 60 minutes long and contains 60 multiple-choice questions.

Ability Tested

The Mathematics Test evaluates your ability to solve mathematical problems by using reasoning, problem-solving insight, logic, and the application of basic and advanced skills learned in high school.

Basic Skills Necessary

The basic skills necessary to do well on this test include those in high school arithmetic, elementary and intermediate algebra, coordinate geometry, plane geometry, and trigonometry, along with some logical insight into problem-solving situations. The three skill levels covered include using the basic skills, applying math skills to different situations, and analyzing when and why operations will and will not yield a solution.

Directions

After solving each problem, choose the correct answer and fill in the corresponding space on your answer sheet. Do not spend too much time on any one problem. Solve as many problems as you can and return to the others if time permits. You are allowed to use a calculator on this test.

Note:

Unless it is otherwise stated, you can assume all of the following:

1. Figures are NOT necessarily drawn to scale.

2. Geometric figures lie in a plane.

3. The word "line" means a straight line.

4. The word "average" refers to the arithmetic mean.

Analysis of Directions

1. You're looking for the *one* correct answer; therefore, although other answers may be close, there is never more than one right answer.

2. Since each problem is of equal value, don't get stuck on any one problem.

3. Take advantage of being allowed to use a calculator, but remember, some of the problems may be easier without using a calculator.

4. All scratch work is to be done in the test booklet; get used to doing this in your practice booklet while practicing because no scratch paper is allowed into the testing area.

5. The math section is slightly graduated in difficulty. That is, the easiest questions are at the beginning and the more difficult ones at the end. Keep in mind that *easy* and *difficult* are relative terms. What's easy for you may be difficult for your friend or vice versa. But generally, the first questions are the easiest and the last questions are the most difficult.

Using Your Calculator. The ACT allows the use of calculators for the Mathematics Test, and the American College Testing Program (the people who sponsor the exam) recommends that each test taker bring a calculator to the test. Even though no question will require the use of a calculator — that is, each question can be answered without one — in some instances, using a calculator will save you valuable time.

You should

- Bring your own calculator, since you can't borrow one during the exam.

- Bring a calculator even if you don't think you'll use it.

- Make sure that you're familiar with the use of your calculator.

- Make sure that your calculator has new, fresh batteries and is in good working order.

- Practice using your calculator on some of the problems to find out when and where it will be helpful.

- Take advantage of being allowed to use a calculator on the test. Learn to use your calculator efficiently by practicing. As you approach a problem, first focus on how to solve that problem and then decide if the calculator will be helpful. Remember, a calculator can save you time on some problems, but also remember that each problem can be solved without one. Also remember that a calculator will not solve a problem for you by itself. You must understand the problem first.

- Check for a shortcut in any problem that seems to involve much computation. But use your calculator if it will be time-effective. If there appears to be too much computation or the problem seems impossible without the calculator, you're probably doing something wrong.

- Before doing an operation, check the number that you keyed in on the display to make sure that you keyed in the right number. You may wish to check each number as you key it in.

- Before using your calculator, set up the problem and/or steps on your paper. Write the numbers on paper as you perform each step on your calculator. (It's generally safer not to use the memory function on your calculator.)

- Be sure to carefully clear the calculator before beginning new calculations.

Be careful that you

- Don't rush out and buy a sophisticated calculator for the test.
- Don't bring a calculator that you're unfamiliar with.
- Don't bring a pocket organizer, handheld minicomputer, laptop computer, or calculator with a typewriter-type keypad or paper tape.
- Don't bring a calculator that requires an outlet or any other external power source.
- Don't bring a calculator that makes noise.
- Don't try to share a calculator.
- Don't try to use a calculator on every problem.
- Don't become dependent on your calculator.

Suggested Approach with Samples

Answering the Right Question. Take advantage of being allowed to mark on the test booklet by always underlining or circling what you're looking for. Using this technique will help you make sure that you're answering the right question.

Sample

---

1. If $x + 6 = 9$ then $3x + 1 =$

   A.   3

   B.   9

   C.   10

   D.   34

   E.   46

You should first circle or underline $3x + 1$ because this is what you're solving for. Solving for x leaves $x + 3$ and then substituting into $3x + 1$ gives $3(3) + 1$ or 10. The most common mistake is to solve for x, which is 3, and mistakenly choose **A.** as your answer. But remember, you're solving for $3x + 1$ not just x. You should also notice that most of the other choices would all be possible answers if you made common or simple mistakes. The correct answer is **C.** *Make sure you're answering the right question.*

Sample

---

2. If $A = \begin{bmatrix} 4 & -1 \\ 3 & 1 \end{bmatrix}$ and $B = \begin{bmatrix} 5 & -1 \\ -4 & 2 \end{bmatrix}$, then $A - B = ?$

   F. $\begin{bmatrix} 9 & -2 \\ -3 & 3 \end{bmatrix}$

   G. $\begin{bmatrix} -1 & -2 \\ 7 & 3 \end{bmatrix}$

   H. $\begin{bmatrix} 9 & 0 \\ -1 & -1 \end{bmatrix}$

   J. $\begin{bmatrix} -1 & 0 \\ 7 & -1 \end{bmatrix}$

   K. $\begin{bmatrix} 20 & 1 \\ -12 & 2 \end{bmatrix}$

You should first underline or circle $A - B$. To find the difference of matrices A and B, subtract the corresponding entries as follows.

$$\begin{bmatrix} 4 & -1 \\ 3 & 1 \end{bmatrix} - \begin{bmatrix} 5 & -1 \\ -4 & 2 \end{bmatrix} \qquad 4 - 5 = -1 \qquad -1 - (-1) = 0 \qquad 3 - (-4) = 7 \qquad 1 - 2 = -1$$

So the correct answer is

$$\begin{bmatrix} -1 & 0 \\ 7 & -1 \end{bmatrix}$$

which is choice **J**.

Work Forward. If you immediately recognize the method or proper formula to solve the problem, then do the work. Work forward.

Sample

3. $\left|-8 + 6\right| + \left|-7\right| = ?$

    A.   21

    B.   9

    C.   7

    D.   −7

    E.   −21

You should work this problem straight through as follows.

$$\left|-8 + 6\right| + \left|-7\right| = \left|-2\right| + \left|-7\right|$$

$$= 2 + 7$$

$$= 9$$

Notice that a quick look at the answer choices enables you to eliminate choices **D.** and **E.**, since they are negative. If you add two absolute values, the answer can't be negative.

Work Backward from the Answers. If you don't immediately recognize a method or formula, or if using the method or formula would take a great deal of time, try working backward — from the answers. Since the answers are usually given in ascending or descending order, always start by plugging in the middle answer choice first if values are given. Then you'll know whether to go up or down with your next try. (Sometimes you might want to plug in one of the simple answers first.)

Sample

> **4.** Which of the following is a value of r for which $r^2 - r - 20 = 0$?
>
> **F.** 4
>
> **G.** 5
>
> **H.** 6
>
> **J.** 7
>
> **K.** 8

You should first underline or circle "value of r." If you've forgotten how to solve this equation, work backward by plugging in answers. Start with choice **H.**; plug in 6.

$$(6)^2 - 6 - 20 \overset{?}{=} 0$$

$$36 - 6 - 20 \overset{?}{=} 0$$

$$30 - 20 \overset{?}{=} 0$$

$$10 \neq 0$$

Since this answer is too large, try choice **G.**, a smaller number. Plugging in 5 gives

$$5^2 - 5 - 20 \overset{?}{=} 0$$

$$25 - 5 - 20 \overset{?}{=} 0$$

$$20 - 20 \overset{?}{=} 0$$

$$0 = 0$$

which is true, so **G.** is the correct answer. *Working from the answers is a valuable technique.*

You could also work this problem by factoring into

$$(r - 5)(r + 4) = 0$$

and then setting $(r - 5) = 0$ and $(r + 4) = 0$ leaving

$$r = 5 \text{ or}$$
$$r = -4$$

Sample

> **5.** Find the counting number that is less than 15 and when divided by 3 has a remainder of 1 and divided by 4 has a remainder of 2.
>
>   **A.**   5
>
>   **B.**   8
>
>   **C.**   10
>
>   **D.**   12
>
>   **E.**   13

By working from the answers, you eliminate wasting time on other numbers from 1 to 14. Choices **B.** and **D.** can be immediately eliminated because they are divisible by 4, leaving no remainder. Choices **A.** and **E.** can also be eliminated because they leave a remainder of 1 when divided by 4. Therefore, the correct answer is **C.**; 10 leaves a remainder of 1 when divided by 3 and a remainder of 2 when divided by 4.

Try a Reasonable Approach. Sometimes you'll immediately recognize the proper formula or method to solve a problem. If that's not the situation, try a reasonable approach and then work from the answers.

Sample

> **6.** Barney can mow the lawn in 5 hours, and Fred can mow the lawn in 4 hours. How many hours will it take them to mow the lawn together?
>
>   **F.**   1
>
>   **G.** $2\frac{2}{9}$
>
>   **H.**   4
>
>   **J.** $4\frac{1}{2}$
>
>   **K.**   5

First underline or circle "hours . . . mow the lawn together." Suppose that you're unfamiliar with the type of equation for this problem. Try the "reasonable" method. Since Fred can mow the lawn in 4 hours by himself, he'll take less than 4 hours if Barney helps him. Therefore, choices **H.**, **J.**, and **K.** are not sensible. Taking this method a little farther, suppose that Barney could also mow the lawn in 4 hours. Then together it would take Barney and Fred 2 hours. But since Barney is a little slower than this, the total time should be a little more than 2 hours. The correct answer is **G.**, $2\frac{2}{9}$ hours.

Using the equation for this problem would give the following calculations.

$$\frac{1}{5} + \frac{1}{4} = \frac{1}{x}$$

In 1 hour Barney could do $\frac{1}{5}$ of the job, and in 1 hour Fred could do $\frac{1}{4}$ of the job; unknown x is that part of the job they could do together in one hour. Now, solving, you calculate as follows.

$$\frac{4}{20} + \frac{5}{20} = \frac{1}{x}$$
$$\frac{9}{20} = \frac{1}{x}$$

Cross multiplying gives

$$9x = 20$$

Therefore,

$$x = \frac{20}{9}, \text{ or } 2\frac{2}{9}$$

Simplify. Sometimes, combining terms performing simple operations, or simplifying the problem in some other way will give you insight and make the problem easier to solve.

Sample

> **7.** If $x = -3$ and $y = 4$ then $xy^2 + 3x^2y + 4xy^2 + 2x^2y =$
>
> A. -420
>
> B. -60
>
> C. 60
>
> D. 420
>
> E. $4{,}500$

Simplifying this problem means first adding the like terms ($xy^2 + 4xy^2$) and ($3x^2y + 2x^2y$). After simplifying this problem to $5xy^2 = 5x^2y$, plug in the value -3 for x and 4 for y, which gives you

$$5(-3)(4)^2 + 5(-3)^2(4) = 5(-3)(16) + 5(9)4$$
$$= -15(16) + 45(4)$$
$$= -240 + 180$$
$$= -60$$

The correct answer is -60, choice **B**.

"Pulling" out Information. "Pulling" information out of the word problem structure can often give you a better look at what you're working with, so you gain additional insight into the problem.

Sample

8. If a mixture is $3/7$ alcohol by volume and $4/7$ water by volume, what is the ratio of the volume of alcohol to the volume of water in this mixture?

   F. $3/7$

   G. $4/7$

   H. $3/4$

   J. $4/3$

   K. $7/4$

The first bit of information you pull out should be what you're looking for: "ratio of the volume of alcohol to the volume of water." Rewrite it as $A:W$ and then into its working form: A/W. Next, you should pull out the volumes of each; $A = 3/7$ and $W = 4/7$

Now the answer can be easily figured by inspection or substitution. Using

$$\frac{\frac{3}{7}}{\frac{4}{7}}$$

invert the bottom fraction and multiply to get

$$3/7 \times 7/4 = 3/4$$

The correct answer is choice **H**. When you pull out information, actually write out the numbers and/or letters to the side of the problem, putting them into some helpful form and eliminating some of the wording.

Substitute Numbers for Variables. Substituting numbers for variables can often help in understanding a problem. Remember to substitute simple numbers, since you have to do the work.

Sample

---

9. If $x > 1$, which of the following decreases as x decreases?

   I. $x + x^2$

  II. $2x^2 - x$

 III. $\dfrac{1}{x+1}$

  A.   I only

  B.   II only

  C.   III only

  D.   I and II only

  E.   II and III only

First underline or circle "decreases as x decreases." This problem is most easily solved by taking each situation and substituting simple numbers. However, for roman numeral I, $x + x^2$, you should recognize that this expression *will* decrease as x decreases.

Trying $x = 2$ gives

$2 + (2)^2 = 6$

Trying $x = 3$ gives

$3 + (3)^2 = 12$

Notice that choices **B.**, **C.**, and **E.** are already eliminated because they don't contain I. You should also realize that now you need only to try the values in II. (Since III isn't paired with I as a possible choice, III can't be one of the answers.)

Trying $x = 2$ in the expression $2x^2 - x$ gives

$2(2)^2 - 2 = 2(4) - 2$

$\qquad\qquad = 6$

Trying $x = 3$ gives

$2(3)^2 - 3 = 2(9) - 3$

$\qquad\qquad = 18 - 3$

$\qquad\qquad = 15$

This expression also decreases as *x* decreases. So the correct answer is **D.** Once again, notice that III shouldn't be attempted because it isn't one of the possible choices.

> **Use 10 or 100. Some problems may deal with percent or percent change. If you don't see a simple method for working the problem, try using values of 10 or 100 and see what you get.**

Sample

> **10.** If 40% of the students in a class have blue eyes and 20% of those with blue eyes have brown hair, then what percent of the original total number have brown hair and blue eyes?
>
> **F.**   4%
>
> **G.**   8%
>
> **H.** 16%
>
> **J.** 20%
>
> **K.** 32%

First, underline or circle "percent of the original number . . . brown hair . . . blue eyes." In this problem, if you don't spot a simple method, try starting with 100 students in the class. Since 40% of them have blue eyes, then 40 students have blue eyes. Now, the problem says that 20% of those students with blue eyes have brown hair. So take 20% of 40, which gives

$$.20 \times 40 = 8$$

Since the question asks what percent of the original total number have blue eyes and brown hair, and since you started with 100 students, the answer is choice **G.,** 8 out of 100, or 8%.

> **Approximate. If it appears that extensive calculations are going to be necessary to solve a problem, check to see how far apart the choices are and then approximate. The reason for checking the answers first is to give you a guide to see how freely you can approximate.**

Sample

> **11.** Sam's promotion earns him a new salary that is an increase of 11% over his present salary. If his present salary is $39,400 per year, what is his new salary?
>
>   **A.** $39,411
>
>   **B.** $39,790
>
>   **C.** $43,734
>
>   **D.** $49,309
>
>   **E.** $53,912

First, underline or circle "new salary." Notice that except for the first two choices, the answers are spread out. Approximate 11% as 10% and $39,400 as $40,000. Now, a quick second look tells you that choices **A.** and **B.** aren't sensible because if you add 10% of $40,000, you get $44,000—eliminate choices **A.** and **B.** Choice **C.** is the only answer that's close to $44,000. Since you're allowed to use a calculator on this test, this problem would be easy to check (or work) with the calculator if the answer choices were close together.

Draw a Diagram. Sketching diagrams or simple pictures can also be very helpful in problem solving because the diagram may tip off either a simple solution or a method for solving the problem.

Sample

> **12.** What is the maximum number of pieces of birthday cake 4 inches by 4 inches in size that can be cut from a cake 20 inches by 20 inches?
>
>   **F.**   5
>
>   **G.** 10
>
>   **H.** 16
>
>   **J.** 20
>
>   **K.** 25

First, underline or circle "maximum number of pieces." Sketching the cake and marking in as follows makes this a fairly simple problem.

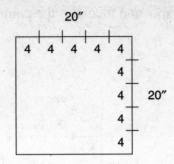

Notice that five pieces of cake will fit along each side. So

$$5 \times 4 = 25$$

The correct answer is **K.** Finding the total area of the cake and dividing it by the area of one of the 4 by 4-inch pieces would also give you the correct answer. But beware of this method because it may not work if the pieces don't fit evenly into the original area.

Sample

13. If points $P(1, 1)$ and $Q(1, 0)$ lie on the same coordinate graph, which of the following must be true?

   I. P and Q are equidistant from the origin.

   II. P is farther from the origin than P is from Q.

   III. Q is farther from the origin than Q is from P.

  A. I only

  B. II only

  C. III only

  D. I and II only

  E. I and III only

First, draw the coordinate graph, and then plot the points as follows.

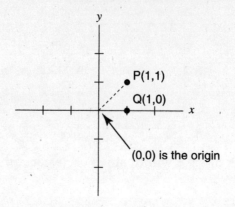

The correct answer is **B.** Only II is true. *P* is farther from the origin than *P* is from *Q*.

Sample

14. The perimeter of the isosceles triangle shown below is 42. The two equal sides, $\overline{AB}$ and $\overline{AC}$ are each three times as long as the third side. What are the lengths of each side?

    F. 21, 21, 21

    G. 6, 6, 18

    H. 18, 21, 3

    J. 18, 18, 6

    K. 4, 19, 19

Mark the equal sides on the diagram. $\overline{AB}$ and $\overline{AC}$ are each three times as long as $\overline{BC}$.

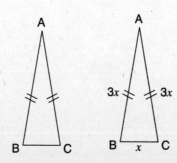

The equation for perimeter is

$$3x + 3x + x = 42$$

$$7x = 42$$

$$x = 6$$

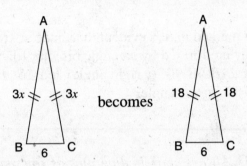

becomes

The answer is **J.** Note that this problem could also be solved by working from the answers given.

Sample

15. In the triangle shown below, $\overline{CD}$ is an angle bisector, $\angle ACD$ is 30° and $\angle ABC$ is a right angle. What is the measurement of $\angle x$ in degrees?

    A. 30°

    B. 45°

    C. 60°

    D. 75°

    E. 80°

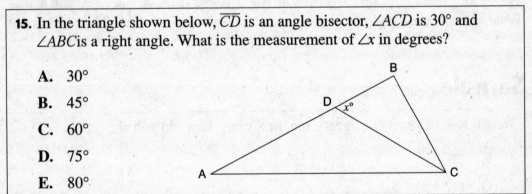

First, underline or circle "measurement of $\angle x$." You should read the problem and mark as follows.

In the triangle shown below, *CD* is an angle bisector (**stop and mark in the drawing**), $\angle ACD$ is 30° and $\angle ABC$ is a right angle (**stop and mark in the drawing**). What is the measurement of $\angle x$ in degrees? (**stop and mark in or circle what you're looking for in the drawing**)

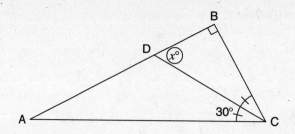

Now, with the drawing marked in, it's evident that since ∠ACD is 30°, then ∠BCD is also 30°, because they are formed by an angle bisector (divides an angle into two equal parts). Since ∠ABC is 90° (a right angle) and ∠BCD is 30°, then ∠x is 60° because there are 180° in a triangle.

$$180 - (90 + 30) = 60$$

The correct answer is **C.** *Always mark in diagrams as you read their descriptions and information about them, including what you're looking for.*

Glance at the Answer Choices on Procedure Problems. Some problems may not ask you to solve for a numerical answer or even an answer including variables. Rather, you may be asked to set up the equation or expression without doing any solving. A quick glance at the answer choices will help you know what is expected.

Sample

> **16.** Uli was 12 years old x years ago. In 8 years, how old will she be?
>
> **F.** $20 - x$
>
> **G.** $(12 + x) + 8$
>
> **H.** $(12 - x) + 8$
>
> **J.** $(8 + x) - 12$
>
> **K.** $(12 + 8) - x$

First, underline or circle "In 8 years, how old." Next, glance at the answers. Notice that none of them gives an actual numerical answer, but rather, each sets up a way to find the answer. Now set up the problem.

"12 years old x years ago" can be written as

$$12 + x$$

"In 8 years" tells you to add 8 more, so the answer is

$$(12 + x) + 8$$

which is choice **G**.

Use Your Calculator. Some questions will need to be completely worked out. If you don't see a fast method but do know that you could compute the answer, use your calculator.

Sample

17. What is the final cost of a watch that sells for $49.00 if the sales tax is 7%?

    A. $49.07

    B. $49.70

    C. $52.00

    D. $52.43

    E. $56.00

The correct answer is **D**. First, underline or circle "final cost." Since the sales tax is 7% of $49.00,

$$7\% \text{ of } \$49.00 = (.07)(\$49.00)$$

$$= \$3.43$$

The total cost of the watch is therefore

$$\$49.00 + \$3.43 = \$52.43$$

Your calculator can be helpful with such calculations.

Content Area Breakdown

The Mathematics Test contains approximately the following number of items and percentages of questions in each category.

CONTENT AREA BREAKDOWN
(Approximate Percentages)

Content/Skills	Number of Items	Percentages
Pre-Algebra and Elementary Algebra	24	40%
Intermediate Algebra and Coordinate Geometry	18	30%
Plane Geometry	14	23%
Trigonometry	4	7%
Total	60	

In addition to the total mathematics score, three subscores are reported in the following areas.

Pre-algebra/elementary algebra (24 items)

Intermediate algebra/coordinate geometry (18 items)

Plane geometry/trigonometry (18 items)

The total Mathematics Test is scored from 1 to 36, with a mean score of 18. The subscores range from 1 to 18, with a mean of 9.

For Additional Study

For additional review and practice in math, you'll find that *Cliffs Math Review for Standardized Tests* will provide you with the help you need. Unlike other general math reviews, this book focuses on *standardized test math* and gives you a practical, personalized test-preparation program. *Cliffs Math Review for Standardized Tests* is available at your local bookstore.

INTRODUCTION TO THE READING TEST

The Reading Test is 35 minutes long and contains 4 reading passages, each followed by 10 multiple-choice questions for a total of 40 questions.

Ability Tested

The Reading Test assesses your ability to understand, interpret, and analyze prose drawn from reading passages:

- **Prose Fiction:** excerpts from short stories or novels
- **Humanities:** architecture, art, dance, music, philosophy, theater
- **Social Studies:** anthropology, economics, history, political science, psychology, sociology
- **Natural Sciences:** biology, chemistry, physical science, physics

The questions test your reading and reasoning abilities, not your prior knowledge of a subject or knowledge of vocabulary or rules of logic.

Common types of questions ask you

- About the main idea, main point, purpose, or possible title of the passage
- About important details or information that is directly stated in the passage
- About the meaning of a word or phrase in a passage
- About information that is assumed, implied, or suggested or that can be reasonably inferred
- To recognize an author's point of view
- To make comparisons between ideas or characters
- To identify cause-effect relationships
- To make generalizations

Basic Skills Necessary

The basic skills necessary to do well on this section include reading skills at the level of a high school senior or college freshman, the ability to understand what is explicitly stated in a passage, the ability to understand what is implied and what can be inferred, and the ability to draw conclusions, comparisons, and generalizations. Students who have read widely and know how to read and mark a passage actively and efficiently tend to do well on the Reading Test.

Directions

Each of the four passages in this test is followed by questions. Read the passage and choose the best answer to each question. Return to the passage as often as necessary to answer the questions.

Analysis of Directions

Answer all the questions for one passage before moving on to the next passage.

Use only the information given or implied in the passage. Do not consider outside information, even if it seems more accurate than the given information.

Suggested General Approaches

- Since there are 4 passages and a total of 40 questions (10 per passage) to complete in 35 minutes, you should spend just under 9 minutes for each passage and set of 10 questions.

- Because of the time allotment and number of questions, you must work quickly. Don't get stuck on any one question.

- There is no penalty for guessing, so if you don't know the answer, take an educated guess if possible, but always fill in an answer.

- As you read the passages, mark the main points and other items you feel are important. Be an active reader.

- You may wish to quickly skim some of the questions (but not the choices) before reading the passage. This prereading can give you a clue about the passage and what to look for.

> **Read the passage actively, marking the main points and other items you feel are important.**

You can mark a passage by underlining or circling important information. But be sure you don't overmark, or you'll defeat the purpose of the technique. The following passage shows one way a test taker might mark a passage to assist in understanding the information given and to quickly return to particular information in the passage when necessary. You may find that circling works better for you or using other marks that you personally find helpful.

Sample Passage

Social science: This passage is from *The Russian Revolution* by Alan Moorehead (© 1958 by Time Inc.).

The war had put a fearful strain upon the Czarist system, and Nicholas II was no Peter the Great to set things right again. It was really a race now to see which would come first: the ending of the war or the revolution. There was always a chance, of course, that the revolution might be staved off indefinitely provided
(5)   that the war ended soon and victoriously; but in December, 1916, there was no sign of this. The Franco-British effort to break through the Dardanelles and come to the aid of their Russian allies had ended in disaster. The United States had not yet come into the war. France was hanging on desperately in the winter mud at Verdun, and at sea the Germans were about to launch their U-boat campaign,
(10) which was designed to starve Britain into surrender. Something like 160 Austrian and German divisions were now entrenched along the Russian front.

The war, then, as far as Russia was concerned, had subsided into a despairing stalemate. And yet, despite all this, it was difficult to see where the revolution was going to come from. A palace revolution, a rising of the nobles to replace the
(15) Czar, was quite feasible; but no single man either in Petrograd or among the generals in the army looked like being the leader of such a movement. Then too, there existed among the liberals as well as among the aristocracy an instinctive fear of what might happen if they upset the throne, if the illiterate masses, the "Dark People," followed their lead and raised a rebellion in the streets. Once let loose
(20) the mob and anything could happen; then all of them from aristocrats to shopkeepers might be swept away.

As for the left-wing revolutionary parties — the people who would accept rebellion at any cost—they too had been weakened by the war and driven underground. Most of the leaders were living in exile abroad or in Siberia: Lenin was in
(25) Switzerland, Trotsky was on his way to New York, Plekhanov, Axelrod, Martov, Dan, and many others were scattered through Europe; and most of them were quarreling bitterly among themselves. None of them were planning to return to Russia, none had any idea that revolution was at hand. Lenin was even saying at this time that he did not believe he would ever live to see it.

(30) And so a strange apathy rests over the scene, and it is something of a marvel that the Russian revolution, the most important political event of modern times, the event which has done more to shape our lives than anything else, should have entered in such an unexpected and rudderless way into history. It seems almost to have come in, as it were, by the back door, and although it was so much talked about before-

(35) hand, it appears to have taken most of the main protagonists by surprise.

One has an entertaining glimpse of just how surprising the whole thing was from *Whitaker's Almanack,* the British reference book which has been issuing the vital statistics about the countries of the world year by year since the middle of the nineteenth century. In the volume dealing with 1916 everything is in order, and in

(40) its place, in the Russian section; the Czar is on his throne, the Duma is sitting, the imports and the exports are listed along with the figures dealing with the rainfall and the average extremes of temperature. But then in the next volume there is a sudden bewildered hiatus. In rather a shocked tone *Whitaker* reports that the Czar has been replaced by an M. Kerensky. "The newly-born freedom of the country,"

(45) the book goes on, "has not up to the present proved an unmixed blessing as several opposing parties have arisen rendering any form of settled administration impossible." A certain "A. Oulianof Lenin" is believed to have seized the reins of power, and a "subaltern" has been named as commander-in-chief. Worse still, "the army is in a state of chaos and the allies are dispatching no more material aid to

(50) Russia." The note ends, "Any news coming to hand under the ruling conditions must obviously be looked on with the greatest suspicion."

> **Preread a few questions. Prereading can give you a clue about the passage and what to look for. Quickly reading a few of the questions before reading the passage may be very helpful, especially if the passage seems difficult or unfamiliar to you.** *When prereading, read only the questions and NOT the answer choices* **(which aren't included in the examples below). Notice that you should mark (underline or circle) what the question is asking. After you read the passage, read the questions again and each of the answer choices. The following questions show examples of ways you can mark the questions and how you can analyze the questions as you preread.**

   1. Which one of the following lines best states the main point of the passage?

   The words "main point" are marked here. You should always read for the main point, but prereading this question is a good reminder.

   2. It can reasonably be inferred from the first paragraph of the passage that:

   Notice that "inferred" and "first paragraph" are marked. To answer this question, you'll need to draw information from the first paragraph by "reading between the lines."

5. From the context of the passage, the "Duma" (line 40) is most likely:

Notice that "Duma" (line 40) is marked. The marking helps you pinpoint where the answer can be found and makes you aware of looking for the meaning as the term is used in the passage.

7. According to the passage, in late 1916, the leaders of the revolutionary parties in Russia were:

Notice that "late 1916" and "leaders of the revolutionary parties" are marked. You need to focus on these specific details to answer this question.

After prereading and marking the questions, you should go back and read the passage actively. The passage is reprinted below without the markings. Try marking it yourself this time before you go on to the sample questions that follow.

Social science: This passage is from *The Russian Revolution* by Alan Moorehead (© 1958 by Time Inc.).

The war had put a fearful strain upon the Czarist system, and Nicholas II was no Peter the Great to set things right again. It was really a race now to see which would come first: the ending of the war or the revolution. There was always a chance, of course, that the revolution might be staved off indefinitely provided
(5) that the war ended soon and victoriously; but in December, 1916, there was no sign of this. The Franco-British effort to break through the Dardanelles and come to the aid of their Russian allies had ended in disaster. The United States had not yet come into the war. France was hanging on desperately in the winter mud at Verdun, and at sea the Germans were about to launch their U-boat campaign,
(10) which was designed to starve Britain into surrender. Something like 160 Austrian and German divisions were now entrenched along the Russian front.

The war, then, as far as Russia was concerned, had subsided into a despairing stalemate. And yet, despite all this, it was difficult to see where the revolution was going to come from. A palace revolution, a rising of the nobles to replace the
(15) Czar, was quite feasible; but no single man either in Petrograd or among the generals in the army looked like being the leader of such a movement. Then too, there existed among the liberals as well as among the aristocracy an instinctive fear of what might happen if they upset the throne, if the illiterate masses, the "Dark People," followed their lead and raised a rebellion in the streets. Once let loose
(20) the mob and anything could happen; then all of them from aristocrats to shopkeepers might be swept away.

As for the left-wing revolutionary parties—the people who would accept rebellion at any cost—they too had been weakened by the war and driven underground. Most of the leaders were living in exile abroad or in Siberia: Lenin was in
(25) Switzerland, Trotsky was on his way to New York, Plekhanov, Axelrod, Martov, Dan, and many others were scattered through Europe; and most of them were

quarreling bitterly among themselves. None of them were planning to return to Russia, none had any idea that revolution was at hand. Lenin was even saying at this time that he did not believe he would ever live to see it.

(30) And so a strange apathy rests over the scene, and it is something of a marvel that the Russian revolution, the most important political event of modern times, the event which has done more to shape our lives than anything else, should have entered in such an unexpected and rudderless way into history. It seems almost to have come in, as it were, by the back door, and although it was so much talked about before-
(35) hand, it appears to have taken most of the main protagonists by surprise.

One has an entertaining glimpse of just how surprising the whole thing was from *Whitaker's Almanack*, the British reference book which has been issuing the vital statistics about the countries of the world year by year since the middle of the nineteenth century. In the volume dealing with 1916 everything is in order, and in
(40) its place, in the Russian section; the Czar is on his throne, the Duma is sitting, the imports and the exports are listed along with the figures dealing with the rainfall and the average extremes of temperature. But then in the next volume there is a sudden bewildered hiatus. In rather a shocked tone *Whitaker* reports that the Czar has been replaced by an M. Kerensky. "The newly-born freedom of the country,"
(45) the book goes on, "has not up to the present proved an unmixed blessing as several opposing parties have arisen rendering any form of settled administration impossible." A certain "A. Oulianof Lenin" is believed to have seized the reins of power, and a "subaltern" has been named as commander-in-chief. Worse still, "the army is in a state of chaos and the allies are dispatching no more material aid to
(50) Russia." The note ends, "Any news coming to hand under the ruling conditions must obviously be looked on with the greatest suspicion."

Read the passage looking for its main point and structure. As you read the passage, try to focus on what the author is really saying or what point the author is trying to make. There are many ways to find the main point of a passage.

Sample

1. Which one of the following lines best states the main point of the passage?

   A. "The war, then, as far as Russia was concerned, had subsided into a despairing stalemate." (lines 12–13)

   B. "A palace revolution, a rising of the nobles to replace the Czar, was quite feasible; but no single man either in Petrograd or among the generals in the army looked like being the leader of such a movement." (lines 14–16)

> **C.** "None of them [that is, the revolutionary leaders] were planning to return to Russian, none had any idea that revolution was at hand." (lines 27–28)
>
> **D.** " . . . it is something of a marvel that the Russian revolution, the most important political event of modern times, the event which has done more to shape our lives than anything else, should have entered in such an unexpected and rudderless way into history." (lines 30–33)

Throughout the passage, the suggestion is that although Russia was ripe for revolution, its occurrence in 1917 was a surprise. So choice **D.** is the best answer. Choice **A.** covers only one aspect of the passage—the status of the war. Choice **B.** covers only the nobility and **C.** only the revolutionary leaders. Therefore, these choices are incomplete as statements of the main idea.

Make sure that your answer is supported by the passage. Every single correct answer is in the passage or can be directly inferred from the passage.

Sample

> **2.** It can reasonably be inferred from the first paragraph of the passage (lines 1–11) that:
>
> **F.** In late 1916, Czarist Russia was dealing with internal problems rather than devoting itself to the war effort.
>
> **G.** The French and English had become disenchanted with Russia's war effort.
>
> **H.** If the United States had entered the war sooner, the Russian revolution wouldn't have occurred.
>
> **J.** At the end of 1916, the Germans appeared to have the upper hand in the war.

The best choice is **J.**, which is supported by several details in the paragraph, such as the Franco-British failure at the Dardanelles, the French plight at Verdun, the imminent German U-boat campaign, and the Austrian and German troops on the Russian front. There is no indication that the Czar is focusing on internal affairs, choice **F.**, and there is no evidence that the French and English are disenchanted with Russia at this point, choice **G.** Choice **H.** might at first appear to be a good choice, but the inference that the United States could have prevented the Russian revolution by entering the war earlier is simplistic and conjectural, and it is not implied by the passage.

As you read, note the purpose or tone of the passage or portions of the passage. The structure and the words that the author uses to describe events, people, or places will help give you an understanding of the author's specific purpose or how the author wants you to feel or think.

Sample

3. The purpose of the last paragraph of the passage (lines 36–51) is to

   A. summarize the problems in prerevolutionary Russia.

   B. suggest that the Allies planned to intervene in Russia.

   C. illustrate that the timing of the revolution came as a surprise.

   D. present the widely held view that Lenin was a vicious man and the power behind the revolution.

A question concerning purpose or tone may be based on the whole passage or a part of the passage, as is the case here. The best choice is **C.** (lines 30–35). The first sentence is the paragraph's topic sentence. This paragraph isn't a summary, choice **A.**; it's an example that supports the author's point. Also, although the paragraph mentions Lenin's position, choice **D.**, nothing in the tone suggests that he was viewed as vicious. The paragraph quotes the *Almanack* as saying that news about Russia must be "looked on with the greatest suspicion" because of the country's unsettled state; the paragraph does *not* state that the Allies had plans to intervene, however, choice **B.**

Make sure that the answer you select answers the question. Some good or true answers are not correct. Even though more than one choice may be true, you're looking for the best answer to the question given.

Sample

4. According to the passage, the mood in Russia in December 1916 could best be described as:

   F. angry

   G. contentious

   H. apathetic

   J. philosophical

It might seem reasonable to think that people who will soon stage a revolution would be "angry," choice **F.** (why would they rebel, you might wonder, if they weren't). But *according to the passage* (see line 30), Russians weren't as angry at that point (December 1916) as they were discouraged. So choice **H.**, "apathetic" (showing little emotion or interest) is the best choice. Choice **G.** would be a good, true answer if the question were about the revolutionary leaders, who are said to be "quarreling bitterly." But the question asks about the mood in Russia as a whole, not only among the revolutionaries. Choice **J.** indicates a calm and reflective mood that isn't indicated in the passage.

Take advantage of the line numbers. All passages show the line numbering, which, in questions that mention specific line numbers, gives you the advantage of being able to quickly spot where the information is located. Once you spot the location, be sure to read the line(s) before and after the lines mentioned. This nearby text can be very helpful in putting the information in the proper context, enabling you to better choose the correct answer to the question.

Sample

5. From the context of the passage, the "Duma" (line 40) is most likely:

    F. a parliament.

    G. a conspirator against the Czar.

    H. an underground revolutionary organization.

    J. the government-sponsored newspaper.

The clue here is the verb in the sentence—"is sitting," which rules out choices **G.**, **J.**, and even **H.** because "sit" in a context such as this generally refers to meetings of official groups. Choices **G.** and **H.** are also eliminated because the phrase "the Duma is sitting" is used as an example of the fact that, according to the "Almanack," everything was in order in 1916 Russia. It's unlikely that either a conspiracy or meetings of an underground organization would be evidence of the stability of the status quo. Choice **F.** is the correct answer.

Read all the choices, since you're looking for the best answer given. *Best* is a relative term; that is, determining what is *best* may mean choosing from degrees of *good, better,* or *best.* Although you may have more than one good choice, you're looking for the *best* of those given. Remember, the answer doesn't have to be perfect, just the best of those presented to you. So don't get stuck on one choice before you read the rest.

Sample

> **6.** Which of the following is the best explanation for the term "Dark People" used in lines 18-19?
>
> **F.** The poor in Russia were unintelligent and prone to violence.
>
> **G.** Those in the masses were dark skinned, while most Russian nobles were fair skinned.
>
> **H.** The poor in Russia were involved in the occult and in witchcraft.
>
> **J.** To the aristocracy, the poor were a great unknown and vaguely sinister.

It's possible that, out of context, choices **F.**, **G.**, and **H.** could be explanations for the term "Dark People," as "Dark" could conceivably refer to violence or to skin color or to the occult, but the passage doesn't link the term to any of these possibilities. Also, choice **F.** is incorrect because the masses are referred to as "illiterate," which is not synonymous with "unintelligent." The *best* choice is **J.**, which is supported by the mention of the fear that if the mob were to rise, the aristocrats might be "swept away," a possibility that would suggest that the poor masses were both "unknown" and "vaguely sinister."

Use an elimination strategy. Often you can arrive at the right answer by eliminating other answers. Watch for key words in the answer choices to help you find the main point given in each choice. Notice that some incorrect choices are too general, too specific, irrelevant, or off topic, or they contradict information given in the passage.

Sample

> **7.** According to the passage, in late 1916, the leaders of the revolutionary parties in Russia were
>
> **A.** in the Russian army and scattered throughout Europe.
>
> **B.** pessimistic about the possibility of an imminent revolution.
>
> **C.** unwilling to take the chance that a revolution at that time would go too far and ruin the country.
>
> **D.** waiting for a major victory in the war before starting the revolution.

You can eliminate choice **A.** Although the revolutionary leaders were scattered throughout Europe, nothing suggests that they were in the "army." You can eliminate choice **C.** because it applies to the nobles, not the revolutionaries. You can eliminate choice **D.** because the revolutionary leaders would have no reason to wait for a major victory, since a major victory could only strengthen the Czar's position. You're left with choice **B.**, the correct choice (see lines 27–29).

Some typical ways of wording questions about the passages are given in the following list. The key words and phrases are underlined to give them special emphasis, but the actual test doesn't do this underlining. You should underline key words and phrases as you read the questions.

- "What is the <u>main point</u> of the passage?"

- "The <u>main emphasis</u> of the second paragraph (lines 11–23) is. . . ."

- "The <u>author claims</u> that. . . ."

- "The <u>passage states</u> that. . . ."

- "It can be <u>reasonably inferred</u> from the passage that. . . ."

- "It can be <u>inferred from the fifth paragraph</u> (lines 55–60) that. . . ."

- "The <u>narrator's point of view</u> is. . . ."

- "According to the author, <u>an important detail</u> is. . . ."

- "According to the passage, the <u>attitude of some people</u> was. . . ."

- "The <u>third paragraph</u> (lines 35–43) <u>suggests</u> that. . . ."

- "The author of the passage would <u>most likely agree</u> with which of the following statements?"

- "As it is used in line 26, the <u>word 'xxxxxx' most nearly means</u>:"

- "According to the passage, which of the following <u>CANNOT</u> be. . . ."

- "<u>An analogy</u> made in the passage is that. . . ."

- "Which of the following <u>best explains the phrase</u>. . . ."

- "Which of the following is <u>reasonable to conclude</u> from the passage?"

- "The author of the pssage makes which of the following <u>comparisons</u>?"

- "The author <u>identifies the cause</u> to be. . . ."

- "According to the author, the <u>generalization</u> that can be made. . . ."

- "How does the discussion of xxxxxx <u>function in the passage</u>?"

Three Final Strategies

If you're having real trouble with a passage or simply running out of time, try one of these three strategies.

Skip a difficult passage. You could skip a difficult passage entirely, along with the questions based on it, and come back to them later. Remember that you can return to those questions only while you're working in the Reading Test. Also, if you use this strategy, take care to mark your answers in the correct spaces on the answer sheet when you skip a group of questions.

Skim the passage. If you're running out of time, you might want to skim the passage and then answer the questions—referring back to the passage when necessary.

Potshot questions and spots in the passage. For this last resort method, if questions on a passage refer to line numbers and you have only a few minutes left (and haven't yet read a passage), simply read the questions that refer to specific lines in the passage and read only those specific lines in the passage (potshot them) to try to answer the question. This final strategy may help you at least eliminate some answer choices and add one or two right answers to your score. And always remember to put down at least a guess answer for all questions.

Content Area Breakdown

The Reading Test contains approximately the following number of items and percentages of questions in each category.

CONTENT AREA BREAKDOWN
(Approximate Percentages)

Reading Context	Number of Items	Percentages
Prose Fiction	10	25%
Humanities	10	25%
Social Studies	10	25%
Natural Sciences	10	25%
Total	40	

In addition to the total reading score, two subscores will be reported in the following areas:

Arts/Literature (Prose Fiction, Humanities: 20 items)

Social Studies/Sciences (Social Studies, Natural Sciences: 20 items)

The total Reading Test will be scored from 1 to 36, with a mean score being 18. The subscores will range from 1 to 18, with a mean of 9.

INTRODUCTION TO THE SCIENCE REASONING TEST

The Science Reasoning Test is 35 minutes long and contains 40 multiple-choice questions.

Ability Tested

In this test, you're given several sets of scientific information, including reading passages, diagrams, and tables. Each set of information is followed by several multiple-choice questions. Your success depends on your ability to quickly understand the information presented to you. There are three formats for the scientific information.

- **The Data Representation format:** The information is presented in tables, graphs, or figures that summarize the results of research.

- **Research Summaries format:** You're given a detailed description of one experiment or a series of related experiments.

- **Conflicting Viewpoints format:** Two or more scientists present different theories about one scientific question.

Basic Skills Necessary

Although the Science Reasoning Test may include information from biology, chemistry, physics, astronomy, or geology, you're not expected to have studied all those fields. You'll be tested on your general reasoning skills applied to the scientific information given to you.

Some questions require you to understand background knowledge, terms, basic facts and concepts about the information. You'll be expected to critically analyze data and scientific arguments, to perceive relationships, to draw conclusions, and to make generalizations. A few questions call for simple mathematical calculations using the data.

The test *emphasizes* scientific reasoning skills rather than your prior knowledge of science, ability to read, or skill at mathematical calculations.

Directions

Each of the seven passages in this test is followed by several questions. After you read each passage, select the correct choice for each of the questions that follow the passage. Refer to the passage as often as necessary to answer the questions. You may NOT use a calculator on this test.

Analysis of Directions

1. Each set of scientific information is called a passage. A passage could be several descriptive paragraphs, a data table, a graph, a diagram of an experiment, or any combination of such information.

2. Each passage does contain the factual information needed to answer the set of questions following the passage.

3. You should refer to the passage for each question rather than attempt to answer using your background knowledge or your memory of the passage.

Suggested Approach with Sample Passages

- Since there's considerable time pressure on this test, you must work quickly. You'll have only about five minutes to read each passage and answer the set of questions.

- Take about two or three minutes to study each passage, leaving about twenty to thirty seconds for each of the questions that follow.

- As you read the passages, mark the main points and other items you feel are important.

- You may wish to quickly skim some of the questions (but *not* the choices) before reading the passage.

- Focus on the key words in the question to make sure you're answering the right question and looking at the right graph, chart, hypothesis, or study.

- Following are sample passages illustrating the three formats on the test. Questions, strategies, and explanations follow each passage.

Data Representation

Sample Passage I

Table 1 shows the total weight of air pollutants for the entire United States during a recent year. The data are cross-tabulated according to both type of pollutant and source of the material. The quantities in the chart represent millions of tons per year.

Table 1

Pollutant	Cars and Trucks	Electric Plants	Industrial Plants	Waste Disposal
Carbon monoxide	67	1	2	2
Sulfur oxides	1	14	9	1
Hydrocarbons	12	1	5	1
Nitrogen oxides	7	3	2	1
Particles	1	4	6	1
Total	88	23	24	6

Sample Questions for Passage I

1. The environmental problem referred to as "acid rain" is caused by sulfur oxide pollution. On the basis of the data presented in Table 1, which source is the major contributor to the acid rain problem?

   A. Cars and trucks

   B. Electric plants

   C. Industrial plants

   D. Waste disposal

You should first focus on understanding what information is given. You're given a table summarizing research on air pollution and asked to answer an interpretive question. Examine the table carefully to comprehend how it organizes the information. In this case, the rows show the various pollutants, and the columns display the various sources of the pollution.

The question asks about the acid rain problem, which it attributes to sulfur oxides. In the second row, the largest quantity is 14, so electric plants are the main contributors to the acid rain problem. The correct answer is choice **B.** Remember to begin by examining the table or figure to see how it organizes the information.

2. Based on the data presented in Table 1, which of the following sources contributes the most carbon monoxide pollutant to the atmosphere?

    F. Cars and trucks

    G. Electric plants

    H. Industrial plants

    J. Waste disposal

Don't memorize the information; refer to the table or graph for each question. Table 1 indicates that cars and trucks contribute the most carbon monoxide to the atmosphere, relative to the other three sources listed. Therefore, the correct answer is choice **F.**

3. The data in Table 1 support which of the following combinations of pollutants as the greatest emissions problem at industrial plants?

    A. Hydrocarbons and particles

    B. Sulfur oxides and hydrocarbons

    C. Sulfur oxides and carbon monoxide

    D. Particles and sulfur oxides

Read tables, charts, and graphs carefully, looking for high points, low points, changes, and trends. Be able to work with the information given. In this case, you need to find the two highest numbers in the Industrial Plants column and then check to be sure that the combination is represented in the answer choices. Those numbers here are 9 and 6, which represent sulfur oxides and particles, respectively. The sum of these pollutants is 15 out of a total of 24, a high ratio. Therefore, **D.** is the correct answer.

4. An environmental regulatory agency decides on the basis of the data presented to implement some tough legislation to combat pollution. Based on the information presented in Table 1, which of the following hypothetical regulations, if passed, would be most likely to have the greatest impact on air pollution in the long run?

    F. A law requiring electric plants to be fined for sulfur oxide emissions

    G. A law requiring automobile owners to be fined for carbon monoxide emissions

    H. A law requiring car manufacturers to make cars that do not emit carbon monoxide

    J. A law requiring electric and industrial plants to be fined for all emissions

Certain questions require you to reason, or draw conclusions, from the information given. According to the data presented, carbon monoxide from cars and trucks is the single greatest contributor to air pollution. Regulation designed to reduce this particular source would therefore present the greatest benefit over the long run. Note also that three of the pieces of legislation involve a monetary penalty for emissions. But there is no indication of the amount of such fines or whether they would be punitive enough to ensure compliance. Choice **H.**, however, directly mandates change to existing technology that is causing much of the problem and is therefore the correct answer.

---

5. The following description is of a particular class of pollutants: "Air Pollutant *X* is emitted mainly from industrial, institutional, utility, and apartment furnaces and boilers, as well as from petroleum refineries, smelters, paper mills, and chemical plants. It is the major source of smog and can aggravate upper-respiratory disorders and cause eye and throat irritation." Based on this description and the information presented in Table 1, Air Pollutant *X* is most likely:

    A. carbon monoxide

    B. sulfur oxides

    C. hydrocarbons

    D. nitrogen oxides

In general, for any graphically presented data, you should review headings, scales, factors, and/or any descriptive information given, noting the correlations between factors, items, or variables. According to the information given in Table 1, sulfur oxides are produced mainly in industrial contexts. Since the information in the question also involves primarily industrial sources of pollution, you can determine that Pollutant *X* is *most likely* sulfur oxides, choice **B.**

Other Points to Be Aware of for Data Representation Questions

- How the data is represented—in tables, graphs, figures, and so on

- How many tables, graphs, figures, and so on, are given

- What correlations exist for items both *within* tables, graphs, and figures and *between* them

- Which specific tables, graphs, or figures (often one or two) a particular question is referring to

- How the terms are used in each representation—total, average, dependent, independent, experimental, control, and so forth

Research Summaries

Sample Passage II

To investigate whether evaporation could cause a liquid to rise within a tube, a researcher placed an open glass tube in a large beaker filled with mercury. Water was then poured slowly into the tube until it was filled. Notice in Figure 1 that the weight of the water displaced the mercury in the tube slightly below its level in the beaker.

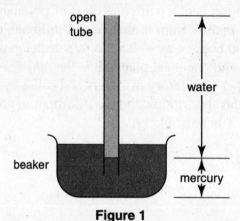

open
tube

water

beaker

mercury

Figure 1

The researcher then fastened a permeable plastic membrane across the top of the tube and turned on a heat lamp to begin evaporating water through the permeable membrane. The mercury slowly rose several inches within the glass tube (see Figure 2).

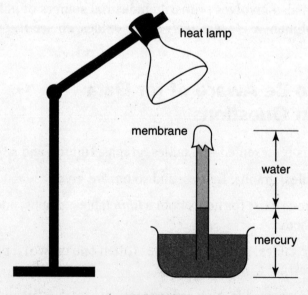

heat lamp

membrane

water

mercury

Figure 2

Sample Questions for Passage II

> **6.** The rate at which the mercury rises in the tube could be accelerated by
>
>   **F.** inserting a smaller bulb in the lamp
>
>   **G.** substituting alcohol for the water
>
>   **H.** using a glass tube of smaller diameter
>
>   **J.** using a larger beaker and more mercury

Here you're given a detailed description of an experiment. For most of the questions in the research summaries format, it's essential that you understand the reason the experiment was conducted. The first sentence of the passage usually states the purpose, so return and reread that sentence. The purpose of the experiment is to "investigate whether evaporation could cause a liquid to rise within a tube."

This question asks how one could get the mercury to rise faster. Since you know that evaporation causes the rise, to increase the rate of rising you must increase the rate of evaporation. The correct answer is choice **G.** because alcohol evaporates much faster than water. Notice how an understanding of the purpose of the experiment aided in answering the question.

> **7.** "Density" is a measurement of the quantity of mass per unit of volume. Based on the information in the description of the experiment and in Figures 1 and 2, and given that water has a density of 1.0 at 20°C, which of the following is most likely the density of mercury at 20°C?
>
>   **A.** 0.35
>
>   **B.** 1.00
>
>   **C.** 1.35
>
>   **D.** 13.50

Pay particular attention to the methods used and the outcome of an experiment. Figure 1 indicates that when water is poured into the tube, it doesn't mix with the mercury already in the beaker. This fact suggests that the density of mercury is significantly greater than the density of water. So choice **D.** is the best answer.

8. Based on the design of the study, it can be concluded that a "liquid" is matter that has

    F. molecules that maintain a fixed position, giving the substance a definite shape

    G. a definite volume but no shape, allowing it to conform to the shape of its container

    H. no fixed shape or volume because its molecules are always in motion

    J. a form that starts out as a solid and then changes shape with heat

You should be able to draw conclusions from the study or experiment. Mercury and water are both liquids. According to the figures in Sample Passage II, it's apparent that the volume of mercury used in the experiment conformed to the shape of the beaker, and the volume of water used conformed to the shape of the tube. So **G.** is the correct answer.

9. At 20°C, the densities ($\times 10^3$ kilograms/meter^3) of ethyl alcohol, chloroform, and water are 0.79, 1.49, and 1.00, respectively. Which of the following combinations and placements of liquids would best reproduce the results of the experiment described in the passage?

    A. water in the beaker, chloroform in the open tube

    B. alcohol in the beaker, water in the open tube

    C. water in the beaker, alcohol in the open tube

    D. alcohol in the beaker, chloroform in the open tube

You should always pay attention to both the design of the experiment and the reasons for the results. In the original experiment, the density of the liquid in the beaker (mercury) is higher than that of the liquid in the tube (water). To get the same experimental results with new liquids, these relative densities must be replicated—a denser liquid should be placed in the beaker, and a less dense liquid should be placed in the tube. Water has a higher density than that of ethyl alcohol, so it should be placed in the beaker. Choice **C.** is the correct answer.

10. Solids, liquids, and gases have physical properties that can be observed and described as behaviors under certain given conditions. From the information provided, it can be hypothesized that:

    F. density is a property that does not depend on the amount of matter being observed.

    G. density is a property that does depend on the amount of matter being observed.

    H. evaporation rate is a property that is related to the boiling point of liquid matter.

    J. evaporation rate is a property that is related to the melting point of solid matter.

Be aware of information or hypotheses not directly stated in the data that *can* or *cannot* be drawn from the experiment. This experiment doesn't specify quantities (volumes) of the matter (liquids) used. But density is an important property of the matter in this study. Melting points and boiling points are properties that are not discussed in the passage text and nothing can be hypothesized about them from the information given or the structure of the experiment. Choice **F.** is the best answer.

---

11. Based on the information given, if the researcher had designed the experiment so that he placed water in the beaker and slowly continued to pour mercury into the tube, his experiment would have become impossible to complete because:

   A. the water would have evaporated before the mercury filled the tube

   B. the mercury would displace the water and no water would enter the tube

   C. the mercury would not penetrate the permeable membrane across the top of the tube

   D. the heat lamp could not generate enough heat to evaporate the water

---

Notice conclusions that can be drawn from the design of the experiment, rather than just from the outcome of the experiment. The experiment could not have been completed because the mercury is much denser than the water, so the water would overflow the beaker and could not get into the tube. At that point, the experiment, as it stands, could not have been performed. Choice **B.** is the best answer.

Other Points to Be Aware of for Research Summaries Questions

- How many experiments or studies were completed
- The similarities and differences in the studies
- The similarities and differences in the outcomes
- How the data were obtained and kept
- How data were displayed (table, graph, and/or figure)
- The amount of information (don't be overwhelmed by it)

Conflicting Viewpoints

Sample Passage III

What caused the extinction of the dinosaurs? Two differing views are presented below.

Scientist 1

Throughout the long Mesozoic era, hundreds of dinosaur species dominated over smaller animals. Some dinosaurs were meat eaters and others ate only plants. Some lived in deserts, some in swamps. There were even dinosaurs swimming through the oceans and soaring through the skies. This extraordinarily successful group of reptiles all disappeared at the end of the Cretaceous period, 65 million years ago. Only a worldwide catastrophe could have simultaneously killed all dinosaurs in their diverse environmental niches (specific areas). The most probable cause of the mass extinction is a close encounter with a comet, which could have abruptly altered the earth's temperatures. Dinosaurs, like all reptiles, were cold-blooded animals and could not adapt to a great temperature change.

Scientist 2

It is almost certain that no single event killed all dinosaurs. Their record during the Mesozoic era is one of species continually evolving to new species; each old species is then said to have become extinct. The extinctions are not at all simultaneous. The early, egg-eating pelycosaurs disappeared in the Permian period. The largest dinosaur of all—Brachiosaurus—became extinct in the Jurassic. The ensuing record during the Cretaceous period is even richer and more complicated, with duck-billed hadrosaurs, predatory tyrannosaurs, and flying pterosaurs appearing and disappearing at various times. By the end of the Cretaceous, the last dinosaur species had vanished. The slow disappearance of the dinosaurs occurred as mammals evolved into more habitats. The last dinosaur and the last dinosaur egg were probably eaten by mammals.

Sample Questions for Passage III

12. A key point that would help settle the dispute about dinosaur extinction would be to know

    F. whether cold-blooded animals could adapt to new temperatures slowly.

    G. when the various dinosaur species disappeared.

    H. whether a comet could cause a minor change of climate.

    J. which environmental niches were occupied by dinosaurs.

You should begin by rereading the opening sentence of the passage to make sure you know the scientific issue in dispute. In this example, it's the cause of dinosaur extinction.

Then try to perceive the main point or points of disagreement in the theories presented, since many of the questions cover these points. Try not to let the details of evidence keep you from recognizing the main points. **Circle or underline the main points of agreement and disagreement.**

In this sample passage, you should notice that Scientist 1 says that all dinosaurs were simultaneously killed, while Scientist 2 states that the different species became extinct at different times—the main point of disagreement between the two theories. You could better choose between the two theories if you definitely knew when the various dinosaur species disappeared, so the correct answer is choice **G.** Understanding the main point or points of disagreement between the rival theories is your best help on the conflicting viewpoints format.

---

13. One of the key differences between the views on extinction of Scientist 1 and Scientist 2 is that:

   A. Scientist 1 credits sudden change; Scientist 2 credits gradual change.

   B. Scientist 1 credits environmental change; Scientist 2 credits killing by mammals.

   C. Scientist 1 credits thermal change; Scientist 2 credits deaths by natural causes.

   D. Scientist 1 credits an astronomical event; Scientist 2 credits a chemical event.

Focus on the *key* differences in the viewpoints. The perspective of Scientist 1 is that the extinctions happened suddenly, at the same time, as a result of an astronomical event. The perspective of Scientist 2 is that the extinctions happened throughout several geologic periods, spanning tens of millions of years. Choice **A.** is the best answer. You might here consider choosing answer **B.**, since Scientist 1 does suggest the astrological event (the comet) caused an environmental change and since Scientist 2 does suggest *some* predation by mammals. It is not as good an answer as **A.**, however, because Scientist 2 doesn't necessarily suggest *only* predation as the reason for extinction. You might also consider choice **C.** to be a possibility, but the problem with this answer is that *both* scientists are speaking of deaths by "natural causes." A close encounter with a comet is just as "natural" as killing by mammals or extinction from some other environmental cause.

14. Which of the following statements would most likely be made by Scientist 2 as an argument against the position taken by Scientist 1?

    F. Dinosaurs could not adapt to the sudden worldwide changes to the environment.

    G. Dinosaurs were so successful in all ecosystems that they out-competed themselves.

    H. There is no evidence for a single astronomical event at the end of the Jurassic period.

    J. There is no evidence for a single astronomical event at the end of the Cretaceous period.

Analyze each viewpoint and the argument given. Scientist 2 believes the extinctions happened gradually over long periods of time. Scientist 1 believes the extinctions happened suddenly, as a (probable) result of climate change due to an encounter with a comet. Scientist 2 would most likely cite the fact that currently known data supply no evidence for a single, large astronomical event that occurred at the end of the Cretaceous period. So choice **J.** is the best answer. Choice **F.** would strengthen the argument of Scientist 1, not weaken it.

15. Which of the following lines of evidence, if true, would most seriously weaken the position of Scientist 1?

    A. Evidence that dinosaurs became extinct in different types of environments

    B. Evidence that dinosaurs became extinct in the same type of environment

    C. Evidence that species of dinosaurs became extinct in different geologic periods

    D. Evidence that all species of dinosaurs became extinct at the same time

Be aware of possible weaknesses in an argument. Scientist 1 believes the extinctions happened at generally the same time (at the end of the Cretaceous period). Evidence that dinosaurs became extinct at widely separated times (different periods) would weaken that position. Choice **C.** is the best answer. Choice **A.** is not the best answer because "types of environments" can refer to many factors, not only temperature. Choice **D.** would strengthen the argument of Scientist 1, not weaken it.

16. All of the following statements, if true, support the position of Scientist 2 EXCEPT:

    F. Brachiosaurs became extinct in the Jurassic period.

    G. Pelycosaurs became extinct in the Permian period.

    H. Encounters with comets can cause extreme temperature changes.

    J. Encounters with comets are uncommon on the earth.

Be aware of what might strengthen or support a viewpoint. Statements **F.** and **G.** contain evidence supporting the position of Scientist 2 that different dinosaurs died out at different times, so these answer choices can be eliminated. If true, the statement alleging that encounters with comets can cause extreme temperature changes would best support the position of Scientist 1 and take away from arguments made by Scientist 2. So **H.** is the best answer.

---

17. Recently, dinosaur extinction research has centered on a crater on the coast of the Yucatan Peninsula in Mexico. It is estimated that this crater could be the remnant of an impact crater that formed 65 million years ago. If true, this new research would lend support to the view of which scientist on dinosaur extinctions?

   A. Scientist 1

   B. Scientist 2

   C. Both Scientist 1 and Scientist 1

   D. Neither Scientist 1 nor Scientist 2

Notice how research supports or weakens an argument. Since Scientist 1 favors a belief that an encounter with a comet transformed the environment of the dinosaurs, the fact that this crater may be evidence of such an encounter would lend the most support to the position of Scientist 1. The correct answer is **A.**

---

18. Current research on extinctions among mammals at the end of the Cretaceous period (65 million years ago) shows that only about 25% of the existing mammals became extinct then. If found to be true, this research would:

   F. weaken the views of Scientist 1.

   G. undermine the views of Scientist 2.

   H. lend support to the views of Scientist 1.

   J. neither support nor undermine the views of either scientist.

Assess additional information given in a question. Since Scientist 1 believes that a comet encounter caused the extinctions of all the dinosaurs, it can be inferred that this scientist would expect this same event to have an impact on all the other life negatively as well. The fact that only 25% of the mammals died off is more supportive of the views of Scientist 2 than of the views of Scientist 1. Choice **F.** is the best answer.

Other Points to Be Aware of for Conflicting Viewpoints Questions

- Conflicts and contradictions between viewpoints
- Underlying assumptions in the viewpoints
- Possible valid criticisms of a viewpoint

Content Area Breakdown

The Science Reasoning Test contains approximately the following number of items and percentages in each category.

CONTENT AREA BREAKDOWN
(Approximate Percentages)

Passage Type	Number of Items	Percentages
Data Representation	15	38%
Research Summaries	18	45%
Conflicting Viewpoints	7	17%
Total	40	

PART II

Four Full-Length Practice Tests

Practice-Review-Analyze-Practice

This section contains four full-length practice simulation ACT exams. The practice tests are followed by answers and complete explanations and analysis techniques. The format, levels of difficulty, question structure, and number of questions are similar to those on the actual ACT. The actual ACT is copyrighted and may not be duplicated, and these questions are not taken directly from the actual tests.

When taking these exams, try to simulate the test conditions by following the time allotments carefully. Remember, the total test is 2 hours and 55 minutes, divided as follows.

English Test	45 minutes
Mathematics Test	60 minutes
Reading Test	35 minutes
Science Reasoning Test	35 minutes

DIRECTIONS FOR ALL PRACTICE TESTS

Directions: Tests in English, mathematics, reading, and science reasoning are contained in the following four practice tests. These tests are designed to measure skills learned in high school and related to success in college. **You may use a calculator on the Mathematics Test only.**

The numbered questions on each test are followed by lettered answer choices. Mark your answer selection next to the corresponding question number on the answer sheet.

After you choose an answer, carefully find the row of letters on your answer sheet that are numbered the same as the question in your question booklet. Using a soft lead pencil, completely blacken the oval of the letter you have selected. **Do NOT use a ballpoint pen.**

Be sure to blacken only one answer to each question. If you wish to change an answer, erase your original answer thoroughly before marking in your new answer. As you mark your answers, pay special attention to make sure that your answer is marked in the right place.

Since only your answer sheet is scored and your score is based completely on the number of questions you answer correctly in the time given, make sure to properly mark the answer you have selected. There is **no penalty** for guessing, so **answer every question, even if you have to guess.**

You are allowed to work on **only** each individual test within the allotted time. If you complete a test before time is up, you may go back and review questions in only that test. You may **NOT** go back to previous tests, and you may **NOT** go forward to another test. You will be disqualified from the exam if you work on another test.

When time is up, be sure to put your pencil down immediately. After time is up, you may **NOT** for any reason fill in answers. This will disqualify you from the exam.

Do **NOT** fold or tear the pages of your test booklet.

TIME WILL BEGIN WHEN YOU TURN TO THE FIRST TEST.

ANSWER SHEETS FOR PRACTICE TEST 1

ENGLISH TEST

```
 1 Ⓐ Ⓑ Ⓒ Ⓓ        26 Ⓕ Ⓖ Ⓗ Ⓙ        51 Ⓐ Ⓑ Ⓒ Ⓓ
 2 Ⓕ Ⓖ Ⓗ Ⓙ        27 Ⓐ Ⓑ Ⓒ Ⓓ        52 Ⓕ Ⓖ Ⓗ Ⓙ
 3 Ⓐ Ⓑ Ⓒ Ⓓ        28 Ⓕ Ⓖ Ⓗ Ⓙ        53 Ⓐ Ⓑ Ⓒ Ⓓ
 4 Ⓕ Ⓖ Ⓗ Ⓙ        29 Ⓐ Ⓑ Ⓒ Ⓓ        54 Ⓕ Ⓖ Ⓗ Ⓙ
 5 Ⓐ Ⓑ Ⓒ Ⓓ        30 Ⓕ Ⓖ Ⓗ Ⓙ        55 Ⓐ Ⓑ Ⓒ Ⓓ
 6 Ⓕ Ⓖ Ⓗ Ⓙ        31 Ⓐ Ⓑ Ⓒ Ⓓ        56 Ⓕ Ⓖ Ⓗ Ⓙ
 7 Ⓐ Ⓑ Ⓒ Ⓓ        32 Ⓕ Ⓖ Ⓗ Ⓙ        57 Ⓐ Ⓑ Ⓒ Ⓓ
 8 Ⓕ Ⓖ Ⓗ Ⓙ        33 Ⓐ Ⓑ Ⓒ Ⓓ        58 Ⓕ Ⓖ Ⓗ Ⓙ
 9 Ⓐ Ⓑ Ⓒ Ⓓ        34 Ⓕ Ⓖ Ⓗ Ⓙ        59 Ⓐ Ⓑ Ⓒ Ⓓ
10 Ⓕ Ⓖ Ⓗ Ⓙ        35 Ⓐ Ⓑ Ⓒ Ⓓ        60 Ⓕ Ⓖ Ⓗ Ⓙ
11 Ⓐ Ⓑ Ⓒ Ⓓ        36 Ⓕ Ⓖ Ⓗ Ⓙ        61 Ⓐ Ⓑ Ⓒ Ⓓ
12 Ⓕ Ⓖ Ⓗ Ⓙ        37 Ⓐ Ⓑ Ⓒ Ⓓ        62 Ⓕ Ⓖ Ⓗ Ⓙ
13 Ⓐ Ⓑ Ⓒ Ⓓ        38 Ⓕ Ⓖ Ⓗ Ⓙ        63 Ⓐ Ⓑ Ⓒ Ⓓ
14 Ⓕ Ⓖ Ⓗ Ⓙ        39 Ⓐ Ⓑ Ⓒ Ⓓ        64 Ⓕ Ⓖ Ⓗ Ⓙ
15 Ⓐ Ⓑ Ⓒ Ⓓ        40 Ⓕ Ⓖ Ⓗ Ⓙ        65 Ⓐ Ⓑ Ⓒ Ⓓ
16 Ⓕ Ⓖ Ⓗ Ⓙ        41 Ⓐ Ⓑ Ⓒ Ⓓ        66 Ⓕ Ⓖ Ⓗ Ⓙ
17 Ⓐ Ⓑ Ⓒ Ⓓ        42 Ⓕ Ⓖ Ⓗ Ⓙ        67 Ⓐ Ⓑ Ⓒ Ⓓ
18 Ⓕ Ⓖ Ⓗ Ⓙ        43 Ⓐ Ⓑ Ⓒ Ⓓ        68 Ⓕ Ⓖ Ⓗ Ⓙ
19 Ⓐ Ⓑ Ⓒ Ⓓ        44 Ⓕ Ⓖ Ⓗ Ⓙ        69 Ⓐ Ⓑ Ⓒ Ⓓ
20 Ⓕ Ⓖ Ⓗ Ⓙ        45 Ⓐ Ⓑ Ⓒ Ⓓ        70 Ⓕ Ⓖ Ⓗ Ⓙ
21 Ⓐ Ⓑ Ⓒ Ⓓ        46 Ⓕ Ⓖ Ⓗ Ⓙ        71 Ⓐ Ⓑ Ⓒ Ⓓ
22 Ⓕ Ⓖ Ⓗ Ⓙ        47 Ⓐ Ⓑ Ⓒ Ⓓ        72 Ⓕ Ⓖ Ⓗ Ⓙ
23 Ⓐ Ⓑ Ⓒ Ⓓ        48 Ⓕ Ⓖ Ⓗ Ⓙ        73 Ⓐ Ⓑ Ⓒ Ⓓ
24 Ⓕ Ⓖ Ⓗ Ⓙ        49 Ⓐ Ⓑ Ⓒ Ⓓ        74 Ⓕ Ⓖ Ⓗ Ⓙ
25 Ⓐ Ⓑ Ⓒ Ⓓ        50 Ⓕ Ⓖ Ⓗ Ⓙ        75 Ⓐ Ⓑ Ⓒ Ⓓ
```

MATHEMATICS TEST

```
 1 Ⓐ Ⓑ Ⓒ Ⓓ Ⓔ      26 Ⓕ Ⓖ Ⓗ Ⓙ Ⓚ      51 Ⓐ Ⓑ Ⓒ Ⓓ Ⓔ
 2 Ⓕ Ⓖ Ⓗ Ⓙ Ⓚ      27 Ⓐ Ⓑ Ⓒ Ⓓ Ⓔ      52 Ⓕ Ⓖ Ⓗ Ⓙ Ⓚ
 3 Ⓐ Ⓑ Ⓒ Ⓓ Ⓔ      28 Ⓕ Ⓖ Ⓗ Ⓙ Ⓚ      53 Ⓐ Ⓑ Ⓒ Ⓓ Ⓔ
 4 Ⓕ Ⓖ Ⓗ Ⓙ Ⓚ      29 Ⓐ Ⓑ Ⓒ Ⓓ Ⓔ      54 Ⓕ Ⓖ Ⓗ Ⓙ Ⓚ
 5 Ⓐ Ⓑ Ⓒ Ⓓ Ⓔ      30 Ⓕ Ⓖ Ⓗ Ⓙ Ⓚ      55 Ⓐ Ⓑ Ⓒ Ⓓ Ⓔ
 6 Ⓕ Ⓖ Ⓗ Ⓙ Ⓚ      31 Ⓐ Ⓑ Ⓒ Ⓓ Ⓔ      56 Ⓕ Ⓖ Ⓗ Ⓙ Ⓚ
 7 Ⓐ Ⓑ Ⓒ Ⓓ Ⓔ      32 Ⓕ Ⓖ Ⓗ Ⓙ Ⓚ      57 Ⓐ Ⓑ Ⓒ Ⓓ Ⓔ
 8 Ⓕ Ⓖ Ⓗ Ⓙ Ⓚ      33 Ⓐ Ⓑ Ⓒ Ⓓ Ⓔ      58 Ⓕ Ⓖ Ⓗ Ⓙ Ⓚ
 9 Ⓐ Ⓑ Ⓒ Ⓓ Ⓔ      34 Ⓕ Ⓖ Ⓗ Ⓙ Ⓚ      59 Ⓐ Ⓑ Ⓒ Ⓓ Ⓔ
10 Ⓕ Ⓖ Ⓗ Ⓙ Ⓚ      35 Ⓐ Ⓑ Ⓒ Ⓓ Ⓔ      60 Ⓕ Ⓖ Ⓗ Ⓙ Ⓚ
11 Ⓐ Ⓑ Ⓒ Ⓓ Ⓔ      36 Ⓕ Ⓖ Ⓗ Ⓙ Ⓚ
12 Ⓕ Ⓖ Ⓗ Ⓙ Ⓚ      37 Ⓐ Ⓑ Ⓒ Ⓓ Ⓔ
13 Ⓐ Ⓑ Ⓒ Ⓓ Ⓔ      38 Ⓕ Ⓖ Ⓗ Ⓙ Ⓚ
14 Ⓕ Ⓖ Ⓗ Ⓙ Ⓚ      39 Ⓐ Ⓑ Ⓒ Ⓓ Ⓔ
15 Ⓐ Ⓑ Ⓒ Ⓓ Ⓔ      40 Ⓕ Ⓖ Ⓗ Ⓙ Ⓚ
16 Ⓕ Ⓖ Ⓗ Ⓙ Ⓚ      41 Ⓐ Ⓑ Ⓒ Ⓓ Ⓔ
17 Ⓐ Ⓑ Ⓒ Ⓓ Ⓔ      42 Ⓕ Ⓖ Ⓗ Ⓙ Ⓚ
18 Ⓕ Ⓖ Ⓗ Ⓙ Ⓚ      43 Ⓐ Ⓑ Ⓒ Ⓓ Ⓔ
19 Ⓐ Ⓑ Ⓒ Ⓓ Ⓔ      44 Ⓕ Ⓖ Ⓗ Ⓙ Ⓚ
20 Ⓕ Ⓖ Ⓗ Ⓙ Ⓚ      45 Ⓐ Ⓑ Ⓒ Ⓓ Ⓔ
21 Ⓐ Ⓑ Ⓒ Ⓓ Ⓔ      46 Ⓕ Ⓖ Ⓗ Ⓙ Ⓚ
22 Ⓕ Ⓖ Ⓗ Ⓙ Ⓚ      47 Ⓐ Ⓑ Ⓒ Ⓓ Ⓔ
23 Ⓐ Ⓑ Ⓒ Ⓓ Ⓔ      48 Ⓕ Ⓖ Ⓗ Ⓙ Ⓚ
24 Ⓕ Ⓖ Ⓗ Ⓙ Ⓚ      49 Ⓐ Ⓑ Ⓒ Ⓓ Ⓔ
25 Ⓐ Ⓑ Ⓒ Ⓓ Ⓔ      50 Ⓕ Ⓖ Ⓗ Ⓙ Ⓚ
```

READING TEST

1 Ⓐ Ⓑ Ⓒ Ⓓ		26 Ⓕ Ⓖ Ⓗ Ⓙ	
2 Ⓕ Ⓖ Ⓗ Ⓙ		27 Ⓐ Ⓑ Ⓒ Ⓓ	
3 Ⓐ Ⓑ Ⓒ Ⓓ		28 Ⓕ Ⓖ Ⓗ Ⓙ	
4 Ⓕ Ⓖ Ⓗ Ⓙ		29 Ⓐ Ⓑ Ⓒ Ⓓ	
5 Ⓐ Ⓑ Ⓒ Ⓓ		30 Ⓕ Ⓖ Ⓗ Ⓙ	
6 Ⓕ Ⓖ Ⓗ Ⓙ		31 Ⓐ Ⓑ Ⓒ Ⓓ	
7 Ⓐ Ⓑ Ⓒ Ⓓ		32 Ⓕ Ⓖ Ⓗ Ⓙ	
8 Ⓕ Ⓖ Ⓗ Ⓙ		33 Ⓐ Ⓑ Ⓒ Ⓓ	
9 Ⓐ Ⓑ Ⓒ Ⓓ		34 Ⓕ Ⓖ Ⓗ Ⓙ	
10 Ⓕ Ⓖ Ⓗ Ⓙ		35 Ⓐ Ⓑ Ⓒ Ⓓ	
11 Ⓐ Ⓑ Ⓒ Ⓓ		36 Ⓕ Ⓖ Ⓗ Ⓙ	
12 Ⓕ Ⓖ Ⓗ Ⓙ		37 Ⓐ Ⓑ Ⓒ Ⓓ	
13 Ⓐ Ⓑ Ⓒ Ⓓ		38 Ⓕ Ⓖ Ⓗ Ⓙ	
14 Ⓕ Ⓖ Ⓗ Ⓙ		39 Ⓐ Ⓑ Ⓒ Ⓓ	
15 Ⓐ Ⓑ Ⓒ Ⓓ		40 Ⓕ Ⓖ Ⓗ Ⓙ	
16 Ⓕ Ⓖ Ⓗ Ⓙ			
17 Ⓐ Ⓑ Ⓒ Ⓓ			
18 Ⓕ Ⓖ Ⓗ Ⓙ			
19 Ⓐ Ⓑ Ⓒ Ⓓ			
20 Ⓕ Ⓖ Ⓗ Ⓙ			
21 Ⓐ Ⓑ Ⓒ Ⓓ			
22 Ⓕ Ⓖ Ⓗ Ⓙ			
23 Ⓐ Ⓑ Ⓒ Ⓓ			
24 Ⓕ Ⓖ Ⓗ Ⓙ			
25 Ⓐ Ⓑ Ⓒ Ⓓ			

SCIENCE REASONING TEST

1 Ⓐ Ⓑ Ⓒ Ⓓ		26 Ⓕ Ⓖ Ⓗ Ⓙ	
2 Ⓕ Ⓖ Ⓗ Ⓙ		27 Ⓐ Ⓑ Ⓒ Ⓓ	
3 Ⓐ Ⓑ Ⓒ Ⓓ		28 Ⓕ Ⓖ Ⓗ Ⓙ	
4 Ⓕ Ⓖ Ⓗ Ⓙ		29 Ⓐ Ⓑ Ⓒ Ⓓ	
5 Ⓐ Ⓑ Ⓒ Ⓓ		30 Ⓕ Ⓖ Ⓗ Ⓙ	
6 Ⓕ Ⓖ Ⓗ Ⓙ		31 Ⓐ Ⓑ Ⓒ Ⓓ	
7 Ⓐ Ⓑ Ⓒ Ⓓ		32 Ⓕ Ⓖ Ⓗ Ⓙ	
8 Ⓕ Ⓖ Ⓗ Ⓙ		33 Ⓐ Ⓑ Ⓒ Ⓓ	
9 Ⓐ Ⓑ Ⓒ Ⓓ		34 Ⓕ Ⓖ Ⓗ Ⓙ	
10 Ⓕ Ⓖ Ⓗ Ⓙ		35 Ⓐ Ⓑ Ⓒ Ⓓ	
11 Ⓐ Ⓑ Ⓒ Ⓓ		36 Ⓕ Ⓖ Ⓗ Ⓙ	
12 Ⓕ Ⓖ Ⓗ Ⓙ		37 Ⓐ Ⓑ Ⓒ Ⓓ	
13 Ⓐ Ⓑ Ⓒ Ⓓ		38 Ⓕ Ⓖ Ⓗ Ⓙ	
14 Ⓕ Ⓖ Ⓗ Ⓙ		39 Ⓐ Ⓑ Ⓒ Ⓓ	
15 Ⓐ Ⓑ Ⓒ Ⓓ		40 Ⓕ Ⓖ Ⓗ Ⓙ	
16 Ⓕ Ⓖ Ⓗ Ⓙ			
17 Ⓐ Ⓑ Ⓒ Ⓓ			
18 Ⓕ Ⓖ Ⓗ Ⓙ			
19 Ⓐ Ⓑ Ⓒ Ⓓ			
20 Ⓕ Ⓖ Ⓗ Ⓙ			
21 Ⓐ Ⓑ Ⓒ Ⓓ			
22 Ⓕ Ⓖ Ⓗ Ⓙ			
23 Ⓐ Ⓑ Ⓒ Ⓓ			
24 Ⓕ Ⓖ Ⓗ Ⓙ			
25 Ⓐ Ⓑ Ⓒ Ⓓ			

CUT HERE

English Test

Time: 45 Minutes

75 Questions

Directions: In the left-hand column, you will find passages in a "spread-out" format with various words and phrases underlined and numbered. In the right-hand column, you will find a set of responses corresponding to each underlined portion. If the underlined portion is correct standard written English, is most appropriate to the style and feeling of the passage, or best makes the intended statement, mark the letter indicating "NO CHANGE." If the underlined portion is not the best choice given, choose the one that is. For these questions, consider only the underlined portions; assume that the rest of the passage is correct as written. You will also see questions concerning parts of the passage or the whole passage. Choose the response you feel is best for these questions.

Passage I

The following paragraphs are given a number in parentheses that appears above each one. The paragraphs may or may not be in the most logical order. Item 16 asks you to choose the paragraph sequence that is the most logical.

The United Vegetable Workers

[1]

[1] Salad lovers, <u>gleefully</u> contemplating the high price of lettuce at the supermarkets, are generally unaware of the several hands outstretched for a share of the retail price. [2] <u>But</u> the growers and the farm workers who harvest

1. A. NO CHANGE
   B. gleeful
   C. glumly
   D. hopefully

2. F. NO CHANGE
   G. For
   H. Because
   J. OMIT the underlined portion.

GO ON TO THE NEXT PAGE

the crop, currently confronting each other <u>in a</u>
<u>strike situation that is violent</u> in the Greenland
₃

Valley, are convinced that <u>one is</u> short-changed
₄
in the division of the harvest revenue. [3] The
United Vegetable Workers Union wants an
increase in minimum wages and <u>that piece-</u>
₅
<u>work rates</u> to bring the earnings of the members
₅

in line <u>with truckers.</u> [4] Farm operators are
₆

reluctant to accept additional costs. ☐7

[2]

<u>In any case, the settlement</u> in the Greenland
₈

3. A. NO CHANGE
   B. in a situation that is a violent strike
   C. in a violent strike situation
   D. striking violently

4. F. NO CHANGE
   G. they are
   H. he is
   J. both are

5. A. NO CHANGE
   B. an increase in piecework rates
   C. piecework rates
   D. a rise of pieceworks

6. F. NO CHANGE
   G. with that of truckers.
   H. with those of truckers.
   J. with the earnings of truckers.

7. Suppose you were obligated to eliminate
   one of the four sentences in Paragraph 1.
   Which of the following sentences can be
   left out with the least damage to the
   meaning and coherence of the
   paragraph?

   A. Sentence 1
   B. Sentence 2
   C. Sentence 3
   D. Sentence 4

8. F. NO CHANGE
   G. (Do NOT begin new paragraph) The
       settlement
   H. (Do NOT begin new paragraph) In
       any case, the settlement
   J. Nevertheless, the settlement

Valley will have an effect on the Presidents' effort to control inflation. The wage and benefit packages adopted at Greenland Valley will have an impact on future farm worker negotiations throughout the country. By adopting an increased minimum wage, an inflationary pressure has already been instituted by the
9.

Congress. The UVW, which wants an increase to $6.00 per hour. Even larger increases are sought in piecework wages, ranging from

$10.00 to $13.00 an hour for a person both skilled in work and industrious when working.

[3]

Because the threat of a lettuce shortage has created a consumer demand that keeps retail prices high, producers unaffected by the strike

have doubled their prices. The lettuce field violence, with several shootings and one death, has shocked the nation. The farm operators

9. A. NO CHANGE
   B. that Presidents'
   C. the President's
   D. the Presidents

10. F. NO CHANGE
    G. an inflationary pressure has already been instituted by Congress.
    H. Congress has already applied an inflationary pressure.
    J. an inflationary pressure has already been applied.

11. A. NO CHANGE
    B. UVW which wants
    C. UVW wants
    D. UVW wanting

12. F. NO CHANGE
    G. skilled and industrious worker.
    H. person industrious at his skill.
    J. person of industry and skill.

13. A. NO CHANGE
    B. Although
    C. Despite the fact that
    D. If

14. F. NO CHANGE
    G. The lettuce field violence of several shootings and one death has shocked the nation.
    H. The violence in the lettuce field has shocked the nation.
    J. OMIT the underlined portion.

GO ON TO THE NEXT PAGE

have offered only small pay <u>hikes. They have</u> <u>however,</u> conceded that a more workable agreement might allow greater increases at the bottom of the farm worker scale with lesser

gains at the top. 16

Passage II

The Mouse and the Rat

[1]

<u>Once, there was</u> a mouse and a rat who lived in a large barn in a fertile country. The rat was happy in this home, for there was always plenty to <u>eat. But</u> the mouse was dissatisfied.

<u>"The food was good," he admitted,</u> but the

winters were cold. He especially <u>disliked to</u> <u>see</u> the smoke from the fireplaces in the farmhouse while he shivered in his nest in the barn. When he could endure the promise of warm fires no longer, he proposed to the rat that they

15. A. NO CHANGE
  B. hikes. They have, however,
  C. hikes; they have however,
  D. hikes: they have however

> Item 16 poses a question about the essay as a whole.

16. Which of the following sequences of paragraphs will make the structure of the passage most logical?

  F. NO CHANGE
  G. 1, 3, 2
  H. 2, 3, 1
  J. 3, 1, 2

17. A. NO CHANGE
  B. Once there was
  C. Once, there were
  D. There was, once

18. F. NO CHANGE
  G. eat, and
  H. eat. And
  J. eat. The

19. A. NO CHANGE
  B. The food is good, he admitted,
  C. The food was good, he admitted,
  D. "The food was good," he would admit,

20. F. NO CHANGE
  G. disliked that he saw
  H. disliked seeing
  J. disliked to have seen

move to the house. "We should have two houses, one for winter and one for summer, <u>like people do,</u>" he said. <u>But the rat was not interested.</u>
21   22

22

[2]

His fur was thicker, his weight greater, <u>and he had a better insulated nest,</u> so he did not
23   23
mind the chill. "I like the change of seasons," he said. "Besides," he went on, "the neighbors here in the barn are friendly and familiar. Who knows <u>what they will be like in the house?</u> I'll
24
stay right here. If you don't go looking for trouble, trouble won't come looking for you.

<u>Nothing ventured, nothing gained.</u> Safety first.
25
A bird in the hand is worth two in the bush." Several more proverbs followed these, and the mouse thought that one more advantage of moving to the farmhouse <u>would be to escape</u>
26

21. **A.** NO CHANGE
   B. as people,
   C. like people,
   D. like people have

22. **F.** NO CHANGE
   G. But the rat was not interested!
   H. OMIT the underlined portion.
   J. (Place at the beginning of Paragraph 2)

23. **A.** NO CHANGE
   B. and his nest was better insulated,
   C. and his was a better insulated nest,
   D. and his nest better insulated,

24. **F.** NO CHANGE
   G. what they are like in the house.
   H. what it is like in the house.
   J. if they will like you in the house.

25. The proverb, compared to the three others in this series, is:

   A. appropriate and briefer.
   B. identical in meaning.
   C. opposite in meaning.
   D. similar in meaning to "Safety first."

26. **F.** NO CHANGE
   G. will be to escape
   H. will be the escape
   J. is to escape

GO ON TO THE NEXT PAGE

from the tedious moralizing and <u>infernal</u>

<u>proverbs</u> of the rat.
27

28

29

Passage III

Annexation Protest

[1]

The city council, Tuesday night, approved the 450-acre annexation of North Belmont by a 5 to 1 vote over the <u>protestations</u> <u>and objections</u> of area residents <u>who attended</u> the meeting. Protesting residents filled the council chambers. Their verbal abuse and

---

27. The word "infernal" is used here because it is the diction of the:

  A. rat.

  B. mouse.

  C. barnyard.

  D. author.

> Items 28 and 29 pose questions about the passage as a whole.

28. The passage uses all of the following devices EXCEPT:

  F. dialogue.

  G. comedy.

  H. contrast of general and specific.

  J. indirect discourse.

29. The longer work of which this passage is a part is probably a:

  A. satire.

  B. novel.

  C. fable.

  D. short story.

30. **F.** NO CHANGE

  G. objections

  H. denouncing

  J. protestation and objection

31. **A.** NO CHANGE

  B. who attended the meeting and filled the

  C. who attended the meeting by filling the

  D. who filled the

threat of an injunction could not alter the two petitions they submitted did not have the needed signatures. To bring the issue before all the voters of the county requires either the signatures of 25% of the registered voters or 10% of the property owners.

32

[34]

[2]

Residents filed petitions signed by 116 alleged registered voters and 48 alleged property owners, some signatures appearing on both lists, at the last city council meeting. But

35

Jack Cope, city manager said in a staff report that only 66 of the registered voters' signatures—far short of the required 25%—

36

---

32. **F.** NO CHANGE
   G. the two petitions which
   H. that of the two petitions
   J. the fact that the two petitions

33. **A.** NO CHANGE
   B. the signatures either of 25% of the registered voters or 10%
   C. the signatures of either 25% of the registered voters or 10%
   D. the signatures of either 25% of the voters or of 10%

34. The probable audience for whom this paragraph was written is:
   F. readers of daily or weekly newspapers.
   G. readers of a monthly news magazine.
   H. members of the city council.
   J. petitioners from North Belmont.

35. The best position in this sentence for the underlined phrase is:
   A. NO CHANGE
   B. at the beginning of the sentence.
   C. after the verb *signed.*
   D. after the noun *owners.*

36. **F.** NO CHANGE
   G. Cope, city manager, said
   H. Cope city manager said
   J. Cope, who is city manager, said

GO ON TO THE NEXT PAGE

was valid. And only 26 of the 48 supposed
37   38

property owners really owned land in the
                    38

county. "Even if all the protest signatures were

accepted," Cope concluded, "the total will still
                                        39

be short of the number required by law. 40

[3]

One of the North Belmont residents told the

council that I have delivered today to the city
               41

clerk the signatures of 21 additional voters

opposed to the annexation. Enough to require
                    42

an election in the county. The city clerk
                    42

acknowledged that she had received the

37. A. NO CHANGE

   B. were valid.

   C. will be valid.

   D. had been valid.

38. F. NO CHANGE

   G. supposedly property owners really
       owned land

   H. supposed property owners really
       owns land

   J. supposed property owners really
       own land

39. A. NO CHANGE

   B. would still

   C. should still

   D. OMIT the underlined portion.

40. Unlike Paragraph 1, Paragraph 2 uses:

   F. loose sentences.

   G. a rhetorical question.

   H. direct quotation.

   J. cause-and-effect reasoning.

41. A. NO CHANGE

   B. I delivered

   C. he delivered

   D. he had delivered

42. F. NO CHANGE

   G. annexation, enough to require an
       election in the county.

   H. annexation. And enough to require
       an election in the county.

   J. annexation. Which is enough to
       require an election in the county.

signatures. <u>Anna Repton, the city clerk, has</u>₄₃ <u>held her office for more than twenty years next</u>₄₃ <u>June.</u>₄₃ But Mayor Schulz, citing the filing deadline of three weeks ago, refused to allow the signatures to be counted. A heated exchange

capped by a series of <u>savagely comic</u>₄₄ insults

followed. 45 The meeting adjourned at

10:35 p.m. 46

Passage IV

Then and Now

[1]

<u>Growing up</u>₄₇ in Maine in the 1930s, my favorite room was the kitchen. Unlike most of the farms nearby, ours had both electricity and gas, woodburning fireplaces in most rooms,

43. A. NO CHANGE

B. Anna Repton, the city clerk, will hold her office for more than twenty years next June.

C. Anna Repton, the city clerk, will have held her office for more than twenty years next June.

D. OMIT the underlined portion.

44. F. NO CHANGE

G. savage

H. comic

J. savage comic

45. The author at this point could strengthen the passage by:

A. discussing the background of Mayor Schulz.

B. discussing the laws governing annexation.

C. citing the names of the North Belmont representatives.

D. quoting one or two of the insults.

46. Which of the following words or phrases does NOT describe the closing sentence of the paragraph?

F. Conventional

G. Terse

H. Deliberately anticlimactic

J. Hortatory

47. A. NO CHANGE

B. When growing up

C. When I was growing up

D. While growing up

GO ON TO THE NEXT PAGE

and <u>the house was centrally heated by oil.</u> Why
should I remember the kitchen as the only

warm room? 49 <u>Because, I suppose,</u> it was
even warmer than the rest of the house. My

mother refused to have <u>a "newfangled"</u> gas
stove and did all her cooking on a huge

woodburning range. <u>And what cooking!</u> There
were four ovens in the range, and my mother
kept all of them full: breads and rolls, pies and
cakes, in the ovens on the left; roasts,

48. **F.** NO CHANGE
    G. the house had central heating.
    H. the house had oil central heating.
    J. oil central heating.

49. The author varies the sentences in the paragraph here by using:
    A. a first person pronoun.
    B. an interrogative verb.
    C. a passive verb.
    D. a periodic sentence.

50. **F.** NO CHANGE
    G. Because I suppose
    H. Because, I suppose
    J. Because.

51. The author puts quotation marks around the adjective "newfangled" because the word is:
    A. not English.
    B. slang.
    C. the one the mother used.
    D. inappropriate in this context.

52. **F.** NO CHANGE
    G. And what cooking?
    H. And what's cooking?
    J. OMIT the underlined portion.

casseroles, and stews, and her giant bean pot in the ovens on the right. ⬚53

⬚54

[2]

I live now in a small, attractive apartment in Manhattan. My rent each month is three or four times as much as my father's farm earned

in a year, and my kitchen is <u>hardly bigger</u> than
                                           55
my mother's four-oven range. I don't know how to make bread (I am a lawyer, specializing in labor law) <u>or how to bake a bean.</u> Most of
                          56

53. The punctuation of this sentence uses a colon after "full" and a semicolon after "left." The correct punctuation would be:

A. NO CHANGE

B. a semicolon after "full" and a colon after "left."

C. a comma after "full" and a comma after "left."

D. a semicolon after "full" and a comma after "left."

54. Which of the following most accurately describes the point of view of Paragraph 1?

F. A male narrator using the third person

G. A narrator using the first person and present tense

H. A female narrator using the first person

J. A narrator using the first person and past tense

55. A. NO CHANGE

B. not hardly bigger

C. not hardly larger

D. smaller

56. F. NO CHANGE

G. or how beans are baked.

H. nor how beans are baked.

J. or know how to bake beans.

GO ON TO THE NEXT PAGE

the time I eat out or <u>fix something from a pack-</u>₅₇
<u>age in the microwave that is quick.</u>₅₇ My kitchen

is <u>no warmer than any room</u>₅₈ in my apartment.

A thermostat keeps all rooms <u>exactly the same,</u>₅₉
<u>identical, temperature of heat.</u>₅₉

[60]

Passage IV

The following paragraphs are given a number in parentheses above each one. The paragraphs may be in the most logical order, or they may not. Question 75 asks you to choose the paragraph sequence that is the most logical.

Domestic Disputes

[1]

[1] A police dispatcher receiving a call about a domestic dispute must decide <u>whether to</u>₆₁
<u>send</u>₆₁ one, two, or no officers at all. [2] If the

57. A. NO CHANGE

    B. fix something from a package quickly in the microwave.

    C. fix something in the microwave from a package that is quick.

    D. fix something that is quick in the microwave from a package.

58. F. NO CHANGE

    G. not warmer than any room

    H. no warmer than any other room

    J. not much warmer than any room

59. A. NO CHANGE

    B. at exactly the same, identical temperature of heat.

    C. at the same, identical temperature.

    D. at the same temperature.

Item 60 poses a question about the essay as a whole.

60. Readers are likely to regard the passage as best described by which of the following terms?

    F. Inspirational

    G. Sarcastic

    H. Confessional

    J. Nostalgic

61. A. NO CHANGE

    B. whether or not to send

    C. weather to send

    D. weather or not to send

disturbance <u>appears to be a routine one</u> a single
₆₂
officer will be dispatched to resolve the dis-

pute. [3] <u>And if it appears</u> that there may be an
₆₃
injury or crime, two or more officers will be
sent to defuse the tensions. [4] In incidents of
domestic violence, women and children are
more often injured than men. ⬚64

[2]

During a family crisis, it is often a member
of the immediate family <u>calling</u> the police
₆₅
department. The neighbors are unlikely, <u>unless</u>
₆₆
<u>the dispute becomes very noisy or threatening,</u>
₆₆
to interfere in someone else's domestic trou-
bles. Sometimes a child of fighting parents
will seek refuge with a neighbor and <u>ask for</u>
₆₇
<u>the neighbor to</u> notify the police. In-laws are
₆₇
frequently responsible for reporting <u>domestic</u>
₆₈
<u>quarrels which have become violent.</u>
₆₈

62. F. NO CHANGE
    G. was routine,
    H. appears to be routine
    J. appears to be routine,

63. A. NO CHANGE
    B. If, however it appears
    C. However if it appears
    D. But if it appears

64. The omission of which of the four sen-
    tences of Paragraph 1 will improve its
    coherence?
    F. Sentence 1
    G. Sentence 2
    H. Sentence 3
    J. Sentence 4

65. A. NO CHANGE
    B. who is calling
    C. who calls
    D. that telephones

66. F. NO CHANGE
    G. OMIT the underlined portion.
    H. (Place after "neighbors")
    J. (Place after "troubles")

67. A. NO CHANGE
    B. ask the neighbor to
    C. ask that the neighbor should
    D. ask of the neighbor to

68. F. NO CHANGE
    G. domestic quarrels, which have
       become violent.
    H. domestic quarrels that are violent.
    J. violent domestic quarrels.

GO ON TO THE NEXT PAGE

[3]

In a crime situation, emotions <u>run high,</u> and
₆₉
officers must <u>maintain a steady attitude of neu-</u>
₇₀
<u>trality,</u> <u>which is not always easy to do.</u> If
₇₀   ₇₁
someone <u>is hurt, they</u> must see to it that proper
₇₂
medical care is obtained. Skilled officers will
be able to reason with the disputants, perhaps
suggesting a separation, with either the
husband or the wife staying with friends or
relatives until <u>the air has cleared.</u>
₇₃

[74]

69. A. NO CHANGE
　　B. run highly,
　　C. ran high,
　　D. have run high,

70. F. NO CHANGE
　　G. keep a steady attitude of neutrality,
　　H. remain neutral,
　　J. steadily maintain an attitude of neutrality,

71. A. NO CHANGE
　　B. and this is not always easy to do.
　　C. and that is not always easy to do.
　　D. something not always easy to do.

72. F. NO CHANGE
　　G. is hurt, then he
　　H. is hurt, he
　　J. is hurt they

73. A. NO CHANGE
　　B. the rain has stopped.
　　C. the air is warmer.
　　D. the air is cooler.

74. From which of the following would a quotation probably be a most effective addition to this passage?

　　F. A social worker who deals with family problems
　　G. A victim of wife abuse
　　H. A police officer
　　J. A judge

75

75. Which of the following sequences of paragraphs will make the structure of the passage most logical?

A. NO CHANGE

B. 1, 3, 2

C. 2, 1, 3

D. 3, 2, 1

IF YOU FINISH BEFORE TIME IS CALLED, CHECK YOUR WORK ON THIS
SECTION ONLY. DO NOT WORK ON ANY OTHER SECTION IN THE TEST.

Mathematics Test

Time: 60 Minutes

60 Questions

Directions: After solving each problem, choose the correct answer and fill in the corresponding oval on your answer sheet. Do not spend too much time on any one problem. Solve as many problems as you can and return to the problems you skipped, or recheck your work, if time permits. You are allowed to use a calculator on this test.

Note: Unless it is otherwise stated, you can assume all of the following.

1. Figures are NOT necessarily drawn to scale.

2. Geometric figures lie in a plane.

3. The word "line" means a straight line.

4. The word "average" refers to the arithmetic mean.

1. The product of x and y is a constant. If the value of x is increased by 50 percent, by what percentage must the value of y be decreased?

   A. 25%

   B. 33⅓%

   C. 40%

   D. 50%

   E. 66⅔%

2. One hundred students will attend a dance if tickets cost 30 cents each. For each 5-cent raise in the price of the ticket, 10 fewer students will attend. What price will deliver the maximum dollar sales?

   F. $0.30

   G. $0.35

   H. $0.40

   J. $0.45

   K. $0.50

3. What is the area of a rectangle, in square inches, if its length is 36 inches and its diagonal is 39 inches?

  A. 1,404
  B.   702
  C.   540
  D.   108
  E.   75

4. Bryan needs 5 shelves for books. The longest shelf is to be the bottom shelf, and each shelf above is to be 4 inches shorter than the one immediately below. If the sum of the lengths of the shelves is 155 inches, what is the length, in inches, of the longest shelf?

  F. 23
  G. 28
  H. 31
  J. 36
  K. 39

5. If $3x + 2y = 14$ and $3x = 2y$, then $x + y = ?$

  A. 6
  B. 5⅚
  C. 5⅙
  D. 4⅚
  E. 3½

6. A square and a circle have the same area. What is the circumference of the circle if the perimeter of the square is $8\sqrt{\pi}$?

  F.   4
  G. 4π
  H. $\sqrt{2}\pi$
  J. 8π
  K. $8\sqrt{\pi}$

7. What is the greatest common factor of 24, 48, 60, and 78?

  A. 2
  B. 6
  C. 12
  D. 18
  E. 78

8. During a season, a tennis team won 21 matches and lost 30 percent of its matches. What is the number of matches that the team lost?

  F. 70
  G. 30
  H. 9
  J. 7
  K. 5

9. In a package of candies, 8 candies are green, 2 are red, and 6 are white. If the first candy chosen is not a white one, what is the probability that the next one randomly chosen will be white?

  A. ⁵⁄₁₆
  B. ⅜
  C. ⅖
  D. ⅗
  E. ⅔

GO ON TO THE NEXT PAGE

10. If the angles of a triangle are $3x$, $x + 10$, and $2x - 40$ what is the measure of the smallest angle?

    F. 30°

    G. 35°

    H. 40°

    J. 45°

    K. 50°

11. $(x + 3)(2x + 4) = ?$

    A. $2x^2 + 10x + 12$

    B. $x^2 + 5x + 6$

    C. $2x^2 + 6x + 12$

    D. $x^2 + 3x + 6$

    E. $2x^2 + 2x + 12$

12. What is the measure of $\angle w$ in the figure shown below?

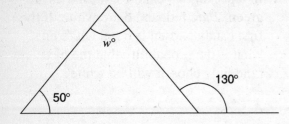

    F. 50°

    G. 60°

    H. 70°

    J. 80°

    K. 90°

13. If A is greater than B, C is less than A, and B is greater than C, then which of the following is true?

    A. $A < B < C$

    B. $B < A < C$

    C. $B < C < A$

    D. $C < A < B$

    E. $C < B < A$

14. Which of the following is (are) true about the figure shown below?

    I. $\angle 1 + \angle 2 = \angle 3$

    II. $\angle 3 > \angle 2$

    III. $180° > \angle 2 + \angle 3$

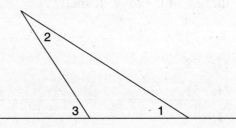

    F. I only

    G. II only

    H. I and II only

    J. I and III only

    K. II and III only

15. Which of the following is a simplified form of $\dfrac{12x^6 y^4 z^2}{6x^2 y^4 z^8}$?

    A. $\dfrac{2x^4}{z^6}$

    B. $2x^8 y^8 z^{10}$

    C. $6x^4 z^{-6}$

    D. $\dfrac{2x^3}{z^4}$

    E. $\dfrac{2x^6}{z^4}$

16. Marlo has a basketball court that measures 30 feet by 50 feet. She needs a grass strip around it. How wide must the strip be, in feet, to provide 900 square feet of grass?

    F. 3
    G. 4
    H. 5
    J. 6
    K. 7

17. Two hikers leave the same point and travel at right angles to each other. After 2 hours, they are 10 miles apart. If one walks 1 mile per hour faster than the other, what is the speed of the slower hiker, in miles per hour?

    A. 2
    B. 3
    C. 4
    D. 5
    E. 6

18. If the 3 sides of a right triangle measure 3 centimeters, 4 centimeters, and 5 centimeters, what is the sine of the angle opposite the side with a length of 4 centimeters?

    F. ⅗
    G. ¾
    H. ⅘
    J. 5/4
    K. 5/3

19. Which equation below has roots that are each 4 less than the roots of $3x^2 + 2x - 4 = 0$?

    A. $3x^2 + 14x - 12 = 0$
    B. $3x^2 + 26x + 52 = 0$
    C. $6x^2 + 3x - 28 = 0$
    D. $6x^2 + 16x + 9 = 0$
    E. $3x^2 - 15x - 18 = 0$

20. Which of the following could NOT be a solution for $4 - 3x < -3$?

    F. 4
    G. 3.5
    H. 3
    J. 2.5
    K. 2

21. What is the area, in square units, of the quadrilateral shown below?

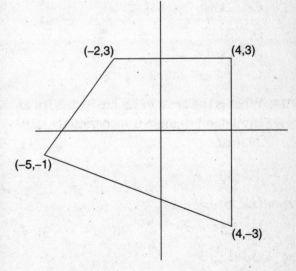

    A. 24
    B. 27
    C. 39
    D. 46
    E. 54

GO ON TO THE NEXT PAGE

Mathematics Test

22. A tank 4 inches high is to be made from a square piece of sheet metal by cutting a square out of each corner and folding up the sides. The volume of the tank is to be 900 cubic inches. What is the width of the piece of sheet metal, in inches?

(Note: $V = lwh$)

  F. 12

  G. 15

  H. 19

  J. 21

  K. 23

23. Macey is 3 times as old as Mike. In 8 years, she will be twice as old as Mike. How old was Macey 3 years ago?

  A. 5

  B. 8

  C. 21

  D. 24

  E. 27

24. What is the area, in square inches, of an equilateral triangle if its perimeter is 30 inches?

  F. 50

  G. $50\sqrt{3}$

  H. 25

  J. $25\sqrt{3}$

  K. $10\sqrt{3}$

25. Ellen can mow a lawn in 2 hours. Dave can mow the same lawn in 1½ hours. Approximately how many minutes will it take to mow the lawn if Ellen and Dave work together?

  A. 210

  B. 90

  C. 51

  D. 48

  E. 30

26. Which of the following is a simplified version equivalent to

$$\frac{\left(x^{2y+2}\right)\left(x^{6y-1}\right)}{x^{4y-3}}?$$

  F. x^{3y+4}

  G. x^{4y+4}

  H. x^{3y-2}

  J. x^{4y-2}

  K. x^{4y+1}

27. The pie graph below represents the relative sizes of a family's per-dollar budget. What is the degree measure of the central angle of the sectors labeled "Food" and "Housing"?

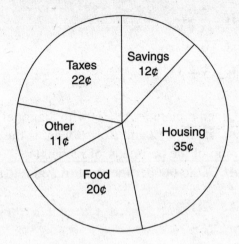

A. 180°

B. 188°

C. 195°

D. 198°

E. 208°

28. In the figure shown below, $\overline{AB} = \overline{BC}, \overline{CD} = \overline{BD}$, and $\angle CAD = 70°$. What is the measure of $\angle ADC$?

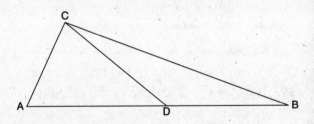

F. 80°

G. 70°

H. 60°

J. 50°

K. 40°

29. In the standard (x, y) coordinate plane, what is the slope of a line that passes through the points $(-2, 3)$ and $(3, -2)$?

A. −2

B. −1

C. 0

D. 1

E. 2

30. Three angles of a pentagon are 130°, 90°, and 80°. Of the remaining 2 angles, one is 30° more than twice the other. What is the sum of the smallest 2 angles?

F. 140°

G. 150°

H. 160°

J. 170°

K. 180°

31. How many liters of 20 percent solution must be added to a 60 percent solution to give 40 liters of a 50 percent solution?

A. 32

B. 30

C. 20

D. 10

E. 8

32. How many times does the equation $y = x^4 - x^5$ intersect the x-axis?

F. 1

G. 2

H. 3

J. 4

K. 5

GO ON TO THE NEXT PAGE

33. Bryan is standing 2,000 feet from objects A and C. The observed angle between the objects is 48°. How far apart are objects A and C?

   A. 4,000 sin 24°

   B. 2,000 sin 48°

   C. 4,000 sin 48°

   D. 2,000 sin 24°

   E. 2,000 cos 48°

34. The current in a river is 4 miles per hour. A boat can travel 20 miles per hour in still water. How many miles up the river can the boat travel if the round trip is to take 10 hours?

   F. 88

   G. 96

   H. 100

   J. 112

   K. 124

35. A man walks from B to C, a distance of x miles, at 8 miles per hour and returns at 12 miles per hour. What is his average speed, in miles per hour?

   A. 10.2

   B. 10

   C. 9.8

   D. 9.6

   E. 9

36. $\dfrac{x}{x-y} - \dfrac{y}{y-x} = ?$

   F. $\dfrac{x+y}{x-y}$

   G. 1

   H. $\dfrac{x-y}{x+y}$

   J. 0

   K. $x-y$

37. Given rectangle $ABCD$ with diagonal $\overline{AC}$ if $\overline{AB} = 12$ and $\overline{BC} = 9$ what is the ratio of the perimeter of rectangle $ABCD$ to the perimeter of triangle ACD?

   A. 2:1

   B. 6:7

   C. 1:2

   D. 7:5

   E. 7:6

38. What is the sum of $4x^3 - 2x^2$, $-3x^3 + 3x^2$, and $-2x^3 - 4x^2$?

   F. $-x^3 - 3x^2$

   G. $x^3 + 3x^2$

   H. $3x^3 - 5x^2$

   J. $-3x^3 + 5x^2$

   K. $4x^5$

39. If $f(x) = x^2 - 2$ and $g(x) = 2x + 2$, then

   $$f\left(g\left(f\left(\tfrac{1}{2}\right)\right)\right) =$$

   A. ¼

   B. ½

   C. 1

   D. 2

   E. 4

40. In the standard (x, y) coordinate plane, what is the equation of the line that passes through the point $(1, 1)$ and is perpendicular to the line with equation

$$y = -\frac{1}{2}x + 3?$$

F. $y = -\frac{1}{2}x - 2$

G. $y = -\frac{1}{2}x + \frac{3}{2}$

H. $y = 2x + 6$

J. $y = 2x - 1$

K. None of these

41. What is the area of the triangle in the figure below?

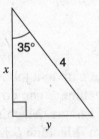

A. $8 \sin 35° \cos 35°$

B. $8 \tan 35°$

C. $\dfrac{8}{\tan 35°}$

D. $4 \sin 35° + 4 \cos 35°$

E. $8(\tan^2 35° + 1)$

42. In the standard (x, y) coordinate plane, what is the equation of a line with slope $\frac{1}{2}$ that passes through the point $(1, 2)$?

F. $x - 2y + 3 = 0$

G. $2x - y = 0$

H. $x + 2y - 5 = 0$

J. $2x + y - 4 = 0$

K. $4x - y - 2 = 0$

43. The length of a rectangle is 6 centimeters greater than its width. The area of the rectangle is 18 square centimeters. What is the width of the rectangle, in centimeters?

A. $3\left(\sqrt{3} - 1\right)$

B. $3\left(\sqrt{3} + 1\right)$

C. $3\left(1 - \sqrt{3}\right)$

D. $3\sqrt{3} - 1$

E. $3\sqrt{3} + 1$

44. Given circle O below, what is the measure of $\angle x$?

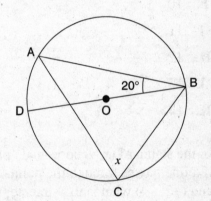

F. $40°$

G. $55°$

H. $70°$

J. $80°$

K. Cannot be determined from the given information

GO ON TO THE NEXT PAGE

45. Consuela biked 20 miles. If she had increased her average speed by 4 miles per hour, the trip would have taken 1 hour less. What is her average speed, in miles per hour?

A. $2\sqrt{21}+2$

B. $2\sqrt{21}-2$

C. $2\sqrt{21}-1$

D. $2\sqrt{21}+1$

E. $\sqrt{21}-2$

46. The sum of two numbers is 25. The sum of their squares is 313. What is the value of the larger number?

F. 10

G. 11

H. 12

J. 13

K. 14

47. In the standard (x, y) coordinate plane, if a line passes through the points $(6, 4)$ and $(-2, -4)$ what is its y-intercept?

A. 1

B. 0

C. −1

D. −2

E. −3

48. In the figure below, $\overline{BC} = 12$ units, $\overline{AC} = 9$ units, and $\angle ACB = 90°$. How many units is the length of the height from C to line $\overline{AB}$?

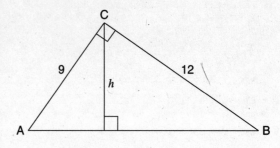

F. 5.4

G. 6.4

H. 6.8

J. 7.2

K. 8

49. Machine A can do a job alone in 10 hours. Machine B can do the same job alone in 12 hours. Machine A is turned on at 6 a.m. Machine B is turned on at 9 a.m. Machine A breaks down at 10 a.m., and Machine B must finish the job alone. When will Machine B finish?

A. 2:30

B. 3:42

C. 4:12

D. 4:40

E. Cannot be determined from the given information

50. The total resistance, R, of two resistors, A and B, connected in parallel, is given by the following formula:

$$\frac{1}{R} = \frac{1}{A} + \frac{1}{B}$$

If $A = 10$ and $R = 4$; what is the value of B?

F. $7\frac{1}{4}$

G. 7

H. $6\frac{3}{4}$

J. $6\frac{2}{3}$

K. 6

51. Two concentric circles have radii of 7 and 13. What is the length of a chord of the larger circle that is tangent to the smaller circle?

A. $4\sqrt{30}$

B. $2\sqrt{30}$

C. $\frac{\sqrt{30}}{2}$

D. $2\sqrt{162}$

E. 22

52. In an isosceles triangle, one angle equals 120°. If one of the legs is 6 inches long, what is the length of the longest side in inches?

F. $3\sqrt{3}$

G. $6\sqrt{2}$

H. $3\sqrt{6}$

J. $3\sqrt{2}$

K. $6\sqrt{3}$

53. Which of the following expressions is a simplified form of

$$\frac{2\sqrt{3} - 4}{\sqrt{3} + 2}?$$

A. $4\sqrt{3} + 7$

B. $2\left(4\sqrt{3} - 7\right)$

C. $2\sqrt{3} - 7$

D. $2\left(7 - 4\sqrt{3}\right)$

E. $2\left(4\sqrt{3} + 7\right)$

54. Which of the following expressions is a simplified form of

$$\sqrt{\frac{78x^5 y^7}{6x^2 y^3}}?$$

F. $\frac{1}{3} x^2 y^2 \sqrt{39x}$

G. $x^2 y \sqrt{13x}$

H. $xy^2 \sqrt{13x}$

J. $\frac{1}{3} xy^2 \sqrt{117x}$

K. $\frac{1}{3} xy^2 \sqrt{13x}$

55. $\dfrac{|8-3||3-8|}{|-3-8||-8+3|} = ?$

A. $-25/121$

B. $-5/11$

C. $25/121$

D. $5/11$

E. 1

56. If $x - 10 = \dfrac{-9}{x}$, then what is the difference between the 2 roots?

F. 1

G. 3

H. 6

J. 8

K. 9

GO ON TO THE NEXT PAGE

Mathematics Test

57. How many degrees are there in each interior angle of a regular decagon (10-sided figure)?

   A. 15

   B. 18

   C. 120

   D. 144

   E. 172

58. If $4x^4 + 2x + A = 0$, which value of A will result in a solution for x of 2 and $-\frac{1}{2}$?

   F. -20

   G. -10

   H. 6

   J. 12

   K. 16

59. What is the length, in feet, of the diagonal of a square if the area of the square is 12 square feet?

   A. $12\sqrt{2}$

   B. 6

   C. $2\sqrt{6}$

   D. $\dfrac{6\sqrt{3}}{2}$

   E. $2\sqrt{3}$

60. Which of the following is a simplified form of
$$\frac{x^2 - 7xy + 12y^2}{x^2 - 4xy + 3y^2}?$$

   F. $\dfrac{x - 3y}{x - y}$

   G. $\dfrac{x - 6y}{x - y}$

   H. $\dfrac{x - 4y}{x - y}$

   J. $3xy - 4$

   K. 12

IF YOU FINISH BEFORE TIME IS CALLED, CHECK YOUR WORK ON THIS
SECTION ONLY. DO NOT WORK ON ANY OTHER SECTION IN THE TEST.

STOP

Reading Test

Time: 35 Minutes

40 Questions

Directions: Each of the four passages in this test is followed by a series of multiple-choice questions. Read the passage and choose the best answer to each question. Return to the passage as often as necessary to answer the questions.

Passage 1

PROSE FICTION: This passage is adapted from Middlemarch *by George Elliott (published in 1876).*

Early in the day Dorothea had returned from the school which she had set going in the village, and was taking her usual place in the sitting-room which divided
(5) the bedrooms of the sisters, bent on finishing a plan for some buildings (a kind of work which she delighted in), when Celia, who had been watching her with a hesitating desire to propose some-
(10) thing, said—

"Dorothea dear, if you don't mind—if you are not very busy—suppose we looked at mamma's jewels to-day, and divided them? It is exactly six months
(15) to-day since uncle gave them to you, and you have not looked at them yet."

Celia's face had the shadow of a pouting expression in it, the full presence of the pout being kept back by an habitual awe
(20) of her sister.

"Well, dear, we should never wear them, you know." Dorothea spoke in a full cordial tone, half caressing, half explanatory. She had her pencil in her
(25) hand, and was making tiny side-plans on a margin.

Celia coloured, and looked very grave. "I think, dear, we are wanting in respect to mamma's memory, to put them by
(30) and take no notice of them. And," she added, after hesitating a little, "necklaces are quite usual now; and women who are stricter in some things even than you are wear ornaments. And
(35) Christians generally—surely there are women in heaven now who wore jewels." Celia was conscious of some mental strength when she really applied herself to argument.

(40) "You would like to wear them?" exclaimed Dorothea, an air of astonished discovery animating her whole person. "Of course, then, let us have them out. Why did you not tell me before?"

(45) The casket was soon open before them, and the various jewels spread out, making a bright parterre on the table. It was no great collection, but a few of the ornaments were really of remarkable
(50) beauty, the finest that was obvious at first being a necklace of purple amethysts set in exquisite gold work, and a pearl cross with five brilliants in it. Dorothea immediately took up the neck-
(55) lace and fastened it round her sister's neck.

GO ON TO THE NEXT PAGE

"There, Celia! you can wear that with your Indian muslin. But this cross you must wear with your dark dresses."

(60) Celia was trying not to smile with pleasure. "O Dodo, you must keep the cross yourself."

"No, no, dear, no," said Dorothea, putting up her hand with careless deprecation.

(65) "Yes, indeed you must; it would suit you—in your black dress, now," said Celia, insistingly. "You *might* wear that."

"Not for the world, not for the world. A cross is the last thing I would wear as a
(70) trinket." Dorothea shuddered slightly.

"Then you will think it wicked in me to wear it," said Celia, uneasily.

"No, dear, no," said Dorothea, stroking her sister's cheek. "Souls have complex-
(75) ions too: what will suit one will not suit another." She was opening some ring boxes, which disclosed a fine emerald, and just then the sun passing beyond a cloud sent a bright gleam over the table.

(80) "How very beautiful these gems are!" said Dorothea, under a new current of feeling, as sudden as the gleam. "It is strange how deeply colours seem to penetrate one, like scent. I suppose that this
(85) is the reason why gems are used as spiritual emblems in the Revelation of St. John. They look like fragments of heaven. I think that emerald is as beautiful as any of them."

(90) "We did not notice this at first," said Celia.

"It's lovely," said Dorothea, slipping the ring on her finely turned finger and holding it towards the window on a
(95) level with her eyes. All the while her

thought was trying to justify her delight in the colours by merging them in her mystic religious joy.

1. From the passage, one can infer that Celia and Dorothea are sisters:

 A. whose mother has very recently died

 B. whose father has very recently died

 C. who are poor and orphaned

 D. whose mother is no longer living and whose father probably is no longer living

2. Which of the following is likely to be the most important reason for Dorothea's decision to examine the jewels?

 F. Her unwillingness to show respect to her mother's memory

 G. Her unrecognized personal vanity

 H. Her realization that Celia would like to wear them

 J. Her deeply seated Christian principles

3. Dorothea gives what at first appear to be the most beautiful and most valuable of the jewels to Celia because she:

 A. knows there are others that are even more valuable

 B. does not understand that the jewels are valuable

 C. wishes to remove temptations from herself

 D. genuinely believes she herself will not wear the jewelry

4. Celia offers the jeweled cross to Dorothea because she:

   F. does not want it herself

   G. believes it is jewelry that Dorothea might wear

   H. does not share Dorothea's religious views

   J. is sure that Dorothea will refuse it

5. The passage suggests that Dorothea's "strictness" is chiefly based upon her:

   A. religious principles

   B. hypocritical wish to be well thought of

   C. hope to marry a rich husband

   D. insensitivity to physical beauty

6. From the presentation of Dorothea in the passage, which of the following can the reader suppose she would be most interested in today?

   F. Red Cross work

   G. Jewelry design

   H. Yachting

   J. Conservative politics

7. Compared to Dorothea, Celia appears to be more:

   A. intellectual

   B. articulate

   C. worldly

   D. quixotic

8. Dorothea attempts to justify her response to the beauty of the jewels by:

   F. pretending she is not interested in them

   G. arguing that jewels are a gift of God

   H. regarding them as religious symbols

   J. hypocritically claiming to have religious feelings

9. Unlike the rest of the passage, lines 83–89 have several examples of:

   A. rhetorical question

   B. simile

   C. irony

   D. dialogue

10. The author's attitude toward Dorothea could best be described as one of:

   F. cool disinterest

   G. affectionate amusement

   H. grudging tolerance

   J. enthusiastic approval

GO ON TO THE NEXT PAGE

Reading Test

Passage II

SOCIAL SCIENCE: This passage is adapted from A Pocket History of the United States *by Allan Nevins and Henry Steele Commager (© 1966 by Simon and Schuster).*

Some of the developments which con- tributed to the growth of industrial America were a positive disadvantage to labor. Two of these we can note briefly:
(5) the mechanization of industry and the rise of the corporation. Mechanization tended, on the whole, to lower the stan- dards of labor. The skills which working men had painfully acquired ceased to
(10) have their old-time value. The creative instinct of craftsmanship was largely de- stroyed, and working men were reduced to a mere part of a mechanical process.

Machinery had a tendency, too, to usurp
(15) the place of the worker in the economy of industry. It represented an enormous capital investment. The fact that furnaces had to be kept going continuously was decisive in maintaining the twelve-hour
(20) day. Machinery was in part responsible, finally, for a great deal of unemploy- ment. It is probably true that in the end machines made more jobs than they eliminated, but it was not always the
(25) same people who got the new jobs.

Several other factors, unique to the United States, conditioned the welfare of labor. The first of these was the pass- ing of good cheap land a generation or
(30) so after the Civil War. It would be an ex- aggeration to say that the West had served as a "safety valve" for labor dis- content or as a refuge for very many working men. But it is clear that for two
(35) or three generations the open land did drain off the surplus population of the countryside, the villages, and even the cities, and the immigrants from abroad. With the rise in the cost of farming and

(40) the disappearance of good cheap land, surplus population did stay in the indus- trial areas. Farming was no longer a practical alternative to the factory. Labor could no longer escape the problems of
(45) an industrialized society, but was forced to stand and face them.

A second factor, peculiar to the United States among industrial nations, was
(50) continuous and unrestricted immigra- tion. In the forty years from 1870 to 1910, more than twenty million people poured into the country. This meant that every year several hundred thousand re-
(55) cruits joined the ranks of labor at almost any wages and under almost any condi- tions. Nor was this the only competition that confronted northern labor. From the South, after the turn of the century,
(60) came tens of thousands of willing blacks ready to take their places beside the Poles, Italians, and Hungarians. For many years, the general tendency of this mass movement was to drive down
(65) wages, depress standards, and disinte- grate labor unions.

A third factor—again one unique to the United States—was the existence, side by side, of a national economy and a
(70) federal political system. The problems of labor were much the same the nation over, but the power to deal with them was lodged, until very recent years, in the states alone. Competition was na-
(75) tionwide, but the right to regulate wages and hours was only statewide.

11. The focus of this passage is upon the:

A. growth of labor unions in the United States

B. problems of labor in the United States

C. expansion of labor in the United States

D. local and federal controls of labor in the United States

12. According to the passage, one reason for the very long working day in the late nineteenth century was the:

F. low hourly wages of the workers

G. greed of the corporate owners

H. need to keep furnaces burning continuously

J. state laws controlling working hours

13. Paradoxically, the development and increased use of specialized machines was

A. an advantage to the growth of American industry and a disadvantage to labor

B. an advantage to the northeast and a disadvantage to the South

C. an advantage to the American worker and a disadvantage to the European

D. an advantage to the European immigrant and a disadvantage to the native American worker

14. The end of free lands in the West had an influence on labor in eastern cities because:

F. the pool of available workers became larger

G. the pool of available workers became smaller

H. farm labor required less training than industrial labor

J. the western farmers were the potential market for food manufactured in the East

15. From information in the passage, it can be inferred that a sharp decline in the number of immigrants would be likely to:

A. bring about an increase in the wages of labor

B. have little or no effect on the economy

C. drive up sharply the number of unemployed workers

D. have a larger influence upon coastal than on inland states

16. Like the United States, industrialized countries in Europe in the late nineteenth century would have to deal with the effects of:

I. a large immigrant population

II. an increasingly mechanized industry

III. the recent unavailability of large areas of farmland

F. I only

G. II only

H. I and III only

J. II and III only

GO ON TO THE NEXT PAGE

17. According to the passage, all of the following contributed to the growth of unemployment EXCEPT:

   A. the development of more sophisticated machines

   B. the rise in the cost of farming

   C. the rise in the number of immigrants

   D. a right-to-work law

18. From information in the passage, it can be inferred that which of the following did NOT exist in the period from 1870 to 1910?

   F. A child-labor law

   G. A federal minimum wage

   H. A law limiting the powers of unions to organize

   J. A right-to-work law

19. According to the passage, the political system in the United States:

   A. encouraged the arrival of foreign workers

   B. encouraged black workers to leave the South

   C. made it difficult to deal with problems of labor

   D. vested too much power in the states and not enough in the federal government

20. As it is used in line 14, the word "usurp" most nearly means:

   F. expand

   G. eliminate

   H. adjust to

   J. seize

Passage III

HUMANITIES: This passage is adapted from Western Philosophy, Volume I, *by Charles Patterson (© 1970 by CliffsNotes, Inc.).*

Medieval thought differed radically from modern thought: Whereas medieval scientists did not doubt that certain precepts of the Church or the
(5) existence of God constituted true knowledge, science today accepts as knowledge only that which can be verified scientifically. In the early Middle Ages, mystical revelation was quite common.
(10) Partly because of the relative isolation of places of learning and the loss of many classics, logical arguments were not accepted, especially in theology— the "queen of the sciences."

(15) When many ancient classics were reintroduced into Europe (by means of translation into Latin from the Arabic, which was translated from the Greek) from Moslem Spain, new patterns of
(20) thought began to emerge: these were considerably expanded by the Crusades. When Aristotle (and the commentaries upon him by Averroës) was translated into Latin, revealed truth was no longer
(25) the accepted authority. The Bible, works of the Church fathers, and Church decrees were not rejected, but it was felt that they should be reconciled with logic and philosophy. The Scholastics were
(30) the group of clerics who undertook the task of applying logic and philosophy to theology. In his work *Sic et Non (Yes and No),* Peter Abelard of Paris stated the conflicting arguments of the various
(35) authorities in order to show their weaknesses. As a consequence, his colleagues considered him a heretic.

Not until the thirteenth century did the Latin translations of Aristotle and
(40) Averroës make their full impact. Two of

the most important Scholastics of this period were Saint Albertus Magnus and Saint Thomas Aquinas. Albertus Magnus tried to reconcile the thought of
(45) Aristotle with medieval ideals. His most famous pupil was Saint Thomas Aquinas. In his major work, the *Summa Theologica,* Thomas Aquinas held that the supreme force in the universe was
(50) God. Both God and His creations could be explained by logic. Thomas Aquinas did not reject faith or revelation; however, he said that certain things beyond the grasp of man (such as the creation of
(55) the universe and the Trinity) should be taken on faith.

By the fourteenth century, mysticism had become widespread and there was a loss of faith in logic; another system of
(60) thought, Nominalism, replaced the theories of Saint Thomas. Among the forerunners of Nominalism was Duns Scotus. Nominalists said that divine matters could be explained only by mys-
(65) tical faith whereas tangible objects were capable of being studied logically. This reversion to mysticism accompanied the desire to look at objects thoroughly, and this desire eventually led to the scien-
(70) tific approach.

21. Which of the following titles best describes the content of the passage?

   A. The Development of Scientific Thought in the Middle Ages

   B. Medieval versus Modern: The Philosophy of the Middle Ages versus Modern Thought

   C. From Aristotle to Nominalism in the Early Middle Ages

   D. Major Christian Thought in the Middle Ages

22. All of the following statements about Europe in the Middle Ages are true EXCEPT:

   F. In the early Middle Ages, many classical texts had not been rediscovered.

   G. Many Greek works were introduced in translation.

   H. Saint Thomas Aquinas and Saint Albertus Magnus were contemporaries.

   J. At the close of the Middle Ages, mystical revelations were no longer credited.

23. As it is used in line 65, the word "tangible" most nearly means:

   A. irrelevant

   B. material

   C. real

   D. valuable

24. According to the account in the third paragraph (lines 38–56), Saint Thomas Aquinas would agree with all of the following EXCEPT:

   F. Logic cannot explain all things.

   G. Good works are more important than faith.

   H. The existence of God can be proven logically.

   J. A mystery like the Trinity must be taken on faith.

GO ON TO THE NEXT PAGE

25. All of the medieval writers discussed in the second and third paragraphs of the passage (lines 15–56) were:

    A. scholars of Greek and Latin

    B. Crusaders

    C. priests

    D. French

26. The term "Scholasticism" is best defined as:

    F. a system of belief that recognizes God as the Supreme Being and the Bible as divinely inspired

    G. Christian and medieval values

    H. a system of medieval schoolmen based on Aristotelian logic and early Christian writings

    J. the philosophical system of Albertus Magnus, Thomas Aquinas, and Duns Scotus

27. The Nominalists may be said to have contributed to the ultimate development of the scientific method because they:

    A. accepted Christian mysticism

    B. revered Aristotle and Aristotelian logic

    C. encouraged careful study of physical objects

    D. avoided the attempt to explain supernatural events by natural laws

28. From the early Middle Ages to the fourteenth century, the attitude of churchmen toward logic:

    F. changed very little

    G. went from ignorance and indifference to favor

    H. went from increasing favor to disfavor

    J. went from extreme disfavor to extreme favor

29. Compared to the earlier thinkers of the Middle Ages, the Nominalists had less respect for:

    A. mysticism

    B. the Church fathers

    C. logic

    D. Church decrees

30. Which of the following best describes the attitude of the author of this passage toward the philosophers mentioned?

    F. The most favored is Saint Thomas Aquinas.

    G. The most disapproved of is Peter Abelard of Paris.

    H. The most favored is Duns Scotus.

    J. The author's personal views are not stated or implied.

Passage IV

NATURAL SCIENCE: This passage is adapted from Chemistry by Linus Pauling and Peter Pauling (© 1975 by W.H. Freeman.).

One of the most interesting recent applications of radioactivity is the determination of the age of carbonaceous materials by measurement of their carbon-14
(5) radioactivity. This technique of radiocarbon dating, which was developed by an American physical chemist, Willard F. Libby, permits the dating of samples containing carbon with an accuracy of
(10) around 200 years. At the present time,

the method can be applied to materials that are not over about 50,000 years old.

Carbon 14 is being made at a steady rate in the upper atmosphere. Cosmic-ray (15) neutrons transmute nitrogen into carbon 14, which is radioactive. The radiocarbon is oxidized to carbon dioxide, which is thoroughly mixed with the nonradioactive carbon dioxide in the at- (20) mosphere, through the action of winds. The steady-state concentration of carbon 14 built up in the atmosphere by cosmic rays is about one atom of radioactive carbon to 10^{12} atoms of ordinary carbon. (25) The carbon dioxide, radioactive and nonradioactive alike, is absorbed by plants, which fix the carbon in their tissues. Animals that eat the plants also similarly fix the carbon, containing a (30) trace of radiocarbon, in their tissues. When a plant or animal dies, the amount of radioactivity of the carbon in its tissues is determined by the amount of radiocarbon present, which corresponds to (35) the concentration in the atmosphere. After 5,760 years (the half-life of carbon 14), however, half of the carbon 14 has undergone decomposition, and the radioactivity of the material is only half (40) as great. After 11,520 years (or two half-lives) only one quarter of the original radioactivity is left, and so on. Accordingly, by determining the radioactivity of a sample of carbon from (45) wood, flesh, charcoal, skin, horn, or other plant or animal remains, the number of years that have gone by since the carbon was originally extracted from the atmosphere can be determined.

(50) In applying the method of radiocarbon dating, a sample of material containing about 30 grams of carbon is burned to carbon dioxide, which is then reduced to elementary carbon in the form of (55) lamp black. The beta-ray activity of the

elementary carbon is then determined, with the use of Geiger counters, and compared with the beta-ray activity of recent carbon. The age of the sample (60) may then be calculated. The method was checked by measurement of carbon from the heartwood of a giant Sequoia tree, for which the number of tree rings showed that 2,928 years had passed (65) since the heartwood was laid down. This check was satisfactory, as were similar checks with other carbonaceous materials, such as wood in First Dynasty Egyptian tombs 4,900 years old, whose (70) dating was considered to be reliable.

31. Carbon dating may be described as:

    I. a useful application of radioactivity

    II. an important technique for historians and anthropologists

    III. a technique that can be used to determine the age of plant or human remains

  A. I only

  B. I and III only

  C. II and III only

  D. I, II, and III

32. One limitation of radiocarbon dating is that it:

  F. cannot be used on objects that do not contain carbon

  G. is not dependably accurate

  H. cannot be used on materials that are less than 2,000 years old

  J. cannot be used on materials that are more than 30,000 years old

GO ON TO THE NEXT PAGE

Reading Test

33. Which of the following is the best title for the passage?

    A. Carbon Dating—Its Strengths and Its Liabilities

    B. Carbon Dating—How It Works

    C. The Use of Carbon to Date Radioactive Materials

    D. Science and History

34. As it is used in line 27, the word "fix" most nearly means:

    F. make fast

    G. prepare

    H. put in order

    J. adjust

35. From the passage, it can be inferred that a carnivore's bones can be dated by using carbon dating because the carnivore would have:

    I. eaten plants

    II. eaten animals which had eaten plants

    III. fixed carbon in its system from breathing air

    A. I and II only

    B. II only

    C. II and III only

    D. I, II, and III

36. Carbon 14 is found in the tissue of plants because:

    F. of the action of cosmic-ray neutrons on plants

    G. of photosynthesis

    H. the plants have absorbed carbon dioxide

    J. the carbon in the air has been caused by fires

37. From the figures given in the second paragraph of the passage (lines 13–49), it can be inferred that one-eighth of the original radioactivity of carbon 14 would be left after:

    A. 5,760 years

    B. 11,520 years

    C. 17,280 years

    D. 23,040 years

38. The reliability of carbon dating has been tested by comparisons with:

    I. wood from an Egyptian tomb

    II. wood dated by annual rings

    III. Geiger counters and beta-ray activity of recent carbon

    F. I only

    G. I and II only

    H. II and III only

    J. I, II, and III

39. Carbon dating depends upon the measurement of:

    A. beta-ray activity

    B. cosmic-ray neutrons

    C. steady-state concentration

    D. carbon dioxide

40. Carbon dating could be used on all of the following ancient objects EXCEPT:

    F. a seal-bone harpoon

    G. a linen burial garment

    H. a turquoise ornament

    J. an ear of corn

IF YOU FINISH BEFORE TIME IS CALLED, CHECK YOUR WORK ON THIS SECTION ONLY. DO NOT WORK ON ANY OTHER SECTION IN THE TEST.

STOP

Science Reasoning Test

Time: 35 Minutes

40 Questions

Directions: Each of the seven passages in this test is followed by several questions. After you read each passage, select the correct choice for each of the questions that follow the passage. Refer to the passage as often as necessary to answer the questions. You may NOT use a calculator on this test.

Passage I

Table 1 displays the results of a series of experiments that measured the viscosities of liquids at several temperatures. *Viscosity* is a property directly proportional to the resistance to flow. For example, molasses is more viscous than coffee.

Table 1

Liquid	Molecular Weight	Viscosity (millipoises)		
		0°C	20°C	40°C
Water	16	17.92	10.05	6.56
Ethanol	46	17.73	12.01	8.34
Pentane	72	3.11	2.43	2.03
Benzene	78	9.12	6.52	5.03
Sulfuric acid	98	13.29	10.04	8.19
Heptane	100	5.24	4.09	3.41
Octane	114	7.06	5.42	4.33
Mercury	201	16.84	15.47	14.83

1. According to the data in Table 1, which of the following liquids has the highest viscosity at normal room temperature?

   A. Ethanol

   B. Mercury

   C. Sulfuric acid

   D. Water

2. Which of the following rules correctly states the variation of viscosity shown in Table 1?

   F. Higher viscosity with higher molecular weight

   G. Lower viscosity with higher temperature

   H. Lower viscosity with lower molecular weight

   J. Higher viscosity with higher temperature

3. Pentane, heptane, and octane are similar hydrocarbons with a linear molecular structure and 5, 7, or 8 carbon atoms, respectively. What is the likely viscosity at 40°C for another such hydrocarbon, hexane?

   A. 2.72 millipoises

   B. 3.87 millipoises

   C. 4.18 millipoises

   D. 5.25 millipoises

4. An experimenter is attempting to measure the rate at which steel ball bearings sink through water. However, at 0°C the water quickly freezes, preventing any experiment. What liquid should be substituted for the water?

   F. Benzene

   G. Ethanol

   H. Mercury

   J. Sulfuric acid

5. Which of the following methods could be used to measure the relative viscosity of liquids?

   A. The amount of liquid passing through a small hole in the base of the beaker in 10 seconds

   B. The diameter of the pool formed when 100 milliliters of liquid are carefully poured onto a table

   C. The distance to which the liquid rises in the core of a very slender capillary tube

   D. The intensity of light measured by a light meter when a beam shines through 5 centimeters of liquid

Passage II

To investigate the response of a primitive animal to light, a researcher selected the Great Burmese Beetle (GBB) as a subject. This large, docile insect lacks any capacity to bite or sting in self-defense. The GBB crawls rapidly enough to complete each experiment within one or two hours. It has two very prominent eyes that bulge at the sides of its head, so it was considered likely to be quite sensitive to illumination from different directions. Each of the following experiments maps the Great Burmese Beetle's movements as seen from above.

Experiment 1
The research began by studying the path of one GBB in a darkened room illuminated only by a dim red glow to permit tracking the beetle. It was found to crawl in a reasonably straight line.

Experiment 2
This experiment began in a darkened room. When the beetle had reached point *P*, shown in Figure 1, the researcher turned on one small white light on the floor to the left of the insect's path. The GBB slowly turned toward the light until it was directly facing the light and then continued straight ahead. In Figure 1, the eyes of the GBB are shown as small open circles.

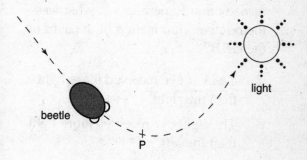

Figure 1

Experiment 3
The researcher then used black enamel to paint over one eye on each of two beetles. In Figure 2, the black circles represent the painted eyes, which cannot perceive light. These GBBs were placed on the floor with one bright light directly overhead. Both beetles crawled in endless circular patterns. The GBB with its right eye painted always turned to the left, while the GBB with its left eye painted invariably turned to the right. Several repetitions of this experiment yielded the same sense of turning for each GBB.

GO ON TO THE NEXT PAGE

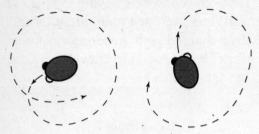

Figure 2

Experiment 4

Finally, the two beetles with painted eyes were studied in the darkened room with dim red illumination. Each GBB tended to move along a straight path.

6. At the moment when the light was turned on in Experiment 2, what was the relative illumination of the eyes of the GBB?

   F. The left eye received more light than the right.

   G. The right eye received more light than the left.

   H. Both eyes were equally illuminated from floor level.

   J. Both eyes were equally illuminated from overhead.

7. What is the most likely reason that the GBB in Experiment 2 wouldn't move in a circular pattern like that of Experiment 3?

   A. The beetle had not yet been trained to crawl along a circular path.

   B. Circular motion could occur only when the source of light is overhead.

   C. It stops turning as soon as it is facing directly toward the light.

   D. Neither eye of the beetle was painted to induce crawling in a circle.

8. Any change of direction of the GBB may be described as:

   F. Turning away from the eye that receives the most light

   G. Turning toward the eye that receives the most light

   H. Turning away from the eye that is covered by paint

   J. Turning toward the eye that is covered by paint

9. According to the experimental results, in a lighted room, the GBB would crawl in a straight line only if:

   A. Its two eyes were equally illuminated.

   B. The light bulb was in the center of the room.

   C. The light was frequently switched off.

   D. Neither of its eyes were covered by paint.

10. What is the most likely reason that the researcher needed to perform Experiment 4?

   F. To prove that dim red light cannot be perceived by the GBB

   G. To prove that the behavior in Experiment 1 was not altered by paint

   H. To prove that the turning in Experiment 3 was not due to the paint alone

   J. To prove that the GBB does not learn during a series of experiments

11. In Experiment 3, it is most likely that a GBB with both eyes covered by paint would:

   A. Stand still

   B. Crawl in a straight line

   C. Always turn in one direction

   D. Turn irregularly in both directions

Passage III

By alteration of the temperature or the pressure, most substances may be transformed from one state (solid, liquid, or gas) into another state. For the chemical element iodine, Figure 1 shows which state exists at each specific combination of temperature and pressure.

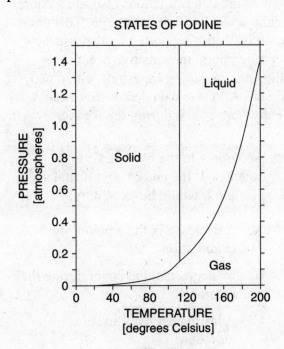

Figure 1

12. According to the data in Figure 1, in which state does iodine exist at 100°C and a pressure of 0.5 atmosphere?

   F. Gas

   G. Liquid

   H. Solid

   J. The information cannot be determined from the data presented

13. Based on the information given, what is the lowest pressure at which iodine may occur as a liquid?

   A. 0.04 atm

   B. 0.12 atm

   C. 0.45 atm

   D. 0.78 atm

14. At what temperature do iodine crystals melt?

   F. 92°C

   G. 114°C

   H. 12°C

   J. 182°C

15. The *boiling point* of any substance is defined as the temperature of the liquid/gas transition at a pressure of 1 atmosphere. What is the boiling point of iodine?

   A. 168°C

   B. 176°C

   C. 184°C

   D. 192°C

GO ON TO THE NEXT PAGE

16. The direct transition from a solid to a gas, without an intermediate liquid state, is called *sublimation*. Which of the following statements describes the conditions under which iodine may sublime?

    F. The pressure must be less than 0.12 atm.

    G. The pressure must be more than 0.05 atm.

    H. The temperature must be less than 94°C.

    J. The temperature must be more than 110°C.

Passage IV

What was the cause of the Ice Age? Two differing viewpoints are presented below.

Scientist 1

Variation in the amount of energy radiated by the sun would change the energy received by the earth. During this century, the sun's radiation has fluctuated by up to 3 percent. It is reasonable to assume a far greater variation over immensely long time spans, like the 3 million years of the Pleistocene Ice Age. If the sun's radiation were considerably higher several million years ago, the warmer atmosphere of the earth would have induced evaporation and greater humidity. The increased cloudiness must have increased the precipitation of both rain and snow. The cloud cover would also have inhibited any melting of snow during the summer months. The abundant snow and its persistence throughout the year must have led to rapid expansion of the polar ice caps, yielding the great continental ice-sheets. Surprisingly, then, the Ice Age may have been initiated by the effects of a temporarily warmer sun.

Scientist 2

It has long seemed self-evident that only a cooler atmosphere could produce the great precipitation of snow needed to nourish continental glaciers. Although a warmer atmosphere might well be more humid due to evaporation from the oceans, it is not likely to precipitate as snow. The central issue seems to be whether the atmosphere was warmer or cooler at the inception of the Pleistocene glaciation. Species of mollusks which live today in cool waters at high latitudes have been found as Pleistocene fossils at numerous sites closer to the equator, indicating that Pleistocene seas were colder than the present. Seawater temperatures of both epochs may also be estimated from oxygen isotope ratios in shells of mollusks, brachiopods, and other marine creatures; these temperature determinations also show cooler oceans several million years ago. That observation is further supported by the distribution of temperature-sensitive ocean sediments, including limestone, chert, and red clay. All these data demonstrate that oceans were colder during the Ice Age.

17. According to the hypothesis of Scientist 1, the end of continental glaciation would be caused by:

    A. A decrease in the amount of evaporation

    B. Inadequate cloud cover during the summer

    C. A lasting decrease in solar radiation

    D. A warmer atmosphere melting the ice

18. The two scientists are in direct disagreement about:

    F. Atmospheric humidity in the past and present

    G. The minimum amount of variation in solar radiation

    H. The reliability of oxygen isotope temperature determinations

    J. Temperature changes over the last 3 million years

19. The theory propounded by Scientist 1 was developed primarily to explain the:

    A. Effects produced by variation in solar radiation

    B. Increased precipitation needed for glacial expansion

    C. Relation between humidity, precipitation, and glaciation

    D. Temperature extremes experienced in the past

20. Although Scientist 2 opposes the theory of Scientist 1, the evidence presented by Scientist 2 is relevant to the dispute only if:

    F. Cooler oceans imply a cooler atmosphere

    G. Oxygen isotope temperature determinations are accurate

    H. Several marine species have survived for millions of years

    J. Solar energy has not varied by more than 3 percent

21. Scientist 1 could best refute the temperatures calculated from oxygen isotope ratios by:

    A. Pointing out that few such measurements have been made

    B. Reminding us that his theory calls for greater atmospheric humidity

    C. Showing that a factor besides temperature can affect the ratios

    D. Suggesting that chemical laws may have been different in the past

22. Coral reefs live only in water exceeding 20°C. According to Scientist 2, how should reefs have changed from the Ice Age to the present?

    F. They have migrated toward the equator.

    G. They have migrated toward the poles.

    H. They have progressively decreased in size.

    J. They have progressively increased in size.

23. The theory of Scientist 1 would be greatly strengthened by a study of data from the last 50 years showing that:

    A. More extensive cloud cover occurred during periods of high precipitation.

    B. More evaporation from the oceans occurred during periods of high air temperature.

    C. More glacial movement occurred during periods of warmer temperature.

    D. More precipitation occurred during periods of high solar radiation.

GO ON TO THE NEXT PAGE

Passage V

A common method of preparing a pure gas sample, as shown in Figure 1, is to pass a mixture of two gases over a substance that reacts with one of the gases to yield a non-volatile solid. The remaining vapor represents the gas that did not react with the substance.

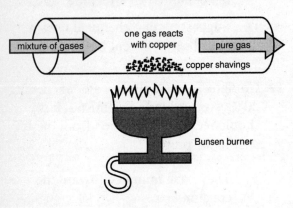

GLASS TUBE WITH HEATED COPPER

Figure 1

Experiment 1

Air is basically a mixture of two gases, oxygen and nitrogen. Many substances react with the former but not the latter, so a purified sample of nitrogen may be obtained by passing air over red-hot copper shavings to form copper oxide. The experiment was carried out and the density of the resulting nitrogen was found to be 1.256 grams per liter.

Experiment 2

A second sample of nitrogen was prepared by mixing dry air with ammonia gas and passing the mixture over heated copper.

$$4NH_3 + 3O_2 \rightarrow 2N_2 + 6H_2O$$
amnonia   oxygen   nitrogen water vapor

After the water vapor was removed from the emerging gas, the sample should have been pure nitrogen, derived partly from the ammonia and partly from the initial air. The density of this nitrogen was measured and found to be very similar to that from the first experiment, as shown in Table 1.

Table 1

	Density of Nitrogen (grams/liter)
Experiment 1	1.256
Experiment 2	1.255

Experiment 3

A third sample of nitrogen was obtained without using any air by simply reacting ammonia with pure oxygen. The density of this nitrogen was also measured, and the results of the three density determinations are tabulated in Table 2.

Table 2

	Density of Nitrogen (grams/liter)
Experiment 1	1.256
Experiment 2	1.255
Experiment 3	1.250

24. Considering the entire set of three experiments, from how many different sources was nitrogen derived?

F. 1

G. 2

H. 3

J. 4

25. Based on the experimental results, how should the differences in densities be reported?

  A. Nitrogen obtained in early experiments is slightly denser than that in later experiments.

  B. Nitrogen obtained in later experiments is slightly denser than that in earlier experiments.

  C. Nitrogen obtained from air is slightly denser than that from ammonia.

  D. Nitrogen obtained from ammonia is slightly denser than that from air.

26. Both of the first two experiments were planned by the researchers before beginning laboratory work. Which of the following best explains why the second experiment was considered necessary?

  F. To check that the oxygen in the air had reacted completely

  G. To compare nitrogen from more than one source

  H. To contrast the properties of dry air and moist air

  J. To ensure the copper shavings were of uniform purity

27. Experiment 3 was not originally planned. Which of the following best explains why it was determined to be desirable?

  A. To avoid contamination by material evaporated from the red-hot copper shavings

  B. To check whether the density difference of the first two experiments was meaningful

  C. To determine whether any residual ammonia was mixed with the emerging nitrogen

  D. To eliminate the problem of having to dehydrate the emerging gas

28. By volume, air contains four times as much nitrogen as oxygen. Experiment 2 yielded ammonia-derived nitrogen equal to two-thirds of the oxygen. In that experiment, what fraction of the emerging nitrogen was derived from ammonia?

  F. One-half

  G. One-third

  H. One-fourth

  J. One-seventh

29. The set of three experiments resulted in the discovery that air contains about 1 percent of a previously unknown gas. What properties of that gas were revealed by the three experiments?

  A. It reacts with copper and is denser than nitrogen.

  B. It reacts with copper and is less dense than nitrogen.

  C. It doesn't react with copper and is denser than nitrogen.

  D. It doesn't react with copper and is less dense than nitrogen.

GO ON TO THE NEXT PAGE

Passage VI

Carbon is the key chemical element in the molecules necessary for life. Figure 1 summarizes the recycling of carbon in our environment.

THE CARBON CYCLE

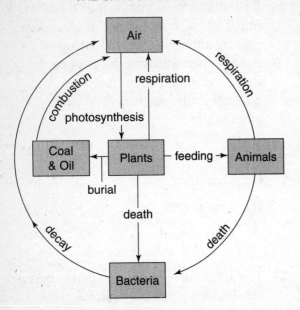

Figure 1

30. The carbon stored in the tissues of living animals is ultimately returned to the atmosphere by:

  F. Burial or respiration

  G. Death or combustion

  H. Decay or respiration

  J. Respiration or feeding

31. Carbon dioxide is removed from the air principally by the:

  A. Combustion of fossil fuels

  B. Decay of dead animals and plants

  C. Photosynthesis of green plants

  D. Respiration of animals

32. In relation only to the carbon cycle, the principal role of bacteria is to:

  F. Prevent the animal population from becoming too large

  G. Provide nourishment for both animals and plants

  H. Release chemical elements stored in plants and animals

  J. Remove waste gases from the atmosphere

33. Photosynthesis in the green leaves of plants produces oxygen. The reverse process, which consumes oxygen, is called:

  A. Combustion

  B. Metabolism

  C. Nutrition

  D. Respiration

34. A modern buildup of carbon dioxide levels threatens our climates with global warming, the highly publicized greenhouse effect. The diagram of the carbon cycle shows four main ways that carbon dioxide is released into the air. Only one of the four sources of carbon is the problem because that stored carbon is being converted rapidly and completely into carbon dioxide. Which source of carbon threatens us with the greenhouse effect?

  F. Animals

  G. Bacteria

  H. Coal and oil

  J. Plants

Passage VII

In an investigation of the metabolism of phosphorous by mammals, a healthy female rat was fed a special meal containing 2 milligrams of sodium phosphate as the sole source of phosphorus. The phosphorous atoms in the sodium phosphate were radioactive P^{32}, which decays with a half-life of 17 days. Measurements of the radioactivity of organic materials permitted tracing the utilization of phosphorous by the rat. The special diet was administered only once. All subsequent meals contained common, nonradioactive phosphorous.

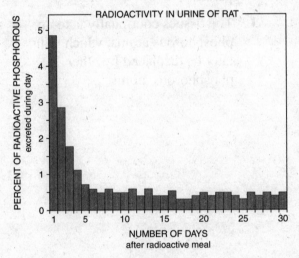

Figure 1

Figure 1 shows the percentage of the radioactive phosphorous excreted daily in the rat's urine. Very similar percentages were excreted each day in the feces. After one month, approximately half of the radioactive phosphorous had been excreted. The animal was then killed and the distribution of the residual phosphorous tracer was studied.

In Table 1, the first percentage shows the fraction of radioactive P^{32} found in the various components of the freshly killed rat, while the second percentage represents the concentration of P^{32} in each gram of dehydrated matter.

Table 1

Material	Radioactive Phosphorous	
	Fresh Material (percent)	Dried Material (percent/gram)
Urine	26.3	
Feces	31.8	
Brain	0.5	14.7
Kidneys	0.2	18.2
Liver	1.7	13.9
Blood	0.4	1.8
Bones	24.8	2.8
Muscles	17.4	7.4

35. According to the data presented, just before the rat was killed, the total percentage of radioactive phosphorous excreted by the rat each day was about:

A. ½%

B. 1%

C. 32%

D. 58%

36. Figure 1 shows high amounts of radioactive phosphorous in the first few days after the special meal. Most of the P^{32} excreted during that early period was:

F. Permanently stored in the bones

G. Temporarily stored in kidney tissue

H. Distributed throughout the tissues of several organs

J. Not utilized in any tissue

GO ON TO THE NEXT PAGE

37. The fact that most of the phosphorous excreted by the rat was not radioactive means that:

   A. Most of the phosphorous comes from the rat's tissues

   B. The phosphorous lost its radioactivity after a few days

   C. The rat could not utilize the radioactive phosphorous

   D. The rat was not harmed by the radioactive phosphorous

38. The average time one phosphorous atom remains in the rat is about:

   F. 1 week

   G. 17 days

   H. 1 month

   J. 2 months

39. Which of the following reasons does NOT help to explain the dramatically different percentages in the two right-hand columns of Table 1?

   A. Some of the phosphorous is lost during the drying procedure.

   B. No dried excreta were analyzed for radioactivity.

   C. Some tissues use much more phosphorous than other tissues.

   D. The tissue systems have very different weights.

40. Which of these statements best describes the metabolism of phosphorous by rats?

   F. Any phosphorous atoms in the tissues are chemically isolated until death disintegrates the tissues and releases the phosphorous.

   G. Only a small percentage of phosphorous atoms in the diet are utilized in the formation of tissues.

   H. As the tissues grow, new phosphorous atoms are required, but this process slows as time passes.

   J. The tissues continually take up phosphorous atoms, which will later be displaced by other phosphorous atoms.

IF YOU FINISH BEFORE TIME IS CALLED, CHECK YOUR WORK ON THIS SECTION ONLY. DO NOT WORK ON ANY OTHER SECTION IN THE TEST.

Answer Key

English Test

1. C	20. H	39. B	58. H
2. F	21. C	40. H	59. D
3. C	22. J	41. D	60. J
4. G	23. D	42. G	61. A
5. C	24. F	43. D	62. J
6. H	25. C	44. F	63. D
7. A	26. F	45. D	64. J
8. F	27. B	46. J	65. C
9. C	28. H	47. C	66. J
10. H	29. C	48. J	67. B
11. C	30. G	49. B	68. J
12. G	31. D	50. F	69. A
13. A	32. J	51. C	70. H
14. J	33. C	52. F	71. D
15. B	34. F	53. A	72. F
16. F	35. B	54. J	73. A
17. C	36. G	55. A	74. H
18. F	37. B	56. F	75. C
19. C	38. F	57. B	

Mathematics Test

1. B	16. H	31. D	46. J
2. H	17. B	32. G	47. D
3. C	18. H	33. A	48. J
4. K	19. B	34. G	49. C
5. B	20. K	35. D	50. J
6. G	21. C	36. F	51. A
7. B	22. K	37. E	52. K
8. H	23. C	38. F	53. B
9. C	24. J	39. A	54. H
10. F	25. C	40. J	55. D
11. A	26. G	41. A	56. J
12. J	27. D	42. F	57. D
13. E	28. F	43. A	58. F
14. H	29. B	44. H	59. C
15. A	30. G	45. B	60. H

Reading Test

1. D	11. B	21. D	31. D
2. H	12. H	22. J	32. F
3. D	13. A	23. B	33. B
4. G	14. F	24. G	34. F
5. A	15. A	25. C	35. B
6. F	16. G	26. H	36. H
7. C	17. D	27. C	37. C
8. H	18. G	28. H	38. G
9. B	19. C	29. C	39. A
10. G	20. F	30. J	40. H

Science Reasoning Test

1. B	11. B	21. C	31. C
2. G	12. H	22. G	32. H
3. A	13. B	23. D	33. D
4. G	14. G	24. G	34. H
5. A	15. C	25. C	35. B
6. F	16. F	26. G	36. J
7. C	17. C	27. B	37. A
8. G	18. J	28. J	38. H
9. A	19. B	29. C	39. A
10. H	20. F	30. H	40. J

Scoring Your ACT Practice Test

To score your practice test, total the number of correct answers for each section. Don't subtract any points for questions attempted but missed, as there is no penalty for guessing. This score is then scaled from 1 to 36 for each section and then averaged for the all-important composite score. The average score is approximately 18.

For Your Own Benefit

To figure out your **percentage right** for each test, use the following formulas.

English Test

$$\frac{\text{Number right}}{75} \times 100 = \underline{\hspace{1cm}} \%$$

Mathematics Test

$$\frac{\text{Number right}}{60} \times 100 = \underline{\hspace{1cm}} \%$$

Reading Test

$$\frac{\text{Number right}}{40} \times 100 = \underline{\hspace{1cm}} \%$$

Science Reasoning Test

$$\frac{\text{Number right}}{40} \times 100 = \underline{\hspace{1cm}} \%$$

Practice Test 1 Analysis Sheet

	Possible	Completed	Right	Wrong
English Test	75			
Mathematics Test	60			
Reading Test	40			
Science Reasoning Test	40			
Overall Totals	215			

Analysis/Tally Sheet for Problems Missed

One of the most important parts of test preparation is analyzing **why** you missed a problem so that you can reduce the number of mistakes. Now that you've taken the practice test and checked your answers, carefully tally your mistakes by marking them in the proper column.

Reason for Mistake				
	Total Missed	Simple Mistake	Misread Problem	Lack of Knowledge
English Test				
Mathematics Test				
Reading Test				
Science Reasoning Test				
Total				

Reviewing the above data should help you determine **why** you're missing certain problems. Now that you've pinpointed the type of errors you made, take the next practice test, focusing on avoiding your most common types of errors.

Answers to English Test

1. **C.** The verb "contemplating" requires an adverb rather than an adjective modifier. A buyer contemplating high prices is more likely to be "glum" than "gleeful."

2. **F.** The conjunction "but" makes clearer that the second sentence will contrast with the first, dealing with people who "are" aware of the fight for a share of the profits.

3. **C.** Although not grammatically incorrect, the original version is wordy. Choice **D.**, the briefest version, is unacceptable because it distorts the meaning. The growers aren't striking.

4. **G.** Since "growers," "farm workers," and "are" are all plurals, the plural "they are" should be used here.

5. **C.** The sentence begins with a noun ("wages") as object of the preposition "in." Using a second noun ("piecework rates") as a second object of the preposition keeps the parallelism of the sentence intact.

6. **H.** The sentence is comparing the earnings of workers with the earnings ("those") of truckers. The plural "earnings" requires a plural pronoun. Without the pronoun, the sentence compares earnings to truckers. Choice **J.** repeats the noun and misuses the apostrophe.

7. **A.** The introductory first sentence is the only one that doesn't include necessary information.

8. **F.** With the move to a new topic (inflation), a new paragraph is necessary. The phrase "in any case" provides a transition.

9. **C.** Since "President" is singular, the possessive is "'s."

10. **H.** The opening phrase of the sentence has no subject. Unless the subject of the verbal "adopting" follows, the phrase will dangle and seem to say that "pressure" adopted the wage increase rather than Congress. Also, the more acceptable idiom is to "apply" pressure rather than "institute" it.

11. **C.** As it stands, the sentence has no main verb. Omission of the "which" solves the problem.

12. **G.** This is the most concise of the choices.

13. **A.** The sentence as a whole makes sense with "because" as the introductory conjunction.

14. **J.** This sentence has no relation to what has gone before or what follows. The paragraph is more coherent if it's omitted.

15. **B.** Although either a period or a semicolon could follow "hikes," the "however" requires two commas.

16. **F.** The passage makes the most sense in the order in which it's printed here.

17. **C.** With the compound subject ("mouse <u>and</u> rat"), a plural verb is necessary.

18. **F.** Since the sentence is to contrast the attitude of the mouse with that of the rat, the conjunction "but" rather than "and" should be used.

19. **C.** The phrase isn't a direct quotation, so no quotation marks should be used. If it were a direct quotation, the mouse would say, "The food is good."

20. **H.** Using the gerund "seeing" rather than the infinitive "to see" is more idiomatic and more concise.

21. **C.** "Like" is a preposition and takes an object ("like people"), while "as" is a conjunction and may be followed by a subject and verb ("as people do").

22. **J.** The sentence fits better as the first sentence of Paragraph 2, which deals with the rat. The existing first sentence of Paragraph 2 follows logically from this sentence.

23. **D.** The parallelism with the second term of the series ("his weight greater") is sustained best by choice **D.**

24. **F.** The sentence as written is correct. The sentence is a question and should be punctuated with a question mark at the end.

25. **C.** The three other proverbs preach caution, standing pat, but "Nothing ventured, nothing gained" urges action to gain a reward.

26. **F.** The "would be" is correct, a subjunctive verb.

27. **B.** The word choice is that of the mouse, who has lost patience with the rat's string of proverbs.

28. **H.** The passage uses dialogue, indirect discourse, and comedy.

29. **C.** The passage is probably part of a fable, a moral story usually using animals as its characters.

30. **G.** "Protestations" and "objections" are so close in meaning that it's unnecessary to use both. Since the next sentence uses "protesting," the use of "objections" in the first sentence avoids the repetition.

31. **D.** Although choices **A.** and **B.** are correct grammatically, they are much wordier than **D.**, which says as much, since you can assume that if they filled the chamber, they attended the meeting.

32. **J.** Here, the use of too few words causes a grammatical error. The verb "alter" requires an object like "fact," since it's the fact, not the petitions, that can't be altered.

33. **C.** The errors in this sentence are of parallelism. The correlatives "either . . . or" should be followed by constructions that are parallel: "either 25%," or "10%." You could also say "either the signatures of 25%" and "or the signatures of 10%," but that construction is wordier than choice **C.**

34. **F.** The council members and petitioners already know what this factual account reports. The use of "Tuesday" and the local nature of the subject suggest that a daily or weekly newspaper is more likely than a monthly news magazine to carry this story.

35. **B.** As a general rule, modifiers should be near the words they modify. This phrase, modifying "filed," fits most naturally at the beginning of the sentence.

36. G. The phrase "city manager" is an appositive and should be set off with two commas. Choice **J.** is wordier and also lacks a necessary comma.

37. B. The subject of this verb is the plural "66." The tense throughout the paragraph is past.

38. F. The adjective "supposed" should be used to modify the noun "owners." The verb should be plural and in the past tense.

39. B. The verb here is the subjunctive "would" required by the conditional sentence.

40. H. The second paragraph uses the direct quotation from the city manager.

41. D. With the use of "that," the quotation is indirect and should use the third person ("he"), not the first person ("I"), and the past perfect tense to indicate an action completed before the main verb ("told") in the past tense.

42. G. As it's written, the sentence beginning with "Enough" is a fragment, lacking a subject and a verb. Adding an "And" makes no difference. Choice **J.** adds a verb, but there is still no subject. As a phrase that's part of a sentence already complete (as in choice **G.**), there's no need for a subject and verb. It's simply an adjectival phrase modifying "signatures."

43. D. This biographical information about a minor character in the passage is unnecessary and intrusive.

44. F. The author wishes to use the adverb "savagely" to modify the adjective "comic." No change is warranted.

45. D. The direct quotation of one or two of these "savagely comic insults" would, no doubt, liven up the passage.

46. J. The author, having reached a climax, ends very quickly with words conventionally used to report a meeting's end. The effect is anticlimactic. The reader isn't to find out what the insults were or what happened next. The adjective "hortatory" means encouraging or exhorting and doesn't at all fit this last sentence.

47. C. As the sentence is written or in versions **B.** and **D.**, the participial phrase dangles. By supplying a subject ("I"), choice **C.** corrects the error.

48. J. The sentence has a series of nouns as the object of the verb "had." By using the phrase "oil central heating," the parallelism is preserved and the meaning is expressed in the fewest words.

49. B. The paragraph here uses a question (an interrogative verb) that the next sentence answers.

50. F. The parenthetical "I suppose" should be set off by two commas. Although, strictly speaking, the phrase is not necessary to the sense of the sentence, it affects the tone, making the speaker appear more casual and conversational.

51. C. The word is a perfectly legitimate English adjective meaning new or novel, usually with disapproval. The author uses quotations because the word is being quoted from the mother.

52. F. The exclamation is correct in this context. The passage loses meaning and tone if the phrase is left out.

53. A. The punctuation is correct. The colon introduces the series, and the semicolon separates the parts of a series that have internal commas.

54. J. There's nothing in the passage to inform a reader of the gender of the speaker. As you find out later, he or she is a lawyer who does not cook. The first paragraph uses the first person and the past tense.

55. A. Choice **D.** changes the meaning. Choices **B.** and **C.** are double negatives.

56. F. As it's written, the sentence is grammatically correct, and the construction in the second half of the sentence is parallel to that in the first ("how to make bread").

57. B. The problem in this sentence is that there are two phrases modifying "something—from a package" and "that is quick." Choice **B.** does the best job of keeping the modifiers as close to the word modified as possible.

58. H. Since the kitchen is a room, the correct phrase is "any other."

59. D. Since "same" and "identical" mean the same thing, only one of the two should be used. The phrase "of heat" is also unnecessary.

60. J. Of the four choices, "nostalgic" is the best.

61. A. The correct word here is the conjunction "whether"; "weather" is the noun. Since the sentence contains a "no" later, the "not" is unnecessary.

62. J. Although not wrong, the "one" is an unneeded word. The correct punctuation sets off the introductory clause with a comma. The meaning of "appears to be," as well as the tense, is different from the meaning and tense of "was." The paragraph uses the present tense.

63. D. The use of "But" or "However" is preferable here because this sentence deals with a different situation, one that is *not* routine. If the "however" is used, it should be set off by commas.

64. J. The first three sentences of this paragraph deal with the police dispatcher, but the fourth moves to a somewhat different subject.

65. C. The verb form here is incorrect. You need a relative pronoun that refers to a family "member" ("who," a person, not "that," a thing) and the present tense of the verb "call."

66. J. Some meaning is lost if the phrase is left out. The best place for the clause is where it won't come between the subject and main verb of the sentence, either at the beginning or at the end.

67. B. The most concise and idiomatic phrase here is "ask . . . to."

68. J. Again, where there's no change of meaning, the shortest version is preferred.

69. A. The rest of the sentence makes it clear that the verb should be in the present. To "run high" is an idiom (and a metaphor) in which "run" is a linking verb, similar in meaning to the verb "to be." For this reason, the adjective ("high") rather than the adverb ("highly") is proper.

70. H. Again, the most concise version is the best.

71. D. Pronouns like "which," "that," and "this" should have specific antecedents. In this sentence, the antecedent of all three pronouns is the whole of the clause ("officers . . . neutrality") but no single word in the clause. The correct version gets rid of the problem pronoun.

72. F. Here, you must know what the "they" or "he" refers to. It's the "officers" of the first sentence, a plural, and a plural again in the third sentence. Choice **J.** has the number right but omits a needed comma.

73. A. The phrase used in the passage is correct, a common idiom that compares clear air with more controlled feelings.

74. H. Since the passage focuses on the police, the words of a police officer who has faced these situations would be especially effective.

75. C. Paragraph 1 talks about the police response to a call, but Paragraph 2 talks about who makes the call in the first place. Paragraph 3 deals with what happens when the police arrive, that is, after the dispatch. The chronological order of the passage is 2, 1, 3, not as it is printed here.

Answers to Mathematics Test

1. **B.** If x is increased by 50%, it can be represented by $\frac{3}{2}x$. This value must be multiplied by $\frac{2}{3}y$ in order to keep the product equal to xy. Since $\frac{2}{3}$ is a $\frac{1}{3}$ reduction, choice **B.** is the correct response.

2. **H.** Although the answer of 40 can be determined by trial and error, there is a better way.

   Maximum = (cost of ticket)(number of tickets)

   $$= (30 + 5x)(100 - 10x)$$
   $$= (5)(10)(6 + x)(10 - x)$$

   The roots of this symmetric curve are 10 and −6. So the line of symmetry is $x = 2$ and

   $$(30 + 5x) = 40$$

   The maximum dollar sales are produced when the ticket price is $0.40.

3. **C.** Because a right triangle is formed, the width of the rectangle can be found with the Pythagorean theorem. You can save time if you note that the triangle is a multiple of a 5, 12, 13 right triangle. The factor is 3, so the width must be 15 inches, and

   $$(15)(36) = 540$$

4. **K.** Because the shelf lengths are 4 inches apart, first find the average shelf length by dividing 155 by 5, which gives 31. This is the middle-length shelf. The shelf measurements are 23, 27, 31, 35, and 39. So the longest shelf is 39 inches long.

   This problem can also be approached algebraically, as follows. If the longest shelf is x, the other shelves can be represented by $x - 4$, $x - 8$, $x - 12$, and $x - 16$. Add these and you get

   $$5x - 40 = 155$$
   $$5x = 155 + 40$$
   $$5x = 195$$
   $$x = 39$$

5. **B.** Substituting,

   $$3x + 3x = 14$$
   $$6x = 14$$
   $$x = \tfrac{14}{6}$$
   $$x = \tfrac{7}{3}$$

   Also

   $$2y + 2y = 14$$
   $$4y = 14$$
   $$y = \tfrac{14}{4}$$
   $$y = \tfrac{7}{2}$$

Therefore,

$$x + y = \frac{1}{3} + \frac{1}{2}$$

$$= \frac{14}{6} + \frac{21}{6}$$

$$= \frac{35}{6}$$

$$= 5\frac{5}{6}$$

The answer is choice **B**.

6. **G.** If the perimeter of the square is $8\sqrt{\pi}$ then each side is $2\sqrt{\pi}$ and the area of the square is 4π. If a circle has an area of 4π its radius is 2, its diameter is 4, and its circumference is 4π.

7. **B.** The greatest common factor can't be larger than the smallest number. This fact eliminates choice **E**. All 4 numbers are divisible by 3, which eliminates choice **A**. None of the numbers is divisible by 12 or 18, which leaves the correct answer of 6.

8. **H.** Because 21 is 70% of the total, the total must be 30. So the team lost 9 matches.

9. **C.** The total number of candies in the package is $8 + 2 + 6 = 16$. After one candy is chosen, 15 are left. Since there are 6 white candies out of 15 candies, the probability of getting a white candy is $\frac{6}{15}$, which equals $\frac{2}{5}$.

10. **F.** Because there are 180° in a triangle,

$$(3x) + (x + 10) + (2x - 40) = 180$$

$$6x - 30 = 180$$

$$6x = 210$$

$$x = 35$$

Therefore, the 3 angles are 105°, 45°, and 30°, and the smallest angle is 30°, choice **F**.

11. **A.** Remember to perform all 4 multiplications if you use the FOIL method: First, Outer, Inner, and Last. An alternate method is to line them up and multiply as follows.

$$\begin{array}{r} 2x + 4 \\ (\times)\ x + 3 \\ \hline 2x^2 + 4x \\ 6x + 12 \\ \hline 2x^2 + 10x + 12 \end{array}$$

12. **J.** The external angle theorem states that an exterior angle of a triangle is equal to the sum of the 2 remote interior angles. Therefore,

$$50 + w = 130$$

$$w = 130 - 50$$

$$= 80$$

13. E. Remember that the symbol "<" means *less than* and ">" means *greater than*. In this problem, the middle condition is repetitious.

"If *A* is greater than *B*"   A > B

"*C* is less than *A*"   C < A

"and *B* is greater than *C*"   B > C

Then, by making the proper connections,

A > B > C

or

C < B < A

14. H. Statement I is the external angle theorem. Statement II follows from statement I. Statement III is true only some of the time.

15. A. When dividing numbers of the same base, subtract the exponents, canceling or dividing as follows:

$$\frac{12x^6 y^4 z^2}{6x^2 y^4 z^8} \text{ leaves } \frac{2x^4}{z^6}$$

16. H. You can sketch the following diagram.

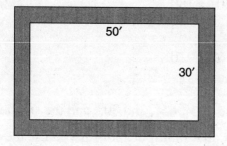

Now you can solve the problem by working from the answers. Since the answers are in order from smallest to largest, you may want to start from the middle answer and then go up or down as needed. If you use the value in choice **H.**, 5, the diagram looks like this.

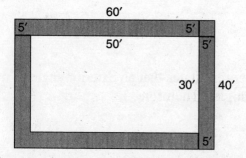

The overall area is 60 feet by 40 feet, or 2,400 square feet. The area of the court is 1,500 square feet. Subtracting the area of the court from the overall area gives the area of the grass strip, which is 900 square feet. So the strip is 5 feet wide.

An algebraic solution for the problem looks like this. If the width of the strip is x, then

$$(2x + 50)(2x + 30) - 1{,}500 = 900$$
$$4x^2 + 160x + 1{,}500 - 1{,}500 = 900$$
$$x^2 + 40x - 225 = 0$$
$$(x + 45)(x - 5) = 0$$

Because distance can't be negative, you're left with x = 5.

17. **B.** The information leads you to the following diagram.

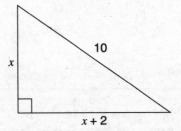

The path taken by the hikers forms a right triangle. Since the hikers hiked 2 hours and one hiker can hike 1 mile per hour faster than the other, that hiker will be 2 miles farther than the slower one after 2 hours. Therefore, the following Pythagorean relationship exists.

$$a^2 + b^2 = c^2$$
$$x^2 + (x + 2)^2 = 10^2$$
$$x^2 + x^2 + 4x + 4 = 100$$
$$2x^2 + 4x - 96 = 0$$
$$x^2 + 2x - 48 = 0$$
$$(x + 8)(x - 6) = 0$$

Now, solving each one independently gives

$x + 8 = 0$, so $x = -8$

or

$x - 6 = 0$, so $x = 6$

Because distance can't be negative, x must be equal to 6. So in 2 hours, the slower hiker walked 6 miles, which is 3 miles per hour. Again, this problem can be solved by working from the answers.

18. **H.** The hypotenuse of the triangle is the longest side, which is 5 centimeters. The sine of an angle is defined as the quotient of the side opposite the angle and the hypotenuse. Therefore, the sine is ⅘.

19. B. Substitute x + 4 in the given equation for *x*.

$$3x^2 + 2x - 4 = 0$$
$$3(x+4)^2 + 2(x + 4) - 4 = 0$$
$$3(x^2 + 8x + 16) + 2x + 8 - 4 = 0$$
$$3x^2 + 24x + 48 + 2x + 8 - 4 = 0$$
$$3x^2 + 26x + 52 = 0$$

20. K. Solving the inequality gives

$$4 - 3x < -3$$
$$-3x < -7$$
$$x > \frac{7}{3}$$

Therefore, *x* is greater than 2⅓.

21. C. To find the area of the quadrilateral, start with the area of the large rectangle and subtract the areas of the 2 triangles. The height of the large rectangle is

$$3 - (-3) = 6$$

and the width of the large rectangle is

$$4 - (-5) = 9$$

Therefore, the area of the large rectangle is 54 square units.

The lower triangle has a width of

$$4 - (-5) = 9$$

and a height of

$$(-1) - (-3) = 2$$

Therefore, its area is

$$\frac{(9)(2)}{2} = 9 \text{ square units}$$

The upper triangle has a width of

$$(-2) - (-5) = 3$$

and a height of

$$3 - (-1) = 4$$

Therefore, its area is

$$\frac{(4)(3)}{2} = 6 \text{ square units}$$

Therefore, the area of the quadrilateral is

$$54 - 9 - 6 = 39 \text{ square units}$$

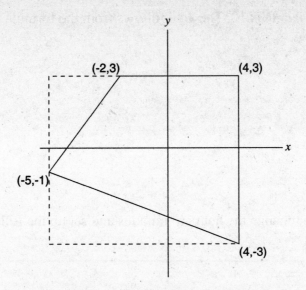

22. **K.** You can sketch a diagram similar to the following:

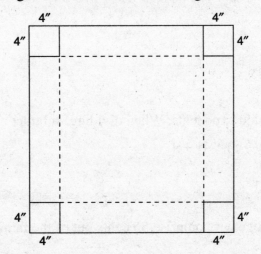

Because the square bottom of the tank can be represented by x^2,

$4x^2 = 900$

$x^2 = 225$

$x = 15$

Therefore, the width of the tank is 15.

Because the 4-inch sides are folded up, you must add 8 to this figure, giving 23 inches.

23. **C.** Let x be Mike's age. Then, $3x$ is Macey's age. Therefore,

$3x + 8 = 2(x + 8)$

$3x + 8 = 2x + 16$

$3x - 2x = 16 - 8$

$x = 8$

So $3x = 24$, which means that Macey is now 24. Therefore, 3 years ago she was 21.

24. J. The side of the triangle is 10. The area follows from the formula for the area of an equilateral triangle.

$$A = \frac{x^2\sqrt{3}}{4}$$

$$A = \frac{10^2\sqrt{3}}{4}$$

$$= \frac{100\sqrt{3}}{4}$$

$$= 25\sqrt{3}$$

25. C. For this problem, change the hours to minutes and set up the following equations.

$$\frac{x}{120} + \frac{x}{90} = 1$$

Multiply by 360.

$$3x + 4x = 360$$

$$7x = 360$$

$$x = 51$$

An alternate equation is

$$\frac{1}{120} + \frac{1}{90} = \frac{1}{x}$$

26. G. When multiplying, add exponents. When dividing, subtract exponents. So

$$(2y + 2) + (6y - 1) - (4y - 3) = 4y + 4$$

or finally,

$$x^{4y + 4}$$

27. D. Housing and Food together comprise 55 cents out of the family's dollar. So 55 cents out of 100 cents is

$$\frac{55}{100} = 55\%$$

Fifty-five percent of the entire central angle of 360° is

$$(55)(360) = 198°$$

28. F. Because AB = BC, ∠CAD = ∠ACB (isosceles triangle *ABC*). So ∠ACB is also 70°. This makes ∠B equal to 40° (180° degrees in a triangle). Also, ∠BCD equals 40°, for the same reason. Therefore, ∠ADC = 80° (external angle theorem).

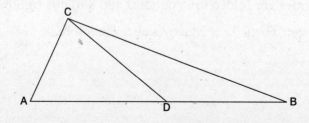

29. B. Drawing the following x-y graph and placing the points can be helpful.

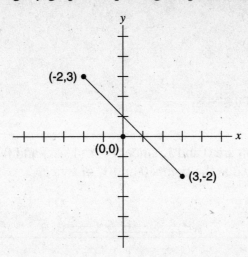

Because the line goes down to the right, the slope is negative, so the answer is either **A.** or **B.** From this drawing you can determine that the answer is −1, choice **B.**

Mathematically, the formula for the slope of a line (where m = slope), given its two endpoints, gives

$$m = \frac{y_2 - y_1}{x_2 - x_1}$$

$$= \frac{3 - (-2)}{-2 - (-3)}$$

$$= \frac{5}{-5}$$

$$= -1$$

30. G. The 5 angles of a pentagon add up to 540°. So 240° are left over for the 2 unknown angles. Therefore,

$$x + (2x + 30) = 240$$

$$3x = 240 - 30$$

$$3x = 210$$

$$x = 70$$

Therefore, the 2 unknown angles are 70° and 170° and the sum of the 2 smallest is

$$70 + 80 = 150$$

31. D. To set up the following equation, let x be the number of liters of 20% solution and $(40 - x)$ be the number of liters of 60% solution. Then

$$(.20)(x) + (.60)(40 - x) = (.50)(40)$$

Simplifying and multiplying by 100 gives

$$20x + 2400 - 60x = 2000$$

$$-40x = -400$$

$$x = 10$$

32. G. Factoring the equation gives

$$y = x^4(1 - x)$$

The roots of this equation are 0 and 1, since $0 = x^4(1 - x)$ and $0 = x^4$ or $0 = 1 - x$. So the x-axis is intersected at the points 0 and 1, or twice.

33. A. From the diagram

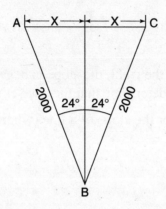

you can see that

$$\sin 24^\circ = \frac{x}{2000}$$

$$x = 2000 \sin 24^\circ$$

Therefore, the distance between A and C is $2x$, or $4000 \sin 24^\circ$.

34. G. You can set up the following chart.

	D	=	R	X	T
Up	D		16		$\frac{D}{16}$
Down	D		24		$\frac{D}{24}$

Since the time is 10 hours for the whole trip,

$$\frac{D}{16} + \frac{D}{24} = 10$$

Multiplying by 48,

$$3D + 2D = 480, 5D = 480, D = 96$$

35. D. Average speed is total distance/total time. The total distance is $2x$. Time going is $x/8$. Time coming back is $x/12$. So average speed is

$$\frac{2x}{\frac{x}{8} + \frac{x}{12}} = \frac{2x}{\frac{3x}{24} + \frac{2x}{24}}$$

$$= \frac{2x}{\frac{5x}{24}}$$

$$= \left(\frac{2x}{1}\right)\left(\frac{24}{5x}\right)$$

$$= \frac{48}{5}$$

$$= 9.6$$

36. F. Given

$$\frac{x}{x-y} - \frac{y}{y-x}$$

Since

$$y - x = -(x - y)$$

then

$$\frac{y}{y-x} = \frac{-y}{x-y}$$

and therefore

$$\frac{x}{x-y} - \frac{y}{y-x} = \frac{x}{x-y} + \frac{y}{x-y}$$

$$= \frac{x+y}{x-y}$$

37. E. From the Pythagorean theorem, you see that the diagonal is 15. So the perimeter of the rectangle is 42, and the perimeter of the triangle is 36. Therefore, the ratio is $42/36 = 7/6$ or 7:6.

38. F. You must combine similar terms.

$$(4x^3) + (-3x^3) + (-2x^3) = -x^3$$

and

$$(-2x^2) + (3x^2) + (-4x^2) = -3x^2$$

Therefore, the sum is $-x^3 - 3x^2$

39. A. Work from the inside out.

$$f\left(\frac{1}{2}\right) = \left(\frac{1}{2}\right)^2 - 2$$

$$= \frac{1}{4} - 2$$

$$= -\frac{7}{4}$$

Then

$$g\left(f\left(\frac{1}{2}\right)\right) = g\left(-\frac{7}{4}\right)$$

$$= 2\left(-\frac{7}{4}\right) + 2$$

$$= -\frac{14}{4} + 2$$

$$= -\frac{14}{4} + \frac{8}{4}$$

$$= -\frac{6}{4}$$

$$= -\frac{3}{2}$$

and

$$f\left(g\left(f\left(\frac{1}{2}\right)\right)\right) = f\left(-\frac{3}{2}\right)$$

$$= \left(-\frac{3}{2}\right)^2 - 2$$

$$= \frac{9}{4} - 2$$

$$= \frac{9}{4} - \frac{8}{4}$$

$$= \frac{1}{4}$$

40. J. Lines that are perpendicular to each other have slopes that are negative inverses of each other. So the equation must be of the form

$y = 2x + b$

If you substitute the given point (1, 1) into this form, you can determine the value of b.

$1 = (2)(1) + b$

So $b = -1$. Thus, $y = 2x - 1$, and choice **J.** is the answer.

41. A. The area of a triangle is

$A = bh/2$

The base and the height are interchangeable.

Since

Sin 35° = $y/4$ and cos 35° = $x/4$

then

$y = 4 \sin 35°$ and $x = 4 \cos 35°$

Therefore, $A = 8 \sin 35° \cos 35°$

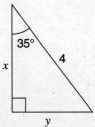

42. F. Using the point slope form of the equation,

$y = \frac{1}{2}x + b$

Substituting the given point into this equation allows you to find b, the y-intercept.

$2 = \frac{1}{2}(1) + b$

$b = \frac{3}{2}$

Therefore,

$y = \frac{1}{2}x + \frac{3}{2}$

Multiplying the whole equation by 2 gives

$2y = x + 3$

Adding $-2y$ to each side gives

$0 = x - 2y + 3$

or

$x - 2y + 3 = 0$

43. A. You can make the following drawing.

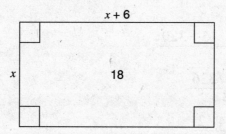

If the width of the rectangle is x, the length can be represented by $x + 6$. So

$x(x + 6) = 18$

$x^2 + 6x = 8$

$x^2 + 6x - 18 = 0$

Using the quadratic formula gives

$x = \dfrac{-6 \pm \sqrt{36 + 72}}{2}$

$= \dfrac{-6 \pm \sqrt{108}}{2}$

$= \dfrac{-6 \pm 6\sqrt{3}}{2}$

$= -3 \pm 3\sqrt{3}$

Since x must be positive, use $+3\sqrt{3}$ giving

$-3 + 3\sqrt{3}$ or $3\sqrt{3} - 3$

Factoring gives

$3(\sqrt{3} - 1)$

44. H. Since $\angle ABD = 20°$, $\overset{\frown}{AD} = 40°$. Since $\overset{\frown}{DAB}$ is a semicircle, $\overset{\frown}{AB}$ must equal 140° and angle x must equal 70°.

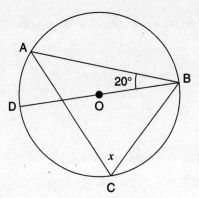

45. B. Time equals distance divided by speed. Therefore,

$$\frac{20}{x} - \frac{20}{x+4} = 1$$

$$20(x+4) - 20x = x^2 + 4x$$

$$20x + 80 - 20x = x^2 + 4x$$

$$x^2 + 4x - 80 = 0$$

$$x = \frac{-4 \pm \sqrt{16+320}}{2}$$

$$= \frac{-4 \pm \sqrt{336}}{2}$$

$$= \frac{-4 \pm 4\sqrt{21}}{2}$$

$$x = -2 \pm 2\sqrt{21}$$

Since speed must be positive, use the $+2\sqrt{21}$ which gives

$-2 + 2\sqrt{21}$ or $2\sqrt{21} - 2$

46. J. You could work this problem by plugging in from the answers. Choices **F., G.,** and **H.** are not reasonable answers because if the sum of 2 numbers is 25, the larger number couldn't be 10, 11, or 12. So, plug in answer **J.**, 13. If 13 is the larger number, 12 is the smaller number. Now square each of them and add them together as follows.

$12^2 + 13^2 =$

$144 + 169 = 313$

Therefore, 13 is the largest number, and the correct answer is **J.**

Algebraically, if x represents one number, then $(25 - x)$ can be used to represent the other number. Therefore,

$$x^2 + (25 - x)^2 = 313$$

$$x^2 + 625 - 50x + x^2 = 313$$

$$2x^2 - 50x + 312 = 0$$

$$x^2 - 25x + 156 = 0$$

$$(x - 12)(x - 13) = 0$$

So the numbers are 12 and 13.

47. D. You can draw the following x-y graph and plot the points.

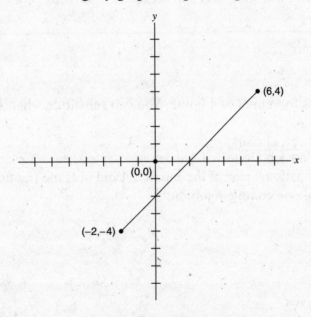

If you understand that the y-intercept is where the line crosses the y-axis, you can eliminate choices **A.** and **B.** From the graph, the y-intercept will be negative. If you draw the graph fairly accurately, you can spot the answer of -2.

To solve for the y-intercept, first determine the slope of the line (m = slope of line).

$$m = \frac{y_2 - y_1}{x_2 - x_1}$$

$$= \frac{4 - (-4)}{6 - (-2)}$$

$$= \frac{8}{8}$$

$$= 1$$

You can use the point slope formula to determine the y-intercept, but there is a faster way. Since the slope is 1, each unit you move to the right results in one unit up. So if you start with the point $(-2, -4)$ and add 2 to each coordinate, you get $(0, -2)$. Therefore, the y-intercept is -2.

48. J. From the Pythagorean theorem, you can see that $\overline{AB}$ is 15.

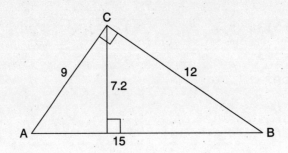

Because the height of a right triangle drawn from the right angle to the hypotenuse divides the triangle into similar triangles, you can set up the following ratio.

$h/9 = {}^{12}/_{15}$

$15h = 12 \times 9$

$h = 7.2$

49. C. Machine A works for a total of 4 hours. You can substitute what is known into the following useful formula.

$$\frac{A \text{ actual work}}{A \text{ do job alone}} + \frac{B \text{ actual work}}{B \text{ do job alone}} = 1$$

In other words, the fractional part of the job that A did plus the fractional part of the job that B did must equal one complete job. So

${}^4/_{10} + {}^x/_{12} = 1$

Since ${}^4/_{10} + {}^6/_{10} = 1$

Then ${}^x/_{12} = {}^6/_{10}$

Cross-multiplying gives

$10x = 72$ or $x = 7.2$

Now, 7.2 hours = 7 hours and 12 minutes. Since B started at 9 a.m., B must finish at 4:12 p.m.

50. J. Simply substitute in the formula.

$\frac{1}{4} = {}^1/_{10} + {}^1/_{B}$

Multiply through by the common denominator $20B$ to get rid of the denominators, giving

$5B = 2B + 20$

$3B = 20$

$B = 6\frac{2}{3}$

51. A. To get additional insight, you should draw the diagram.

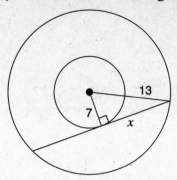

From the Pythagorean theorem,

$$7^2 + x^2 = 13^2$$
$$x^2 = 169 - 49$$
$$x^2 = 120$$
$$x = \sqrt{120} = 2\sqrt{30}$$

Because the length of the chord is twice the length of the leg of the right triangle,

$$2x = 4\sqrt{30}$$

52. K. The drawing would look like this.

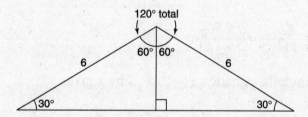

If you divide the triangle in half, you get two 30—60—90 right triangles. The longest side is 6. So the shortest side is 3, and the third side is $3\sqrt{3}$. Therefore, the length of the longest side of the large triangle is $6\sqrt{3}$.

53. B. Perform the following.

$$\frac{2\sqrt{3}-4}{\sqrt{3}+2} \times \frac{\sqrt{3}-2}{\sqrt{3}-2} = \frac{6-8\sqrt{3}+8}{3-4}$$

To get the above numerator,

$$2\sqrt{3}-4$$
$$\underline{(\times)\sqrt{3}-2}$$
$$6-4\sqrt{3}$$
$$\underline{-4\sqrt{3}+8}$$
$$6-8\sqrt{3}+8$$

To get the above denominator,

$$\sqrt{3}+2$$

$$(\times)\sqrt{3}-2$$

$$3+2\sqrt{3}$$

$$\frac{-2\sqrt{3}-4}{3 \qquad -4}$$

Now simplifying,

$$=\frac{14-8\sqrt{3}}{-1}=8\sqrt{3}-14=2\left(4\sqrt{3}-7\right)$$

54. H. Given $\sqrt{\dfrac{78x^5y^7}{6x^2y^3}}$

$$\sqrt{\frac{78x^5y^7}{6x^2y^3}}=\sqrt{13x^3y^4}$$

$$=\sqrt{13(x^2)x(y^4)}$$

$$=xy^2\sqrt{13x}$$

55. D. Solve as follows.

$$\frac{|8-3||3-8|}{|-3-8||-8+3|}=\frac{5\times5}{11\times5}=\frac{25}{55}=\frac{5}{11}$$

56. J. Multiplying through the equation $x-10=\frac{-9}{x}$ by x gives

$$x^2-10x=-9$$

$$x^2-10x+9=0$$

$$(x-9)(x-1)=0$$

Therefore, the roots are 9 and 1. Their difference is 8.

57. D. The formula for the total number of degrees in an n-sided polygon is $(n-2)180$ where n is the number of sides. Since a decagon has 10 sides, there are $(10-2)180=1440$ degrees total. Since the polygon is regular, all angles are the same size. Therefore, dividing by 10, $\frac{1440}{10}=144$.

58. F. Simply substitute either value into the equation and solve. Using the value of 2,

$$4x^2+2x+A=0$$

$$4(2)^2+(2)(2)+A=0$$

$$16+4+A=0$$

$$A=-20$$

59. C. To gain insight, you could draw a diagram such as the following.

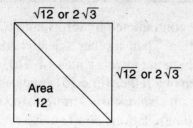

If the area of a square is 12, then each side of the square is $\sqrt{12}$ or $2\sqrt{3}$. From the relationship in the 45—45—90-degree right triangle, you know that the hypotenuse, and in this case the diagonal, is equal to the product of a side and $\sqrt{2}$. Therefore,

$$d = \left(\sqrt{2}\right)\left(2\sqrt{3}\right)$$
$$= 2\sqrt{6}$$

60. H. First factor the numerator and denominator.

$$\frac{x^2 - 7xy + 12y^2}{x^2 - 4xy + 3y^2} = \frac{(x-3y)(x-4y)}{(x-3y)(x-y)}$$
$$= \frac{x-4y}{x-y}$$

Answers to Reading Test

1. **D.** All answers except **D.** are contradicted by information in the passage or by reasonable inferences from that information. Their mother's death had taken place at least six months earlier when the uncle gave them the jewels (lines 14–15), so choice **A.** is incorrect. The reference to the uncle rather than a father (line 15) suggests that both parents are no longer living and that the father's death also occurred more than six months before. **C.** is a poor choice; the sisters' living accommodations don't suggest poverty (lines 3–5).

2. **H.** The passage is ironic when it speaks of the strength of Celia's arguments. But because Dorothea isn't interested in jewels herself, it hasn't occurred to her that Celia might be. See lines 40–44. As soon as Dorothea realizes Celia's desires, she is eager to please her sister, whom she loves. Dorothea's reactions throughout the passage give no indication that she doesn't respect her mother's memory (choice **F.**). Although she does react to the beauty of the gems (lines 80–82), nothing suggests that she wishes to adorn herself with them out of personal vanity (choice **G.**)—quite the contrary. Choice **J.** is also incorrect; her decision to look at the jewels has nothing to do with her Christian principles but rather with her feelings for her sister.

3. **D.** Dorothea doesn't fully understand herself why she believes she will not wear the jewelry, but she is sincere when she first states that she won't wear jewels. Had she been concerned with jewelry, she wouldn't have forgotten about the jewels. Choice **A.** is clearly incorrect; it contradicts the picture of Dorothea's character in the passage. Choice **B.** is also wrong; as well as being religious, Dorothea is presented as an intelligent woman (lines 1–7, for example), and it is unlikely that she would be unaware of the jewels' value. Also, nothing implies that she is herself tempted to wear the jewels (lines 68–70, for example), making choice **C.** incorrect.

4. **G.** Celia would like Dorothea to wear at least one jewel, and she hopes the cross might appeal to her sister's religious feelings. Nothing suggests that choice **F.** is true; Celia simply doesn't want her sister to think ill of her for wearing the cross (line 71–72). Although Celia obviously doesn't share Dorothea's religious strictness, this wouldn't affect her desire to wear the cross; its beauty is much more important to her than its religious significance. Choice **H.** is therefore incorrect. Choice **J.** also isn't a good choice. Neither Celia's behavior nor her words (lines 65–67) indicate that she is sure Dorothea will refuse the cross.

5. **A.** Celia's words (lines 30–37, 71–72) suggest that Dorothea's strictness is attributable to her religious beliefs. Also, throughout the passage, Dorothea is shown as dedicated to her religious principles. Choice **B.** is incorrect; Dorothea's reactions and words do not indicate hypocrisy, and nothing in the passage implies that she simply wants to be well thought of. Choice **C.** is completely irrelevant; marriage hopes are not addressed or implied in this passage. Finally, choice **D.** is directly contradicted (lines 80–89, 96–98).

6. **F.** The passage presents Dorothea as indifferent to the jewels her mother has left her (making **G.** a poor choice), but interested in good works, such as a school in the village (lines 1–10). Nothing implies that she is interested in recreation for the rich (choice **H.**). **J.** may seem like a good choice, but Dorothea, though strict in religion, isn't shown as political, and it's unlikely that she would be in favor of conservative polices regarding the poor.

7. **C.** Celia is more worldly than Dorothea, as Celia's attitude about the jewels makes clear. *Intellectual* (choice **A.**) and *articulate* (choice **B.**) aren't good choices (see lines 11–20, for example). (Lines 37–39 are ironic.) *Quixotic* (choice **D.**) means extravagantly chivalrous or foolishly idealistic, neither of which describes Celia as she is presented in the passage.

8. **H.** Dorothea refers to jewels as *spiritual emblems* (lines 85–86) and *like fragments of heaven* (lines 87–88). Choice **F.** is contradicted by her open reaction to the jewels (lines 80–89, 92–98). She doesn't argue anywhere in the passage that the jewels are a gift of God (choice **G.**). Dorothea isn't shown as a hypocrite about religion (choice **J.**), even though she can't help but be affected by the beauty of the jewels.

9. **B.** Similes, comparisons using *like* or *as,* are used in lines 80–88 but not in the rest of the passage. On the other hand, irony (choice **C.**) is used throughout (lines 27–39, for example), and the entire passage is a dialogue between the sisters (choice **D.**). Rhetorical questions (choice **A.**), which are questions that are asked for effect and to which no answer is expected, aren't used in the passage.

10. **G.** Although the author is aware of some limitations in Dorothea, the attitude toward the character is tolerant, not *grudgingly* tolerant (choice **H.**). Nor is the attitude enthusiastically approving (choice **J.**). She is presented here in a scene of light comedy. Choice **F.** may seem a possibility, but the tone in the presentation of Dorothea is *affectionate amusement*, not *cool disinterestedness*.

11. **B.** The problems in U.S. labor from 1870 to 1910 is the overall subject of this passage. Choice **A.** is incorrect; labor unions are mentioned only once (line 66). The word *expansion* in choice **C.** is vague and misleading, and choice **D.** is mentioned only in the final paragraph.

12. **H.** Lines 17–20 state that the maintenance of the furnaces was *decisive* in maintaining the twelve-hour day. Choices **F.**, **G.**, and **J.**, while they may appear to be possible answers, aren't mentioned as causes of the long work day and are therefore irrelevant to the question.

13. **A.** It seems odd that industry should grow at the expense of the worker, but this was the effect of specialized machinery (lines 1–6). No evidence in the passage suggests choice **B.**, although it may in fact be true. Neither choice **C.** nor choice **D.** is stated or implied.

14. **F.** With fewer people leaving the eastern cities for farms in the West, the eastern labor force grew larger (lines 39–42). Choice **G.** is therefore incorrect, and choices **H.** and **J.** are irrelevant.

15. **A.** If the labor pool is small, wages are likely to rise. See lines 53–66. Choice **B.** is contradicted in the passage in the same lines. Choice **C.** is also incorrect; with fewer immigrants, more American workers would be required and therefore unemployment could be expected to fall. Choice **D.** is irrelevant; this issue isn't addressed or implied in the passage.

16. **G.** The large immigrant population and the recent unavailability of farmland are specifically mentioned as uniquely American experiences in the period and therefore wouldn't affect European countries (lines 26–30, 48–51). On the other hand, an increasingly mechanized industry would present problems for Europe as well as America. Therefore, choices **F.**, **H.**, and **J.** are all incorrect.

17. **D.** Notice the word *EXCEPT* in this question. Right-to-work laws aren't discussed in the passage. Choice **A.** is indicated in lines 14–16, **B.** in lines 39–42, and **C.** in lines 48–57; all are mentioned as contributing to the growth of unemployment.

18. **G.** Lines 67–76 explain that only the states, not the federal government, had the authority to regulate wages. Therefore, there couldn't be a *federal minimum wage*. Of the possible answers, this is the only one for which there is direct evidence. Nothing in the passage implies choice **F.**, **H.**, or **J.**

19. **C.** The political system left most labor laws at this time to the states (lines 70–74). **D.** might seem a good choice, but the passage refers specifically to labor problems, not other issues. Although immigration was unrestricted in the United States (choice **A.**), the political *system* is the issue being addressed in the question. Choice **B.** is unsupported in the passage.

20. **J.** From the context of the passage, *usurp the place* means to take or *seize* the place. Choice **G.**, which may seem reasonable, is incorrect because the place of the worker wasn't eliminated. In addition to being incorrect definitions of *usurp*, the context of the word makes it clear that choices **F.** and **H.** are incorrect (lines 20–22).

21. **D.** Both choices **A.** and **B.** misrepresent the contents. The passage isn't about scientific or modern thought. The passage covers more than the early Middle Ages (choice **C.**), so choice **D.**, although uninspired, is at least accurate.

22. **J.** See lines 57–70. Notice the word *EXCEPT* in this question. Choice **F.** is supported in lines 8–14, **G.** in lines 15–19, and **H.** in lines 40–47.

23. **B.** Since the word *tangible* is used as the opposite of *mystical faith* in the sentence, the best definition is *material*. Choice **C.** may seem like a good answer, but *real* is vague and not a good contrast to *mystical faith*. Choices **A.** and **D.** aren't definitions of *tangible* and make no sense in context.

24. **G.** The issue of faith versus works isn't mentioned in this passage. Choices **F.** and **J.** are supported in lines 51–56 and choice **H.** in lines 50–51.

25. **C.** The passage identifies the Scholastics as *clerics,* that is, priests (lines 29–32). Choice **A.** is incorrect; the writers read translations of the Greek (lines 22–25). Choice **B.** is also incorrect; although the Crusades are mentioned in line 21, the writers are identified as clerics, not Crusaders. Except for Peter Abelard, the nationality of the writers isn't stated, making choice **D.** incorrect as well.

26. **H.** The inclusion of Scotus should eliminate choice **J.**; he is identified in lines 62–63 as a forerunner of Nominalism. Choice **F.** describes most Christian belief of any era, and choice **G.** is too vague; Scholasticism refers to a specific system of medieval Christian thought.

27. **C.** See lines 66–70. Although choice **D.** is true, it wouldn't contribute so much to the development of the scientific method as would the more positive choice **C.** Choice **B.** is contradicted in lines 57–59. Choice **A.** wouldn't contribute to the development of the scientific method.

28. **H.** According to lines 58–59, in the fourteenth century *there was a loss of faith in logic*. This followed a period when faith in logic had grown (lines 25–56). Choice **F.** is incorrect; the attitude toward logic had clearly changed (paragraphs 3 and 4). The word *indifference* in choice **G.** is incorrect, and the answer is also incomplete, ignoring the last paragraph of the passage. Choice **J.** is also incorrect; *extreme disfavor* isn't indicated anywhere in the passage, and the final paragraph contradicts *extreme favor*.

29. **C.** The last paragraph explicitly states that the Nominalists had lost faith in logic (lines 58–59). Choice **A.** is contradicted by these same lines. Choices **B.** and **D.** aren't mentioned in the passage.

30. **J.** Nothing in this passage reveals the author's bias for or against the schoolmen discussed. The passage is disinterested (unbiased) in tone.

31. **D.** All three are accurate statements. See lines 1–5 and 43–49. The entire passage makes it clear that the technique is valuable to both historians and anthropologists. Choices **A.**, **B.**, and **C.** exclude one or two of the statements and are therefore incorrect.

32. **F.** Carbon dating can be used only on carbonaceous materials (materials that contain carbon) (line 3). It is accurate to about 200 years (line 3), making choice **G.** incorrect, and is unusable on objects older than 50,000 years (line 12), not 30,000 (choice **J.**). The passage doesn't indicate that materials must be over 2,000 years old (choice **H.**).

33. **B.** The passage doesn't deal with liabilities (choice **A.**). Choice **C.** is misleading because it isn't radioactive materials that are being dated but plant and animal remains that contain radioactivity. Choice **D.** is incorrect because it's too broad, and little is said in the passage about history.

34. **F.** According to the context of the passage, the word *fix* means to hold tight, or to *make fast* (permanent, secure). At different times, *fix* can mean to *prepare* (choice **G.**), *put in order* (choice **H.**), or *adjust* (choice **J.**), but none of these is appropriate in this context.

35. **B.** While a carnivore, by definition, would have eaten animals and not plants (ruling out choices **A.** and **D.**), it can be assumed that some of the animals the carnivore ate would themselves have eaten plants. Choice **C.** can be eliminated because III (fixing carbon in the system by breathing) is not indicated in the passage.

36. **H.** According to the passage (lines 25–28), plants absorb the carbon dioxide and fix the carbon in their tissues. Choice **F.** is incorrect; cosmic-ray neutrons act on nitrogen, not on plants (lines 14–16). Choice **G.** isn't mentioned in the passage; photosynthesis is the production of organic substances by light acting on carbon dioxide and water. Choice **J.** is also irrelevant to carbon dating.

37. **C.** Three half-lives, or 17,280 years, would reduce the original radioactivity to one–eighth of what it was. Choice **A.** represents only one half-life, **B.** two half-lives, and **D.** four half-lives. With each half-life, the amount of radioactivity is reduced by half.

38. **G.** Lines 60–70 allude to both I and II, making choice **F.** incorrect. III (present in both choices H and J) is the way carbon dating is done, not a method for checking its reliability.

39. **A.** According to lines 55–59, Geiger counters measure the beta-ray activity. Cosmic-ray neutrons (choice **B.**) are related to the production of carbon 14, not measurement (lines 14–16). Carbon dioxide (**D.**) is absorbed by plants; it isn't directly measured in carbon dating. Choice **C.** refers to the carbon 14 built up in the atmosphere (lines 21–23).

40. **H.** A turquoise ornament is made from neither animal nor vegetable, and therefore carbon dating couldn't be used on it. See lines 43–49. On the other hand, choice **F.** is made from an animal and choice **G.** from a plant, and choice **J.** is itself a plant.

Answers to Science Reasoning Test

1. **B.** You should be aware that normal room temperature is about 68°F or 20°C. Therefore, the answer is in the middle of the three viscosity columns in the chart. Mercury has the highest viscosity, 15.47 millipoises.

2. **G.** For each of the eight liquids in the chart, the viscosity decreases as you go from low temperature (0°C) toward high temperature (40°C) No simple rule relating viscosity to molecular weight is evident.

3. **A.** The prefix *hex-* means six; you can deduce, then, that hexane must have six carbon atoms. Therefore, its viscosity is likely to be midway between those of pentane (five carbons) and heptane (seven carbons). The average of those two values is 2.72 millipoises.

4. **G.** In the column with viscosities at 0°C, the liquid most similar to water is ethanol. The steel bearing should sink in either liquid at nearly the same rate.

5. **A.** At the beginning of the passage, viscosity is defined as a quantity measuring the resistance to flow. The first method would accomplish that task: The higher the viscosity, the less liquid would flow through the hole in the base of the beaker. Methods **B.** and **C.** are related to surface tension, not viscosity.

6. **F.** The light is on the floor to the left of the beetle, so its left eye received much more light than its right eye.

7. **C.** All the experiments show that the beetle turns only if one eye receives more light. As soon as the beetle in Experiment 2 was facing directly toward the light, the beetle would see equal amounts of light with both eyes, and it would stop turning.

8. **G.** Experiment 2 clearly showed that the beetle would turn toward the eye that received the most light. Experiment 4 showed that paint alone would not cause the beetle to turn.

9. **A.** The beetle turns if either eye receives more light, so it would crawl in a straight line only if both eyes received equal amounts of light. The beetle would have to be heading directly toward any light.

10. **H.** The beetle may have turned in Experiment 3 either because of more light going into the open eye or by the paint causing irritation to the other eye. Experiment 4 proved that paint alone would not cause the beetle to turn.

11. **B.** Since the beetle turns only if one eye receives more light, a beetle with both eyes covered with paint should crawl in a straight line even if the room contained a lone bright light off to one side of the beetle's path.

12. **H.** Read the graph upward from 100°C and rightward from 0.5 atmospheres. That point falls in the solid field, so iodine would occur as crystals under such conditions.

13. **B.** The lowest point in the liquid field is where it touches both the gas field and the solid field. The pressure at that triple point is 0.12 atmosphere. At any lower pressure, iodine can exist only as a solid or a gas.

14. **G.** The vertical line between the solid field and the liquid field represents the transition from solid to liquid iodine. That vertical boundary is at a temperature of 114°C. Iodine crystals would melt to a liquid if heated to that temperature.

15. **C.** Go directly to the right from a pressure of 1 atmosphere until you come to the line between the liquid and gas fields; then look downward to read the temperature. The boiling point of iodine is 184°C. Notice that the temperature of the liquid/gas transition depends on the pressure.

16. **F.** Sublimation can occur only at those conditions where the solid and gas fields are in direct contact, toward the bottom of the graph. The pressure must be less than 0.12 atmosphere and the temperature must be less than 114°C.

17. **C.** The fundamental idea proposed by Scientist 1 is that an increase in solar radiation causes glaciation. Therefore, an end to continental glaciation would require a lasting decrease in solar radiation, removing the condition that triggered glaciation.

18. **J.** They are in direct disagreement about temperatures. Scientist 1 says that high temperatures started the Ice Age, while Scientist 2 says that low temperatures started the Ice Age.

19. **B.** Both scientists agree that more snowfall is needed to start a glacial episode. The first scientist realized that a warmer atmosphere could well be more humid and have more precipitation. Choice **A.** is wrong because the scientist is proposing only what effects might be produced by variation in the sun's energy.

20. **F.** Scientist 2 makes a strong case for colder oceans during the Pleistocene epoch. However, the main issue is the temperature of the atmosphere. The implication is that if the oceans were cooler, then so would be the atmosphere.

21. **C.** Unless Scientist 1 can show that some factor besides temperature affects the oxygen isotope ratios in marine shells, one would have to accept the assertion by Scientist 2 that they record temperatures accurately. Choice **A.** is not the best answer because even a few measurements can be meaningful.

22. **G.** According to Scientist 2, ocean waters have become progressively warmer from the Ice Age to the present. During the Ice Age, coral reefs must have been near the equator only. As the seas warmed, the reefs could migrate toward the poles.

23. **D.** If data showed that periods of high solar radiation occurred during periods of high precipitation, then the theory of Scientist 1 would be greatly strengthened. As it now stands, he or she simply *asserts* that high solar radiation would lead to more precipitation.

24. **G.** The nitrogen was derived from two sources, air and ammonia.

25. **C.** Look at Table 2. The highest density nitrogen came from air, while the lowest density nitrogen was derived solely from ammonia. Choice **A.** isn't the best answer because the order of the experiments is only incidental. The source of the nitrogen is the fundamental difference between the three experiments.

26. **G.** The second experiment was considered necessary because then nitrogen from two sources, air and ammonia, could be compared. Without that scientific precaution, the researcher would have missed the important discovery of the unknown gas making up about 1 percent of air.

27. **B.** Look at Table 1. Although the densities of the gases are very similar, the researcher decided to perform Experiment 3 to see whether the initial difference (only 0.001 grams/liter) was meaningful. Experiment 3 then proved that the density difference was important.

28. **J.** Look at the balanced chemical reaction in Experiment 2. The numbers of molecules (4, 3, 2, and 6) are proportional to the volumes of gases. Three volumes of oxygen yield

two volumes of nitrogen derived from ammonia. However, air with three volumes of oxygen must have four times as much nitrogen, so this sample has *twelve volumes of nitrogen derived from air*. Of the total fourteen volumes of nitrogen, two were derived from ammonia. So two of fourteen, or one seventh of the total nitrogen, came from ammonia.

29. **C.** The unknown gas doesn't react with copper or it wouldn't have contaminated the "pure nitrogen" produced in the first two experiments. The densities measured in those early experiments show that the unknown gas is denser than nitrogen. The inert gas, argon, was actually discovered by this set of experiments.

30. **H.** The box labeled *Air* represents carbon dioxide in the atmosphere. The carbon in animals is returned to the atmosphere either by respiration or by decay.

31. **C.** The only arrow leaving the box labeled *Air* is the one for photosynthesis. In photosynthesis, green plants use carbon dioxide and water to produce sugar and oxygen.

32. **H.** Without bacteria, the chemical elements in plant and animal tissues would not be recycled. Bacterial decay disintegrates the tissues and releases the elements, including carbon.

33. **D.** The pair of arrows between the boxes labeled *Air* and *Plants* show that respiration is the reverse of photosynthesis. In respiration, organisms release stored energy by oxidizing sugar and producing carbon dioxide and water.

34. **H.** For half a billion years, some dead organic material has been buried and gradually transformed into coal and oil. That immense quantity of stored carbon is now being used as fuel. The deposits of coal and oil will last only another century at the present rate. The vast volumes of carbon dioxide produced by burning those fuels has changed the composition of our atmosphere.

35. **B.** The graph shows ½% excreted in urine each day after one month of study. The passage states that a similar amount was excreted in feces. The total amount excreted must have been 1%.

36. **J.** The high amounts of radioactive phosphorous excreted during the first four days must represent phosphorous that was never utilized to build any tissues of the rat.

37. **A.** Throughout the study, most of the phosphorous atoms were nonradioactive. For the first few days, these nonradioactive phosphorous atoms must have been previously stored in the rat's tissues. Later in the study, the nonradioactive phosphorous came both from tissue storage and from later nonradioactive meals.

38. **H.** The passage states that after one month, half the radioactive phosphorous had been excreted. The other half must still be in the live rat. Thus, the average time one phosphorous atom remains in the rat is one month.

39. **A.** There is no suggestion that phosphorous is lost during drying. Look at Table 1. In the first column, the high values for bones and muscles merely mean those tissues make up most of the body. The second column reveals that the kidneys, brain, and liver use much more phosphorous than equal weights of bones and muscles.

40. **J.** About 90% of the radioactive phosphorous atoms were temporarily stored in the various tissues of the rat. The tissues, then, must continually take up new phosphorous atoms, which displace the old ones. This study demonstrated that phosphorous atoms are not simply locked into body tissues until the animal dies.

ANSWER SHEETS FOR PRACTICE TEST 2

ENGLISH TEST

1 Ⓐ Ⓑ Ⓒ Ⓓ	26 Ⓕ Ⓖ Ⓗ Ⓙ	51 Ⓐ Ⓑ Ⓒ Ⓓ
2 Ⓕ Ⓖ Ⓗ Ⓙ	27 Ⓐ Ⓑ Ⓒ Ⓓ	52 Ⓕ Ⓖ Ⓗ Ⓙ
3 Ⓐ Ⓑ Ⓒ Ⓓ	28 Ⓕ Ⓖ Ⓗ Ⓙ	53 Ⓐ Ⓑ Ⓒ Ⓓ
4 Ⓕ Ⓖ Ⓗ Ⓙ	29 Ⓐ Ⓑ Ⓒ Ⓓ	54 Ⓕ Ⓖ Ⓗ Ⓙ
5 Ⓐ Ⓑ Ⓒ Ⓓ	30 Ⓕ Ⓖ Ⓗ Ⓙ	55 Ⓐ Ⓑ Ⓒ Ⓓ
6 Ⓕ Ⓖ Ⓗ Ⓙ	31 Ⓐ Ⓑ Ⓒ Ⓓ	56 Ⓕ Ⓖ Ⓗ Ⓙ
7 Ⓐ Ⓑ Ⓒ Ⓓ	32 Ⓕ Ⓖ Ⓗ Ⓙ	57 Ⓐ Ⓑ Ⓒ Ⓓ
8 Ⓕ Ⓖ Ⓗ Ⓙ	33 Ⓐ Ⓑ Ⓒ Ⓓ	58 Ⓕ Ⓖ Ⓗ Ⓙ
9 Ⓐ Ⓑ Ⓒ Ⓓ	34 Ⓕ Ⓖ Ⓗ Ⓙ	59 Ⓐ Ⓑ Ⓒ Ⓓ
10 Ⓕ Ⓖ Ⓗ Ⓙ	35 Ⓐ Ⓑ Ⓒ Ⓓ	60 Ⓕ Ⓖ Ⓗ Ⓙ
11 Ⓐ Ⓑ Ⓒ Ⓓ	36 Ⓕ Ⓖ Ⓗ Ⓙ	61 Ⓐ Ⓑ Ⓒ Ⓓ
12 Ⓕ Ⓖ Ⓗ Ⓙ	37 Ⓐ Ⓑ Ⓒ Ⓓ	62 Ⓕ Ⓖ Ⓗ Ⓙ
13 Ⓐ Ⓑ Ⓒ Ⓓ	38 Ⓕ Ⓖ Ⓗ Ⓙ	63 Ⓐ Ⓑ Ⓒ Ⓓ
14 Ⓕ Ⓖ Ⓗ Ⓙ	39 Ⓐ Ⓑ Ⓒ Ⓓ	64 Ⓕ Ⓖ Ⓗ Ⓙ
15 Ⓐ Ⓑ Ⓒ Ⓓ	40 Ⓕ Ⓖ Ⓗ Ⓙ	65 Ⓐ Ⓑ Ⓒ Ⓓ
16 Ⓕ Ⓖ Ⓗ Ⓙ	41 Ⓐ Ⓑ Ⓒ Ⓓ	66 Ⓕ Ⓖ Ⓗ Ⓙ
17 Ⓐ Ⓑ Ⓒ Ⓓ	42 Ⓕ Ⓖ Ⓗ Ⓙ	67 Ⓐ Ⓑ Ⓒ Ⓓ
18 Ⓕ Ⓖ Ⓗ Ⓙ	43 Ⓐ Ⓑ Ⓒ Ⓓ	68 Ⓕ Ⓖ Ⓗ Ⓙ
19 Ⓐ Ⓑ Ⓒ Ⓓ	44 Ⓕ Ⓖ Ⓗ Ⓙ	69 Ⓐ Ⓑ Ⓒ Ⓓ
20 Ⓕ Ⓖ Ⓗ Ⓙ	45 Ⓐ Ⓑ Ⓒ Ⓓ	70 Ⓕ Ⓖ Ⓗ Ⓙ
21 Ⓐ Ⓑ Ⓒ Ⓓ	46 Ⓕ Ⓖ Ⓗ Ⓙ	71 Ⓐ Ⓑ Ⓒ Ⓓ
22 Ⓕ Ⓖ Ⓗ Ⓙ	47 Ⓐ Ⓑ Ⓒ Ⓓ	72 Ⓕ Ⓖ Ⓗ Ⓙ
23 Ⓐ Ⓑ Ⓒ Ⓓ	48 Ⓕ Ⓖ Ⓗ Ⓙ	73 Ⓐ Ⓑ Ⓒ Ⓓ
24 Ⓕ Ⓖ Ⓗ Ⓙ	49 Ⓐ Ⓑ Ⓒ Ⓓ	74 Ⓕ Ⓖ Ⓗ Ⓙ
25 Ⓐ Ⓑ Ⓒ Ⓓ	50 Ⓕ Ⓖ Ⓗ Ⓙ	75 Ⓐ Ⓑ Ⓒ Ⓓ

MATHEMATICS TEST

1 Ⓐ Ⓑ Ⓒ Ⓓ Ⓔ	26 Ⓕ Ⓖ Ⓗ Ⓙ Ⓚ	51 Ⓐ Ⓑ Ⓒ Ⓓ Ⓔ
2 Ⓕ Ⓖ Ⓗ Ⓙ Ⓚ	27 Ⓐ Ⓑ Ⓒ Ⓓ Ⓔ	52 Ⓕ Ⓖ Ⓗ Ⓙ Ⓚ
3 Ⓐ Ⓑ Ⓒ Ⓓ Ⓔ	28 Ⓕ Ⓖ Ⓗ Ⓙ Ⓚ	53 Ⓐ Ⓑ Ⓒ Ⓓ Ⓔ
4 Ⓕ Ⓖ Ⓗ Ⓙ Ⓚ	29 Ⓐ Ⓑ Ⓒ Ⓓ Ⓔ	54 Ⓕ Ⓖ Ⓗ Ⓙ Ⓚ
5 Ⓐ Ⓑ Ⓒ Ⓓ Ⓔ	30 Ⓕ Ⓖ Ⓗ Ⓙ Ⓚ	55 Ⓐ Ⓑ Ⓒ Ⓓ Ⓔ
6 Ⓕ Ⓖ Ⓗ Ⓙ Ⓚ	31 Ⓐ Ⓑ Ⓒ Ⓓ Ⓔ	56 Ⓕ Ⓖ Ⓗ Ⓙ Ⓚ
7 Ⓐ Ⓑ Ⓒ Ⓓ Ⓔ	32 Ⓕ Ⓖ Ⓗ Ⓙ Ⓚ	57 Ⓐ Ⓑ Ⓒ Ⓓ Ⓔ
8 Ⓕ Ⓖ Ⓗ Ⓙ Ⓚ	33 Ⓐ Ⓑ Ⓒ Ⓓ Ⓔ	58 Ⓕ Ⓖ Ⓗ Ⓙ Ⓚ
9 Ⓐ Ⓑ Ⓒ Ⓓ Ⓔ	34 Ⓕ Ⓖ Ⓗ Ⓙ Ⓚ	59 Ⓐ Ⓑ Ⓒ Ⓓ Ⓔ
10 Ⓕ Ⓖ Ⓗ Ⓙ Ⓚ	35 Ⓐ Ⓑ Ⓒ Ⓓ Ⓔ	60 Ⓕ Ⓖ Ⓗ Ⓙ Ⓚ
11 Ⓐ Ⓑ Ⓒ Ⓓ Ⓔ	36 Ⓕ Ⓖ Ⓗ Ⓙ Ⓚ	
12 Ⓕ Ⓖ Ⓗ Ⓙ Ⓚ	37 Ⓐ Ⓑ Ⓒ Ⓓ Ⓔ	
13 Ⓐ Ⓑ Ⓒ Ⓓ Ⓔ	38 Ⓕ Ⓖ Ⓗ Ⓙ Ⓚ	
14 Ⓕ Ⓖ Ⓗ Ⓙ Ⓚ	39 Ⓐ Ⓑ Ⓒ Ⓓ Ⓔ	
15 Ⓐ Ⓑ Ⓒ Ⓓ Ⓔ	40 Ⓕ Ⓖ Ⓗ Ⓙ Ⓚ	
16 Ⓕ Ⓖ Ⓗ Ⓙ Ⓚ	41 Ⓐ Ⓑ Ⓒ Ⓓ Ⓔ	
17 Ⓐ Ⓑ Ⓒ Ⓓ Ⓔ	42 Ⓕ Ⓖ Ⓗ Ⓙ Ⓚ	
18 Ⓕ Ⓖ Ⓗ Ⓙ Ⓚ	43 Ⓐ Ⓑ Ⓒ Ⓓ Ⓔ	
19 Ⓐ Ⓑ Ⓒ Ⓓ Ⓔ	44 Ⓕ Ⓖ Ⓗ Ⓙ Ⓚ	
20 Ⓕ Ⓖ Ⓗ Ⓙ Ⓚ	45 Ⓐ Ⓑ Ⓒ Ⓓ Ⓔ	
21 Ⓐ Ⓑ Ⓒ Ⓓ Ⓔ	46 Ⓕ Ⓖ Ⓗ Ⓙ Ⓚ	
22 Ⓕ Ⓖ Ⓗ Ⓙ Ⓚ	47 Ⓐ Ⓑ Ⓒ Ⓓ Ⓔ	
23 Ⓐ Ⓑ Ⓒ Ⓓ Ⓔ	48 Ⓕ Ⓖ Ⓗ Ⓙ Ⓚ	
24 Ⓕ Ⓖ Ⓗ Ⓙ Ⓚ	49 Ⓐ Ⓑ Ⓒ Ⓓ Ⓔ	
25 Ⓐ Ⓑ Ⓒ Ⓓ Ⓔ	50 Ⓕ Ⓖ Ⓗ Ⓙ Ⓚ	

CUT HERE

READING TEST

1 Ⓐ Ⓑ Ⓒ Ⓓ	26 Ⓕ Ⓖ Ⓗ Ⓙ
2 Ⓕ Ⓖ Ⓗ Ⓙ	27 Ⓐ Ⓑ Ⓒ Ⓓ
3 Ⓐ Ⓑ Ⓒ Ⓓ	28 Ⓕ Ⓖ Ⓗ Ⓙ
4 Ⓕ Ⓖ Ⓗ Ⓙ	29 Ⓐ Ⓑ Ⓒ Ⓓ
5 Ⓐ Ⓑ Ⓒ Ⓓ	30 Ⓕ Ⓖ Ⓗ Ⓙ
6 Ⓕ Ⓖ Ⓗ Ⓙ	31 Ⓐ Ⓑ Ⓒ Ⓓ
7 Ⓐ Ⓑ Ⓒ Ⓓ	32 Ⓕ Ⓖ Ⓗ Ⓙ
8 Ⓕ Ⓖ Ⓗ Ⓙ	33 Ⓐ Ⓑ Ⓒ Ⓓ
9 Ⓐ Ⓑ Ⓒ Ⓓ	34 Ⓕ Ⓖ Ⓗ Ⓙ
10 Ⓕ Ⓖ Ⓗ Ⓙ	35 Ⓐ Ⓑ Ⓒ Ⓓ
11 Ⓐ Ⓑ Ⓒ Ⓓ	36 Ⓕ Ⓖ Ⓗ Ⓙ
12 Ⓕ Ⓖ Ⓗ Ⓙ	37 Ⓐ Ⓑ Ⓒ Ⓓ
13 Ⓐ Ⓑ Ⓒ Ⓓ	38 Ⓕ Ⓖ Ⓗ Ⓙ
14 Ⓕ Ⓖ Ⓗ Ⓙ	39 Ⓐ Ⓑ Ⓒ Ⓓ
15 Ⓐ Ⓑ Ⓒ Ⓓ	40 Ⓕ Ⓖ Ⓗ Ⓙ
16 Ⓕ Ⓖ Ⓗ Ⓙ	
17 Ⓐ Ⓑ Ⓒ Ⓓ	
18 Ⓕ Ⓖ Ⓗ Ⓙ	
19 Ⓐ Ⓑ Ⓒ Ⓓ	
20 Ⓕ Ⓖ Ⓗ Ⓙ	
21 Ⓐ Ⓑ Ⓒ Ⓓ	
22 Ⓕ Ⓖ Ⓗ Ⓙ	
23 Ⓐ Ⓑ Ⓒ Ⓓ	
24 Ⓕ Ⓖ Ⓗ Ⓙ	
25 Ⓐ Ⓑ Ⓒ Ⓓ	

SCIENCE REASONING TEST

1 Ⓐ Ⓑ Ⓒ Ⓓ	26 Ⓕ Ⓖ Ⓗ Ⓙ
2 Ⓕ Ⓖ Ⓗ Ⓙ	27 Ⓐ Ⓑ Ⓒ Ⓓ
3 Ⓐ Ⓑ Ⓒ Ⓓ	28 Ⓕ Ⓖ Ⓗ Ⓙ
4 Ⓕ Ⓖ Ⓗ Ⓙ	29 Ⓐ Ⓑ Ⓒ Ⓓ
5 Ⓐ Ⓑ Ⓒ Ⓓ	30 Ⓕ Ⓖ Ⓗ Ⓙ
6 Ⓕ Ⓖ Ⓗ Ⓙ	31 Ⓐ Ⓑ Ⓒ Ⓓ
7 Ⓐ Ⓑ Ⓒ Ⓓ	32 Ⓕ Ⓖ Ⓗ Ⓙ
8 Ⓕ Ⓖ Ⓗ Ⓙ	33 Ⓐ Ⓑ Ⓒ Ⓓ
9 Ⓐ Ⓑ Ⓒ Ⓓ	34 Ⓕ Ⓖ Ⓗ Ⓙ
10 Ⓕ Ⓖ Ⓗ Ⓙ	35 Ⓐ Ⓑ Ⓒ Ⓓ
11 Ⓐ Ⓑ Ⓒ Ⓓ	36 Ⓕ Ⓖ Ⓗ Ⓙ
12 Ⓕ Ⓖ Ⓗ Ⓙ	37 Ⓐ Ⓑ Ⓒ Ⓓ
13 Ⓐ Ⓑ Ⓒ Ⓓ	38 Ⓕ Ⓖ Ⓗ Ⓙ
14 Ⓕ Ⓖ Ⓗ Ⓙ	39 Ⓐ Ⓑ Ⓒ Ⓓ
15 Ⓐ Ⓑ Ⓒ Ⓓ	40 Ⓕ Ⓖ Ⓗ Ⓙ
16 Ⓕ Ⓖ Ⓗ Ⓙ	
17 Ⓐ Ⓑ Ⓒ Ⓓ	
18 Ⓕ Ⓖ Ⓗ Ⓙ	
19 Ⓐ Ⓑ Ⓒ Ⓓ	
20 Ⓕ Ⓖ Ⓗ Ⓙ	
21 Ⓐ Ⓑ Ⓒ Ⓓ	
22 Ⓕ Ⓖ Ⓗ Ⓙ	
23 Ⓐ Ⓑ Ⓒ Ⓓ	
24 Ⓕ Ⓖ Ⓗ Ⓙ	
25 Ⓐ Ⓑ Ⓒ Ⓓ	

CUT HERE

English Test

Time: 45 Minutes

75 Questions

Directions: In the left-hand column, you find passages in a spread-out format with various words and phrases underlined and numbered. In the right-hand column, you find a set of responses corresponding to each underlined portion. If the underlined portion is correct standard written English, is most appropriate to the style and feeling of the passage, or best makes the intended statement, mark the letter indicating "NO CHANGE." But if the underlined portion is *not* the best choice, choose the best of the remaining choices. For these questions, consider only the underlined portions; assume that the rest of the passage is correct as written. You will also see questions that refer to parts of the passage or the whole passage. Choose the response that you feel best answers each of these questions.

Passage I

Human Rights and Scientific Cooperation

Notwithstanding <u>its</u> scientific excellence in
selected fields, the Soviet Union badly needed
the collaboration of the rest of the world's
scholars. During the Cold War, a number of
American scientists <u>who chose to restrict</u> their
cooperation as a protest against Moscow's
suppression of human rights. <u>Computers are an area in which the Russians are far behind.</u> The
list of American scientists who joined in this
collective expression of conscience included
thirteen Nobel laureates and eighteen directors
of major laboratories. What most of them

1. **A.** NO CHANGE
   B. it's
   C. their
   D. there

2. **F.** NO CHANGE
   G. whose choice to restrict
   H. who choose to restrict
   J. chose to restrict

3. **A.** NO CHANGE
   B. Computers is an area in which the Russians are far behind.
   C. In computers, the Russians are far behind.
   D. OMIT the underlined portion.

GO ON TO THE NEXT PAGE

157

found <u>in the Soviet regime that most disturbed</u>
₄

<u>them</u> was <u>a contempt for</u> the notion that each
₄   ₅

individual has intrinsic moral worth. "Détente

and the promises of Helsinki are empty catch-

words to those dissenters locked up in the vast

Gulag Archipelago," said Yale biologist Arthur

Martins. Physicists and chemists from univer-

sities <u>all over the country agree.</u> <u>The response</u>
₆   ₇

<u>to the Western scientists from Moscow was icy</u>
₇

<u>silence.</u> The release of scientists like Liepa and
₇

<u>Tchelikov, who the</u> authorities had imprisoned
₈

on vague and unproved charges, might have

<u>untied the deadlock</u> with the scientists in the
₉

West but would have had potentially dangerous

effects in Russia. There was some restlessness

4. F. NO CHANGE

   G. in the Soviet regime that disturbed them most

   H. most disturbing in the Soviet regime

   J. OMIT the underlined portion.

5. A. NO CHANGE

   B. a contemptuous attitude toward

   C. a feeling of contempt for

   D. OMIT the underlined portion.

6. F. NO CHANGE

   G. throughout the country agree.

   H. throughout the country are in agreement.

   J. all over the country agreed.

7. A. NO CHANGE

   B. The response from Moscow to the Western scientists was icy silence.

   C. From Moscow, the response to the Western scientists was icy silence.

   D. (Begin new paragraph) The response from Moscow to the Western scientists was icy silence.

8. F. NO CHANGE

   G. Tchelikov who the

   H. Tchelikov whom the

   J. Tchelikov, whom the

9. A. NO CHANGE

   B. severed the deadlock

   C. broken the deadlock

   D. overturned the deadlock

already in the <u>predominant Moslem</u> states.
10

Once again, the grain harvest in the Ukraine

was <u>expected to be</u> <u>as small, if not smaller</u>
11   12

<u>than, the previous year's.</u> And <u>there was, as</u>
12   13

<u>usual, a dearth</u> of consumer goods in the shops
13

of the cities.

Passage II

The following paragraphs are given a number in parentheses above each one. The paragraphs may be in the most logical order, or they may not. Question 32 asks you to choose the paragraph sequence that is the most logical.

Cooking

[1]

Even as a small child, <u>cooking had inter-</u>
14

<u>ested me.</u> My mother encouraged my curiosity,
14

10. F. NO CHANGE
   G. predominant Muslim
   H. predominantly Moslem
   J. Muslim

11. A. NO CHANGE
   B. predominant Muslim
   C. predominantly Moslem
   D. Muslim

12. F. NO CHANGE
   G. as small if not smaller than the previous year's
   H. as small, if not smaller than the previous year's.
   J. as small as, if not smaller than the previous year's.

13. A. NO CHANGE
   B. there was as usual, a dearth
   C. there was usually, a dearth
   D. there was, as usual a dearth

14. F. NO CHANGE
   G. cooking interested me.
   H. cooking was of interest to me.
   J. I was interested in cooking.

GO ON TO THE NEXT PAGE

since in those days cooking was thought <u>to be</u>
15
<u>a suitable interest</u> for a little girl, and I was the
15
only daughter among six children. Not, of
course, that anyone ever imagined I would
cook professionally. ☐16 Anyway, <u>before I had</u>
17

graduated from high school, I was very good
17
by American standards. I did most of the

cooking at home and sold my <u>cakes cookies,</u>
18
<u>and breads</u> to neighbors. I had learned enough
18
French in school to be able to make my way
through the articles and recipes I found in the
illustrated European <u>magazines, which I</u>
19
<u>bought</u> at the second-hand book shops. I'm
19
certain that mine were the first croissants

ever put on sale in New <u>Hampshire, though</u>
20

15. A. NO CHANGE
B. suitably interesting
C. of interest
D. interesting

16. The preceding sentence differs from the others in this paragraph because it:

F. has no direct object.
G. uses a metaphor.
H. is not a complete sentence.
J. poses a rhetorical question.

17. A. NO CHANGE
B. before I had been graduated from
C. before graduating from
D. before I graduated from

18. F. NO CHANGE
G. cakes, cookies, and my breads
H. cakes, cookies, and breads
J. cakes, my cookies, and my breads

19. A. NO CHANGE
B. magazines I bought
C. magazines, which I purchased
D. magazines which had been bought

20. F. NO CHANGE
G. Hampshire and
H. Hampshire, and
J. Hampshire, because

nowadays you can buy them in any store that sells Wonder Bread. 21

[2]

While in the first two years of college, cooking more or less slipped my mind. I went to a women's college, where we all ate the appalling institutional food in elegant dining rooms with spotless linen on the tables. In my junior year, I was living in a small dorm when the college workers, they were criminally underpaid, went out on strike. We divided up the chores in the dorm, and I volunteered to cook the dinners. It was really not greatly different than cooking for my large family. Compared to the college cooks I looked like Escoffier. My studies slipped badly because I was clearly more interested in crisp vegetables than in Russian history and more engaged by the problems of nutrition than I was by the problems of mathematics.

21. In Paragraph 1, the author uses all of the following devices to give a conversational time EXCEPT:

   A. contraction

   B. incomplete sentence

   C. specific, commonplace detail

   D. simile

22. F. NO CHANGE

   G. While in my freshman and sophomore years,

   H. When in the two first years of college,

   J. In my first two years of college,

23. A. NO CHANGE

   B. they were criminal and underpaid,

   C. —they were criminally underpaid—

   D. which was criminally underpaid,

24. F. NO CHANGE

   G. no different than

   H. not really greatly different than

   J. really not greatly different from

25. A. NO CHANGE

   B. cooks I looked as good as Escoffier.

   C. cooks, I looked like Escoffier.

   D. cooks—I looked like Escoffier.

26. F. NO CHANGE

   G. than I was by mathematics.

   H. than by the problems of mathematics.

   J. than mathematics.

GO ON TO THE NEXT PAGE

[3]

One of the other residents of my dorm was a <u>rich, rather snooty girl</u> from New York who
                                                    27
had hardly spoken to me before the strike. Nancy loved good food, and for the first time since she came to college could now actually look forward to dinner. She knew more about cooking than anyone I had ever met. It turned out that her family owned <u>a post hotel and two</u>
                                                    28
<u>restaurants in New York City, one Italian and a</u>
                                                    28
<u>French one.</u> We were soon best friends. She
    28
had a crazy idea of running the family business

herself, in those days as likely as a <u>woman be-</u>
                                                    29
<u>ing an astronaut, a college president, or on the</u>
                                                    29
<u>Supreme Court.</u> And she <u>said "I was to become</u>
    29   30
<u>the best chef in the city."</u>
    30

27. A. NO CHANGE
  B. rich and conceited girl
  C. rich, conceited girl
  D. rich girl

28. F. NO CHANGE
  G. a posh hotel and an Italian and a French restaurant in New York City.
  H. in New York City a posh hotel and two restaurants, one Italian and one that was French.
  J. a posh hotel, a French restaurant, and an Italian restaurant, all in New York City.

29. A. NO CHANGE
  B. woman's being an astronaut, a college president, or on the Supreme Court.
  C. woman astronaut, college president, or Supreme Court justice.
  D. female astronaut, college president, or being on the Supreme Court.

30. F. NO CHANGE
  G. said "I would be the best chef in the city."
  H. said, "I was to become the best chef in the city."
  J. said that I was to become the best chef in the city.

Items 31 and 32 pose questions about the passage as a whole.

[31]

[32]

Passage III

Armed Robberies
[1]

The number of local armed robberies in the past week <u>rose by two more</u> Tuesday night,
₃₃

<u>but they reported two suspects arrested this</u>
₃₄
<u>morning by city police.</u> One suspect, John
₃₄

Hugo, was arrested <u>after spotting</u> in the
₃₅
Eastview Mall carrying a suspicious looking package. Security guards at the mall held the

suspect until city police <u>had arrived and the</u>
₃₆
<u>package</u> proved to be cash and jewels taken
₃₆
earlier this week from an Astromart. Hugo has

31. The passage is best described as:

    A. didactic

    B. autobiographical

    C. formal

    D. inspirational

32. Which of the following sequences of paragraphs make the passage's structure most logical?

    F. NO CHANGE

    G. 2, 1, 3

    H. 2, 3, 1

    J. 1, 3, 2

33. **A.** NO CHANGE

    B. rose by two

    C. has risen by two more

    D. had risen by two

34. **F.** NO CHANGE

    G. but two reported suspects were arrested this morning by city police.

    H. but city police reported the arrest of two suspects this morning.

    J. but city police reportedly arrested two suspects this morning.

35. **A.** NO CHANGE

    B. having been spotted

    C. after he is spotted

    D. after spotting him

36. **F.** NO CHANGE

    G. arrived, and the package

    H. had arrived. The package

    J. arrived. The package

GO ON TO THE NEXT PAGE

a long history of criminal activity. <u>Later this morning, a second suspect was arrested while attempting to break into the storage room of an electronics store.</u>
37

[2]

Michael Marshall was armed <u>according to the sheriff's deputy who arrested him with a handgun and a knife.</u> He attempted to escape
38

<u>by commandeering</u> an automobile from a
39
worker in the parking lot, but the deputy blocked the only exit from the area before Marshall could get his car started. Described as a heavy man of unusual height, <u>police said the suspect</u> is almost certainly the man they
40
have been looking for in connection with the Western Savings robbery.

[3]

<u>Police spokesman were</u> especially eager to
41

37. A. NO CHANGE
   B. OMIT the underlined portion.
   C. (Place at beginning of Paragraph 2)
   D. (Place at the end of Paragraph 2)

38. F. NO CHANGE
   G. according to a sheriff's deputy, who arrested him with a handgun and a knife.
   H. with a handgun and a knife, according to the sheriff's deputy who arrested him.
   J. with a handgun and a knife, according to the sheriff's deputy, who arrested him.

39. A. NO CHANGE
   B. by commandeering of
   C. by commanding
   D. by commandment of

40. F. NO CHANGE
   G. police said that the suspect
   H. the suspect, according to police,
   J. the suspect, say the police,

41. A. NO CHANGE
   B. Police spokesman was
   C. (Do NOT begin new paragraph) Police spokesmen were
   D. (Do NOT begin new paragraph Police spokesmen was

discuss the arrest of Marshall, <u>who they have been pursuing</u> for more than four months. If he is convicted of the Western robbery, he can be sentenced to as many as ten years in prison, since two innocent bystanders were injured <u>committing that crime.</u> <u>As a repeat offender,</u> the sentence for Hugo could be just as long.

42. **F.** NO CHANGE
   G. who they have pursued
   H. whom they have been pursuing
   J. whom has been pursued

43. **A.** NO CHANGE
   B. while committing that crime.
   C. when committing that crime.
   D. when that crime was committed.

44. **F.** NO CHANGE
   G. A repeat offender,
   H. Because a repeat offender,
   J. Because he is a repeat offender,

Question 45 poses a question about the passage as a whole.

45. The passage may best be described as an example of:
   A. analytical expository prose
   B. news writing
   C. editorial prose
   D. biography

45

Passage IV

Interest Rates
[1]

In the 1980s, the Treasury Department took a close look at regulations limiting the interest that banks and savings and loan associations were permitted to pay on deposits. Small depositors rarely got more than four percent interest and <u>often got less.</u> At the time, Americans saved just under five percent of their personal income. Supply-side government economists argued that if the interest

46. **F.** NO CHANGE
   G. often received a lower rate.
   H. frequently received less interest.
   J. often received less than four percent interest.

rates paid by banks <u>were allowed to increase,</u>₄₇ Americans would soon be saving eight to ten

percent of their personal income. <u>At the time,</u>₄₈ <u>treasury bills in denominations of $10,000</u>₄₈ <u>paid up to six percent interest.</u>₄₈

[2]

[1] <u>With the removal of the cap on bank in-</u>₄₉<u>terest rates,</u>₄₉ savers received twice as much

interest on bank deposits. [2] <u>And many new</u>₅₀ <u>safe savings vehicles</u>₅₀ became <u>available such as</u>₅₁

<u>money market accounts.</u>₅₁ [3] And how much of personal income did Americans save? [4] Three and one half percent, compared to six percent in Europe or eight percent in Japan.

[52] [5] More savings and loan institutions failed in the ten years following deregulation that in the first seventy years of the twentieth century. [6] The percentage of personal income saved by Americans continued to decline each year. [7] Supply-side economists continued to

47. A. NO CHANGE
B. increased,
C. went up,
D. should go up,

48. F. NO CHANGE
G. (Place following the first sentence of Paragraph 1)
H. (Place at the beginning of Paragraph 2)
J. OMIT the underlined portion.

49. A. NO CHANGE
B. Having removed the cap on bank interest rates,
C. The cap on bank interest rates having been removed,
D. OMIT the underlined portion.

50. F. NO CHANGE
G. Many new safe savings vehicles
H. And many are the new safe savings vehicles
J. Many new, safe, savings vehicles

51. A. NO CHANGE
B. available, such as money market accounts.
C. available as money market accounts.
D. available, one being the money market account.

52. Sentence 3 and Sentence 4 of this paragraph are different from the rest of the passage because they:
F. both contain errors of grammar
G. are a question and an exclamation
H. are a question and an incomplete sentence
J. ask and answer a question by using a metaphor

argue that deregulation would solve all our problems. 53

Passage V

The Pilgrim's Scrip

[1]

Some years ago a small book called *The Pilgrim's Scrip* <u>was published anonymously.</u> A
₅₄

collection of <u>aphorisms the book was</u> notice-
₅₅
able for its quaint earnestness and its perversity

of view of <u>women who</u> the writer appeared to
₅₆
rank as creatures in service to the Serpent. The

author, if he did not always say things new,

evidently spoke from <u>reflection, feeling, and</u>
₅₇
<u>experience.</u> His thoughts were sad enough, oc-
₅₇
casionally dark, here and there comical in their

oddness, and yet with an element of hope.

[2]

[1] <u>Curious enough, the objectionable</u> fea-
₅₈
ture in this little book preserved it from

Question 53 poses a question about the passage as a whole.

53. The passage is probably best described as an example of:

   A. news writing

   B. editorial prose

   C. investigative journalism

   D. economic analysis

54. F. NO CHANGE

   G. is anonymously published.

   H. had been published anonymously.

   J. anonymously was published.

55. A. NO CHANGE

   B. aphorism the book was

   C. aphorisms, the book was

   D. aphorisms were

56. F. NO CHANGE

   G. woman who

   H. women, whom

   J. women, who

57. A. NO CHANGE

   B. reflex, feeling and experience.

   C. reflection feeling, and experience.

   D. reflection feeling and experiences.

58. F. NO CHANGE

   G. Curiously enough, the objectionable

   H. Curiously, the objectionable

   J. Curiously, the objective

GO ON TO THE NEXT PAGE

obscurity. 59 [2] Men read it and tossed it aside, amused or weary. By the ladies,

however, the book <u>was welcomed.</u> These ex-
₆₀
traordinary creatures, whose actions it is

impossible to predict and <u>who will now and</u>
₆₁
<u>then love, or affect to love, their enemies</u> better
₆₁
than their friends, cherished the book, and asked for its author. He had not put his name on the title page. In place of an author's name was a griffin between <u>wheat-</u>
₆₂
<u>sheaves, perhaps a symbol or</u> a family crest.
₆₂
Many inquired of the publisher for further enlightenment, but he kept the author's secret and increased the mystery.

[3]

One adventurous lady went to the Herald's College and there, after immense labor, <u>ascer-</u>
₆₃
<u>tained that</u> griffin between wheatsheaves was
₆₃
the crest of Sir Austin Feverel, a man of wealth, honor, and a somewhat lamentable

59. A. (Keep new paragraph beginning with preceding sentence)

B. (Do NOT begin new paragraph with Sentence 1)

C. (OMIT Sentence 1 and begin new paragraph with Sentence 2)

D. (End Paragraph 1 with Sentence 1 and begin Paragraph 2 with Sentence 2)

60. F. NO CHANGE

G. had been welcomed.

H. is welcomed.

J. was welcome.

61. A. NO CHANGE

B. who will now and then love, or effect to love, their enemies

C. who will love, or effect to love their enemies.

D. who will now and then love or affect to love their enemies.

62. F. NO CHANGE

G. wheatsheaves, perhaps symbolic of

H. wheatsheaves, perhaps, a symbol, or

J. wheatsheaves, perhaps

63. A. NO CHANGE

B. found out the discovery that

C. made the discovery that

D. discovered the fact that

history. Sir Austin had been married, <u>and he had been deserted by his wife for another man.</u> He must surely be the author the lady concluded and published her conclusions to the world. 65

Passage VI

Hospital Costs

[1]

<u>When usual, conservative</u> business people call for government controls on hospital costs, it's a sure sign that the hospitals are losing the public opinion battle to the regulators. And no wonder. The cost of hospital care <u>quadrupling</u> in the last ten years, while the consumer price index has not quite doubled in the same period. Nationwide, hospital costs are now rising at rate of sixteen percent yearly, <u>and this is three times the current state of inflation.</u> To impose a form of price control would be to use a method

64. F. NO CHANGE

G. and he was deserted by his wife for another man.

H. and his wife deserted him for another man.

J. and for another man he had been deserted by his wife.

Question 65 poses a question about the passage as a whole.

65. The passage is probably an excerpt taken from:

A. a newspaper editorial

B. a novel

C. a biography

D. a history

66. F. NO CHANGE

G. usual conservative

H. usual and conservative

J. usually conservative

67. A. NO CHANGE

B. having quadrupled

C. has quadrupled

D. having increased four times

68. F. NO CHANGE

G. which is a rate three times the current inflation rate.

H. and this is three times the current rate of inflation.

J. three times the current inflation rate.

GO ON TO THE NEXT PAGE

with a poor tract record. 69 The average hospital bill today is $4,000, three times the overage only four years ago. 70 These dismal statistics [71] translate into steadily rising insurance premiums for companies which offer health insurance to their workers.

[2]

Hospital economics are simply too insulated from the normal competitive pressures that restrains [72] costs elsewhere in the economy. With ninety percent of all hospital bills paid by government health care programs on a cost incurred basis, hospitals have no insistence [73] to control costs. A government task force has urged insurers to negotiate directly with hospitals to revise payment formulas and impose economizing discipline [74] on hospital

---

69. **A.** NO CHANGE
   B. (Place the preceding sentence at the beginning of Paragraph 1)
   C. (Place the preceding sentence at the end of Paragraph 1)
   D. (OMIT the preceding sentence)

70. The preceding statistic would be more significant if we were also told:
   F. what the average bill two years ago was
   G. how long a hospital stay this bill represents
   H. how many hospitals have a higher average bill
   J. what the average doctor's bill is

71. **A.** NO CHANGE
   B. These statistics
   C. These figures
   D. Figures like these

72. **F.** NO CHANGE
   G. which restrains
   H. that restrain
   J. to restrain

73. **A.** NO CHANGE
   B. instinct
   C. insurance
   D. incentive

74. **F.** NO CHANGE
   G. economic discipline
   H. economic discretion
   J. economics and discipline

English Test

expenditures. But <u>the key to blocking the sky-rocket of hospital cost spiral</u> without government interference remains in the hands of hospital administrators.
₇₅

75. A. NO CHANGE

B. the key to stopping the skyrocketing hospital cost spiral

C. unlocking the skyrocket of hospital costs

D. stopping fast-rising hospital costs

IF YOU FINISH BEFORE TIME IS CALLED, CHECK YOUR WORK ON THIS SECTION ONLY. DO NOT WORK ON ANY OTHER SECTION IN THE TEST.

STOP

Mathematics Test

Time: 60 Minutes

60 Questions

Directions: After solving each problem, choose the correct answer and fill in the corresponding space on your answer sheet. Do not spend too much time on any one problem. Solve as many problems as you can and return to the others if time permits. You are allowed to use a calculator on this test.

Note:

Unless it is otherwise stated, you can assume all of the following.

1. Figures are NOT necessarily drawn to scale.

2. Geometric figures lie in a plane.

3. The word "line" means a straight line.

4. The word "average" refers to the arithmetic mean.

1. If 20% of a class averages 80% on a test, 50% of the class averages 60% on the test, and the remainder of the class averages 40% on the test, what is the overall class average?

   A. 64%

   B. 60%

   C. 58%

   D. 56%

   E. 54%

2. A full container holds ⅝ gallon of liquid. If the container is ⅘ full and then 25% of the liquid is lost due to evaporation, how much liquid, in gallons, is left in the container?

   F. ¼

   G. ⅜

   H. ½

   J. ⅝

   K. ¾

3. Two similar polygons have perimeters in the ratio of 3 to 4. If the smaller polygon has an area of 36 square inches, what is the area of the larger polygon, in square inches?

   A. 20¼

   B. 27

   C. 48

   D. 64

   E. 72

4. If $f(x) = 2x + 4$ and $g(x) = x^2 - 2$ then $f(g(3)) =$

F. 12

G. 14

H. 18

J. 70

K. 98

5. What is the tenth term in the following sequence: 5, 6, 8, 11, 15, . . .?

A. 20

B. 35

C. 41

D. 50

E. 60

6. In 6 years, Tony will be twice as old as he was 4 years ago. How old, in years, will Tony be in 4 years?

F. 12

G. 14

H. 16

J. 18

K. 20

7. The chart below represents an inventory of the number of toys in the storeroom of Acme Toy Company. If a child were to choose one of these toys at random, what would be the probability that the chosen toy is worth under $5.00?

Number of Toys	Value Each
140	$3.98
60	$4.98
178	$5.98
122	$6.98
500 total	

A. $\frac{3}{25}$

B. $\frac{7}{25}$

C. $\frac{2}{5}$

D. $\frac{1}{2}$

E. $\frac{3}{5}$

8. Olga's collection of 50 coins consists of dimes and quarters totaling $7.10. How many more dimes than quarters does Olga have?

F. 14

G. 20

H. 22

J. 26

K. 36

9. Which of the following is a simplified version equivalent to $3 + \cfrac{3}{3 + \cfrac{3}{3 + \cfrac{3}{3 + 3}}}$?

A. $3\,\frac{23}{27}$

B. $3\,\frac{7}{8}$

C. $3\,\frac{19}{27}$

D. $3\,\frac{17}{27}$

E. $3\,\frac{1}{3}$

GO ON TO THE NEXT PAGE

10. If you bicycle 10 miles per hour for y hours and y miles per hour for 10 hours, how far, in miles, have you bicycled?

   F. $20 + 2y$

   G. $20y$

   H. $\dfrac{y^2 + 100}{10y}$

   J. $\dfrac{100}{y^2}$

   K. $100y^2$

11. In the figure below, $\angle w + \angle z = 170°$.

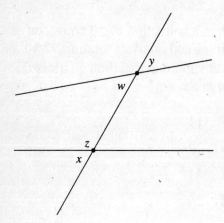

Which of the following is (are) true?

  I. $\angle x > \angle y$

  II. $\angle x$ and $\angle z$ are supplementary

  III. $\angle x < 90°$

   A. I only

   B. I and II only

   C. I and III only

   D. II and III only

   E. I, II, and III

12. An empty fuel tank is filled with brand Z gasoline. When the tank is half empty, it is filled with brand Y gasoline. When the tank is half empty again, it is filled with brand Z gasoline. When the tank is half empty again, it is filled with brand Y gasoline. At this time, what percent of the gasoline in the tank is brand Z?

   F. 50%

   G. 40%

   H. 37½%

   J. 25%

   K. None of these

13. What is 0.7% of 30?

   A.   0.021

   B.   0.21

   C.   2.1

   D.   21

   E.   210

14. $\dfrac{\left(4^{2x}\right)\left(4^{x}\right)\left(2^{4x}\right)}{\left(2^{6x}\right)\left(4^{3x}\right)\left(2^{2x}\right)} = ?$

   F. 2^{4x}

   G. 4^{2x}

   H. $\frac{1}{4}^{2x}$

   J. $\frac{1}{2}^{2x}$

   K. $\frac{1}{4}^{x}$

15. How many 3-person committees can be formed in a club with 8 members?

    A.   8

    B.   24

    C.   48

    D.   56

    E.   336

16. In rectangle *ABCD* shown below, $\overline{BC} = 4$, $\overline{CD} = 10$, and $\overline{BE} = x$ What is the area of the shaded region?

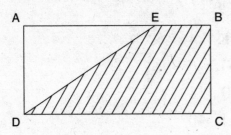

    F. $20 + 2x$

    G. $2 + 4x$

    H. $\dfrac{40 - x}{2}$

    J. $20 + x$

    K. $40 + 2x$

17. At a party, there are 5 times as many females as males. There are 3 times as many adults as children. Which of the following could NOT be the number of people at the party?

    A.   72

    B.   120

    C.   216

    D.   258

    E.   384

18. Which of the following is the largest?

    F.   Half of 30% of 280

    G.   One third of 70% of 160

    H.   Twice 50% of 30

    J.   Three times 40% of 40

    K.   60% of 60

19. $\dfrac{12\sqrt{6} - 6\sqrt{50}}{\sqrt{72}} = ?$

    A.   2

    B. $\dfrac{\sqrt{3} - \sqrt{2}}{2}$

    C. $3\sqrt{2} - 6\sqrt{3}$

    D. $2\sqrt{3} - 5$

    E.   None of these

20. If electricity costs x cents per kilowatt hour for the first 30 kilowatt hours and y cents per kilowatt hour for each additional kilowatt hour, what is the cost of z kilowatt hours?

    (Note: $z > 30$)

    F. $30(x - y) + yz$

    G. $(z - 30)x + 30y$

    H. $30y - 30x + yz$

    J. $20x + (y - 30)z$

    K. $30(x + y) - yz$

21. In the standard (x, y) coordinate plane, what is the point of intersection of the two lines with the equations $3y + 2x = 18$ and $y = 4x - 8$?

    A.   (8,–3)

    B.   (4,3)

    C.   (3,4)

    D.   (2,0)

    E.   (–3,8)

GO ON TO THE NEXT PAGE

22. In the figure below, $\overline{AB}$ and $\overline{CE}$ are parallel, $\overline{AE}$ = 12 inches, $\overline{DE}$= 6, and $\overline{CE}$= 4 inches. What is the length of $\overline{AB}$ in inches?

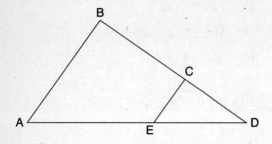

   F.   6

   G.   8

   H.   10

   J.   12

   K.   18

23. Using 3 standard dice, what is the approximate probability of rolling a combination totaling 4?

   A. $\frac{1}{18}$

   B. $\frac{1}{36}$

   C. $\frac{1}{64}$

   D. $\frac{1}{72}$

   E. $\frac{1}{108}$

24. In the standard (x, y) coordinate plane, at which of the following does the graph of the equation $y + 4 = 2x^2$ cross the graph of the equation $x = -1$?

   F.   −6

   G.   −2

   H.   0

   J.   2

   K.   6

25. If $6x - 3y = 30$ and $4x = 2 - y$, then what is the value of $x + y$?

   A.   −8

   B.   −6

   C.   −4

   D.   2

   E.   8

26. If a 32-inch chord is drawn in a circle of radius 20 inches, how far, in inches, is the chord from the center of the circle?

   F.   4

   G.   6

   H.   8

   J.   10

   K.   12

27. If $7x = 3y$, what is the ratio of x to y?

   A. $\frac{1}{3}$

   B. $\frac{1}{4}$

   C. $\frac{4}{3}$

   D. $\frac{4}{7}$

   E. $\frac{3}{7}$

28. If $\frac{3}{y} + \frac{1}{2y} = \frac{3}{4}$, what is the value of y?

   F.   8

   G. $6\frac{2}{3}$

   H. $4\frac{1}{2}$

   J. $2\frac{3}{4}$

   K. $1\frac{1}{3}$

29. In the standard (x, y) coordinate plane, what are the coordinates of one endpoint of a segment if the other endpoint has coordinates (x, y) and the midpoint has coordinates $(3x, -3y)$?

  A. $(2x, -y)$

  B. $(-2x, y)$

  C. $(5x, -7y)$

  D. $(4x, -2y$

  E. $(7x, -5y)$

30. Tim's weight is 12 kilograms more than twice Jane's weight. What is Tim's weight, in kilograms, if they weigh 135 kilograms together?

  F. 94

  G. 82

  H. 73.5

  J. 61.5

  K. 41

31. If $i = \sqrt{-1}$ which of the following is a simplified form of $\dfrac{1}{3+i}$?

  A. $\dfrac{3-i}{10}$

  B. $\dfrac{i-3}{10}$

  C. $\dfrac{3-i}{8}$

  D. $\dfrac{i-3}{8}$

  E. $\dfrac{1}{3i}$

32. What is the product of $(5x^2y)$, $(-2xy^2)$, and $(-3y^4)$?

  F. $30x^2y^8$

  G. $-30x^3y^7$

  H. $30x^3y^7$

  J. $-30x^2y^8$

  K. $60x^3y^7$

33. An item that normally sells for \$40.00 has been marked down 10%. If 10% sales tax is added to the discount price, how much will the item cost including tax?

  A. \$36.10

  B. \$39.60

  C. \$40.00

  D. \$40.40

  E. \$44.00

34. In the figure shown below, $\overline{AB} \perp \overline{BC}$, $\overline{BD} \perp \overline{AC}$, and each triangle is scalene. If $\overline{AD}$ is 4 inches and $\overline{BD}$ is 8 inches, what is the length, in inches, of $\overline{AC}$?

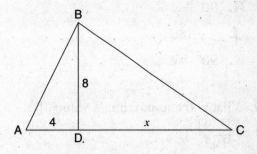

  F. 12

  G. 16

  H. 20

  J. 32

  K. Cannot be determined from the given information

GO ON TO THE NEXT PAGE

35. If 6 apples and 2 pears weigh the same as 3 apples and 6 pears, how many apples will it take to balance 12 pears?

A.   3

B.   5

C.   6

D.   9

E.   12

36. In the figure shown below, $\angle x$ and $\angle z$ are complementary. In terms of $\angle y$ what is the measure of $\angle z$?

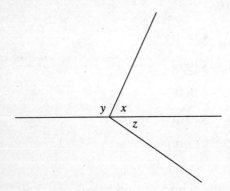

F. $y - 90°$

G. $180° - y$

H. $90° + y$

J. $y + 180°$

K. $90° - y$

37. What is the approximate value of $\sqrt{\dfrac{2,491}{103}}$?

A.   50

B.   25

C.   24

D.   5

E.   4

38. $1 - 2 + 3 - 4 + 5 - \ldots + 99 = ?$

F.   100

G.   50

H.   0

J.   −50

K.   −100

39. Twenty-seven cubes are arranged as shown in the figure below and placed on a flat board. Then the exposed surfaces are painted. Not counting the bottom surfaces on the board, how many unpainted sides are there?

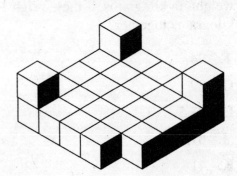

A.   41

B.   44

C.   76

D.   82

E.   84

40. If $12 < 2x < 18$ and $-9 < 3y < 6$, then which of the following is (are) true?

   I. $3 < x + y < 11$

   II. $-12 < y - x < -4$

   III. $x > 7$

   F. I only

   G. III only

   H. I and II only

   J. I and III only

   K. II and III only

41. A student received the following scores on 5 exams: 32, 20, 40, 42, 36. Which of the following scores would the student need to receive on the sixth test so that the median score and the mean score would be the same?

   A. 46

   B. 48

   C. 52

   D. 58

   E. 60

42. Three consecutive odd numbers add up to 15 more than twice the smallest. What is the sum of the 3 numbers?

   F. 33

   G. 31

   H. 29

   J. 28

   K. 26

43. $\dfrac{\left(5^2 + 5\right)\left(5^3 + 5^2\right)}{5^2} = ?$

   A. 625

   B. 180

   C. 156

   D. 150

   E. 15

44. The longest side of a right triangle is 6 feet long. The second side is half the length of the third side. What is the length of the third side, in feet?

   F. $\dfrac{6\sqrt{5}}{5}$

   G. $\dfrac{3\sqrt{5}}{5}$

   H. $\dfrac{12\sqrt{5}}{5}$

   J. $5\sqrt{5}$

   K. $12\sqrt{5}$

45. If parallelogram *ABCD* below has a height of 6 inches and a base of 8 inches and $\angle A$ is equal to $60°$, what is the perimeter of the parallelogram, in inches?

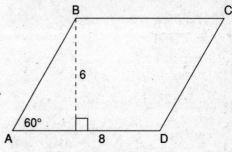

   A. $16\left(1 + 3\sqrt{3}\right)$

   B. $8\left(4 + \sqrt{3}\right)$

   C. $4\left(4 + \sqrt{3}\right)$

   D. $8\left(1 + \sqrt{3}\right)$

   E. $8\left(2 + \sqrt{3}\right)$

GO ON TO THE NEXT PAGE

46. Line *A* has a slope of ¾. In the standard (*x, y*) coordinate plane, what is the equation of a line that passes through the point (0,1) and is perpendicular to line *A*?

F. $4x - 3y = 3$

G. $3x - 4y = -4$

H. $3x + 4y = 4$

J. $4x - 3y = -3$

K. $4x + 3y = 3$

47. If the supplement of $\angle x$ is 4 times its complement, what is the measure of $\angle x$?

A. 30°

B. 45°

C. 60°

D. 120°

E. 150°

48. Which of the following is equivalent to

$\dfrac{\sqrt{5} + 2}{\sqrt{3}}$?

F. $\dfrac{\sqrt{5} + \sqrt{6}}{3}$

G. $\sqrt{15} + \sqrt{6}$

H. $\dfrac{\sqrt{5} + 2\sqrt{3}}{3}$

J. $\dfrac{2\sqrt{15} + \sqrt{3}}{3}$

K. $\dfrac{\sqrt{15} + 2\sqrt{3}}{3}$

49. In the standard (*x, y*) coordinate plane, △*ABC* has its vertices at (2,8), (9,7), and (4,2). What is the area of △*ABC*?

A. 20

B. 24

C. 24.5

D. 28

E. 32

50. As shown in the figure below, a tower casts a shadow 60 feet long. If the angle of elevation of the sun is 40°, what is the height of the tower?

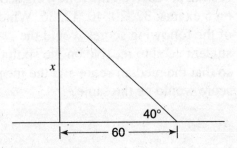

F. 60 sin 40°

G. 60 tan 40°

H. 60 tan 50°

J. 60 cot 40°

K. 60 cot 50°

51. If a regular hexagon has a perimeter of 48 inches, what is its area, in inches?

A. $60\sqrt{2}$

B. $96\sqrt{3}$

C. $48\sqrt{3}$

D. $96\sqrt{2}$

E. $72\sqrt{3}$

52. Three lines intersect as shown in the figure below to form the indicated angles. If $\angle b + \angle c = 160°$ and if $\angle a = 50°$, what is the measure of $\angle d$?

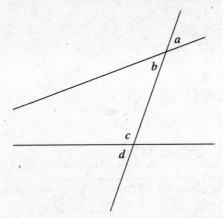

F. 50°

G. 60°

H. 70°

J. 80°

K. Cannot be determined from the given information

53. Fernando scored an average of 60 on his first 4 tests. What must he score on his fifth test so that the average of the 5 tests will be 70?

A. 80

B. 90

C. 95

D. 100

E. 110

54. A circle and a square have the same area. What is the ratio of the perimeter of the square to the circumference of the circle?

F. 1:1

G. $\pi:3$

H. $4:\pi$

J. $\sqrt{\pi}:2$

K. $2\sqrt{\pi}:\pi$

55. $\dfrac{9 - \dfrac{1}{p^2}}{3 - \dfrac{1}{p}} = ?$

A. $3 - \dfrac{1}{p}$

B. $3 + \dfrac{1}{p^2}$

C. $\dfrac{3p-1}{p}$

D. $\dfrac{3p+1}{p}$

E. $6 - p$

56. A racetrack is made up of 2 straight sections of equal length and 2 semicircular sections with a radius 10m as shown in the figure below. How many meters is it around the racetrack?

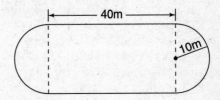

F. $20(4+\pi)$

G. $20(6+\pi)$

H. $100(8+\pi)$

J. $40(2+\pi)$

K. None of the above

GO ON TO THE NEXT PAGE

57. $\dfrac{\left(m^6 n\right)^{-2} \left(mn^{-2}\right)^3}{\left(m^{-2} n^{-2}\right)^{-2}} = ?$

A. $\dfrac{1}{m^{13} n^{12}}$

B. $m^6 n^4$

C. $\dfrac{m^2}{n^8}$

D. $\dfrac{n^3}{n^4}$

E. $\dfrac{m}{n^8}$

58. What is the measure of $\angle x$ in the figure below?

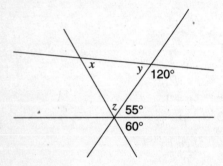

F. 65°

G. 60°

H. 55°

J. 50°

K. 45°

59. Given the figure shown below, what is the value, in meters, of x?

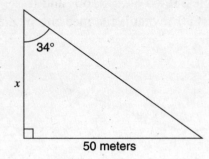

A. 50 sin 34°

B. 50 cos 34°

C. 50 tan 34°

D. $\dfrac{50}{\tan 34°}$

E. $\dfrac{50}{\cos 34°}$

60. One half a number is 6 greater than twice a second number. If the second number is 9 greater than the first number, then what is the value of the larger number?

F. −20

G. −16

H. −7

J. 4

K. 10

IF YOU FINISH BEFORE TIME IS CALLED, CHECK YOUR WORK ON THIS SECTION ONLY. DO NOT WORK ON ANY OTHER SECTION IN THE TEST.

STOP

Reading Test

Time: 35 Minutes

40 Questions

Directions: Each of the four passages in this test is followed by several questions. Read the passage and then choose the best answer to each question that follows the passage. Refer to the passage as often as necessary to answer the questions.

Passage I

Prose fiction: This passage (published in 1865) is adapted from Huckleberry Finn *by Mark Twain.*

I had shut the door to. Then I turned around, and there he was. I used to be scared of him all the time, he tanned me so much. I reckoned I was scared now, (5) too; but in a minute I see I was mistaken—that is, after the first jolt, as you may say, when my breath sort of hitched, he being so unexpected; but right away after, I see I warn't scared of (10) him worth bothering about.

He was most fifty, and he looked it. His hair was long and tangled and greasy, and hung down, and you could see his eyes shining through like he was behind (15) vines. It was all black, no gray; so was his long, mixed-up whiskers. There warn't no color in his face, where his face showed; it was white; not like another man's white, but a white to make a (20) body sick, a white to make a body's flesh crawl—a tree-toad white, a fish-belly white. As for his clothes—just rags, that was all. He had one ankle resting on t'other knee; the boot on that foot (25) was busted, and two of his toes stuck through, and he worked them now and then. His hat was laying on the floor—an old black slouch with the top caved in, like a lid.

(30) I stood a-looking at him; he set there a-looking at me, with his chair tilted back a little. I set the candle down. I noticed the window was up; so he had clumb in by the shed. He kept a-looking me all (35) over. By and by he says:

"Starchy clothes—very. You think you're a good deal of a big-bug, *don't* you?

"Maybe I am, maybe I ain't," I says.

"Don't you give me none o' your lip," (40) says he. "You've put on considerable many frills since I been away. I'll take you down a peg before I get done with you. You're educated, too, they say—can read and write. You think you're (45) better'n your father, now, don't you, because he can't? *I'll* take it out of you. Who told you you might meddle with such hifalut'n foolishness, hey?—who told you you could?"

(50) "The widow. She told me."

"The widow, hey?—and who told the widow she could put in her shovel about a thing that ain't none of her business?"

"Nobody never told her."

(55) "Well, I'll learn her how to meddle. And looky here—you drop that school, you hear? I'll learn people to bring up a boy to put on airs over his own father and let

GO ON TO THE NEXT PAGE

on to be better'n what *he* is. You lemme
(60) catch you fooling around that school
again, you hear? Your mother couldn't
read, and she couldn't write, nuther,
before she died. None of the family
couldn't before *they* died. *I* can't; and
(65) here you're a-swelling yourself up like
this. I ain't the man to stand it—you
hear? Say, lemme hear you read."

I took up a book and begun something
about General Washington and the wars.
(70) When I'd read about a half a minute, he
fetched the book a whack with his hand
and knocked it across the house. He
says:

"It's so. You can do it. I had my doubts
(75) when you told me. Now looky here; you
stop that putting on frills. I won't have
it. I'll lay for you, my smarty; and if I
catch you about that school I'll tan you
good. First you know you'll get religion,
(80) too. I never see such a son."

1. The two characters who appear in the
   scene are:

   A. an uncle and his nephew

   B. a father and his daughter

   C. a father and his son

   D. two former friends meeting again
      after a separation

2. From details in the passage, it can be
   inferred that this scene takes place:

   F. out of doors in warm weather

   G. indoors in winter

   H. indoors at night

   J. indoors during the day

3. The state of mind of the speaker in the
   first paragraph (lines 1–10) is best
   described as:

   A. terrified

   B. startled, but not frightened

   C. frightened at first, then pleased

   D. unaffected

4. The description in the second paragraph
   (lines 11–35) differs from the rest of the
   passage because several times it uses:

   F. indirect discourse

   G. simile and metaphor

   H. denotative language

   J. incorrect grammar

5. The effect of the description in the
   second paragraph (lines 11–35) is to
   make the man described appear:

   A. pitiable

   B. interesting

   C. repulsive

   D. mysterious

6. When the visitor says "Starchy
   clothes—very. You think you're a good
   deal of a big-bug, *don't* you?" (lines
   36–37), he is expressing his:

   F. surprise at how much the other has
      grown

   G. admiration of the clothes the other
      is wearing

   H. contempt at the other's supposed
      complacence

   J. amusement at the way the other is
      dressed

7. In narrating the passage, the author uses which of the following?

    A. A first-person narrator, dialogue, and action that took place in the past

    B. A third-person narrator, action taking place in the present, and monologue

    C. A second-person narrator, dialogue, and action taking place in the present

    D. A first-person narrator, action taking place in the present, and monologue

8. From details in the passage, it can be inferred that the narrator's mother:

    F. is a widow

    G. was uneducated and is no longer alive

    H. came from a social position above that of the father

    J. deserted his father before her death

9. It can reasonably be inferred from the passage that the second speaker asks to hear the first speaker read because he:

    A. is interested in war

    B. wishes to find out if the other can read

    C. hates reading and readers

    D. cannot read himself

10. In the course of the passage, the visitor expresses his contempt for all of the following EXCEPT:

    F. school

    G. decent clothes

    H. ignorance

    J. religion

Passage II

Social science: This passage is adapted from Origins *by Robert E. Leakey and Roger Lewin (©1977 by Robert E. Leakey and Roger Lewin, published by E.P. Dutton).*

Scholars concede that Tutankhamen's is "the richest royal tomb of antiquity ever found." Yet, since it belonged to an obscure "boy king" who ruled only nine
(5) years (from about 1334 to 1325 B.C.), it has been assumed that mightier pharoahs must indeed have had richer tombs, although most of the evidence has long since vanished.

(10) Tutankhamen was more than a pharaoh. He was a milestone, a symbol of restored order after an interlude of chaos. Egypt had long been dominated by the vast priesthood of the state god Amun-
(15) Re. The priests profited from the spoils of Egypt's foreign conquests, and they shared power with the pharoahs. Then, under Amenophis III, the stage was set for the dwindling of the priests' power,
(20) and under his son, who became known as Akhenaten, disaster struck. Akhenaten had the effrontery to sponsor a universal sun god called Aten. He abandoned the priestly stronghold at
(25) Thebes, sailed down the Nile to a site he called Akhenaten, and built a new religious capital.

The priests were irate, and the rest of Egypt worried. The populace hated to
(30) give up all their beloved gods, and when Akhenaten died, the reaction was inevitable. The priests recaptured their power, and the boy Tutankhamen became pharaoh. To many of his subjects,
(35) he represented a welcome return to "old times." For this reason, one modern scholar suggests that, when Tutankhamen died at about the age of

GO ON TO THE NEXT PAGE

18, this tomb may have been outfitted
(40) with extra elegance.

Whatever the case, the contents of the
tomb are full of clues to Egyptian history. Take the little alabaster unguent jar.
Represented in the handle are two long-
(45) stemmed flowers, the lotus of Upper
Egypt and the papyrus plant of Lower
Egypt. After a fierce battle, these two regions were united about 3000 B.C. and
subsequently the flowers were often pic-
(50) tured with their stems knotted together
as an emblem of peaceful unity.

The early Egyptian, like most of
mankind, tried to protect himself against
misfortune. His gods, amulets, and
(55) magic writings were all part of his protective equipment. Tutankhamen's mir-
ror case was shaped like an ankh, a
cross with a loop at the top. Potent symbols of life, ankhs were seen every-
(60) where. Another ubiquitous emblem was
the eye, which appears on the clasp on
Tutankhamen's bracelet. One of the
holiest symbols of Egyptian religion, the
eye at different periods was identified
(65) with the sun and moon.

The uses of tomb treasure were both
magical and practical, with no sharp line
between them. An example of double
usefulness is Tutankhamen's ivory head-
(70) rest, with two lions on its base and Shu,
the god of air, holding up the curved
head support. This would serve the king
in a practical way in the afterworld—
just as it did on earth—but, also, since
(75) the human head was regarded as the seat
of life, a headrest had a magical efficacy
in the attempt to defy death.

11. The central concern of the passage is:

A. Egyptian gods

B. Egyptian dynastic history

C. Egyptian symbols

D. Tutankhamen's tomb

12. The first paragraph (lines 1–9) is
logically related to the second and third
paragraphs (lines 10–27 and 28–40)
because:

F. all three deal with Egyptian
pharaohs

G. paragraphs two and three discuss
the pharaohs who followed
Tutankhamen

H. paragraphs two and three discuss
Egyptian religion in the reigns
before Tutankhamen

J. paragraphs two and three offer an
explanation for the richness of
Tutankhamen's tomb

13. Tutankhamen was probably born in:

A. 1325 B.C.

B. 1334 B.C.

C. 1343 B.C.

D. 1352 B.C.

14. The words "disaster" (line 21) and
"effrontery" (line 22) represent the
point of view of:

F. the author of the passage

G. scholars of Egyptian history

H. Akhenaten

J. the priests

15. According to the passage, the accession of Tutankhamen was welcomed by many Egyptians because:

    A. the religious capital at Thebes was restored

    B. polytheism was restored

    C. the kingdoms of Upper and Lower Egypt were reunited

    D. the priests were removed from power

16. It can be inferred from information in the passage that the priests were able to reclaim their authority at the death of Akhenaten because:

    I. the people wished to return to the old religion

    II. the new king was only a child

    III. the populace was enraged by the cost of Akhenaten's tomb

    F. I and II only

    G. I and III only

    H. II and III only

    J. I, II, and III

17. On Egyptian artifacts, the representation of a lotus and papyrus plant together most likely signified:

    A. the importance of flowers to the Egyptians

    B. the unification of Upper and Lower Egypt

    C. the rivalry between Upper and Lower Egypt

    D. the importance of water to the Egyptians

18. From details of the passage, it can be inferred that ancient Egyptians were believers in:

    I. a life after death

    II. magic

    III. the efficacy of the priesthood

    F. I and II only

    G. I and III only

    H. II and III only

    J. I, II, and III

19. As it is used in line 60, the word "ubiquitous" most nearly means:

    A. symbolic

    B. potent

    C. visionary

    D. omnipresent

20. That the kings who ruled longer and were more important historically than Tutankhamen had richer and larger tombs is:

    F. disproved in this passage

    G. unresolved by this passage

    H. an issue this passage never raises

    J. proven in this passage

GO ON TO THE NEXT PAGE

Reading Test

187

Passage III

Humanities: This passage (published in 1893) is adapted from Modern Painters *by John Ruskin, a nineteenth-century art critic.*

Is it useful to compare the works of the greatest artists? Should an art student be encouraged to paint like Leonardo *and* Goya, though one is Italian and the other
(5) Spanish, and they lived in different centuries? It is, indeed, true that there *is* a relative merit, that a peach is nobler than a hawthorn berry. But in each rank of fruits, as in each rank of masters, one is
(10) endowed with one virtue, and another with another; their glory is their dissimilarity, and they who propose in the training of an artist that he should unite the coloring of Tintoretto, the finish of
(15) Durer, and the tenderness of Correggio are no wiser than a horticulturist would be who made it the object of his labor to produce a fruit which should unite in itself the lusciousness of the grape, the
(20) crispness of the nut, and the fragrance of the pine.

And from these considerations one most important practical corollary is to be deduced, namely, that the greatness or
(25) smallness of a man is, in the most conclusive sense, determined for him at his birth, as strictly as it is determined for a fruit whether it is to be a currant or an apricot. Education, favorable circum-
(30) stances, resolution, and industry can do much; in a certain sense they do *everything;* that is to say, they determine whether the apricot shall fall blighted by the wind, or whether it shall reach matu-
(35) rity. But apricot out of currant—great man out of small—did never yet art or effort make; and, in a general way, men have their excellence nearly fixed for them when they are born; a little
(40) cramped and frostbitten on one side, a little sun-burned and fortune-spotted on the other, they reach between good and evil chances, such size and taste as generally belong to the men of their caliber.

(45) Therefore it is, that every system of teaching is false which holds forth "great art" as in any wise to be taught to students or even to be aimed at by them. Great art is precisely that which never
(50) was, nor will be, taught. It is preeminently and finally the expression of the spirits of great men; so that the only wholesome teaching is that which simply endeavors to fix those characters of
(55) nobleness in the pupil's mind, without holding out to him, as a possible or even probable result, that he should ever paint like Titian or carve like Michelangelo. Such teaching enforces upon him the as-
(60) sured duty of endeavoring to draw in a manner at least honest and intelligible and cultivates in him those general charities of heart, sincerities of thought, and graces of habit which are likely to lead
(65) him, throughout life, to prefer openness to affectation, realities to shadows, and beauty to corruption.

21. Which of the following is the best title for this passage?

  A. The Comparison of Great Artists

  B. The Uniqueness of Artistic Genius

  C. How to Train an Artist

  D. Artists Are Made, Not Born

22. According to the first paragraph (lines 1–21), the great artists are:

  F. alike

  G. dissimilar

  H. poor models for student artists

  J. no wiser than horticulturists

23. The development of the first paragraph (lines 1–21) depends chiefly upon:

   A. the posing of a question and the offering of a series of answers

   B. an extended analogy

   C. a series of rhetorical questions

   D. a contrast of the specific and the general

24. In the second paragraph (lines 22–44), the author compares men to fruits to stress:

   F. the importance of inborn ability

   G. the importance of good luck

   H. the importance of determination and hard work

   J. humans' ability to control their destiny

25. The comparison of artists to fruits is employed in:

   A. the second paragraph (lines 22–44) only

   B. the first and second paragraphs (lines 1–21 and 22–44) only

   C. the first and third paragraphs (lines 1–21 and 45–67) only

   D. all three paragraphs

26. The author of the passage would probably believe that a great dancer achieved success chiefly because of:

   F. hard work

   G. an intense will to succeed

   H. inborn ability

   J. excellent coaching

27. As it is used in line 14, the word "finish" most nearly means:

   A. completeness

   B. polish

   C. reticenc

   D. perspective

28. The author would probably disagree with all of the following EXCEPT:

   F. all artists are equally valuable

   G. contemporary artists should be taught to imitate the works of the great artists of the past

   H. greatness in art is unteachable

   J. birth alone will determine artistic success

29. The author would be likely to condemn a work of art for all of the following reasons EXCEPT:

   A. dishonesty

   B. simplicity

   C. unreality

   D. affectation

GO ON TO THE NEXT PAGE

Reading Test

30. What the last paragraph (lines 45–67) suggests should be taught to prospective artists implies that the author believes:

   F. there is no significant connection between the character of the artists and the work of art

   G. an evil artist might produce noble art

   H. there is a relation between the character of the artist and the work of art

   J. a virtuous artist may produce corrupt art

Passage IV

Natural science: This passage is adapted from Cold Blooded Vertebrates *(©1931 by Samuel F. Hildebrand, published by the Smithsonian Institute).*

Comparatively few freshwater species of fishes are limited in their distribution to a single river system, yet not many are found on both sides of a high moun-

(5) tain ridge, such as the Rocky Mountains in North America. That is to say, the fishes of the Mississippi Valley are generally different and distinct from those of the Pacific slope.

(10) While it is a well-known fact that the fish life in no two river systems, even though they empty into the sea on the same side of a divide, is identical, such streams do have many species in com-

(15) mon. The principal rivers of the Atlantic slope of the United States, for example, contain several species common to all of them, including the bullhead catfish, the bluegill sunfish, and the largemouth

(20) bass. None of these species can endure salt water, so they cannot now migrate from one river system to another. On the other hand, the more northern streams

contain species not found in the south-
(25) ern ones, and vice versa. The common pike, for example, is found in the Atlantic streams from Maryland northward, and the brook trout and yellow perch occur only in the streams from
(30) North Carolina southward.

How the present distribution came about must remain a matter of conjecture. It is quite probable that some of the streams, including those on opposite sides of a
(35) divide, may have been connected at one time. Again, streams may be entirely separate during normal weather, but an exceptionally heavy rainfall or the sudden melting of snow in the uplands
(40) sometimes causes floods which may form a temporary connection between them, providing a passageway for fishes. It is possible, also, that water birds may accidentally carry fish or
(45) spawn from one stream to another, or that man may be instrumental in such a transfer.

Evidently, then, freshwater fishes may become distributed far beyond the con-
(50) fines of the stream of their origin. The chief factor in limiting the still wider distribution of species is temperature. This forms such an efficient barrier that comparatively few species of freshwater
(55) fishes of the United States extend their range into Mexico. In Panama only one fish common to the fresh waters of the States has been found, and that is the eel, which is not strictly a freshwater
(60) form, as it enters salt water to spawn and is taken in fairly salty water at other times.

31. According to the first paragraph (lines 1–9), in which of the following pairs of states are freshwater fishes expected to be most similar?

    A. Oregon and New Jersey

    B. New York and Delaware

    C. California and Kentucky

    D. Washington and Vermont

32. The freshwater fish life found in two river systems at approximately the same latitude and on the same side of a continental divide is:

    F. never just the same

    G. likely to be very different

    H. always just the same

    J. often just the same

33. Which of the following are three species of freshwater fish that are all likely to be found in waters of South Carolina?

    A. Bullhead catfish, largemouth bass, pike

    B. Bluegill sunfish, pike, largemouth bass

    C. Largemouth bass, yellow perch, pike

    D. Bullhead catfish, brook trout, bluegill sunfish

34. According to the passage, exceptionally heavy rains or the melting of large amounts of snow may explain:

    F. sudden rises in freshwater fish populations

    G. sudden declines in freshwater fish populations

    H. why fish of the same species may be found in different water systems

    J. why fish of different species are seldom found in water systems on different sides of a high mountain ridge

35. Which of the following statements helps to explain why the freshwater system on one side of a high mountain ridge has so few species in common with the freshwater system on the other side?

    I. It is possible that the streams on both sides of the ridge were once connected.

    II. Most species of freshwater fish cannot endure salt water.

    III. Water birds that cross mountain ridges often carry fish spawn from one stream to another.

    A. I only

    B. II only

    C. I and III only

    D. II and III only

36. As it is used in line 32, the word "conjecture" most nearly means:

    F. experimentation

    G. speculation

    H. history

    J. assertion

GO ON TO THE NEXT PAGE

37. According to the last paragraph (lines 48–62), in which of the following pairs of states should the species of freshwater fish be expected to be most similar?

  A. New York and Rhode Island

  B. Michigan and Georgia

  C. Maine and Florida

  D. Minnesota and Mississippi

38. According to the passage, the chief deterrent to a wider distribution of the species of freshwater fish is:

  F. water pollution

  G. the loss of habitat due to human encroachment on nature

  H. temperature

  J. the salinity of the oceans

39. One should expect the largest number of freshwater fish species found in the northeastern United States to be found also in:

  A. Mexico

  B. Canada

  C. Panama

  D. Peru

40. The best title for this passage would be:

  F. Temperature, Geography, and the Distribution of Fish

  G. North American Fish and Their Separation by Mountain Ridges

  H. The Distribution of Freshwater Fish Species in North America

  J. The Distribution of Freshwater Fish and Its Results

IF YOU FINISH BEFORE TIME IS CALLED, CHECK YOUR WORK ON THIS SECTION ONLY. DO NOT WORK ON ANY OTHER SECTION IN THE TEST.

STOP

Science Reasoning Test

Time: 35 Minutes

40 Questions

Directions: Each of the seven passages in this test is followed by several questions. Read each passage and then choose the best answer to each question that follows the passage. Refer to the passage as often as necessary to answer the questions. You may NOT use a calculator on this test.

Passage I

Figure 1 shows the variation of temperature with altitude in our atmosphere. The four layers of different shades correspond to atmospheric zones, which are named in the right side of the graph.

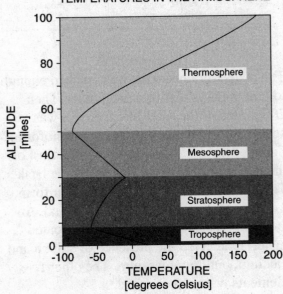

TEMPERATURES IN THE ATMOSPHERE

Figure 1

1. What is the temperature of the atmosphere at an altitude of 70 miles?

    A. −80°C

    B. −15°C

    C. 27°C

    D. 50°C

2. Which of the four atmospheric zones has the smallest range of temperature?

    F. The mesosphere

    G. The stratosphere

    H. The thermosphere

    J. The troposphere

3. Which two atmospheric zones show decreasing temperature with increasing altitude?

    A. The mesosphere and troposphere

    B. The stratosphere and thermosphere

    C. The thermosphere and mesosphere

    D. The troposphere and stratosphere

4. Air pressure at any given altitude is caused by the weight of the air above that level. Which of the atmospheric zones has the highest air pressure?

    F. The mesosphere

    G. The stratosphere

    H. The thermosphere

    J. The troposphere

GO ON TO THE NEXT PAGE

5. Conditions are most favorable in the stratosphere for the formation of ozone molecules from oxygen. At that altitude, oxygen absorbs ultraviolet radiation and is transformed into ozone. How does ozone formation explain the temperature pattern in the stratosphere?

A. The absorption of solar energy causes a rise in temperature.

B. Energy released by ozone formation causes a rise in temperature.

C. The loss of oxygen molecules causes a fall in temperature.

D. Ozone molecules absorb energy and cause a fall in temperature.

Passage II

To determine the types of crystals making up a coarse-grained rock, a researcher had only two analytical methods available.

The semiquantitative *x-ray fluorescence unit* could detect the presence of certain chemical elements, but it could not measure their abundances precisely. The chemical compositions for all crystals likely to be found in the rock are given in Table 1.

Table 1

CRYSTAL VARIETIES	ATOMIC PERCENTAGES							
	Oxygen	*Silicon*	*Aluminum*	*Iron*	*Magnesium*	*Calcium*	*Sodium*	*Potassium*
Magnetite	57	0	0	43	0	0	0	0
Olivine	57	14	0	13	16	0	0	0
Hypersthene	60	20	0	9	11	0	0	0
Augite	60	20	0	4	6	10	0	0
Hornblende	57	19	5	7	5	5	2	0
Biotite	60	15	5	9	6	0	0	5
Plagioclase	61	19	12	0	0	4	4	0
Quartz	67	33	0	0	0	0	0	0
Orthoclase	61	23	8	0	0	0	0	8

The second apparatus available was a *heavy liquids kit* containing three bottles of organic liquids of known specific gravity, an alternate method of reporting density. The specific gravity of crystals may be estimated by seeing whether they sink or float in each liquid. Table 2 states the specific gravity for each liquid and all crystal varieties suspected to be in the rock.

Table 2

		SPECIFIC GRAVITY
LIQUIDS	Methylene Iodide	3.33
	Bromoform	2.89
	Acetone	0.79
CRYSTALS	Magnetite	5.18
	Olivine	3.65
	Hypersthene	3.45
	Augite	3.25
	Hornblende	3.20
	Biotite	3.00
	Plagioclase	2.69
	Quartz	2.65
	Orthoclase	2.57

Experiment 1

The coarse-grained rock was crushed enough to free the crystals from each other. Then 200 grams of the sand-like material was stirred into a beaker containing bromoform. Some of the material floated, while most of the material sank to the bottom of the beaker. The fraction that floated appeared uniform, as if it were only one variety of crystal. An x-ray fluorescence analysis of the floated material detected the presence of silicon and calcium, but not potassium. The other five elements were not checked.

Experiment 2

The fraction of the material that sank in Experiment 1 was then washed free of bromoform and dried. It was then stirred into another beaker containing methylene iodide; again the material separated into two fractions. Each fraction appeared to be homogeneous and composed of only one crystal type. The part that had floated in the methylene iodide was analyzed with the x-ray fluorescence unit and found to contain silicon and magnesium, but not sodium. The other five elements were not checked.

Experiment 3
The rock fraction that sank in the previous experiment was quickly analyzed for the presence of silicon. After that element was found to be present, the investigator discontinued her work.

6. The crystals that were analyzed by x-ray fluorescence in Experiment 1 must be:

    F. Hornblende

    G. Magnetite

    H. Plagioclase

    J. Quartz

7. The three liquids in the kit are mutually *miscible* (capable of being mixed), so by mixing them, a liquid of intermediate specific gravity may be obtained. Which pair of crystals may be separated by using a liquid produced by mixing equal volumes of bromoform and methylene iodide?

    A. Augite and hornblende

    B. Hornblende and biotite

    C. Hypersthene and augite

    D. Olivine and hypersthene

8. To specifically identify the crystals that were analyzed in Experiment 2, the researcher should try to detect any of the following elements EXCEPT:

    F. Aluminum

    G. Calcium

    H. Iron

    J. Potassium

9. The usefulness of the x-ray fluorescence unit could be most improved if it could:

    A. Analyze two samples at the same time

    B. Detect the presence of oxygen

    C. Measure the amount of each element

    D. Work with wet or dry samples

10. Why would it be fruitless for the researcher to analyze the material in Experiment 3 for the remaining elements?

    F. The material could not contain any of those elements.

    G. The possible crystals had already been narrowed to only one.

    H. The two likely crystals contain the same elements.

    J. The three possible crystals are all known to contain iron.

11. All rock-forming crystals are denser than the acetone included in the heavy liquids kit. How can that light liquid best be used in crystal separations?

    A. Mix a small amount of it into bromoform to produce a liquid with a specific gravity of less than 2.89.

    B. Mix a small amount of it into bromoform to produce a liquid with a specific gravity of more than 2.89.

    C. Mix a small amount of it into methylene iodide to produce a liquid with a specific gravity of less than 3.33.

    D. Mix a small amount of it into methylene iodide to produce a liquid with a specific gravity of more than 3.33.

GO ON TO THE NEXT PAGE

Passage III

Figure 1 shows the feeding relationships in one woodland community. The arrows point toward the dependent organism. For example, frogs eat insects.

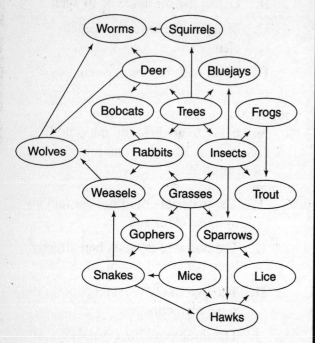

Figure 1

12. According to Figure 1, sparrows feed on:

   F. Grasses and mice

   G. Insects and grasses

   H. Lice and insects

   J. Mice and trees

13. The longest food chain in the diagram links six different organisms. That longest chain runs from:

   A. Grasses to deer

   B. Trees to lice

   C. Grasses to worms

   D. Trees to wolves

14. Which of the following animals are natural enemies of snakes?

   F. Gophers and mice

   G. Hawks and weasels

   H. Mice and hawks

   J. Weasels and gophers

15. At the base of the network of feeding relationships are independent organisms that do not feed on other organisms. In this woodland, which organisms are at the base of the network?

   A. Worms and lice

   B. Frogs and snakes

   C. Grasses and trees

   D. Wolves and bobcats

16. A campaign by chicken farmers to eradicate weasels throughout the area could lead indirectly to:

   F. A decrease of hawks

   G. A decrease of snakes

   H. An increase of bluejays

   J. An increase of bobcats

Passage IV

To investigate the ionization of air by alpha radiation, the apparatus shown in Figure 1 was assembled.

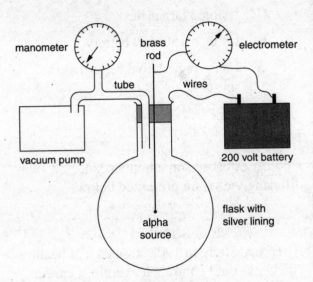

Figure 1

A large, round, glass flask was coated with a silver lining so it could conduct electricity. Through a cork at the top, a slender brass rod supported a 10-milligram sample of polonium-210 at the center of the flask. Po^{210} is strongly radioactive, decaying by emitting alpha particles. The half-life is 138 days; in that period, half of all Po^{210} atoms decay to nonradioactive lead-206 plus high-velocity alpha particles. As the alpha particles travel through the air in the flask, some of their kinetic energy is dissipated by ionizing some of the nitrogen and oxygen molecules to electrons and positive ions. Normal air is a good electrical insulator, but ionized air allows an electrical current to flow around the circuit: battery/brass/air/silver/battery. The electrometer measures the amount of current flowing, which is directly proportional to the degree of ionization in the air.

The cork is also pierced by a tube to a pump that can lower the air pressure within the flask. The manometer permits reading the pressure at any time. Beginning at 1

atmosphere air pressure, the researcher made nine readings of the electrical current flowing at progressively lower pressures. The prior hypothesis was that as the pressure was lowered, less of the energy of the alpha particles would be spent in ionizing air molecules. The results of the study are shown in Figure 2.

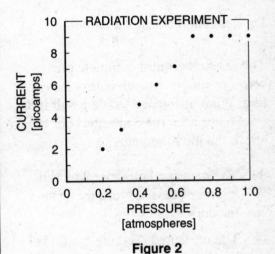

Figure 2

17. The prior hypothesis that the amount of ionization would be proportional to air pressure is supported by readings made over the range:

   A. 0.2 to 0.7 atmosphere

   B. 0.3 to 0.8 atmosphere

   C. 0.4 to 0.9 atmosphere

   D. 0.5 to 1.0 atmosphere

18. At the moment when the researcher records one data point to be graphed, which one of the four instruments may be switched off without affecting the measurement?

   F. The battery

   G. The electrometer

   H. The manometer

   J. The pump

GO ON TO THE NEXT PAGE

19. The low currents measured at low air pressures may be explained by:

    A. the electrical resistance of a vacuum

    B. fewer air molecules to be ionized

    C. fewer alpha particles reaching the silver

    D. less energetic alpha radiation

20. The researcher must complete one series of measurements within a day or two. What difference would result if the researcher tried three months later to check the measurements?

    F. The measured pressure would be higher because of leakage around the cork.

    G. The measured pressure would be lower because the pump slowly removes the air.

    H. The measured current would be lower because the radioactive source is weaker.

    J. The measured current would be higher because the silver lining will have tarnished.

21. The nearly constant current measured at high air pressures can be explained only if:

    A. All the alpha particles reach the silver lining without ionizing air molecules

    B. All the energy of the alpha particles is dissipated in ionizing air molecules

    C. All the nitrogen and oxygen molecules in the flask have been ionized

    D. All the silver atoms have been ionized by alpha particles

22. Which of the following alterations to the apparatus would NOT significantly alter the measured current?

    F. Using aluminum to line the flask

    G. Using a larger flask

    H. Using a 150-volt battery

    J. Using radioactive cerium as the source

Passage V

Do viruses cause some human cancers? Two differing views are presented below.

Scientist 1

A seminal study in 1908 showed that healthy chickens could contract leukemia, a cancer afflicting blood, by being injected with a highly filtered extract from diseased birds. Three years later, another researcher found that a connective-tissue cancer could likewise be transferred among chickens. The latter cancer originally appeared spontaneously in one hen; highly filtered plasma injected into other chickens caused highly malignant tumors of the same kind, called *sarcomas*. Extended investigation showed that the tumor-causing agent in the filtrate was one specific virus. In 1932, a virus causing tumors in a mammal was discovered. Again, cell-free filtrates from a skin tumor in a rabbit induced malignant skin tumors, *carcinomas,* in healthy rabbits. A few years later, the first of many tumor viruses in mice was isolated. The mouse viruses are capable of causing leukemias, sarcomas, and solid tumors (*lymphomas*). Some of these cancer-inducing viruses can be transmitted from a mother mouse to her suckling offspring through the milk. By the 1950s, scientists had found tumor viruses in other mammals, including primates like the Rhesus monkey. Especially disturbing was the discovery that human adenoviruses induced cancers in laboratory mice and rats. It seems highly probable that some human cancers are caused by viral infections. The herpes viruses are prime suspects.

Scientist 2

Eighty years of searching for human viruses that induce cancerous growth have been fruitless. Not a single variety of human cancer has been shown to be due to a viral infection. Researchers have looked, and looked long, and looked well. There is not a single known human tumor virus. Cancers have been shown to be caused by genetic defects, radioactivity, light, x-rays, and numerous chemicals. Modern cancer research techniques are so advanced and sensitive that new mutagenic agents are identified each day. The widely used Ames test is capable of identifying a carcinogen that causes cancer in as few as five out of a billion bacterial cells. If viruses were a significant cause of human cancer, at least one tumor virus would have been found after our extensive search. In fact, even the case for viral cancer in other animals has not been positively established. Most animals infected with a virus supposed to induce malignancy in that species do not develop any tumors. Therefore, the cause of the tumors in the few cancerous animals is uncertain. Possibly the viral infection simply weakens the animals' resistance until a cancer is induced by another agent, such as an ingredient of the diet. The reports of animal tumor viruses are too frequently from researchers seeking yet another grant. Surely it is time to shift our entire research budget onto known causes of cancer in humans. The search for a human tumor virus needed to be made, but by now it is known to have failed.

23. Which type of animal mentioned by Scientist 1 would be most relevant to human medicine?

   A. Chickens

   B. Mice

   C. Primates

   D. Rabbits

24. The strongest point that Scientist 2 raises against the belief that viral infections cause tumors in animals is that:

   F. The infections may be bacterial rather than viral.

   G. Laboratory animals eat an unnatural diet.

   H. Most animal researchers need results to receive grants.

   J. Not all infected animals develop cancer.

25. Scientist 1 also refers to a cancer of connective tissues as a:

   A. Carcinoma

   B. Leukemia

   C. Lymphoma

   D. Sarcoma

26. All of the following points support the belief of Scientist 2 EXCEPT:

   F. The cause of many human cancers is already known.

   G. New cancer-causing agents are discovered often.

   H. No virus has been shown to be the sole cause of any cancer.

   J. Present techniques should be capable of detecting human viruses.

GO ON TO THE NEXT PAGE

27. In the rabbit research reported by Scientist 1, why is it important to specify that the injected liquid be cell-free?

   A. The disease was not transmitted as cancerous cells.

   B. Cancer might not develop in the presence of cells.

   C. The liquid must not be contaminated with any virus.

   D. Some cells could kill any viruses in the liquid.

28. The argument presented by Scientist 2 would be considerably weakened if Scientist 1 could prove that:

   F. Human tumor viruses will be discovered soon.

   G. No animal is truly resistant to cancer.

   H. Research on viruses uses only 10% of cancer research grants.

   J. Some animal tumors are definitely caused by viruses.

29. The evidence presented by Scientist 1 for animal tumor viruses could be shaken if Scientist 2 showed that:

   A. Adenoviruses occur in other animals as well as humans.

   B. Herpes infections are not associated with any specific type of cancer.

   C. Leukemia may be induced in mice by exposure to radioactivity.

   D. Some particles besides the viruses passed through the filters.

Passage VI

Table 1 gives both the chemical symbols and atomic sizes of six nonmetallic elements. The last four elements are referred to as *halogens* in the questions for this passage.

Table 1

Element	Symbol	Diameter of Atom (angstrom units)
Hydrogen	H	0.74
Oxygen	O	1.21
Fluorine	F	1.42
Chlorine	Cl	1.99
Bromine	Br	2.28
Iodine	I	2.67

Atoms of each of the six elements form chemical bonds to identical atoms and to each of the other five elements. A research project measured the energy required to break those chemical bonds, and the results are given in Table 2. A higher energy corresponds to a greater force of attraction between the two atoms. Note that the chemical symbols are defined in Table 1.

Table 2

Bond	Energy kcal/mole
F-H	135
F-O	45
F-F	37
Cl-H	103
Cl-O	49
Cl-F	61
Cl-Cl	58
Br-H	88
Br-F	57
Br-Cl	52
Br-Br	46
I-H	71
I-Cl	50
I-Br	43
I-I	36

30. Which halogen forms the weakest bond to hydrogen?

   F. Bromine

   G. Chlorine

   H. Fluorine

   J. Iodine

31. The pure halogen elements occur as molecules with two identical atoms, such as F_2. Which of these elements would have to be heated to the highest temperature to decompose the molecule into atoms?

   A. Bromine

   B. Chlorine

   C. Fluorine

   D. Iodine

32. Hydrogen and the halogens all react with carbon to form organic compounds with four such atoms bonded to a central carbon atom. Which of these organic compounds has the largest molecules?

   F. Carbon tetrachloride, CCl_4

   G. Methyl bromide, CH_3Br

   H. Methylene Fluoride, CH_2F_2

   J. Methyl iodide, CH_3I

33. The bond study did not measure the energy of a bromine-oxygen bond. Based on the information given concerning chlorine bonds to oxygen and fluorine, which of the following is an estimate of that energy?

   A. 25 kcal/mole

   B. 45 kcal/mole

   C. 65 kcal/mole

   D. 85 kcal/mole

34. Which of the following statements best summarizes the relative strengths of bonds between any two halogen atoms?

   F. The bond is weakest between identical atoms.

   G. The bond is stronger with hydrogen than with oxygen.

   H. The bond is weakest if iodine is involved.

   J. The bond is stronger between smaller atoms.

Passage VII

To investigate the possibility of gene transfer between different strains of bacteria, the following series of experiments was performed. In each case, the bacterial culture was carefully plated onto Petri dishes containing a sterilized growth medium composed of glucose and various salts. The medium did not contain any amino acids, although it is known that all organisms require amino acids for metabolism.

GO ON TO THE NEXT PAGE

Experiment 1

As shown in Figure 1, in the first experiment, a culture of normal bacteria was plated onto the growth medium that lacked any amino acids. The cluster of circular colonies that appeared was the evidence of bacterial growth. The normal bacteria were able to internally synthesize any necessary amino acids.

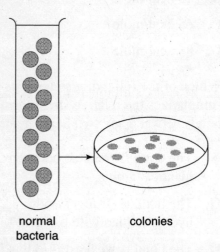

normal   colonies
bacteria

Figure 1

Experiment 2

In the second experiment, the researcher used two mutant strains of the same bacterial species. These mutant bacteria lacked the ability to synthesize certain amino acids, leucine and cystine. One strain (L) could not synthesize leucine, but it could synthesize cystine. The other strain (C) could not synthesize cystine. As shown in Figures 2 and 3, neither strain could grow on the Petri medium.

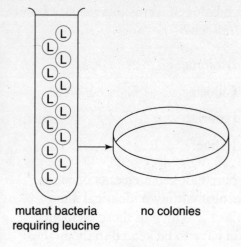

mutant bacteria   no colonies
requiring leucine

Figure 2

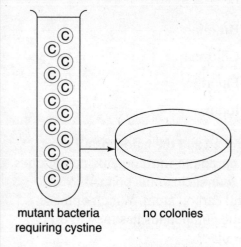

mutant bacteria   no colonies
requiring cystine

Figure 3

Experiment 3

In Experiment 3, the two mutant strains of bacteria were mixed. That mixed culture remained in the test tube for three hours to allow the bacteria an opportunity to exchange genes. When the culture was plated onto the nutritionally deficient medium, a number of colonies appeared, as shown in Figure 4.

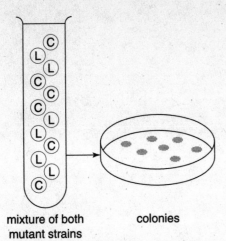

mixture of both   colonies
mutant strains

Figure 4

35. The fundamental assumption of the entire set of experiments is that the ability of bacteria to synthesize specific amino acids is:

  A. due to environmental requirements

  B. governed by specific genes

  C. inhibited by glucose and salts

  D. the result of genetic mutations

36. In the set of experiments, the crucial term "synthesize" must mean:

  F. Digest

  G. Manufacture

  H. Require

  J. Utilize

37. The fact that the L strain of bacteria required only leucine in order to grow on the glucose-salts medium shows that it must have a gene to synthesize:

  A. Cystine

  B. Glucose

  C. Leucine

  D. All amino acids

38. If cystine had been added to both Petri dishes in Experiment 2, the result would have been growth of:

  F. The C strain only

  G. The L strain only

  H. Both C and L strains

  J. Neither mutant strain

39. The appearance of colonies in Experiment 3 can best be explained by which of these descriptions of genetic exchange?

  A. The C strain must have received the cystine-synthesizing gene from the L strain.

  B. The L strain must have received the leucine-synthesizing gene from the C strain.

  C. Both the L strain received the leucine-synthesizing gene and the C strain received the cystine-synthesizing gene.

  D. Either the C strain received the cystine-synthesizing gene or the L strain received the leucine-synthesizing gene or both.

40. If no colonies had appeared in Experiment 3, one interpretation would be that no genes were transferred between strains in the test tube. What would be another valid interpretation?

  F. All bacteria may have starved during the three hours.

  G. Both strains lacked at least one identical, vital gene.

  H. One strain had mutated to synthesize all amino acids.

  J. Some normal bacteria may have contaminated the culture.

IF YOU FINISH BEFORE TIME IS CALLED, CHECK YOUR WORK ON THIS
SECTION ONLY. DO NOT WORK ON ANY OTHER SECTION IN THE TEST.

Answer Key

English Test

1. A	20. F	39. A	58. G
2. J	21. D	40. H	59. A
3. D	22. J	41. C	60. F
4. H	23. C	42. H	61. A
5. A	24. J	43. D	62. F
6. J	25. C	44. J	63. A
7. D	26. H	45. B	64. H
8. J	27. A	46. F	65. B
9. C	28. G	47. A	66. J
10. H	29. C	48. J	67. C
11. D	30. J	49. A	68. J
12. J	31. B	50. J	69. D
13. A	32. F	51. B	70. G
14. J	33. B	52. H	71. A
15. A	34. H	53. B	72. H
16. H	35. B	54. F	73. D
17. A	36. J	55. C	74. F
18. H	37. C	56. H	75. D
19. B	38. H	57. A	

Mathematics Test

1. C	16. F	31. A	46. K
2. G	17. D	32. H	47. C
3. D	18. J	33. B	48. K
4. H	19. D	34. H	49. A
5. D	20. F	35. D	50. G
6. J	21. C	36. F	51. B
7. C	22. J	37. D	52. H
8. H	23. D	38. G	53. E
9. B	24. G	39. D	54. K
10. G	25. C	40. H	55. D
11. B	26. K	41. D	56. F
12. K	27. E	42. F	57. A
13. B	28. G	43. B	58. H
14. H	29. C	44. H	59. D
15. D	30. F	45. E	60. H

Reading Test

1. C	11. D	21. B	31. B
2. H	12. J	22. G	32. F
3. B	13. C	23. B	33. D
4. G	14. J	24. F	34. H
5. C	15. B	25. B	35. B
6. H	16. F	26. H	36. G
7. A	17. B	27. B	37. A
8. G	18. J	28. H	38. H
9. B	19. D	29. B	39. B
10. H	20. G	30. H	40. H

Science Reasoning Test

1. B	11. A	21. B	31. B
2. G	12. G	22. F	32. F
3. A	13. C	23. C	33. B
4. J	14. G	24. J	34. J
5. A	15. C	25. D	35. B
6. H	16. J	26. G	36. G
7. B	17. A	27. A	37. A
8. H	18. J	28. J	38. F
9. C	19. B	29. D	39. D
10. H	20. H	30. J	40. G

Scoring Your ACT Practice Test

To score your practice test, total the number of correct answers for each section. Don't subtract any points for questions attempted but missed, as there is no penalty for guessing. This score is then scaled from 1 to 36 for each section and then averaged for the all-important composite score. The average score is approximately 18.

For Your Own Benefit

To figure out your **percentage right** for each test, use the following formulas.

English Test

$$\frac{\text{Number right}}{75} \times 100 = \underline{\hspace{1.5cm}} \%$$

Mathematics Test

$$\frac{\text{Number right}}{60} \times 100 = \underline{\hspace{1.5cm}} \%$$

Reading Test

$$\frac{\text{Number right}}{40} \times 100 = \underline{\hspace{1.5cm}} \%$$

Science Reasoning Test

$$\frac{\text{Number right}}{40} \times 100 = \underline{\hspace{1.5cm}} \%$$

Practice Test 2 Analysis Sheet

	Possible	Completed	Right	Wrong
English Test	75			
Mathematics Test	60			
Reading Test	40			
Science Reasoning Test	40			
Overall Totals	215			

Analysis/Tally Sheet for Problems Missed

One of the most important parts of test preparation is analyzing **why** you missed a problem so that you can reduce the number of mistakes. Now that you've taken the practice test and checked your answers, carefully tally your mistakes by marking them in the proper column.

Reason for Mistake				
	Total Missed	Simple Mistake	Misread Problem	Lack of Knowledge
English Test				
Mathematics Test				
Reading Test				
Science Reasoning Test				
Total				

Reviewing the above data should help you determine **why** you're missing certain problems. Now that you've pinpointed the type of errors you made, take the next practice test, focusing on avoiding your most common types of errors.

COMPLETE ANSWERS AND EXPLANATIONS FOR PRACTICE TEST 2

Answers to English Test

1. **A.** The singular possessive "its" is correct here. The spelling "it's" is the contraction of "it is."

2. **J.** If the "who" is preserved, the sentence has no main verb, only a verb in a relative clause. The subject of the sentence ("number") needs a main verb to make the sentence complete.

3. **D.** The paragraph is greatly improved if this sentence is left out. It might have followed the opening sentence as an example, but the paragraph moves on to its real subject, the American scientists, in the second sentence. As it stands, the third sentence is now an interruption.

4. **H.** This shortest version of the phrase is the best choice. To omit the phrase altogether would completely change the meaning of the sentence.

5. **A.** As in question 4, the shortest version is again the best choice, and omission changes the meaning of the sentence.

6. **J.** The distinction between "all over" and "throughout" is a red herring here. Both are acceptable. The error is the verb tense. The paragraph has so far used only the past tense. There's no reason to shift to the present tense in this sentence.

7. **D.** The sentence begins a new subject, the Moscow response to the American scientists, and a new paragraph should begin with this sentence. Whether the prepositional phrase "from Moscow" precedes or follows "the response" isn't important.

8. **J.** In the relative clause, the subject is "authorities," the verb is "had imprisoned," and the object of the verb is "whom," the objective case. The comma should set off the clause because it's nonrestrictive.

9. **C.** The issues here are idiom and metaphor. You untie a knot or sever it, and these metaphors can be used to mean to end an impasse. But the idiom with the word "deadlock" is to "break" or to "release."

10. **H.** The adverbial form is needed to modify the adjective "Moslem" (or "Muslim"). By omitting the adverb, choice **J.** changes the meaning.

11. **D.** The singular "was expected" is needed with the singular subject "harvest." Choices **B.** and **C.** aren't grammatically wrong, but they change the meaning of the sentence.

12. **J.** The phrase must include "as" twice. If the phrase "if not smaller than" is left out, the incompleteness of "as small the previous year's" is very easy to see.

13. **A.** "Dearth" is a singular noun meaning shortage. The parenthetical "as usual" should be wholly set off by commas.

14. **J.** The sentence begins with a phrase ("Even as a small child") that will dangle unless the noun or pronoun that it modifies follows immediately. It is the "I," not "cooking," who had been a small child, so **J.** is the only possible correct answer.

15. **A.** The sentence is correct as it's written. The changes save words but they change the meaning. The real subject is what's suitable for a girl, not what's interesting.

16. **H.** Strictly speaking, this sentence is a fragment. But in informal writing like this passage, authors will often deliberately ignore rules of grammar to give the prose naturalness. The use of "Anyway" at the beginning of the next sentence also works to give the prose a relaxed tone.

17. **A.** The past perfect tense, to express an action completed before the past tense ("was") later in the sentence is correct. Choice **B.** is the same tense using the passive, which isn't wrong, but given a choice between active and passive, take the active. It will be at least one word shorter.

18. **H.** The series should be parallel (**G.** isn't) and punctuated with commas. Choice **J.** isn't wrong, but it's wordier than **H.**

19. **B.** The best punctuation of this phrase is "that" with no comma, since the clause is restrictive. But by omitting the pronoun altogether, the problem of punctuation is solved and words are saved.

20. **F.** The best word here is "though," to indicate the difference between then and now. The "and" suggests a continuity, not a change.

21. **D.** All of the first three devices are used in the paragraph. There are no similes.

22. **J.** Like the opening of the first sentence of the first paragraph, this initial phrase dangles, seeming to say that "cooking" had two years of college. By using the simple prepositional phrase of **J.**, you eliminate the implied but unstated "I was," which makes choices **F.**, **G.**, and **H.** dangling phrases.

23. **C.** The dash is the better way to set off this interruption.

24. **J.** The preferred idiom is "different from" rather than "different than." Although you should always be alert for ways to get rid of unneeded words, be sure that cutting out a word doesn't alter the meaning, as in choice **G.**

25. **C.** The introductory phrase here should be followed by a comma.

26. **H.** The sentence has established a pattern by using the phrases "in crisp vegetables . . . ," "in Russian history" and "by the problems of nutrition . . . ." To maintain the parallel, use choice **H.** The original version is wordy as well as not parallel. The other choices are briefer but lose the balanced phrasing.

27. **A.** The passage is written in a relaxed, conversational style, one that would certainly admit a word like "snooty" in place of the more formal "conceited." Both are legitimate English words. In this context, the livelier word is the better choice. Note the use of the word "posh" later in this paragraph, a similar choice of level of diction.

28. **G.** Choice **G.** is the most concise and direct way of ordering all the elements of the sentence. The other versions repeat words.

29. **C.** By using the parallel nouns ("astronaut," "president," "Justice"), choice **C.** maintains parallelism and uses fewer words.

30. **J.** This sentence illustrates indirect discourse. If the quotation had been direct, she would have said, "You . . ."

31. **B.** None of the other three choices is at all appropriate.

32. **F.** The paragraphs are in a logical, chronological order.

33. **B.** The paragraph uses the past tense, so the correct verb form here is "rose." The "more" is unnecessary, as "rose" means "increased."

34. **H.** As written, the sentence is muddled and the "they" can't be identified. In choice **G.**, the adjective "reported" and in **J.**, the adjective "reportedly" are unclear or misleading. Choice **H.** clarifies the confusion.

35. **B.** The main verb of the sentence ("was arrested") is a passive in the past tense. Since he was seen before he was arrested, the form of the verb "spot" should indicate an action earlier than that of the main verb.

36. **J.** Since the clause about the package presents different information, it's clearer as an independent sentence. The basic verb tense of the paragraph is the past ("arrived").

37. **C.** The passage is clearer if this sentence begins the second paragraph. The first paragraph tells of two arrests, with details about the first. The second paragraph deals wholly with the second arrest.

38. **H.** The problem in this sentence is placing modifiers near what they modify. It's "Marshall," not the "deputy," who is armed with a handgun and knife, so that prepositional phrase must be close to "armed." The "who" clause shouldn't be set off by commas, and there should be an apostrophe in "sheriff's."

39. **A.** To "commandeer" is to seize by force and is the best choice of word here. The "of" isn't needed.

40. **H.** The participial phrase that begins this sentence dangles unless the word it modifies ("the suspect") follows the comma. Choice **J.** corrects the dangling participle but changes from the tense of the other verbs in the paragraphs.

41. **C.** A case could be made on both sides of the new paragraph question. Separated, both paragraphs are short. Both do deal with Marshall. In any event, the noun "spokesman" must be changed to a plural in the absence of any article ("the" or "a"), so the verb must be the plural "were."

42. **H.** In the "who" clause, the subject is "they," the verb is "have been pursuing," and the object of this verb is "whom," in the objective case.

43. **D.** The phrase "committing the crime" must be closer to the word it modifies ("he") or rephrased. It's now another dangling participle. Adding "while" or "when" doesn't change the error. Choice **D.** gets rid of the participle.

44. **J.** Another dangling modifier. By adding a subject to the phrase ("he is"), the problem is corrected.

45. B. Although there are one or two details that could be called biographical, this is much more obviously a sample of news writing.

46. F. Although all of the four answers are grammatical, the original version is clear and more concise.

47. A. Here the shorter versions don't say exactly what the original longer version says. The economists are concerned with changing the law to allow an increase in interest rates. The briefer versions leave out the issue of "allowing."

48. J. This sentence has no real connection with the concerns of either paragraph. The passage is improved if the sentence is omitted.

49. A. Choices **B.** and **C.** are dangling participles. To omit the opening phrase is to remove essential information from the sentence, although the sentence will still make grammatical sense.

50. J. The commas make the sentence clearer.

51. B. The comma is helpful here. Choice **D.** is wordy.

52. H. The third sentence is a question; the fourth is an incomplete sentence that answers the question but doesn't use a metaphor.

53. B. This is an editorial piece, written chiefly to criticize economists who argue for deregulation. Although the subject is economics, the passage isn't really economic analysis so much as it is using a few economic facts to make a case against a political position.

54. F. Reading through the rest of the paragraph will show that the past tense is used throughout. If possible, a subject and its verb should be kept together, so there's no reason to move the adverb between them as in choice **J.**

55. C. The opening phrase should be separated from "the book." The past tense singular is the correct verb form.

56. H. The clause is nonrestrictive and should be set off by a comma. In the clause, the subject is "the writer," the verb is "appeared to rank," and the object of this verb is "whom." So the objective "whom" should be used.

57. A. The diction of the series is correct as it stands, and the series is properly punctuated with commas.

58. G. The adjective that fits best here is "objectionable," which means disagreeable or offensive. The point is that the book attracted interest because of its criticism of women.

59. A. The author has moved from the book itself (Paragraph 1) to its reception. The sentence should begin the second paragraph.

60. F. The passage is written in the past tense. Since the sentence uses the preposition "by" ("by the ladies"), the use of "welcome" would be unidiomatic. We say "welcome to," "welcomed by."

61. A. The punctuation in the passage is correct. The phrase "or affect to love" is parenthetical and should be set off by commas. The verb "affect" means to feign (compare "affectation"), while the verb "effect" means to bring about.

62. **F.** Choices **G.** and **J.** alter the meaning. The punctuation in the passage is correct.

63. **A.** The verb "ascertain" means to find out and is appropriate here. There's no reason to use three or four words to accomplish what one word can.

64. **H.** All things being equal, the active verb is less wordy than the passive.

65. **B.** The passage is the opening of a Victorian novel, George Meredith's *The Ordeal of Richard Feverel* (1859).

66. **J.** The "usual" here modifies the adjective "conservative," not the noun "business people," so the adverb "usually" should be used.

67. **C.** This clause needs a main verb—one that's consistent with "has . . . doubled" in the second half of the sentence. Choices **A.**, **B.**, and **D.** are all participles, not main verbs.

68. **J.** The phrase "and this is" isn't wrong, but it's a wordy construction. The word "state" is evidently a diction error for "rate."

69. **D.** The sentence isn't closely connected to the rest of the paragraph. The passage is improved if this sentence is left out.

70. **G.** If the reader doesn't know how long a stay this bill represents (one day? one month?), it's much less meaningful. None of the information of choices **F.**, **H.**, or **J.** would make this statistic more significant.

71. **A.** The author has chosen the adjective "dismal" to express a personal view of the situation. To omit this important adjective is to alter the effect of the paragraph.

72. **H.** Choice **J.** changes the meaning of the sentence. The antecedent of "that" is the plural "pressures," so the verb must be the plural "restrain."

73. **D.** The context should make it clear that "incentive," that is, a motive or encouragement, is the right word here.

74. **F.** The meaning here of the adjective is money-saving ("economizing"), not the same thing as "economic" or "economics."

75. **D.** The problem here is the mixture of metaphors. There's a "key," a "blocking," a "sky-rocket," and a "spiral" all in the same clause. Choices **A.** and **B.** are only slightly better. Choice **D.** gets rid of the metaphors.

Answers to Mathematics Test

1. **C.** The answer to this problem is a weighted average, which is found as follows.

$$\frac{(20)(80)+(50)(60)+(30)(40)}{100}=\frac{5,800}{100}=58\%$$

2. **G.** If 25% is lost, 75%, or ¾, remains. So

$$\frac{5}{8}\times\frac{4}{5}\times\frac{3}{4}=?$$

Simplifying gives an answer of $\frac{3}{8}$.

3. **D.** If the linear measure is in the ratio of 3 to 4, the areas are in the ratio of 9 to 16.

So, $\frac{9}{16}=\frac{36}{x}$

Therefore, $\frac{(16)(36)}{9}=64$

4. **H.** Since $f(g(3))$, working inside to outside gives

$g(x)=x^2-2$

$g(3)=3^2-2$

$g(3)=9-2$

$g(3)=7$

Next, $f(g(3))=f(7)$

And since $f(x)=2x+4$

then $f(7)=2(7)+4$

$=14+4$

$=18$

5. **D.** To determine the next numbers in the sequence, use differences between pairs of consecutive numbers.

$5+1=6$

$6+2=8$

$8+3=11$

$11+4=15$

Continuing this process,

$15+5=20$

$20+6=26$

$26+7=33$

$33+8=41$

$41+9=50$

Another method of solution is to notice that the tenth number in this sequence would be the sum of the integers 1 through 9 and the starting number of 5. The formula for finding the sum of the integers from 1 to n is

$$\frac{n(n+1)}{2}$$

So if $n = 9$, the tenth number in the sequence is $5 + 45 = 50$.

6. J. If x represents Tony's age now,

$$x + 6 = 2(x - 4)$$
$$x + 6 = 2x - 8$$
$$x = 14$$

So Tony's age now is 14, and in 4 years he will be 18.

7. C. Two hundred toys are worth under \$5.00, $(140 + 60)$. So the probability of choosing one of these toys is 200 out of a total of 500 toys, or $^{200}\!/_{500} = \frac{2}{5}$

8. H. Since the collection contains 50 coins, you can use x and $50 - x$ as the quantity of quarters and dimes, respectively. So

$$25x + 10(50 - x) = 710$$
$$25x + 500 - 10x = 710$$
$$15x = 210$$
$$x = 14$$

Since the number of quarters is 14, the number of dimes is $50 - 14$, or 36. The difference is 22.

9. B. Start solving at the bottom right with the fraction $\frac{3}{3+3}$ and continue as follows.

$$3 + \cfrac{3}{3 + \cfrac{3}{3 + \cfrac{3}{3 + 3}}}$$

$$= 3 + \cfrac{3}{3 + \cfrac{3}{3 + \cfrac{3}{6}}}$$

$$= 3 + \cfrac{3}{3 + \cfrac{3}{3\frac{1}{2}}}$$

$$= 3 + \cfrac{3}{3 + \cfrac{3}{\frac{7}{2}}}$$

$$= 3 + \cfrac{3}{3 + \frac{6}{7}}$$

$$= 3 + \frac{3}{3\frac{6}{7}}$$

$$= 3 + \frac{3}{\frac{27}{7}}$$

$$= 3 + \frac{21}{27}$$

$$= 3\frac{21}{27} = 3\frac{7}{9}$$

10. G. Distance equals rate times time. If you travel 10 miles per hour for y hours, you've traveled $10y$ miles. If you travel y miles per hour for 10 hours, you've also traveled $10y$ miles. So you traveled $20y$ miles all together.

11. B. Statement II is correct, since the measures of angle x and angle z add up to the measure of a line. Statement I is correct, since the two lines aren't parallel and meet on the left. The lower line can be rotated clockwise, or the top line can be rotated counterclockwise, or a combination of these. In each case, the measure of $\angle x$ is greater than the measure of $\angle y$. Statement III is not necessarily true all the time.

12. H. You can tabulate the data as follows.

	part of tank brand Z	part of tank brand Y
after first fill up	1	0
before second fill up	$^1/_2$	0
after second fill up	$^1/_2$	$^1/_2$
before third fill up	$^1/_4$	$^1/_4$
after third fill up	$^3/_4$	$^1/_4$
before fourth fill up	$^3/_8$	$^1/_8$
after fourth fill up	$^3/_8$	$^5/_8$

Since the tank is now full, $^3/_8$, or $37\frac{1}{2}\%$, is brand Z.

13. B. Change the question into an algebraic sentence and solve.

$$x = 0.7\% \text{ of } 30$$

$$= (.007)(30)$$

$$= 0.21$$

14. H. Change all factors to a base of 4.

$$\frac{(4^{2x})(4^{x})(2^{4x})}{(2^{6x})(4^{3x})(2^{2x})} = \frac{(4^{2x})(4^{x})(4^{2x})}{(4^{3x})(4^{3x})(4^{x})} = \frac{4^{5x}}{4^{7x}} = \frac{1}{4^{2x}}$$

15. D. The formula for combinations is, for n things taken r at a time,

$$\binom{n}{r} = \frac{n!}{r!(n-r)!}$$

Therefore, $\quad \binom{8}{3} = \frac{8!}{3!5!} = \frac{8\times7\times6\times5\times4\times3\times2\times1}{3\times2\times1\times5\times4\times3\times2\times1} = 56$

16. F. The shaded region is a trapezoid. The formula for the area of a trapezoid is

$$\left[\text{Area} = \left(\frac{b_1 + b_2}{2} \right) h \right]$$

So the area of this trapezoid is

$$\text{area} = \left(\frac{x+10}{2} \right)4 = (x+10)(2)$$
$$= 2x + 20, \text{ or } 20 + 2x$$

17. D. From the first sentence, you see that the total number of people at the party must be divisible by 6 (5:1). From the second sentence, the total must be divisible by 4 (3:1). So the total must be divisible by 6 and 4, or 12. The only number given that *isn't* divisible by 12 is 258.

18. J. Calculate the value of each.

  F. $(.5)(.3)(280) = 42$

  G. $(.33)(.7)(160) = 36.96$

  H. $(2)(.5)(30) = 30$

  J. $(3)(.4)(40) = 48$

  K. $(.6)(60) = 36$

19. D. Simplifying and factoring gives

$$\frac{12\sqrt{6} - 6\sqrt{50}}{\sqrt{72}} = \frac{12\sqrt{2}\sqrt{3} - 6\cdot5\sqrt{2}}{6\sqrt{2}}$$

and simplifying gives

$$2\sqrt{3} - 5$$

20. F. From the given information, it costs $30x$ for the first 30 kilowatt hours. So $z - 30$ kilowatt hours remain at y cents per kilowatt hour. Therefore,

$$30x + (z - 30)y = (30x) - (30y) + yz$$
$$= 30(x - y) + yz$$

21. C. Solve the 2 equations simultaneously.

$$3y + 2x = 18$$
$$y - 4x = -8$$

Multiply the first equation by 2 and add it to the second equation.

$$6y + 4x = 36$$
$$\underline{y - 4x = -8}$$
$$7y \quad\;\; = 28$$
$$\text{or } y = 4$$

Note that the only point with a y-coordinate of 4 is (3,4), choice **C**.

Substituting back into one of the original equations gives

$$3(4) + 2x = 18$$
$$12 + 2x = 18$$
$$2x = 6$$
$$x = 3$$

So (3,4) is the point.

22. **J.** You can set up a proportion, since the triangles are similar.
$$\frac{AB}{AD} = \frac{CE}{DE}$$
So,
$$\frac{AB}{18} = \frac{4}{6}$$
Therefore, $AB = 12$

23. **D.** There are 216, or $(6 \times 6 \times 6)$, ways of rolling 3 dice. Of these, there are 3 ways of rolling a 4. So, $3/216 = 1/72$.

24. **G.** The point of intersection of these 2 graphs has an x-coordinate of -1. Substitute -1 into the equation and solve for y.

$$y + 4 = 2x^2$$
$$y + 4 = 2(-1)^2$$
$$y + 4 = 2$$
$$y = -2$$

25. **C.** Solve simultaneously.

$$6x - 3y = 30$$
$$4x + y = 2$$

Multiply the bottom equation by 3 and add the 2 equations together.

$$6x - 3y = 30$$
$$\underline{12x + 3 = 6}$$
$$18x \quad\quad = 36$$
$$x = 2$$

Substituting 2 for x in one of the original equations gives $y = -6$. So the sum of x and y is $2 + (-6) = -4$.

26. **K.** Based on the information in the figure, use the Pythagorean theorem to find the missing side, x.

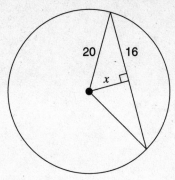

$$x^2 + 16^2 = 20^2$$

$$x^2 + 256 = 400$$

$$x^2 = 400 - 256$$

$$x^2 = 144$$

$$x = 12$$

27. **E.** To get a ratio of $\frac{3}{7}$, divide both numbers by 7, leaving

$$x = \frac{3y}{7}$$

and then divide by y, giving

$$\frac{x}{y} = \frac{3}{7}$$

28. **G.** Multiplying each term by the lowest common denominator, $4y$, you get

$$12 + 8 = 3y$$

$$20 = 3y$$

Dividing each side by 3 gives $y = 6\frac{2}{3}$

29. **C.** Because the coordinates of the midpoint are the average of the endpoints, you have the following.

Let (a,b) be the coordinates of the missing endpoint. Since no two points given as choices have the same first (or second) coordinates, it's necessary to find only the first *or* second coordinate.

So $\dfrac{(a)+(x)}{2} = 3x$ and $\dfrac{(b)+(y)}{2} = -3y$

Therefore, $a + x = 6x$ and $b + y = -6y$

So, $a = 5x$ and $b = -7y$

So the coordinates are $(5x, -7y)$.

30. F. Let x = Jane's weight. Then $2x + 12$ = Tim's weight. Therefore,

$$x + 2x + 12 = 135$$
$$3x + 12 = 135$$
$$3x = 135 - 12$$
$$x = 41$$

So Tim's weight is $(2)(41) + 12 = 94$

31. A. Given that

$$\left(\frac{1}{3+i}\right)\left(\frac{3-i}{3-i}\right) = \frac{3-i}{9-i^2} = \frac{3-i}{10}$$

32. H. When you multiply, you add exponents. The product of 2 negative numbers is a positive number. Rearranging and simplifying gives

$$\left(5x^2 y\right)\left(-2xy^2\right)\left(-3y^4\right) = (5)(-2)(-3)\left(x^2\right)(x)(y)\left(y^2\right)\left(y^4\right) = 30x^3 y^7$$

33. B. First calculate the discount. Ten percent of $40.00 is $4.00. Subtract this discount from the normal price of $40.00, giving $36.00 after the discount. The 10% tax is calculated on this $36.00 amount, or $3.60. Add this $3.60 to $36.00, giving $39.60.

34. H. The number 8 is the geometric mean between 4 and x. Therefore, $\frac{4}{8} = \frac{8}{x}$ thus $x = 16$. Thus $\overline{AC} = 20$.

35. D. Set up an equation: $6a + 2p = 3a + 6p$. Thus, $3a = 4p$

Multiplying both sides by 3 gives $9a = 12p$. So the answer must be **D.**

36. F. Since x and z are complementary, $x = 90 - z$. Since x and y are supplementary, $x = 180 - y$. So, $180 - y = 90 - z$, and solving for z, $z = y - 90$.

37. D. Rounding off the numbers gives $\sqrt{2500/100}$ which reduces to $\sqrt{25} = 5$

38. G. If the term -100 were at the end, the answer would be -50 (Take the series in pairs, each pair being equal to -1. There are 50 pairs.) Since the -100 is missing at the end, add 100 to -50 giving 50.

39. D. Count 2 surfaces for each edge where cubes are connected. Don't forget the 6 surfaces for the 3 cubes on the top of the first layer.

40. H. Divide the first inequality by 2, giving $6 < x < 9$. Divide the second inequality by 3, giving $-3 < y < 2$. If you add these 2 inequalities, you see that statement I is true. If you multiply the first inequality by -1, you get $-6 > -x > -9$ or $-9 < -x < -6$. Now adding the two inequalities gives $-12 < y - x < -4$. So statement II is true.

41. D. To find the mean, average the 6 scores (add the scores and then divide by the number of scores). The median is the middle score when the scores are in order from lowest to highest or highest to lowest. With an even number of scores, the median is the average of the 2 middle scores. Putting the scores in order,

$20, 32, 36, 40, 42, x$

Since the 5 answer choices are each greater than the first 5 scores, the median must be the average of 36 and 40, or 38. Multiplying 38 times 6 gives the sum of the 6 needed numbers.

$$38 \times 6 = 228$$

Since the sum of the first 5 numbers is 170, the sixth number must be 58. You can also work this problem by plugging in from the answer choices.

42. F. If x represents the smallest number, then the 3 numbers can be represented by

$$x + (x + 2) + (x + 4) = 2x + 15$$
$$3x + 6 = 2x + 15$$
$$x = 9$$

So the numbers are 9, 11, and 13, which total 33. Again, you could use a trial-and-error method of working from the answers. In this particular problem, only 33, choice **F.**, can be obtained by adding 3 consecutive odd numbers.

43. B. Solving, $\dfrac{\left(5^2 + 5\right)\left(5^3 + 5^2\right)}{5^2} = \dfrac{(30)(150)}{25} = 180$

44. H.

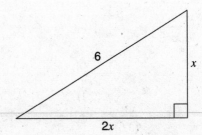

If the shortest side of the triangle is x, using the Pythagorean theorem,

$$x^2 + (2x)^2 = 6^2$$
$$x^2 + 4x^2 = 36$$
$$5x^2 = 36$$
$$x^2 = \frac{36}{5}$$
$$x = \sqrt{\frac{36}{5}}$$
$$x = \frac{\sqrt{36}}{\sqrt{5}}$$
$$x = \frac{6}{\sqrt{5}}$$

Now multiplying by $\dfrac{\sqrt{5}}{\sqrt{5}}$

$$x = \frac{\sqrt{6}}{\sqrt{5}} \times \frac{\sqrt{5}}{\sqrt{5}} = \frac{6\sqrt{5}}{5}$$

Since the third side is twice the second side, the answer is $\dfrac{12\sqrt{5}}{5}$

45. E.

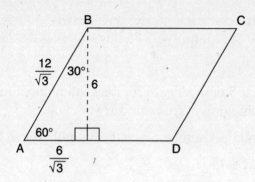

Using the 30° –60° –90° relationship in a right triangle, you can see that the slant height is $\frac{12}{\sqrt{3}}$, which can be changed to $4\sqrt{3}$

$$\left(\frac{12}{\sqrt{3}}\cdot\frac{\sqrt{3}}{\sqrt{3}}=\frac{12\sqrt{3}}{3}=4\sqrt{3}\right)$$

So the perimeter is $4\sqrt{3}+4\sqrt{3}+8+8=8\left(2+\sqrt{3}\right)$

46. K.

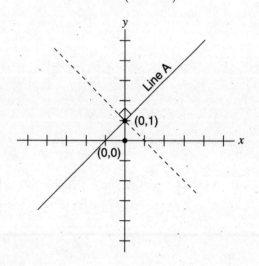

Use the point slope formula.

$y = mx + b$ (where the slope $m = \frac{3}{4}$)

A perpendicular line has a slope that is the negative reciprocal of ¾, which is –⅘. This leaves the equation as

$$y=-\frac{4}{3}x+1$$

You know that the y-intercept is 1, since the line passes through (0,1). The slope is the negative reciprocal. Now multiply through by 3.

$$3y=-4x+3$$

Then add $-4x$ to both sides giving

$$4x+3y=3$$

47. C. If x is the angle, then $(90 - x)$ is its complement and $(180 - x)$ is its supplement. So,

$$180 - x = 4(90 - x)$$
$$180 - x = 360 - 4x$$
$$3x = 180$$
$$x = 60$$

48. K. Multiply by $\dfrac{\sqrt{3}}{\sqrt{3}}$

$$\frac{\left(\sqrt{5}+2\right)}{\sqrt{3}} \cdot \frac{\sqrt{3}}{\sqrt{3}} = \frac{\sqrt{15}+2\sqrt{3}}{3}$$

49. A. Since the slope of the line between (4,2) and (9,7) is 1, the line can be extended in both directions giving the following diagram.

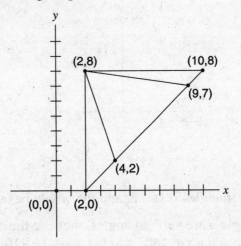

There are now several triangles. The large right triangle has an area of 32. The 2 smallest triangles have areas of 4 and 8. Subtract these from 32, giving 20.

50. G.

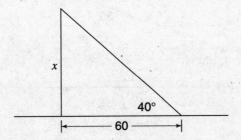

Since $\tan 40° = \dfrac{x}{60}$

then $x = 60 \tan 40°$

51. B. The hexagon is made up of 6 equilateral triangles, each having side length of 48/6 = 8.

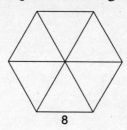

The area of an equilateral triangle is $\frac{1}{2}$ the base times the height. The triangle is a $30° - 60° - 90°$ right triangle with the sides in the ratio of $1:2:\sqrt{3}$. So the area of each equilateral triangle is

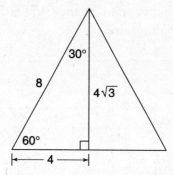

$$A = \frac{1}{2} \times \left(8\right) \times 4\sqrt{3}$$

So the area of one of the triangles is $16\sqrt{3}$, and the whole hexagon is $96\sqrt{3}$

52. H. Since angle a and angle b are vertical angles, they are the same size. So angle $b = 50°$. Since angle b and angle c add up to $160°$, angle c must be $110°$. So angle d, which is supplementary to angle c, must be $70°$.

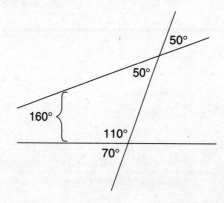

53. E. If Fernando averaged 60 on his first 4 tests, then his total points must have been 240. In order to average 70 on 5 tests, the total must be 350. So he must score 110 on the fifth test.

54. K. If r is the radius and s is an edge of the square, you could equate the areas.

$$\left(\begin{array}{l} \text{Area of circle} = \pi r^2 \\ \text{Area of square} = s^2 \end{array}\right)$$

$$\pi r^2 = s^2$$

Dividing by r^2, $\pi = \dfrac{s^2}{r^2}$

Taking the square root, $\dfrac{s}{r} = \sqrt{\pi}$

Now you have a ratio of side to radius. Then multiply both sides by 4 and divide both sides by 2π. Simplify.

$$\frac{\text{perimeter of square}}{\text{circumference of circle}} = \frac{4s}{2\pi r} = \frac{4\sqrt{\pi}}{2\pi} = \frac{2\sqrt{\pi}}{\pi}$$

55. D. Proceed as follows. Multiply both the numerator and denominator by p^2. This gives

$$\frac{9p^2 - 1}{3p^2 - p}$$

$$= \frac{(3p + 1)(3p - 1)}{p(3p - 1)}$$

$$= \frac{3p + 1}{p}$$

56. F. The distance around the track is equal to 2 straight sections plus the circumference of the circle.

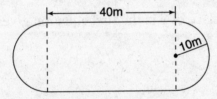

So, $\quad 40 + 40 + (2)(10\pi) = 80 + 20\pi = 20(4 + \pi)$

57. A. Solve as follows.

$$\frac{\left(m^6 n\right)^{-2}\left(mn^{-2}\right)^3}{\left(m^{-2} n^{-2}\right)^{-2}} = \frac{m^{-12} n^{-2} m^3 n^{-6}}{m^4 n^4}$$

$$= \frac{m^{-9} n^{-8}}{m^4 n^4}$$

$$= \frac{1}{m^{13} n^{12}}$$

58. H.

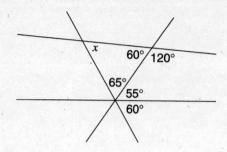

Since ∠y is supplementary to 120° it must be 60°. And ∠z plus 55° plus 60° add up to a straight angle of 180°. So ∠z is 65°. Since the 3 angles of a triangle add up to 180°, ∠x must be 55°.

59. D. Use the definition of a tangent.

$$\tan\theta = \frac{\text{opposite side}}{\text{adjacent side}}$$

$$\tan 34° = \frac{50}{x}$$

$$x = \frac{50}{\tan 34°}$$

60. H. Two equations are represented.

½x = 2y + 6

y = x + 9

Now, substituting x + 9 in place of y in the first equation gives

½x = 2(x + 9) + 6

Simplifying gives

½x = 2x + 18 + 6

or ½x = 2x + 24

Multiplying through by 2 gives

x = 4x + 48

Adding −4x to each side gives

−3x = 48

And dividing by −3 leaves x = −16

Plugging back into one of the original equations,

y = x + 9

y = (−16) + 9 = −7

So the larger value is −7. Using another method, the 2 equations could be written like this.

$\frac{1}{2}x - 2y = 6$

$x - y = -9$

Multiply the first equation by −2, giving $-x + 4y = -12$, and add the first equation to the second equation, $x - y = -9$, which gives

$3y = -21$ or $y = -7$

So, $x = -16$. The larger value is −7.

Answers to Reading Test

1. **C.** The two are father and son. The son narrates the passage after not having seen his father for some time. The relationship is made clear in lines 44–46, 57–59, and 80.

2. **H.** There are references to a door and a window through which the father has entered his son's room (lines 1 and 32–34), making it clear that the scene is indoors, ruling out choice **F.** The reference to a candle in line 32 sets the scene at night, eliminating choice **J.** Choice **G.** might seem reasonable, but nothing in the passage indicates the season.

3. **B.** The speaker corrects his first expression ("I reckoned I was scared . . . but . . . I was mistaken," lines 4–6). Although terrified of his father in the past (choice **A.**), here he is only startled. There is no suggestion anywhere in the passage that he is pleased (choice **C.**), and lines 1–10, as well as his description of his father in lines 11–29, rule out choice **D.**

4. **G.** The second paragraph, unlike the rest of the passage, uses similes ("like he was behind vines," lines 14–15; "with the top caved in, like a lid," lines 28–29) and metaphors ("a tree-toad white, a fish-belly white," lines 21–22). On the other hand, denotative language (choice **H.**), which refers to the use of words for their primary dictionary definitions, is seen throughout the passage, as is incorrect grammar (choice **J.**). Dialogue, not indirect discourse (choice **F.**), makes up most of the scene.

5. **C.** The paragraph is at pains to make the visitor repulsive (for example, "a white to make a body sick," "a white to make a body's flesh crawl"). Although he is described as dressed in rags, he isn't shown as pitiable (choice **A.**). Choice **B.** is vague and doesn't take into account the negative details in the description, and although the visitor may seem menacing, he isn't shown as mysterious (choice **D.**).

6. **H.** Throughout the passage the father is obsessed with the notion that his son now looks down on him as a social inferior. In fact, the son dislikes him for reasons having nothing to do with class. Choice **G.** is clearly incorrect; none of the father's words indicate admiration. Choice **J.**, amusement, is too gentle a word to describe the way in which the father reacts to his son's appearance; he makes fun of the boy, but in a cruel, menacing way. He expresses no interest in or surprise about his son's growth (choice **F.**).

7. **A.** The passage is a first-person ("I") narration that quotes dialogue (more than one speaker) from a scene that took place in the past. Choice **D.**, the only other answer that specifies first-person narration, is incorrect because of the second two elements. (In a monologue, there is only one speaker.)

8. **G.** Lines 61–63 reveals that the mother is dead and, like the father, was illiterate. There is no indication that she came from a higher social class (choice **H.**), that she deserted him (choice **J.**) or that she was a widow when she married him (choice **F.**).

9. **B.** Although choices **C.** and **D.** are accurate, his motive is to find out if the report is true. This is made clear in lines 74–75. Given the nature of the father's words and behavior in the passage, choice **A.** can be immediately eliminated.

10. **H.** Notice the word "EXCEPT" in this question. The father is hostile toward all choices except ignorance. His approval of ignorance is made clear in lines 55–67. His hostility toward school (choice **F.**) is shown in lines 55–61, toward decent clothes (choice **G.**) in lines 36–37 and 75–77, and toward religion in line 79.

11. **D.** Although choices **A.**, **B.**, and **C.** are mentioned in the passage, the organizing subject matter is Tutankhamen's tomb and its treasures.

12. **J.** The first paragraph raises the question of why an apparently minor boy king should have been given so rich a tomb; the second and third paragraphs propose an answer to this question. Choice **F.** is too general and doesn't logically relate the first paragraph, which is about the tomb, to the second and third paragraphs. The second and third paragraphs don't discuss the pharaohs who followed Tutankhamen but those who preceded him (choice **G.**), and although they do discuss Egyptian religion (choice **H.**), this subject isn't set up in the first paragraph.

13. **C.** The third paragraph (lines 37–39) says he died when he was about 18, and the first paragraph that he ruled until 1325 B.C. (line 5). Eighteen years before would be 1343 B.C.

14. **J.** These words reflect the attitude of the outraged priests. The author is objective in the passage, and these words indicate a bias, making choice **F.** incorrect. Nothing in the passage suggests choice **G.**, and Akhenaten (choice **H.**) wouldn't share the view suggested by these words.

15. **B.** Lines 29–30 assert that the populace "hated to give up all their beloved gods," so it can be assumed that the return of many gods was welcomed. Although choice **A.** is true, the passage doesn't cite this as the reason the people welcomed Tutankhamen. The priests recaptured their power (lines 32–33), making choice **D.** incorrect, and Upper and Lower Egypt were not reunited when Tutankhamen became the ruler (lines 47–48), making choice **C.** also incorrect.

16. **F.** Both the first and second statements are plausible inferences. See lines 28–34. The passage says nothing about Akhenaten's tomb, however (the third statement); it is Tutankhamen's tomb that is described as rich. Therefore, choices **G.**, **H.**, and **J.** are incorrect.

17. **B.** Lines 45–51 support this choice. Although both the lotus and papyrus are water plants and choice **D.** is true, this explanation isn't presented in the passage. Choice **A.** also isn't suggested in the passage, and choice **C.** is contradicted.

18. **J.** The passage suggests that the Egyptians believed in all three: a life after death (lines 72–74), magic (lines 54–56), and the efficacy (effectiveness) of the priesthood (lines 13–17). Choices **F.**, **G.**, and **H.** all exclude one of these three.

19. **D.** In the context of the passage and in view of the preceding sentence ("ankhs were seen everywhere"), the word "ubiquitous" refers to being everywhere, or "omnipresent." "Symbolic" (choice **A.**) would be a redundant adjective with the noun that follows ("emblem"). "Visionary" (choice **C.**) means seen in a vision, or impractical; neither definition is appropriate to the context. Choice **B.** might seem to fit the context, but it isn't a definition of "ubiquitous."

20. **G.** The passage neither proves (choice **J.**) nor disproves (choice **F.**) the idea that those who ruled longer and were more important historically had richer tombs. It asserts only that Tutankhamen's is, so far, "the richest" tomb that has been discovered (line 2). The passage does raise this issue (lines 5–9), making choice **H.** incorrect.

21. **B.** Choice **A.** is only a minor concern; the main thrust of the passage isn't to compare great artists. Choice **D.**, according to the passage, is untrue, as made clear in, for example, "greatness or smallness . . . determined for him at his birth" (lines 24–27). The passage asserts that choice **C.**, training an artist, can't be done (lines 45–48).

22. **G.** The passage calls their "dissimilarity" the glory of artists (lines 11–12). Choice **F.** is therefore obviously incorrect. Choice **H.** is also not a good choice. The passage indicates that artists shouldn't imitate the masters or be told they can learn to be as good, but it doesn't call great artists "poor models." Choice **J.** is irrelevant to the question; it's a reference to a poor method of training.

23. **B.** The extended comparison in the first paragraph of the passage likens the unique qualities of certain paintings to qualities of fruit. The passage opens with two questions, but the questions aren't the chief method used to develop the paragraph (choices **A.** and **C.**); the extended analogy is much more significant. Choice **D.** is simply incorrect; there is no contrast of specific and general.

24. **F.** Although the passage grants education some importance, its chief point is that the artist's talent is inborn. See lines 22–52. Choices **H.** and **J.** are conventional ideas, but they have nothing to do with the fruit analogy or with the author's central point. See lines 35–39. Similarly, choice **G.** is irrelevant.

25. **B.** The comparison is introduced in the first paragraph and further developed in the second (lines 27–44). This eliminates choice **A.** It doesn't appear in the third paragraph, eliminating choices **C.** and **D.**.

26. **H.** Although the other elements are important, inborn ability, according to this writer, is the most important factor. See lines 35–44. A commonly held idea is that hard work (choice **F.**) and an intense will to succeed (choice **G.**) are the keys to artistic success, but remember to answer the question according to the points made in the passage itself. Choice **J.** also isn't relevant to the central idea of the passage.

27. **B.** The artist refers to the virtue possessed by each master. In this context, "finish" means polish. Choice **A.** may seem reasonable, but "polish" is more appropriate. Choices **C.** and **D.** are definitions that have nothing to do with the word "finish," nor does **C.** fit the context. "Reticence" means a disinclination to speak.

28. **H.** Notice the word "EXCEPT" in the question. The idea that greatness in art can't be taught is central to the passage, and therefore choice **H.** is the only statement that the author would be likely to agree with. Choice **F.** is incorrect; although the author recognizes the merits of different artists, he states in lines 6–7 that "there is a relative merit." He would also disagree with choice **G.** (lines 52–58) and with choice **J.**; lines 29–35 indicate that factors other than birth play a role.

29. **B.** In the last paragraph, the author specifically objects to dishonesty (choice **A.**), unreality (choice **C.**), and affectation (choice **D.**). The approval of honesty and intelligibility suggests that the author wouldn't object to simplicity. See lines 59–67.

30. **H.** The last paragraph suggests teaching artists about the nobility of other artists and virtues including charity, sincerity, and honesty. The implication is that the better a person the artist is, the more likely (though "not" certain) it is that the artist's work will be good.

Lines 49–58 make a connection between character and artistic achievement, and therefore **F.** is a poor choice, as are **G.** and **H.**. The author sees great art as the "expression of the spirits of great men."

31. **B.** According to the passage, the species of fish on opposite sides of a high mountain range will, for the most part, be different (lines 1–6). Therefore, the states west of the Rockies (Oregon, California, and Washington) are likely to have species different from those in states east of the mountains, such as New York, Kentucky, and Vermont. So choices **A.**, **C.**, and **D.** are incorrect. The fish can be expected to be most similar in New York and Delaware because they are both east of the Rockies.

32. **F.** The second paragraph (lines 5–7) asserts that fish life in any two river systems is never "identical." Therefore, choices **H.** and **J.** are incorrect. Choice **G.** also is incorrect (lines 13–15: "such streams do have many species in common").

33. **D.** The pike is found north of Maryland (lines 25–28). The catfish and sunfish are found in both the North and South, but the brook trout occurs only in the South (lines 15–20 and 28–30). At least one species is wrong in choices **A, B,** and **C.**

34. **H.** It is possible that river systems that appear to be separate were connected at times because of heavy rain or snow melt (lines 36–43). Choices **F.** and **G.** aren't addressed in the passage. Choice **J.** is incorrect; fish of different species are seldom found on different sides of a mountain range because of the range itself, not because of heavy rain or melting snow.

35. **B.** Because many freshwater species can't survive in salt water, it's impossible for them to migrate to another water system by way of the ocean (lines 20–22). The first and third statements could be used to explain how species got from one system to the other, thus eliminating choices **A.**, **C.**, and **D.**

36. **G.** The best definition would be "speculation." According to the context of the passage, "conjecture" refers to a probable, but not certain, cause, ruling out choice **J.** ("assertion"). Choice **F.** doesn't fit the context; "experimentation" wouldn't be reasonable on something that had already occurred. "History" (choice **H.**) also isn't appropriate; "a matter of history" suggests that the issue is closed, but in the next sentence a theory is presented.

37. **A.** According to the last paragraph, temperature is the chief factor in limiting wider distribution of species. Of the pairs listed here, the temperatures would be most alike in New York and Rhode Island.

38. **H.** The last paragraph cites temperature (lines 50–52). Choice **J.** explains why some species can't migrate (lines 20–22), but according to the passage, temperature is a more important factor. Both choices **F.** and **G.** are environmental issues, but neither is addressed in this passage, which is concerned with the distribution of freshwater fish species.

39. **B.** Since the area most similar in temperature would be most likely to have similar species, Canada is the best answer. Choices **A.**, **C.**, and **D.** are all farther from the northeast and likely to have warmer waters.

40. **H.** Neither choice **F.** nor choice **G.** refers to fresh water, an important aspect of the subject of this passage. Choice **J.** doesn't have the geographical specificity of **H.**, and "results" aren't considered in the passage.

Answers to Science Reasoning Test

Passage I

1. **B.** Find the mark representing 70 miles on the left scale, halfway between 60 and 80. Trace rightward to the temperature line, then downward to the bottom scale. The temperature at that altitude is −15°C.

2. **G.** The stratosphere varies in temperature from −60° at its base to −10° at its top, for a total range of only 50°. The range of the troposphere is 80°, the mesosphere 70°, and the thermosphere at least 270°.

3. **A.** The mesosphere and troposphere both show lower temperatures as you move upward to higher altitudes. In contrast, the stratosphere and thermosphere both display increasing temperature with increasing altitude.

4. **J.** The troposphere has the highest air pressure because it has the most air overlying that level. The variation of air pressure is much simpler than the variation of temperature because the air pressure always decreases with increasing altitude.

5. **A.** The rise in temperature upward through the stratosphere is caused by the solar energy absorbed by oxygen molecules at that height.

Passage II

6. **H.** Since those crystals floated in bromoform, they must have a specific gravity less than 2.89. The detection of calcium proves that they must be plagioclase, not quartz or orthoclase.

7. **B.** The liquid would have a specific gravity of 3.11, which is the average of the values for bromoform and methylene iodide. In such a liquid, biotite (3.00) would float and hornblende (3.20) would sink. To separate any two crystal varieties, it is necessary to have a liquid of intermediate specific gravity.

8. **H.** The crystals must be either augite or biotite, and those crystals could be distinguished by detecting aluminum (biotite), calcium (augite), or potassium (biotite). The absence of sodium in Experiment 2 shows that the crystals could not be hornblende.

9. **C.** The x-ray fluorescence unit would be much more useful if it could measure the amount of each element detected. For example, a silicon abundance of 20% would indicate hypersthene, augite, hornblende, or plagioclase.

10. **H.** The crystals must be either olivine or hypersthene because they have a specific gravity over 3.33 and contain silicon. Unfortunately, olivine and hypersthene have the same elements present and therefore cannot be distinguished with the available apparatus.

11. **A.** Possessing a liquid of specific gravity less than 2.89 would permit separating light crystals like plagioclase, quartz, and orthoclase. Choice C. is not the best because such a liquid could be prepared by mixing bromoform and methylene iodide, without any acetone.

Passage III

12. **G.** Sparrows feed on insects and grasses. Notice the arrows pointing from insects and grasses toward sparrows.

13. **C.** The longest food chain on the diagram is as follows: grasses to mice to snakes to weasels to wolves to worms.

14. **G.** According to the diagram, the only animals that eat snakes are hawks and weasels. You must look at the arrows in the diagram to answer the questions dealing with the network of feeding relationships.

15. **C.** Grasses and trees are the only independent organisms in the diagram. The photosynthesis of green plants derives energy from solar radiation. All the animals in the diagram are dependent on plants or other animals.

16. **J.** Because weasels eat rabbits, a reduction in the number of weasels would allow an increase in the number of rabbits. Since bobcats eat rabbits, the larger number of rabbits would allow an increase in the number of bobcats. Probably the chicken farmers do not realize that their weasel campaign could lead to more bobcats.

Passage IV

17. **A.** Within the range 0.2 to 0.7 atmosphere, it is true that lower current accompanied the lower pressure. Since the current is proportional to the amount of ionization, the prior hypothesis holds for that pressure range.

18. **J.** The battery must be present to produce the current that flows around the circuit. Both meters must be present to measure the current and pressure. However, the vacuum pump could be switched off during one reading; it would have to be switched back on to lower the pressure for the next reading.

19. **B.** At lower pressures, there are fewer molecules of nitrogen and oxygen in the flask. So the alpha particles encounter fewer molecules to ionize. The lower degree of ionization results in lower currents.

20. **H.** The polonium-210 loses half of its radioactivity every 138 days. If the researcher tried to repeat the experiment 90 days later, there would be fewer alpha particles emitted from the source and less ionization of the air. The new current readings would be lower than the original readings.

21. **B.** In the pressure range 0.7 to 1.0 atmosphere, the energy of the alpha particles must be completely dissipated in ionization. This would explain why a change of pressure within that range doesn't affect the degree of ionization. It's as high as it can get.

22. **F.** The lining of the flask serves only to conduct current. Substituting aluminum—or any other metal—for the silver should not affect the results. Choice **G.** affects the degree of ionization, **H.** affects the current directly, and **J.** affects the number of alpha particles.

Passage V

23. C. The passage mentions Rhesus monkeys as an example of primates. Apes and monkeys are closely related to humans (also classified as primates), so any primate studies would be relevant to human medicine.

24. J. The statement that few of the animals infected with a supposedly carcinogenic virus actually develop cancers certainly suggests that the case for animal tumor viruses is still uncertain.

25. D. In the second sentence, Scientist 1 mentions connective-tissue cancer. The following sentence says that cancers of the same kind are called sarcomas.

26. G. If new cancer-causing agents are discovered frequently, then all causes of cancer are not known. Perhaps viruses are a "new" cause yet to be discovered.

27. A. It is accepted that cancer may be spread by injecting cancerous cells into a healthy animal. To show that some other material in the injected liquid causes the cancer, it is necessary to filter out any cancer cells.

28. J. Scientist 2 doesn't accept the evidence that some animal cancers are induced by viruses. If Scientist 1 could prove that point, it would weaken the argument presented by Scientist 2.

29. D. Scientist 1 implies that only minuscule virus particles are small enough to pass through the filters and remain in the liquid to be injected. If some material besides viruses also passes through the filters, that other material could be the cause of the induced cancers.

Passage VI

30. J. Iodine forms the weakest bond with hydrogen. The I–H bond has an energy of 71 kcal/mole, less than the value for F–H, Cl–H, or Br–H. It is important to realize that a high energy means a strong bond, while a low energy means a weak bond.

31. B. The Cl–Cl bond has a higher energy and thus is stronger than the F–F, Br–Br, or I–I bonds. Notice that the question refers to molecules with two identical halogen atoms.

32. F. Carbon tetrachloride would be the largest molecule because the central carbon atom is surrounded by four large chlorine atoms. Look at Table 1 to see the relative sizes of the atoms. Molecules G and J aren't as large as carbon tetrachloride because they have only one large halogen atom.

33. B. In the chlorine bonds, Cl–O is 12 kcal/mole less than Cl–F. By analogy, Br–O should be about 12 kcal/mole less than the value for Br–F, which is 57 kcal/mole. 57 minus 12 equals 45 kcal/mole.

34. J. The best generalization of bond strengths is that the bond is stronger (energy is higher) between smaller atoms. This explains the very strong bonds with the small hydrogen atom and the very weak bonds with the large iodine atom.

Passage VII

35. **B.** The experiments were performed to explore the possibility of gene exchange. The assump-tion is that the abilities to synthesize leucine and cystine are governed by different genes.

36. **G.** Since all organisms need amino acids for metabolism and growth, yet the normal bacteria don't require an external source, they must manufacture the needed amino acids internally.

37. **A.** Since the L strain needed a supply of leucine to survive, that strain can't manufacture its own leucine. However, the strain didn't require any cystine nutrient, so it must be able to synthesize its own cystine.

38. **F.** The C strain would have been able to grow if supplied with a source of cystine because it could synthesize all other needed amino acids. The L strain wouldn't have been able to grow under those conditions because it still had no possible means of obtaining the leucine that it needed but couldn't synthesize.

39. **D.** At least one of the two strains must have received the gene, permitting it to manufacture the one amino acid that it originally couldn't manufacture. However, the mere growth of colonies doesn't reveal whether the growing bacteria come from the C strain, the L strain, or both strains.

40. **G.** It is possible that the mutant C and L strains lacked more than one gene apiece compared to the normal bacteria. If they each were missing the same gene (plus other missing genes to differentiate the two strains), then even perfect gene exchange in the mixed culture couldn't have reconstructed the normal gene set. This difficult question is best answered by eliminating the other three choices.

ANSWER SHEETS FOR PRACTICE TEST 3

ENGLISH TEST

1 Ⓐ Ⓑ Ⓒ Ⓓ	26 Ⓕ Ⓖ Ⓗ Ⓙ	51 Ⓐ Ⓑ Ⓒ Ⓓ
2 Ⓕ Ⓖ Ⓗ Ⓙ	27 Ⓐ Ⓑ Ⓒ Ⓓ	52 Ⓕ Ⓖ Ⓗ Ⓙ
3 Ⓐ Ⓑ Ⓒ Ⓓ	28 Ⓕ Ⓖ Ⓗ Ⓙ	53 Ⓐ Ⓑ Ⓒ Ⓓ
4 Ⓕ Ⓖ Ⓗ Ⓙ	29 Ⓐ Ⓑ Ⓒ Ⓓ	54 Ⓕ Ⓖ Ⓗ Ⓙ
5 Ⓐ Ⓑ Ⓒ Ⓓ	30 Ⓕ Ⓖ Ⓗ Ⓙ	55 Ⓐ Ⓑ Ⓒ Ⓓ
6 Ⓕ Ⓖ Ⓗ Ⓙ	31 Ⓐ Ⓑ Ⓒ Ⓓ	56 Ⓕ Ⓖ Ⓗ Ⓙ
7 Ⓐ Ⓑ Ⓒ Ⓓ	32 Ⓕ Ⓖ Ⓗ Ⓙ	57 Ⓐ Ⓑ Ⓒ Ⓓ
8 Ⓕ Ⓖ Ⓗ Ⓙ	33 Ⓐ Ⓑ Ⓒ Ⓓ	58 Ⓕ Ⓖ Ⓗ Ⓙ
9 Ⓐ Ⓑ Ⓒ Ⓓ	34 Ⓕ Ⓖ Ⓗ Ⓙ	59 Ⓐ Ⓑ Ⓒ Ⓓ
10 Ⓕ Ⓖ Ⓗ Ⓙ	35 Ⓐ Ⓑ Ⓒ Ⓓ	60 Ⓕ Ⓖ Ⓗ Ⓙ
11 Ⓐ Ⓑ Ⓒ Ⓓ	36 Ⓕ Ⓖ Ⓗ Ⓙ	61 Ⓐ Ⓑ Ⓒ Ⓓ
12 Ⓕ Ⓖ Ⓗ Ⓙ	37 Ⓐ Ⓑ Ⓒ Ⓓ	62 Ⓕ Ⓖ Ⓗ Ⓙ
13 Ⓐ Ⓑ Ⓒ Ⓓ	38 Ⓕ Ⓖ Ⓗ Ⓙ	63 Ⓐ Ⓑ Ⓒ Ⓓ
14 Ⓕ Ⓖ Ⓗ Ⓙ	39 Ⓐ Ⓑ Ⓒ Ⓓ	64 Ⓕ Ⓖ Ⓗ Ⓙ
15 Ⓐ Ⓑ Ⓒ Ⓓ	40 Ⓕ Ⓖ Ⓗ Ⓙ	65 Ⓐ Ⓑ Ⓒ Ⓓ
16 Ⓕ Ⓖ Ⓗ Ⓙ	41 Ⓐ Ⓑ Ⓒ Ⓓ	66 Ⓕ Ⓖ Ⓗ Ⓙ
17 Ⓐ Ⓑ Ⓒ Ⓓ	42 Ⓕ Ⓖ Ⓗ Ⓙ	67 Ⓐ Ⓑ Ⓒ Ⓓ
18 Ⓕ Ⓖ Ⓗ Ⓙ	43 Ⓐ Ⓑ Ⓒ Ⓓ	68 Ⓕ Ⓖ Ⓗ Ⓙ
19 Ⓐ Ⓑ Ⓒ Ⓓ	44 Ⓕ Ⓖ Ⓗ Ⓙ	69 Ⓐ Ⓑ Ⓒ Ⓓ
20 Ⓕ Ⓖ Ⓗ Ⓙ	45 Ⓐ Ⓑ Ⓒ Ⓓ	70 Ⓕ Ⓖ Ⓗ Ⓙ
21 Ⓐ Ⓑ Ⓒ Ⓓ	46 Ⓕ Ⓖ Ⓗ Ⓙ	71 Ⓐ Ⓑ Ⓒ Ⓓ
22 Ⓕ Ⓖ Ⓗ Ⓙ	47 Ⓐ Ⓑ Ⓒ Ⓓ	72 Ⓕ Ⓖ Ⓗ Ⓙ
23 Ⓐ Ⓑ Ⓒ Ⓓ	48 Ⓕ Ⓖ Ⓗ Ⓙ	73 Ⓐ Ⓑ Ⓒ Ⓓ
24 Ⓕ Ⓖ Ⓗ Ⓙ	49 Ⓐ Ⓑ Ⓒ Ⓓ	74 Ⓕ Ⓖ Ⓗ Ⓙ
25 Ⓐ Ⓑ Ⓒ Ⓓ	50 Ⓕ Ⓖ Ⓗ Ⓙ	75 Ⓐ Ⓑ Ⓒ Ⓓ

MATHEMATICS TEST

1 Ⓐ Ⓑ Ⓒ Ⓓ Ⓔ	26 Ⓕ Ⓖ Ⓗ Ⓙ Ⓚ	51 Ⓐ Ⓑ Ⓒ Ⓓ Ⓔ
2 Ⓕ Ⓖ Ⓗ Ⓙ Ⓚ	27 Ⓐ Ⓑ Ⓒ Ⓓ Ⓔ	52 Ⓕ Ⓖ Ⓗ Ⓙ Ⓚ
3 Ⓐ Ⓑ Ⓒ Ⓓ Ⓔ	28 Ⓕ Ⓖ Ⓗ Ⓙ Ⓚ	53 Ⓐ Ⓑ Ⓒ Ⓓ Ⓔ
4 Ⓕ Ⓖ Ⓗ Ⓙ Ⓚ	29 Ⓐ Ⓑ Ⓒ Ⓓ Ⓔ	54 Ⓕ Ⓖ Ⓗ Ⓙ Ⓚ
5 Ⓐ Ⓑ Ⓒ Ⓓ Ⓔ	30 Ⓕ Ⓖ Ⓗ Ⓙ Ⓚ	55 Ⓐ Ⓑ Ⓒ Ⓓ Ⓔ
6 Ⓕ Ⓖ Ⓗ Ⓙ Ⓚ	31 Ⓐ Ⓑ Ⓒ Ⓓ Ⓔ	56 Ⓕ Ⓖ Ⓗ Ⓙ Ⓚ
7 Ⓐ Ⓑ Ⓒ Ⓓ Ⓔ	32 Ⓕ Ⓖ Ⓗ Ⓙ Ⓚ	57 Ⓐ Ⓑ Ⓒ Ⓓ Ⓔ
8 Ⓕ Ⓖ Ⓗ Ⓙ Ⓚ	33 Ⓐ Ⓑ Ⓒ Ⓓ Ⓔ	58 Ⓕ Ⓖ Ⓗ Ⓙ Ⓚ
9 Ⓐ Ⓑ Ⓒ Ⓓ Ⓔ	34 Ⓕ Ⓖ Ⓗ Ⓙ Ⓚ	59 Ⓐ Ⓑ Ⓒ Ⓓ Ⓔ
10 Ⓕ Ⓖ Ⓗ Ⓙ Ⓚ	35 Ⓐ Ⓑ Ⓒ Ⓓ Ⓔ	60 Ⓕ Ⓖ Ⓗ Ⓙ Ⓚ
11 Ⓐ Ⓑ Ⓒ Ⓓ Ⓔ	36 Ⓕ Ⓖ Ⓗ Ⓙ Ⓚ	
12 Ⓕ Ⓖ Ⓗ Ⓙ Ⓚ	37 Ⓐ Ⓑ Ⓒ Ⓓ Ⓔ	
13 Ⓐ Ⓑ Ⓒ Ⓓ Ⓔ	38 Ⓕ Ⓖ Ⓗ Ⓙ Ⓚ	
14 Ⓕ Ⓖ Ⓗ Ⓙ Ⓚ	39 Ⓐ Ⓑ Ⓒ Ⓓ Ⓔ	
15 Ⓐ Ⓑ Ⓒ Ⓓ Ⓔ	40 Ⓕ Ⓖ Ⓗ Ⓙ Ⓚ	
16 Ⓕ Ⓖ Ⓗ Ⓙ Ⓚ	41 Ⓐ Ⓑ Ⓒ Ⓓ Ⓔ	
17 Ⓐ Ⓑ Ⓒ Ⓓ Ⓔ	42 Ⓕ Ⓖ Ⓗ Ⓙ Ⓚ	
18 Ⓕ Ⓖ Ⓗ Ⓙ Ⓚ	43 Ⓐ Ⓑ Ⓒ Ⓓ Ⓔ	
19 Ⓐ Ⓑ Ⓒ Ⓓ Ⓔ	44 Ⓕ Ⓖ Ⓗ Ⓙ Ⓚ	
20 Ⓕ Ⓖ Ⓗ Ⓙ Ⓚ	45 Ⓐ Ⓑ Ⓒ Ⓓ Ⓔ	
21 Ⓐ Ⓑ Ⓒ Ⓓ Ⓔ	46 Ⓕ Ⓖ Ⓗ Ⓙ Ⓚ	
22 Ⓕ Ⓖ Ⓗ Ⓙ Ⓚ	47 Ⓐ Ⓑ Ⓒ Ⓓ Ⓔ	
23 Ⓐ Ⓑ Ⓒ Ⓓ Ⓔ	48 Ⓕ Ⓖ Ⓗ Ⓙ Ⓚ	
24 Ⓕ Ⓖ Ⓗ Ⓙ Ⓚ	49 Ⓐ Ⓑ Ⓒ Ⓓ Ⓔ	
25 Ⓐ Ⓑ Ⓒ Ⓓ Ⓔ	50 Ⓕ Ⓖ Ⓗ Ⓙ Ⓚ	

READING TEST

1 Ⓐ Ⓑ Ⓒ Ⓓ		26 Ⓕ Ⓖ Ⓗ Ⓙ
2 Ⓕ Ⓖ Ⓗ Ⓙ		27 Ⓐ Ⓑ Ⓒ Ⓓ
3 Ⓐ Ⓑ Ⓒ Ⓓ		28 Ⓕ Ⓖ Ⓗ Ⓙ
4 Ⓕ Ⓖ Ⓗ Ⓙ		29 Ⓐ Ⓑ Ⓒ Ⓓ
5 Ⓐ Ⓑ Ⓒ Ⓓ		30 Ⓕ Ⓖ Ⓗ Ⓙ
6 Ⓕ Ⓖ Ⓗ Ⓙ		31 Ⓐ Ⓑ Ⓒ Ⓓ
7 Ⓐ Ⓑ Ⓒ Ⓓ		32 Ⓕ Ⓖ Ⓗ Ⓙ
8 Ⓕ Ⓖ Ⓗ Ⓙ		33 Ⓐ Ⓑ Ⓒ Ⓓ
9 Ⓐ Ⓑ Ⓒ Ⓓ		34 Ⓕ Ⓖ Ⓗ Ⓙ
10 Ⓕ Ⓖ Ⓗ Ⓙ		35 Ⓐ Ⓑ Ⓒ Ⓓ
11 Ⓐ Ⓑ Ⓒ Ⓓ		36 Ⓕ Ⓖ Ⓗ Ⓙ
12 Ⓕ Ⓖ Ⓗ Ⓙ		37 Ⓐ Ⓑ Ⓒ Ⓓ
13 Ⓐ Ⓑ Ⓒ Ⓓ		38 Ⓕ Ⓖ Ⓗ Ⓙ
14 Ⓕ Ⓖ Ⓗ Ⓙ		39 Ⓐ Ⓑ Ⓒ Ⓓ
15 Ⓐ Ⓑ Ⓒ Ⓓ		40 Ⓕ Ⓖ Ⓗ Ⓙ
16 Ⓕ Ⓖ Ⓗ Ⓙ		
17 Ⓐ Ⓑ Ⓒ Ⓓ		
18 Ⓕ Ⓖ Ⓗ Ⓙ		
19 Ⓐ Ⓑ Ⓒ Ⓓ		
20 Ⓕ Ⓖ Ⓗ Ⓙ		
21 Ⓐ Ⓑ Ⓒ Ⓓ		
22 Ⓕ Ⓖ Ⓗ Ⓙ		
23 Ⓐ Ⓑ Ⓒ Ⓓ		
24 Ⓕ Ⓖ Ⓗ Ⓙ		
25 Ⓐ Ⓑ Ⓒ Ⓓ		

SCIENCE REASONING TEST

1 Ⓐ Ⓑ Ⓒ Ⓓ		26 Ⓕ Ⓖ Ⓗ Ⓙ
2 Ⓕ Ⓖ Ⓗ Ⓙ		27 Ⓐ Ⓑ Ⓒ Ⓓ
3 Ⓐ Ⓑ Ⓒ Ⓓ		28 Ⓕ Ⓖ Ⓗ Ⓙ
4 Ⓕ Ⓖ Ⓗ Ⓙ		29 Ⓐ Ⓑ Ⓒ Ⓓ
5 Ⓐ Ⓑ Ⓒ Ⓓ		30 Ⓕ Ⓖ Ⓗ Ⓙ
6 Ⓕ Ⓖ Ⓗ Ⓙ		31 Ⓐ Ⓑ Ⓒ Ⓓ
7 Ⓐ Ⓑ Ⓒ Ⓓ		32 Ⓕ Ⓖ Ⓗ Ⓙ
8 Ⓕ Ⓖ Ⓗ Ⓙ		33 Ⓐ Ⓑ Ⓒ Ⓓ
9 Ⓐ Ⓑ Ⓒ Ⓓ		34 Ⓕ Ⓖ Ⓗ Ⓙ
10 Ⓕ Ⓖ Ⓗ Ⓙ		35 Ⓐ Ⓑ Ⓒ Ⓓ
11 Ⓐ Ⓑ Ⓒ Ⓓ		36 Ⓕ Ⓖ Ⓗ Ⓙ
12 Ⓕ Ⓖ Ⓗ Ⓙ		37 Ⓐ Ⓑ Ⓒ Ⓓ
13 Ⓐ Ⓑ Ⓒ Ⓓ		38 Ⓕ Ⓖ Ⓗ Ⓙ
14 Ⓕ Ⓖ Ⓗ Ⓙ		39 Ⓐ Ⓑ Ⓒ Ⓓ
15 Ⓐ Ⓑ Ⓒ Ⓓ		40 Ⓕ Ⓖ Ⓗ Ⓙ
16 Ⓕ Ⓖ Ⓗ Ⓙ		
17 Ⓐ Ⓑ Ⓒ Ⓓ		
18 Ⓕ Ⓖ Ⓗ Ⓙ		
19 Ⓐ Ⓑ Ⓒ Ⓓ		
20 Ⓕ Ⓖ Ⓗ Ⓙ		
21 Ⓐ Ⓑ Ⓒ Ⓓ		
22 Ⓕ Ⓖ Ⓗ Ⓙ		
23 Ⓐ Ⓑ Ⓒ Ⓓ		
24 Ⓕ Ⓖ Ⓗ Ⓙ		
25 Ⓐ Ⓑ Ⓒ Ⓓ		

CUT HERE

English Test

Time: 45 Minutes

75 Questions

Directions: In the left-hand column, you will find passages in a "spread-out" format with various words and phrases underlined and numbered. In the right-hand column, you will find a set of responses corresponding to each underlined portion. If the underlined portion is correct standard written English, is most appropriate to the style and feeling of the passage, or best makes the intended statement, mark the letter indicated "NO CHANGE." If the underlined portion is not the best choice given, choose the one that is. For these questions, consider only the underlined portions; assume that the rest of the passage is correct as written. You will also see questions concerning parts of the passage or the whole passage. Choose the response you feel is best for these questions.

Passage I

What's in a Name?

[1]

Have you heard the one about the student who said to the science teacher, "I can understand how astronomers discovered the positions and distances of the stars, but how did they <u>find out their names"</u>. The names of the
1
stars, as the teacher explained, tell us more about life on earth than about the stars. The stars that we have fitted together to form the

1. **A.** NO CHANGE
   B. find out their names?"
   C. find out their names"?
   D. find out their names?".

constellations <u>that outline</u> dippers or archers or
₂
twins would appear totally unconnected with

each other <u>from any perspective in space other</u>
₃
<u>than ours.</u>
₃

[2]

Named after gods and goddesses, beasts and
heroes, <u>the inhabitants of the Northern</u>
₄
<u>Hemisphere have found words for their con-</u>
₄
<u>stellations in Greek mythology.</u> It was chiefly
₄
the Greeks who long ago gave these stars their

names. <u>Additionally,</u> many of the stars of the
₅
Southern Hemisphere, which were not named
until much later, reflect more modern notions
such as instruments or geometric figures.
Similarly, the rocks on Mars that have acquired
names in the 1990s are called after late
twentieth-century cartoon characters, like
Calvin and Hobbes. [6]

2. **F.** NO CHANGE
   G. that outlined
   H. outlining the form of
   J. making an outline of

3. **A.** NO CHANGE
   B. in any perspective in space different than ours.
   C. from any other perspective in space that is different than ours.
   D. from any perspective in space.

4. **F.** NO CHANGE
   G. the Greek myths gave names to the constellations of the Northern Hemisphere.
   H. the Northern Hemisphere called the constellations after Greek myths.
   J. the constellations of the Northern Hemisphere have names from Greek myth.

5. **A.** NO CHANGE
   B. On the other hand,
   C. And
   D. Yet,

6. The writer has decided NOT to end the second paragraph with this sentence:

   One of the Mars rocks is named Scooby Doo.

   Which of the following is the best reason NOT to use this sentence?

   F. The sentence is unrelated to the rest of the paragraph.
   G. The sentence is ungrammatical.
   H. The paragraph has given other examples of the names of rocks.
   J. Scooby Doo is a silly name and out of place in a serious essay.

[3]

As we approach the year 2000 and draw near to the turn of the century, many people expect a significant planetary event, as if the idea of the millennium had some important meaning throughout the universe. They fail to see that any point we name in time is arbitrary meaningless in the natural world. The whole

idea of time is totally and completely created by humans. All any date can tell us is the

position of the earth in relation to the sun. As the names of the stars, numbers are useful fictions that make relationships easier to grasp or

to remember. [11]

7. A. NO CHANGE

B. As we approach and draw near to the year 2000,

C. As the year 2000, the turn of the century, draws near,

D. As we approach the year 2000,

8. F. NO CHANGE

G. arbitrary, meaningless

H. arbitrary: meaningless

J. arbitrary; meaningless

9. A. NO CHANGE

B. completely the total creation of humans.

C. wholly created by humans.

D. created by humans.

10. F. NO CHANGE

G. Like the names of the stars,

H. As are the names of the stars,

J. Similar to the names of the stars,

11. Which of the following best explains the connection of Paragraph 3 to Paragraphs 1 and 2?

A. Paragraphs 1 and 2 are concerned with space, and Paragraph 3 is concerned with time.

B. All deal with the names we have given to places and times.

C. All deal with words that are conveniences but have no effect on the natural world.

D. Paragraphs 1 and 2 present the natural world as it appears from the earth, while Paragraph 3 encompasses spiritual meaning

GO ON TO THE NEXT PAGE

[4]

At times scientists have explained the natural world by giving names to something <u>that never did and never will exist.</u> <u>For example</u>
₁₂
₁₃

<u>"phlogistin,"</u> the element invented to explain
₁₃

combustion, is now discredited. <u>In spite of this,</u> valuable terms have also been invented
₁₄
long before their reality could be proven.

<u>The truth is that terms like</u> "molecule" or
₁₅
"quark" were once just figures of speech. Only years later did scientists have the technology to

prove their reality. 16

12. **F.** NO CHANGE
   G. that never will and never has existed.
   H. that will never, and has never existed.
   J. that never existed, and it never will exist.

13. **A.** NO CHANGE
   B. "Phlogistin" for example
   C. For example, "phlogistin,"
   D. For example, phlogistin

14. **F.** NO CHANGE
   G. However,
   H. Additionally
   J. Thus,

15. **A.** NO CHANGE
   B. The fact is that terms like
   C. It is true that terms like
   D. Terms like

Question 16 asks about the essay as a whole.

16. The writer is thinking of changing the title of the essay to reflect its contents more clearly. Which of the following is the most effective?
   F. The Names of the Constellations
   G. The Limited Usefulness of Names and Numbers
   H. Real and Imaginary Names in Science
   J. The Historical Development of Scientific Naming

Passage II

For more than a year, I have helped to pay for my education by working as a waiter. It is not an easy job, and it is made harder by the fact that there are so few good clients. To a waiter, a good client is a customer who is

well-mannered, thoughtful, and has feelings.

just like the same qualities a diner looks for in a good waiter. The patron-waiter relationship

should be reciprocity.

[1] Good clients should be prepared to wait a little longer if a restaurant is very busy. [2] He should be prepared to make all their needs clear from the beginning so the waiter doesn't have to make extra trips when they forget to say they want mushrooms with their steak; salad dressing on the side; and a hamburger well done. [3] Extra trips to one table will slow

17. A. NO CHANGE
  B. the fact that so few good clients.
  C. the fact that there being so few good clients.
  D. the scarcity of good clients.

18. F. NO CHANGE
  G. is sensitive,
  H. sensitive,
  J. has understanding,

19. A. NO CHANGE
  B. the same qualities
  C. just the qualities as
  D. the exact same qualities as

20. F. NO CHANGE
  G. reciprocated
  H. reciprocal
  J. reciprocally

21. A. NO CHANGE
  B. He or she should
  C. He ought to
  D. They should

22. F. NO CHANGE
  G. steak—salad dressing on the side—
  H. steak, salad dressing on the side,
  J. steak: salad dressing on the side:

GO ON TO THE NEXT PAGE

down the service at all the other tables at a
waiter's station. 23

Good customers listen when the waiter explains that the turkey burger takes longer to
cook and don't keep calling the waiter over to
ask "why it is taking so long?" If the waiter
tells them the chili is very spicy today, they

don't order the chili and they send it back
when they find out it's too hot for their delicate
stomachs.

Many restaurants train their staff to try to
sell certain foods or drinks. 26 Customers
should be patient with a sales pitch, since it is

part of a waiter's job. At the same time, waiters
must try to sound interested, even though they

23. The writer is considering adding the
following sentence to this paragraph:

Most patrons know that a waiter is
concerned with the size of his or her tip.

This sentence should:

A. be added after Sentence 1.
B. be added after Sentence 2.
C. be added after Sentence 3.
D. NOT be added to this paragraph.

24. F. NO CHANGE
G. "why it is taking so long"?
H. why it is taking so long?
J. why it is taking so long.

25. A. NO CHANGE
B. sending
C. send
D. will send

26. The writer wishes to add the following to
this sentence after the word "drinks":

usually those that produce more profit or
are in oversupply

In addition to the period at the end of the
sentence, this clause should be
punctuated with:

F. a colon at the beginning.
G. a hyphen at the beginning.
H. parentheses at the beginning and end.
J. a semicolon at the beginning.

27. A. NO CHANGE
B. Conversely,
C. However,
D. Therefore,

are saying something they have said thirty times that day. 28

Though probably willing to forgive some rudeness if the tip is large, and resentful of even the most thoughtful customer who leaves

no tip at all, <u>money is not the only thing a good waiter thinks about.</u> Any regular job that has
29

no rewards <u>except</u> money eventually becomes
30
unsatisfying, and waiters who dislike their jobs will, in time, communicate their discontent to their customers. Sullen waiters will soon have unhappy clients. 31

Passage III

Each of the following paragraphs are given a number in brackets. The paragraphs may or may not be in the most logical order. Items 47 and 48 ask you questions about the essay as a whole.

28. The writer wishes to add the adverb "already" to this sentence. It should be placed:

   F. after "saying"
   G. after "have"
   H. after "said"
   J. after "times"

29. A. NO CHANGE
   B. money should not be the only focus of a good waiter.
   C. the size of the tip is not all that a good waiter thinks about.
   D. good waiters think about more than the size of the tips.

30. F. NO CHANGE
   G. accept
   H. with the exception of
   J. excepting

31. The writer is considering adding the following conclusion to this essay:

   And waiters with too many unhappy clients will soon have no job at all.

   Should the writer add this conclusion?

   A. Yes, because it adds a personal note to this personal essay.
   B. Yes, because it effectively completes a logical argument.
   C. No, because it is redundant.
   D. No, because it fails to support the point of the final paragraph.

GO ON TO THE NEXT PAGE

The Flight of the Butterfly

[1]

Like many birds, the familiar orange and black monarch butterfly <u>are migratory.</u> Each year more than a hundred million of the insects fly from their summer homes in Washington, Oregon, and northern California to areas in southern California and northern <u>Mexico meanwhile,</u> the monarchs on the eastern side of the Rockies fly more than two thousand miles from Canada and the United States to mountain retreats in Mexico. Covering as much as sixty miles a day, <u>the seasonal winds propel the butterflies more than</u> the power of their wings.

[2]

[1] The migration raises a question that scientists are trying to answer. [2] How does this tiny creature find its way to a wintering place several thousand miles <u>away?</u> [3] Larger migratory animals like those of the great herds of Africa learn their routes from their parents or older members of the species. [4] So do birds like the swallow, or sea animals like the salmon or sea turtle. [5] These creatures are helped to navigate by the position of the sun,

32. F. NO CHANGE
   G. is migratory.
   H. migrate.
   J. are migrating.

33. A. NO CHANGE
   B. Mexico, meanwhile,
   C. Mexico—Meanwhile,
   D. Mexico. Meanwhile,

34. F. NO CHANGE
   G. the seasonal wind propels the butterfly more than
   H. the butterflies are propelled more by the seasonal winds than by
   J. and, propelled by the seasonal winds that carry the butterflies more than

35. A. NO CHANGE
   B. away.
   C. away!
   D. away?" (And add a quotation mark at the beginning of the sentence)

by the magnetic field, <u>or scenting</u> certain sea
₃₆

currents. [6] <u>Consequently,</u> an older generation
₃₇

of butterflies cannot instruct a younger one. 38

[3]

The life span of a monarch is likely to be less than ninety days, so the butterflies that make their way down south are several

generations away from their ancestors <u>who</u>
₃₉
<u>make</u> the same trip. <u>Not anyone</u> of the insects
₃₉   ₄₀
that flew north in the spring is alive to fly south in the fall. How, then, do they find their way to Mexico from points as far apart as Maine and Wisconsin?

36. **F.** NO CHANGE

G. or by the scent of

H. or recognizing the scent of

J. or the scenting of

37. **A.** NO CHANGE

B. But

C. Also,

D. At the same time,

38. Assume that the writer must eliminate one of the six sentences in this paragraph. Which of the following is the best choice and reason?

F. OMIT Sentence 2 because the rest of the paragraph is about animals other than the butterfly.

G. OMIT Sentence 3 because it is not about the butterfly, the subject of the essay.

H. OMIT Sentence 5 because it is not related to the topic of one generation's instruction of the next.

J. OMIT Sentence 6 because it fails to answer the question that the paragraph raises.

39. **A.** NO CHANGE

B. who are making

C. that made

D. making

40. **F.** NO CHANGE

G. Not one

H. No one

J. Nobody

GO ON TO THE NEXT PAGE

[4]

Insect ecologists have recently established that the monarchs use the position of the sun to determine their flight direction on long-distance journeys. [41] But this cannot be the whole story. It may be that the butterfly can sense the force lines of the earth's magnetic field and use this as navigational information.

Another theory raises the possibility that maybe the butterflies find directional clues in the changing length of the days. How so small an insect can find its way is still a mystery? We still do not have an explanation. [44]

41. The author wishes to add the detail explaining that this discovery was made "at the University of Kansas." The best place to add this phrase is

A. after "ecologists"

B. after "recently"

C. after "established"

D. after "sun"

42. F. NO CHANGE

G. theorizes that

H. proposes the idea that

J. is

43. A. NO CHANGE

B. mystery.

C. mystery. (And also change the capital on "We" to lowercase)

D. mystery? (And also change the capital on "We" to lowercase)

44. The writer is considering deleting the last sentence of this paragraph. Which of the following is the best choice and reason?

F. Do NOT delete the sentence because it effectively summarizes the paragraph.

G. Do NOT delete the sentence because it answers the question raised in the sentence that precedes it.

H. Delete the sentence because it is irrelevant.

J. Delete the sentence because it is repetitive.

[5]

Twenty-five years ago, scientists <u>in an acci-₄₅</u> <u>dent discovered</u> the location of the monarch ₄₅ butterflies' winter home. An American ento- mologist found millions of the North American insects in the Sierra Chinchua. Now butter- flies, like birds, are tagged, watched, and counted by hundreds of American schoolchild- ren and college students. One insect (tagged in Virginia) <u>arrived, safe</u> in Mexico, more than ₄₆ two thousand miles away. Exactly how it found its way there is still uncertain.

47

45. A. NO CHANGE
   B. made the accidental discovery of
   C. accidental discovered
   D. accidentally discovered

46. F. NO CHANGE
   G. arrived safe
   H. arrived safely
   J. arrived in safety

Questions 47 and 48 ask about the essay as a whole.

47. Which of the following is the best order for the five paragraphs of this essay?
   A. 1, 2, 3, 4, 5
   B. 1, 3, 2, 4, 5
   C. 1, 3, 2, 5, 4
   D. 1, 2, 3, 5, 4

GO ON TO THE NEXT PAGE

48

48. Suppose the author has been asked to supply a one-sentence summary of this essay. Which of the following does so most effectively?

    F. Scientists have traced the migration of the monarch butterfly from Canada and the United States to locations in Mexico.

    G. Now that we know their routes, insect ecologists can trace the migrations of the monarch butterflies.

    H. Although we know, in part, how migrating butterflies find their way, we still do not fully understand the phenomenon.

    J. That a creature as small and delicate as the monarch butterfly can find its way over thousands of miles is an inspiring lesson to humans.

Passage IV

Growing up in the Midwest, <u>Sundays were</u> ₄₉ <u>very hard to take.</u> There was the thought of go-₄₉ ing back to school on Monday morning and the

homework that <u>would have to be done by me</u> ₅₀ on Sunday night. Nothing was open except, perhaps, a little convenience store, and no one

was around. <u>This made Sundays</u> always the ₅₁

same and <u>dull as dishwater.</u> ₅₂

49. A. NO CHANGE

    B. Sundays were unbearable.

    C. I used to hate Sundays,

    D. Sundays were the days I hated most.

50. F. NO CHANGE

    G. was finished

    H. I would have finished

    J. had to be finished

51. A. NO CHANGE

    B. Sundays were

    C. Which made Sundays

    D. This resulted in Sundays being

52. F. NO CHANGE

    G. dull and boring.

    H. real dull.

    J. dull.

After church, I'd have to get in the car and drive the ten miles to pick up my grandmother. Then, on the way home, I'd have to listen to her complaints about how she disliked our car and my clothes or <u>my haircut turned her off.</u>
53

After dropping her off, <u>I'd get back</u> in the car
54
and drive the twelve miles in the other direction to pick up my other grandmother and my <u>grandfather on</u> the way home he would com-
55
plain about politics or taxes or my haircut. 56

The Sunday dinner was good. However, I don't like big meals in the middle of the day because I always feel overstuffed and sleepy all afternoon long. The talk at dinner was usually <u>along the same lines like</u> the conversations
57

53. A. NO CHANGE
   B. my haircut rubbed her the wrong way.
   C. was offputting.
   D. (End the sentence with a period after haircut.)

54. F. NO CHANGE
   G. I get
   H. I'll get
   J. I had gotten

55. A. NO CHANGE
   B. grandfather, and on
   C. grandfather, on
   D. grandfather: on

56. The writer is considering the following edits. Which of the four edits would result in the most effective paragraph?
   F. Eliminate the use of the repeated word "I'd," a contraction that does not belong in a formal essay.
   G. Eliminate the repetition of phrases like "get . . . in the car" or the references to haircut.
   H. Include some details that present the grandparents more favorably.
   J. Leave the content of the paragraph unchanged.

57. A. NO CHANGE
   B. along the same lines as were
   C. like
   D. as

GO ON TO THE NEXT PAGE

in the car — how taxes were too high, how the
              58
government was stupid, or how my hair was

too long. 59

[1] An hour or two after Sunday dinner, I'd
get back in the car and take my grandparents
home. [2] Every week there would be an argu-
                                    60
ment about who would go first. [3] They all
              60
wanted to stay longer, although I could never
figure out why. [4] The late afternoon drives
were just like the morning's, except it was

58. F. NO CHANGE

    G. car. How

    H. car how

    J. car; how

59. The writer is considering adding the following text after the first sentence of this paragraph:

Usually there was a roast of chicken, beef, or pork, potatoes and gravy, two or three vegetables, hot homemade rolls, and a large Jello salad. For dessert, we had pie (apple mostly, but sometimes cherry or custard) or chocolate cake.

Which of the following is the most convincing reason to reject this addition?

    A. It does not add crucial information and disrupts the flow of the paragraph.

    B. It calls into question the writer's reasons for disliking Sundays.

    C. It places too much emphasis on the physical pleasures of food.

    D. It suggests that the writer is selfish and ungrateful.

60. F. NO CHANGE

    G. they're would be an argument about who would go first.

    H. there would be an argument about whom would be the first to go.

    J. they would argue about whom would go first?

darker. [5] Usually it was raining, too. [61]

By the spring of my senior year in high school, I finally realized I had no reason to dread my Sunday night homework and
Monday school days. It was better than listening to complaints about my hair. I began to look forward to my Sunday night homework when I'd be alone. And Mondays, I realized, were full of activity with friends my own age. At last I understood that Sundays were invented to make us appreciate the rest of the week.

Passage V

Nowadays, more and more high school seniors have access to the Web. Most of them don't like pulling out their old typewriters to fill out long forms. So the old paper

61. The writer is considering adding the following sentence to this paragraph:

In the car, my grandmother would whisper to my grandfather that the pie was not flaky or the meat must have cost a fortune.

If added, it should be placed after:

A. Sentence 1.

B. Sentence 2.

C. Sentence 3.

D. Sentence 4.

62. F. NO CHANGE

G. By the spring of the year in which I was a senior

H. By the time in the spring when I was a senior

J. In the springtime when I was a senior

63. A. NO CHANGE

B. They were

C. It is

D. They are

GO ON TO THE NEXT PAGE

application to college may soon be <u>as rarely as</u> the inkwell, as more and more colleges are hurrying to set up on-line application forms to be used by the fall class of applicants.

The Web page allows a school to advertise itself <u>more conveniently, more economically, and more widely</u> than a catalog. <u>Which saves</u> paper and postal costs. <u>Conversely, it</u> sends a message to potential applicants that the school is advanced technologically <u>and on the cutting edge ahead of its time.</u>

A few glitches have already appeared. Some site browsers have managed to gain access to such classified information as a school's crime reports or faculty ratings. A professor whose e-mail address may appear can be overwhelmed with questions from <u>perspective</u> applicants. Still, most colleges find the

64. F. NO CHANGE
   G. as rare as
   H. as rare used as
   J. as rare in use

65. A. NO CHANGE
   B. in a manner more convenient, more economically, and wider
   C. more conveniently, economically, and more wide
   D. more conveniently and more widely, and more economically

66. F. NO CHANGE
   G. It saves
   H. They save
   J. Saving

67. A. NO CHANGE
   B. But, it
   C. Also, it
   D. However, it

68. F. NO CHANGE
   G. and on the cutting edge, ahead of its time.
   H. and on the cutting edge.
   J. (End the sentence with a period after technologically.)

69. A. NO CHANGE
   B. prospective
   C. prescriptive
   D. proscriptive

advantages outweigh the disadvantages and have subscribed to services to set up programs that <u>permits</u> high school seniors to use a single
₇₀
web location to apply and pay application fees to several schools over the computer.

Many of the large state university systems are taking advantage of these new services. The State University of New <u>York, a system of</u>
₇₁
<u>sixty-four campuses,</u> has been online for sev-
₇₁
eral years. Online applications have quadrupled each year since the system joined the College Net service to facilitate applications from out of state.

The twenty-three-campus California State University system will soon begin to use the Web to work with students just beginning high school. <u>They hope</u> to help students plan their
₇₂
high school class work more carefully so when

they reach college <u>they will</u> be no need for
₇₃

remedial classes. <u>Through the current rate</u> of
₇₄
growth in Web use, in only a few years most of the high school seniors will complete their

70. F. NO CHANGE
    G. enables
    H. allow
    J. makes it possible for

71. A. NO CHANGE
    B. York a system of sixty-four campuses
    C. York, a system of sixty-four campuses
    D. York a system of sixty-four campuses,

72. F. NO CHANGE
    G. It hopes
    H. It is hoped
    J. Hoping

73. A. NO CHANGE
    B. they're will
    C. there will
    D. their will

74. F. NO CHANGE
    G. For the current rate
    H. At the current rate
    J. Of the current rate

GO ON TO THE NEXT PAGE

college applications without setting a pen to paper or a typewriter or licking a single stamp.

₇₅

75. **A.** NO CHANGE

   B. to paper (or a typewriter)

   C. (or a typewriter) to paper

   D. to a paper or to a typewriter

IF YOU FINISH BEFORE TIME IS CALLED, CHECK YOUR WORK ON THIS SECTION ONLY. DO NOT WORK ON ANY OTHER SECTION IN THE TEST.

Mathematics Test

Time: 60 Minutes

60 Problems

Directions: After solving each problem, choose the correct answer and fill in the corresponding space on your answer sheet. Do not spend too much time on any one problem. Solve as many problems as you can and return to the others if time permits. You are allowed to use a calculator on this test.

Note:

Unless it is otherwise stated, you can assume all of the following:

1. Figures are NOT necessarily drawn to scale.

2. Geometric figures lie in a plane.

3. The word "line" means a straight line.

4. The word "average" refers to the arithmetic mean.

1. Mike opened a new box of crackers and ate 16 of the crackers. These 16 crackers represent exactly 25% of the crackers in the box. How many crackers were there in the unopened box?

   A. 20

   B. 24

   C. 36

   D. 48

   E. 64

2. In the figure below, the 3 diameters intersect at the center of the circle. What is the measure of $\angle x$?

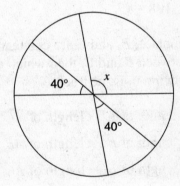

   F. 10°

   G. 40°

   H. 80°

   J. 100°

   K. 120°

GO ON TO THE NEXT PAGE

3. What is the eleventh term in the sequence $-20, -17, -14, -11, \ldots$?

A. -41

B. 3

C. 10

D. 16

E. 22

4. What value of x solves the following proportion?

$$x/3 = 4/9$$

F. $7/9$

G. $1\frac{1}{3}$

H. $6\frac{3}{4}$

J. 12

K. 108

5. If points A, B, and C are colinear and A is between B and C, then which of the following must be true?

A. length of $\overline{AB}$ < length of $\overline{AC}$

B. length of $\overline{BC}$ < length of $\overline{AB}$

C. length of $\overline{BC}$ < length of $\overline{AC}$

D. length of $\overline{AC}$ < length of $\overline{AB}$

E. length of $\overline{AB}$ < length of $\overline{BC}$

6. Dee has $42 to spend on presents. If she buys 4 books at $7.60 each, how much money does she have left?

F. $11.40

G. $11.60

H. $12.40

J. $12.60

K. $14.00

7. If $y = -5$, then what is the value of $y + 2(6 - y)$?

A. -33

B. -3

C. 3

D. 6

E. 17

8. What is the value of $-|2 - |6 - (-2)||$?

F. -6

G. -4

H. -2

J. 2

K. 4

9. A $4,500 computer is scheduled for a 12% price drop. What will be the new price?

A. $3,300

B. $3,960

C. $4,104

D. $4,446

E. $4,488

10. If $x^3 + x^2 = 250$, then what is the approximate value of x?

F. 4

G. 5

H. 6

J. 7

K. 8

11. If $-24 = -8 - y$, then $y =$?

   A. −32

   B. −16

   C. −3

   D. 16

   E. 32

12. *R* is 8 years younger than *S*, and *S* is 3 times the age of *T*. If *x* represents the age of *R*, what is the age of *T*?

(Note: All ages are in years.)

   F. $(\frac{1}{3})(x+8)$

   G. $3(x-8)$

   H. $3x+8$

   J. $3x-8$

   K. $(\frac{1}{3})(x-8)$

13. In the standard (x, y) coordinate plane, a rectangle is drawn such that one corner has coordinates of $(4,-2)$ and the center has coordinates of $(1,3)$. What is the area in square units of the rectangle?

   A. 6

   B. 15

   C. 30

   D. 60

   E. 100

14. Which of the following is equivalent to $2(x+y)-(x-y)$?

   F. $3x$

   G. $3x+3y$

   H. $x+3y$

   J. $x+y$

   K. $x-y$

15. Given $\overline{BD}$ is a median of $\triangle ABC$ below, what is the measure of $\angle ABC$?

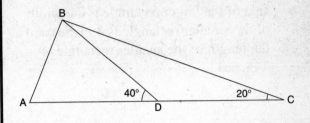

   A. 60°

   B. 70°

   C. 80°

   D. 90°

   E. 100°

16. If line *m* is perpendicular to the line $5x - 2y = -2$, what is the slope of line *m*?

   F. $-\frac{5}{2}$

   G. $-\frac{2}{5}$

   H. $\frac{2}{3}$

   J. $\frac{5}{2}$

   K. −10

17. If *x* represents the length of a pencil and $3x^2 - 10x = 8$, then $x =$?

   A. $\frac{2}{3}$

   B. $\frac{3}{2}$

   C. 4

   D. 8

   E. 10

GO ON TO THE NEXT PAGE

18. Two rectangles are similar, and the area of one is 4 times that of the other. What is the length, in inches, of the shorter side of the larger rectangle if the width of the smaller rectangle is 4 inches and the length of the smaller rectangle is 7 inches?

   F. 8

   G. 14

   H. 16

   J. 28

   K. 56

19. A stock that sold for \$32.75 3 years ago has increased in value by 30%. What is the current value of the stock rounded to the nearest dollar?

   A. \$9

   B. \$10

   C. \$42

   D. \$43

   E. \$63

20. Which of the following is a factored form of $9a^2 c - 9ac^2$?

   F. $9ac(a - c)$

   G. $(3a^2 c + 3ac^2)(3a^2 c - 3ac^2)$

   H. $9(a - c)^2$

   J. ac

   K. $a^2 c^2$

21. If $3p + 2q = 8$ and $p - 4q = 5$, then $q =$?

   A. −2

   B. −½

   C. ½

   D. 2

   E. 3

22. One kilogram is approximately 2.2 pounds. If each kilogram of fertilizer can feed 800 square feet of lawn, approximately how many pounds of fertilizer would be needed to feed 1,200 square feet of lawn?

   F. 0.7

   G. 1.5

   H. 3.0

   J. 3.3

   K. 3.7

23. The overall figure shown below is made up of congruent rectangles. What is the perimeter of the overall figure, in inches, if the area of the shaded portion is 25 square inches?

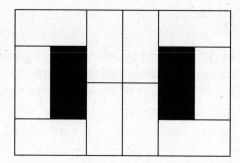

   A. 25

   B. 50

   C. 60

   D. 75

   E. 150

24. A water company charges 20 cents per day in service fees and 95 cents per 100 cubic feet of water usage. What would be the cost of 4,200 cubic feet of water usage during a 31-day month?

    F. $39.90

    G. $40.10

    H. $46.10

    J. $54.40

    K. $101.90

25. What is the area (in square meters) of the figure shown below?

    (Note: All angles are right angles and all measurements are in meters.)

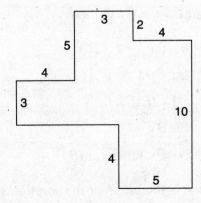

    A. 80

    B. 100

    C. 108

    D. 112

    E. 132

26. What is the graph of the solution set of $4 - y > -2$?

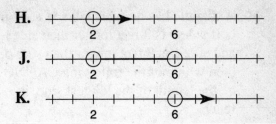

27. Which of the following fractions has the largest value?

    A. $3/7$

    B. $4/9$

    C. $5/11$

    D. $6/13$

    E. $8/17$

28. The area of a triangle can be determined if you know the lengths of the 3 sides. What is the area of a triangle in square inches if the lengths of its sides are 10 inches, 24 inches, and 26 inches?

    F. 24

    G. 60

    H. 120

    J. 125

    K. 240

29. A certain number of plants have been purchased to be planted in rows in a garden. If the plants are planted 6 plants per row, 8 plants per row, or 10 plants per row, there is always 1 plant left over. What is the minimum number of plants that were purchased?

    A. 49

    B. 61

    C. 81

    D. 121

    E. 481

GO ON TO THE NEXT PAGE

Mathematics Test

30. A triangle has its sides labeled a, b, and c. If side b is 2 feet longer than side a and side c is 3 feet longer than side b, then which of the following CANNOT be the length of the longest side, in feet?

    F. 7

    G. 9

    H. 10.5

    J. 12

    K. 13

31. If $a > 0$ and $b < 0$, then $\frac{2b}{a} + \frac{a}{b} = $?

    A. $\dfrac{a + 2b}{a + b}$

    B. $\dfrac{a + 2b}{ab}$

    C. $\dfrac{a^2 + 2b^2}{ab}$

    D. $\dfrac{2a^2 + b^2}{ab}$

    E. $\dfrac{a^2 + 4b^2}{a + b}$

32. Given the figure below, which of the following is true?

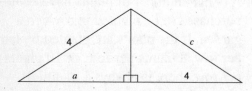

    F. $c^2 = 32 - a^2$

    G. $c^2 = a^2 - 16$

    H. $c^2 = a^2 + 32$

    J. $c = \frac{10}{a}$

    K. $c^2 = \frac{32}{a^2}$

33. The length of a rectangle is 4 inches longer than the width of the rectangle. If the width is increased by 1 inch and the length is decreased by 1 inch, how does the area of the new rectangle compare to the area of the old rectangle?

    A. There is a decrease by more than 4 square inches.

    B. There is a decrease by less than 4 square inches.

    C. They are the same.

    D. There is an increase by less than 4 square inches.

    E. There is an increase by more than 4 square inches.

34. If $\sin\theta > \cos\theta > 0$, then:

    F. $0 < \tan\theta < 1$

    G. $\tan\theta > 1$

    H. $-1 < \tan\theta < 0$

    J. $\tan\theta < -1$

    K. $\cos\theta < \tan\theta < \sin\theta$

35. What is the graph of the solution set of the inequality $|x - 2| < 3$?

    A.

    B.

    C.

    D.

    E.

36. A class of students was given a quiz consisting of 4 questions. If 25% of the class answered all 4 questions correctly, 30% answered exactly 3 questions correctly, 20% answered exactly 2 questions correctly, 10% answered exactly 1 question correctly, and 15% answered none correctly, what was the average number of questions answered correctly per student?

F. 1.8

G. 2.1

H. 2.2

J. 2.4

K. 2.7

37. In the figure below, if $BC = 8$ feet, $\angle BAC = 45°$, and $\angle BCA = 30°$ then how many feet long is AB?

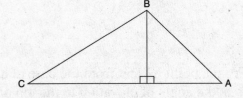

A. 4

B. $4\sqrt{2}$

C. $4\sqrt{3}$

D. $4\sqrt{6}$

E. $8\sqrt{3}$

38. The perimeter of a rectangle is 48 inches. What is the maximum possible area of the rectangle in square inches if the lengths of all 4 sides are odd integers?

F. 109

G. 135

H. 143

J. 144

K. 156

39. Given parallelogram $ABCD$ below, with $\overline{EF}$ parallel to $\overline{CD}$, what is the measure of $\angle y$?

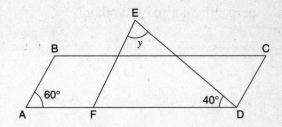

A. 60°

B. 70°

C. 80°

D. 90°

E. 100°

40. In the standard (x,y) coordinate plane, what is the x-intercept of the line $2x + 3y = -12$?

F. −12

G. −6

H. −4

J. 4

K. 6

41. If the following points were graphed on the standard number line, which one would be the closest to 7?

A. $6\sqrt{2}$

B. $2\sqrt{6}$

C. $5\sqrt{3}$

D. $3\sqrt{5}$

E. $4\sqrt{4}$

GO ON TO THE NEXT PAGE

Mathematics Test

42. If the following pair of equations represent lines drawn in the standard (x,y) coordinate plane, what must be the value of k if these 2 lines are perpendicular to each other?

$$2x + 4y = -3$$
$$kx - 2y = 6$$

   F. -8

   G. -4

   H. -1

   J. 1

   K. 4

43. What is the measure of angle θ if the supplement of θ is equal to 4 times the complement of θ?

   A. $30°$

   B. $45°$

   C. $60°$

   D. $90°$

   E. $120°$

44. If $a^2 - b^2 = -12$, and $a + b = -6$, then $a - b = ?$

   F. -18

   G. -6

   H. -2

   J. 2

   K. 6

45. If two sides of a triangle measure 9 inches and 12 inches, what must the length of the third side be, in inches, so that the area of the triangle is a maximum?

   A. $3\sqrt{3}$

   B. 10.5

   C. 15

   D. $9\sqrt{3}$

   E. $12\sqrt{2}$

46. In the standard (x,y) coordinate plane, if $(2,-4)$ and $(-4, a)$ are 2 points on a given line, then what must be the value of a if the slope of the line is -3?

   F. -2

   G. 2

   H. 10

   J. 14

   K. 22

47. From a point 62 feet from the base of a tree, the angle of elevation to the top of the tree is $38°$. What is the height, in feet, of the tree?

   A. $62 \sin 38°$

   B. $62 \cos 38°$

   C. $62 \tan 38°$

   D. $\dfrac{62}{\cos 38°}$

   E. $\dfrac{62}{\tan 38°}$

48. Two numbers have a lowest common multiple that is 10 times their greatest common factor. Which of the following could be the numbers?

   F.   4 and 30

   G.   6 and 15

   H.   8 and 22

   J.   9 and 24

   K.   12 and 40

49. If $f(x) = x^2 - x - 2$ and $g(x) = 2x - 1$, then $f(g(x)) = ?$

   A. $4x^2 - 6x$

   B. $4x^2 - 6x - 3$

   C. $4x^2 - 2x - 3$

   D. $x^2 + x - 3$

   E. $x^2 - 3x - 1$

50. Given a cube with point A and point B as centers of opposite faces of the cube, and point C as one of the corners of the face that contains point B, what is the cosine of $\angle ABC$?

   F. $\dfrac{\sqrt{3}}{3}$

   G. $\dfrac{\sqrt{2}}{2}$

   H. $\dfrac{\sqrt{2}}{3}$

   J. $\dfrac{\sqrt{3}}{2}$

   K. $\dfrac{\sqrt{6}}{4}$

51. The areas of 2 circles are in the ratio of 9 to 4. If the sum of the radii of these circles is 20π, what is the area of the larger circle?

   (Note: The radii are measured in inches, and the areas are measured in square inches.)

   A. $9\pi^2$

   B. 36π

   C. $36\pi^2$

   D. $72\pi^2$

   E. $144\pi^3$

52. In the standard (x,y) coordinate plane, 3 lines are drawn with different slopes. These 3 lines each have a y-intercept of $-b$ and have x-intercepts of -4, 6, and k, respectively. What is the value of k such that the sum of the slopes of these 3 lines is 0?

   F.   2

   G.   4

   H.   8

   J.   12

   K.   16

53. The sum of the 2 roots of the equation $y = x^2 + kx - 46$ is 0. What is the value of k?

   A. -8

   B. -4

   C.   0

   D.   4

   E.   8

GO ON TO THE NEXT PAGE

54. In the standard (x,y) coordinate plane, the line $2x + ky = a$ is parallel to the line $x - 3y = -2$ and passes through the point $(-3,4)$. What is the value of a?

   F. −30

   G. −6

   H.   6

   J. 12

   K. 20

55. If $\left| \left(\dfrac{1}{x+y} \right)(x-y) \right| > 1$, then which of the following CANNOT be true?

   A. $xy > 0$

   B. $x < 0$

   C. $x > 0$

   D. $y < 0$

   E. $y > 0$

56. If a 4-foot walkway borders a rectangular lawn that is 10 feet longer than it is wide, what is the area of the walkway, in square feet, in terms of the length of the lawn (x)?

   F. $16x + 144$

   G. $16x - 16$

   H. $4x + 16$

   J. $4x + 144$

   K. $16x - 144$

57. For which of the following values of x does $\sin 3x = \frac{1}{2}$?

   A. $\pi/18$

   B. $\pi/9$

   C. $\pi/6$

   D. $\pi/3$

   E. $\pi/2$

58. In the standard (x,y) coordinate plane, what is the equation of the line whose points are equidistant from the points $(2,4)$ and $(-4,6)$?

   F. $5x - y = -10$

   G. $3x + y = 2$

   H. $3x - y = -8$

   J. $x - 3x = -16$

   K. $x + 3y = 14$

59. One bag contains 2 red marbles and 1 white marble. A second bag contains 2 red marbles and 2 white marbles. A marble is randomly selected from the first bag and dropped into the second bag. If a marble is now randomly selected from the second bag, what is the probability that it is red?

   A. $\frac{1}{2}$

   B. $\frac{8}{15}$

   C. $\frac{5}{9}$

   D. $\frac{4}{7}$

   E. $\frac{3}{5}$

60. How many different integer values of x satisfy this inequality?

$$\frac{8}{x} < \frac{2-x}{x}$$

   F. 2

   G. 3

   H. 4

   J. 5

   K. 6

IF YOU FINISH BEFORE TIME IS CALLED, CHECK YOUR WORK ON THIS SECTION ONLY. DO NOT WORK ON ANY OTHER SECTION IN THE TEST.

Reading Test

Time: 35 Minutes

40 Questions

Directions: Each of the four passages in this test is followed by several questions. Read each passage and then choose the best answer to each question that follows the passage. Refer to the passage as often as necessary to answer the questions.

Passage I

Prose fiction: This passage is from the first chapter of Migrant Souls, *a novel by Arturo Islas (©1990 by Arturo Islas).*

In their mother's eyes, Josie Salazar knew, she and her sister Serena were more like the Indians than the Spanish ladies they were brought up to be.

(5) When they were children and growing up on the "American" side of the Mexican Texas border, it was, "Serena, get that braid out of your mouth. Do you want to be taken for an Indian?" Or,
(10) "Josie, how many times do I have to tell you that a young lady does not cross her legs like an Indian?"

Later, when they were teenagers in the late forties and still on the border, Serena
(15) was criticized for wearing clothes that were too bright and immodest and Josie was told that if her hair got any stringier because she refused to wash it every day, the Indians were going to claim her
(20) as their own and drag her off to Ysleta, or worse yet, to San Elizario, even farther into the lower valley.

Secretly, Josie longed to be dragged by anyone, to anywhere as long as it was
(25) out of her mother's house. "I wonder what life with the Indians is like?" she asked Serena, who remained silent.

Only Ofelia, the eldest of the three sisters, came close to fulfilling their
(30) mother Eduviges' dream of producing delicate and tactful young women worthy of their connection to the Angel family name and strong enough to endure the rigorous demands of marriage
(35) and motherhood. Even before the age of reason, which the Church had set at seven years old, the girls learned very quickly that their mother's side of the family—the Angel clan—was more im-
(40) portant than their father's, the plain old Salazars. Sancho Salazar, ever wary of large concepts, ignored his relatives altogether and devoted himself to his wife, his daughters, and, as often as pos-
(45) sible, to hunting and fishing in the mountains and lakes of northern Chihuahua. In that wild country, he told the girls, his Indian blood came to life and made him feel at home with the
(50) land and sky. "Don't tell your mother I said these things to you."

Ofelia ignored him when he talked about Mexico. But Serena and Josie sensed that their blood was closer to the
(55) earth than an Angel's ought to be. And except for the annual Christmas Eve get-together, they saw that their father made certain he had something else to do whenever his wife reminded him that
(60) the Angels were gathering at so-and-so's house to celebrate something or other.

GO ON TO THE NEXT PAGE

"I am not about to sit through another of those phony family exercises," Sancho said to Eduviges. "I've got more impor-
(65) tant things to do. I'm going fishing." And, kissing the girls good-bye after pitching his gear into Serapio Fuentes' beat-up Buick station wagon, he went.

Only Josie did not kiss him back and
(70) refused to keep waving along with her sisters until Serapio honked the horn one last time and turned the corner on Cotton Street. Her spirit went with Sancho and she was often thought to be unwell at
(75) most Angel family celebrations.

"Are you sick, Josie?" her aunt Mema asked. They were at their great-aunt Cuca's apartment after a baptism party for the girls' cousin Joel. "Are you miss-
(80) ing your daddy?"

Josie looked at her without blinking while Mema felt her forehead and face. She wanted to tell her aunt that they were all lizards shedding their skins in
(85) the sun, but just then her grandmother said in Spanish, "Oh, she's all right. She's only being a baby. Always has been. That's what happens to girls who are their father's favorite."

(90) "She'll be all right if you don't tease her," Serena said and put her arm around her sister.

"She's simply acting like an Indian, that's all," their mother said. "Everyone
(95) knows they don't talk and can't answer politely when someone asks them a question." '

Whispering in her ear, Serena was promising to show Josie the new kittens
(100) in Tia Cuca's closet. She knew that if she were not led away, her little sister would remain staring at the older

women until they stopped talking about her as if Josie were invisible.

(105) The girls walked quietly down the short hallway into Tia Cuca's bedroom. Shaded by the deep green leaves of the mulberry trees on West Yandell Street, the room was cool and dark and smelled
(110) of lavender toilet water.

"Ladies are like flowers," their great-aunt told them often. "They must smell good. Fortunes have been won and lost through the noses of gentlemen." And
(115) then, in a velvety voice full of charm, she sang a ditty that always made the girls laugh.

Adios, Mama Carlota, narices de pelota,
Adios, Papa Joaquin, narices de violin.

(120) Josie was not able to understand what a woman with two noses like a ball and a man with two noses like a violin had to do with being a lady.

1. This passage is set in:

   A. Chihuahua

   B. Southern Texas

   C. San Elizario

   D. Northern Mexico

2. Which of the following best describes Eduviges Salazar's attitude toward Josie and Serena?

   F. She berates them because of their intrusion on her life and her relationship with her family.

   G. She scoffs at their preference for Sancho and belittles him and them with constant insults.

H. She criticizes them so that they will lose their Indian ways and be assimilated into American culture.

J. She attributes any of their behavior and feelings that she doesn't approve of to their Indian blood.

3. It is reasonable to infer from the passage that Ofelia Salazar:

A. Identifies with her mother's family

B. Is envious of Josie

C. Acts as the peacemaker in the family

D. Is ignored by her father

4. From information in the passage, which of the following does Eduviges Salazar identify with Indians?

F. Kinship with nature

G. Immodest behavior

H. Poverty

J. Laziness

5. It is reasonable to infer from the passage that the reason Josie does not kiss her father (line 69) is that she:

A. Is afraid of her mother's reaction.

B. Disapproves of his irresponsibility.

C. Is angry at him for leaving her behind.

D. Doesn't like being thought of as the "favorite."

6. Serena and Josie believe the Angel clan is more important than the Salazar clan because:

F. They feel closer to their mother's family than to their father's relatives.

G. The Angels have no Indian blood.

H. Eduviges Salazar has indoctrinated them.

J. The Salazars are irresponsible and the Angels are not.

7. For Josie, Indian blood is associated with:

A. Creativity

B. Freedom

C. Determination

D. Loss

8. Josie probably "wanted to tell her aunt that they were all lizards shedding their skins" (lines 83–85) because she:

F. Was upset

G. Wanted them to understand their connection with other living things

H. Was disoriented because of a fever

J. Was acting like an Indian

9. From the passage, which of the following best describes Sancho Salazar?

A. He is easy-going and generally does what he wants to.

B. His wife controls his behavior.

C. He despises his wife but stays with her because of the children.

D. He is ashamed of his Indian heritage and feels uncomfortable around his wife's relatives.

GO ON TO THE NEXT PAGE

10. It is reasonable to infer from Josie's reaction to her great-aunt's ditty (lines 118–119) that she:

    F. Is scornful of her mother's family

    G. Tries, sometimes unsuccessfully, to understand the adult world

    H. Is smarter and more cynical than her sisters, even though she is the youngest

    J. Doesn't take advice seriously but rather turns it into a joke

Passage II

Social science: This passage is from Presidential Campaigns *by Paul F. Boller, Jr. (©1984 by Paul F. Boller, Jr.).*

The campaign of 1840 was boisterous. To oust Martin Van Buren from the White House and put William Henry Harrison in his place the Whigs pulled
(5) out all the stops. "The whole country," observed John Quincy Adams, "is in a state of agitation upon the approaching Presidential election such as was never before witnessed. . . . Not a week has
(10) passed within the last few months without a convocation of thousands of people to hear inflammatory harangues against Martin Van Buren and his Administration!" He went on worriedly:
(15) "Here is a revolution in the habits and manners of the people. Where will it end? These are party movements, and must in the natural progress of things become antagonistical. . . . Their mani-
(20) fest tendency is to civil war."

The election of 1840 was neither civil war nor revolution; it was mainly fun and games. More people voted that year than in any previous presidential
(25) contest. The participation of the average citizen, moreover, in the energetic elec-tioneering—parades, barbecues, rallies, songfests—reached astonishing propor-tions. During the 1830s, the lowering
(30) or abolition of property or tax-paying qualifications for voting in most states meant the gradual democratization of American politics. Presidential contests ceased to be the private preserve of the
(35) rich and well-born. They became in part great entertainments in which even peo-ple who could not vote joined in on the fun. By 1840 it was necessary for all the presidential aspirants to do what
(40) Andrew Jackson had done when he first entered the hustings: bid for the support of the masses. In 1840 the Whigs de-cided to take a leaf or two from the Jacksonian book and present their candi-
(45) date as a man of the people and a mili-tary hero. Their strategy worked beautifully. As the *Democratic Review* admitted with chagrin after Harrison beat Van Buren in November: "They
(50) have at last learned from defeat the art of victory. We have taught them how to conquer us!"

Harrison was an unlikely "people's can-didate." Unlike Jackson, who had been
(55) born in poverty, the Whig nominee was well-born and college-educated; and he was living on a comfortable farm in North Bend, Ohio, when the Whigs first became interested in him. His military
(60) career, compared with Jackson's, was not particularly distinguished. He had, as governor of the Indiana Territory, led the forces that engaged the Shawnee chief, Tecumseh, in a battle at
(65) Tippecanoe in 1811; but though he beat off the Indians, his men suffered heavy casualties in the encounter. He had been, moreover, merely competent, at best, as

commander in the Northwest during the
(70) War of 1812. But the Whigs blithely re-
shaped Harrison's persona. They called
him "Old Buckeye" to prove he was just
as plain and forthright as "Old Hickory";
and they hailed him as "the Hero of
(75) Tippecanoe" to elevate him to the status
of "the Hero of New Orleans." In vain
did the Democrats point to his unim-
pressive record. The names, Harrison
and Tippecanoe, soon became
(80) interchangeable.

To some extent the Whigs stumbled
onto their major campaign theme. When
they passed over Henry Clay and picked
Harrison to run for President at their
(85) convention in Harrisburg, Pennsylvania,
in December 1839, the *Baltimore
Republican* gleefully reported a remark
made about the Whig candidate by one
of Clay's friends: "Give him a barrel of
(90) hard cider and a pension of two thousand a year and, my word for it, he will
sit the remainder of his days in a log
cabin, by the side of a 'sea-coal' fire and
study moral philosophy." Whig leaders
(95) quickly turned the sneer into a slogan
and began presenting Harrison as the
log-cabin–hard-cider candidate, who unlike the high-falutin' Martin Van Buren,
was plain, simple, down-to-earth, and
(100) very much of, by, and for the people.
The Democrats pointed out that it was a
Whig, not a Democrat who, had first
cast the slur, but the Whigs paid no attention to them. They had decided (as
(105) one of them admitted) "that passion and
prejudice, properly aroused and di-
rected, would do about as well as principle and reason in a party contest." The
log cabin and hard cider soon became
(110) the central symbols of their campaign
against Van Buren.

The log-cabin–hard-cider campaign had
to be seen to be believed. There was
no dearth of spectators. Estimates of
(115) crowds assembled for Whig rallies
ranged from one thousand to one hundred thousand and sometimes were
reckoned in terms of acreage covered.
Whig parades got longer and longer as
(120) the campaign went on: one mile, three
miles, ten miles long. And Whig gather-
ings—replete with speeches, songs,
cheers, and hard cider—were almost in-
terminable: two, three, five hours long.
(125) Log cabins decorated with coonskins
(after the fashion of frontier huts) became ubiquitous: erected at party rallies,
drawn along in parades, and stationed in
just about every city, town, village, and
(130) hamlet in the land. Hard cider was plentiful: the latchstring at the door of the
log cabins was always drawn; and there
was also sweet cider for the temperate.
Slogans, mottos, nicknames and catch-
(135) words abounded: "The Farmer's
President"; "The Hero of Tippecanoe";
"Harrison, Two Dollars a Day and Roast
Beef"; and, best of all (since John Tyler
of Virginia was Harrison's running
(140) mate), "Tippecanoe and Tyler Too!"

11. The quotation from John Quincy Adams
(lines 5–20) in the first paragraph is
used to show:

A. Adams's rejection of both
candidates

B. The people's general disgust with
campaign tactics

C. The atmosphere of the 1840
campaign

D. Adams's intuition that the Civil
War would soon take place

GO ON TO THE NEXT PAGE

273

12. According to the passage, the election of 1840 was different from previous elections because of:

    F. Greater involvement by a wider electorate

    G. The similarity of the candidates' backgrounds and views

    H. The role played by the press

    J. The strong desire of the Whigs to win

13. As it is used in line 41, "hustings" most nearly means:

    A. Barns or other farm buildings

    B. A receptacle for holding ballots in an election

    C. A place where campaign speeches are made

    D. A voting booth

14. It is reasonable to infer from the second paragraph (lines 21–52) that more people voted in the 1840 election because:

    F. They were violently opposed to Van Buren.

    G. There were more literate, educated people than there had been previously.

    H. William Henry Harrison had long been a popular favorite of the average citizen.

    J. People who didn't own property or pay taxes could now vote.

15. From information in the second paragraph (lines 21–52), it can reasonably be inferred that the *Democratic Review*:

    A. Presented an image of William Henry Harrison as a military hero

    B. Supported Harrison's bid for the presidency in spite of the Whigs' tactics

    C. Had supported Andrew Jackson when he ran for President

    D. Represented the interests of the rich and well-born

16. Harrison's military career is described as:

    F. Similar to Andrew Jackson's

    G. Unimpressive

    H. Fabricated by the Whigs

    J. A disaster

17. The Whigs called Harrison:

    A. "Old Hickory"

    B. "The Hero of New Orleans"

    C. "Hard Cider"

    D. "Old Buckeye"

18. The "log-cabin–hard-cider" theme used in Harrison's campaign came from a:

    F. Derogatory remark made by a fellow Whig

    G. Compliment from a fellow Whig

    H. Newspaper reporter criticizing Harrison's drinking

    J. Speech by Henry Clay

19. The campaign slogan "Tippecanoe and Tyler Too!" is an indication of the Whigs':

A. Desire to stress Harrison's humble background

B. Use of catchy slogans and mottos

C. Unscrupulous exploitation of people's prejudices

D. Efforts to identify Harrison with the popular Andrew Jackson

20. It can reasonably be inferred from the passage that one of the reasons Harrison won the 1840 election was that:

F. The newspapers unanimously supported him because Van Buren was seen as an elitist.

G. The Whigs were able to create a lively campaign and a persona for him that people liked.

H. The Whigs spent vast amounts of money on campaign activities such as barbecues and songfests.

J. He, unlike Van Buren, was from a humble background.

Passage III

Humanities: This passage is from Jazz Styles: History and Analysis, *Second Edition, by Mark C. Gridley (©1985 by Prentice-Hall, Inc.).*

Why did jazz originate in New Orleans? New Orleans had always had a unique culture. In the late 1700s and early 1800s New Orleans was largely occu-
(5) pied by the French, who maintained a high regard for the arts and enjoyed the pleasures of music and dancing more than their more conservative northern neighbors. In fact, relative to its size,
(10) New Orleans had more musical organizations than any other American city during that period.

Another factor that made New Orleans a good place for jazz to form was the
(15) city's having been a magnet for freed and escaped slaves in the South throughout the 1800s. New Orleans was especially attractive for its work opportunities, social activity, and diverse
(20) ways of life. And the city was convenient to several slave states, actually being closer to several parts of Mississippi and Alabama than to much of Louisiana itself. Much of the South is only a short
(25) boat ride or a few days on a raft away from New Orleans because, on its way to New Orleans, the Mississippi River touches the states of Kentucky, Arkansas, Missouri, and Tennessee as
(30) well as Mississippi and Louisiana. Together with the 1809 arrival of many Haitian Creoles and an already high proportion of blacks in the city's population, these geographical conveniences
(35) made New Orleans a center for black culture in the United States. And, of course, several types of music were included in that culture.

Not only did New Orleans have a fes-
(40) tive French tradition contributing to an atmosphere of pleasure, it also had its role as host to travelers from all over the world because the city was a seaport, and it was a center for commerce be-
(45) cause of its nearness to the mouth of the Mississippi River, a flourishing trade route for America and the Caribbean. New Orleans therefore maintained its party atmosphere and had one of
(50) America's largest and most famous brothel districts. ("The district," as musicians called it, eventually became

GO ON TO THE NEXT PAGE

known as Storyville, in honor of an alderman named Story whose idea it was
(55) to section off a portion of the town in 1897 and limit prostitution to that area. Because of Storyville's legendary importance in jazz history, jazz record companies, book publishers, and night
(60) clubs have been given the same name.) The singing and dancing, sex and liquor that was so plentiful in New Orleans was important to the birth of jazz because it generated work for musicians.
(65) And, in this way, it furnished a context, in addition to that of church music, for mixing the musical traditions of European colonists with those of African slaves.

(70) New Orleans was a whirlwind of musical activity. Diverse styles bumped into each other, with characteristics of one rubbing off on another. Opera coexisted with sailors' hornpipes. Music for the
(75) formal European dances of the minuet and the quadrille coexisted with African music used in voodoo ceremonies. Band music, in the style of Sousa, was especially popular during the late 1800s.
(80) There were also the musical cries of street vendors selling their wares.

Another factor that promoted the mixing of African and European traditions was a considerable amount of sex and inter-
(85) marriage occurring in New Orleans between blacks and whites prior to the mid-1800s. The offspring of these unions, whose ancestry was part African and part French, were called Creoles of
(90) Color, or simply "Creoles" for short. However, a sharp separation existed between the two groups of New Orleans residents who had African ancestry. Creoles were not referred to as Negro.
(95) That term was reserved for blacks who had little or no white blood. Creoles were usually well-educated and successful

people such as businessmen, physicians, landowners, and skilled craftsmen. They
(100) spoke French. Many owned slaves and often required their slaves to speak French, too. Children in Creole families often received high quality, formal musical training, some even traveling to Paris
(105) for study at a conservatory. Creoles lived downtown in the area of New Orleans today known as The French Quarter. Negroes lived uptown and worked primarily as laborers. Creoles embraced al-
(110) most exclusively European music. Negroes played less formal music and forms which retained some African elements. Though many uptown musicians received formal training, their music was
(115) generally somewhat rougher than that of the Creoles. (Only sketchy information exists about the uptown music of that period, and it remains unclear whether improvisation was used and, if so, how
(120) much. According to some reports, however, little improvisation was used, and it was mostly in the form of simple embellishment upon existing material instead of being totally fresh melodic invention.) In
(125) summary, some African traditions were preserved in Negro music while many European concert traditions were absorbed and maintained by Creole music.

21. According to the passage, New Orleans in the late 1700s had a unique flavor primarily because of:

A. A large population of runaway slaves

B. The large number of French inhabitants

C. Its ideal position on the Mississippi

D. Its proximity to Haiti

22. New Orleans was attractive to African-Americans for which of the following reasons?

    I. The availability of jobs

    II. Its role as a seaport

    III. Its location between slave and free states

    F. I only

    G. II only

    H. I and III only

    J. II and III only

23. It can reasonably be inferred from the third paragraph (lines 39–69) that in nineteenth-century New Orleans:

    A. The French were irreverent and encouraged a loose morality.

    B. African-American musicians were responsible for creating "the district."

    C. Class distinctions didn't exist.

    D. Prostitution was legal.

24. Storyville was named after a:

    F. City alderman

    G. Jazz musician

    H. Famous night club

    J. Book publisher

25. Storyville was especially important to musicians in New Orleans because it:

    A. Was occupied by people who combined a variety of musical traditions

    B. Was a source of inspiration because of its lively atmosphere

    C. Provided jobs

    D. Was integrated

26. It is reasonable to infer from the passage that Creoles in early nineteenth-century New Orleans:

    F. Were descended from runaway slaves

    G. Formed the ruling class

    H. Identified with the French more than with African-Americans

    J. Were rejected by both races because of their mixed-race status

27. According to the passage, uptown music differed from Creole music in that it:

    A. Included African elements

    B. Was the product of untrained musicians

    C. Included both band and church music

    D. Was improvisational

28. The purpose of the fourth paragraph of the passage (lines 70–81) is to:

    F. Illustrate the importance of Creole influence on jazz

    G. Identify the music that was most popular in New Orleans

    H. Emphasize the importance of European music, such as opera, on jazz

    J. Provide concrete examples of the variety of musical styles coexisting in New Orleans

GO ON TO THE NEXT PAGE

29. "The French Quarter" refers to the:

    A. Center of musical activity in New Orleans

    B. Area in New Orleans where most Creoles lived

    C. Part of New Orleans originally settled by the French

    D. Birthplace of jazz

30. As it is used in the passage, "improvisation" (lines 119 and 121) most likely refers to:

    F. Adding African rhythms to a piece of music

    G. Inventing a melody while performing

    H. Combining different styles of music in a piece

    J. Performing an instrumental solo in the middle of a piece

Passage IV

*Natural science: This passage is from David Schneider's "The Rising Seas" (*Scientific American, *March 1997).*

Many people were awakened by the air-raid sirens. Others heard church bells sounding. Some probably sensed only a distant, predawn ringing and returned to
(5) sleep. But before the end of that day—February 1, 1953—more than a million Dutch citizens would learn for whom these bells tolled and why. In the middle of the night, a deadly combination of
(10) winds and tides had raised the level of the North Sea to the brim of the Netherlands' protective dikes, and the ocean was beginning to pour in.

As nearby Dutch villagers slept, water
(15) rushing over the dikes began to eat away at these earthen bulwarks from the back side. Soon the sea had breached the perimeter, and water freely flooded the land, eventually extending the sea in-
(20) ward as far as 64 kilometers from the former coast. In all, more than 200,000 hectares of farmland were inundated, some 2,000 people died, and roughly 100,000 were left homeless. One sixth
(25) of the Netherlands was covered in seawater.

With memories of that catastrophe still etched in people's minds, it is no won-der that Dutch planners took a keen in-
(30) terest when, a quarter century later, scientists began suggesting that global warming could cause the world's oceans to rise by several meters. Increases in sea level could be expected to come
(35) about for various reasons, all tied to the heating of the earth's surface, which most experts deem an inevitable conse-quence of the mounting abundance of carbon dioxide and other heat-trapping
(40) "greenhouse gases" in the air.

First, greenhouse warming of the earth's atmosphere would eventually increase the temperature of the ocean, and sea-water, like most other substances, ex-
(45) pands when heated. That thermal expansion of the ocean might be suffi-cient to raise sea level by about 30 cen-timeters or more in the next 100 years.

A second cause for concern has already
(50) shown itself plainly in many of Europe's Alpine valleys. For the past century or two, mountain glaciers there have been shrinking, and the water released into streams and rivers has been adding to
(55) the sea. Such meltwaters from mountain glaciers may have boosted the ocean by as much as five centimeters in the past

100 years, and this continuing influx will most likely elevate sea level even (60) more quickly in the future.

But it is a third threat that was the real worry to the Dutch and to the people of other low-lying countries. Some scientists began warning more than 20 years (65) ago that global warming might cause a precariously placed store of frozen water in Antarctica to melt, leading to a calamitous rise in sea level—perhaps five or six meters' worth.

(70) Yet predicting exactly how—or whether—sea level will shift in response to global warming remains a significant challenge. Scientists trained in many separate disciplines are attempting (75) to glean answers using a variety of experimental approaches, ranging from drilling into the Antarctic ice cap to bouncing radar off the ocean from space. With such efforts, investigators (80) have learned a great deal about how sea level has varied in the past and how it is currently changing. For example, most of these scientists agree that the ocean has been creeping upward by two mil- (85) limeters a year for at least the past several decades. But determining whether a warmer climate will lead to a sudden acceleration in the rate of sea level rise remains an outstanding question.

(90) One of the first prominent geologists to raise concern that global warming might trigger a catastrophic collapse of the Antarctic ice cap was J. H. Mercer of Ohio State University. Because the thick (95) slab of ice covering much of West Antarctica rests on bedrock well below sea level, Mercer explained in his 1979 article "West Antarctic Ice Sheet and the CO_2 Greenhouse Effect: A Threat of

(100) Disaster," this "marine ice sheet" is inherently unstable. If the greenhouse effect were to warm the south polar region by just five degrees Celsius, the floating ice shelves surrounding the (105) West Antarctic ice sheet would begin to disappear. Robbed of these buttresses, this grounded ice sheet—a vestige of the last ice age—would quickly disintegrate, flooding coastlines around the (115) world in the process.

Mercer's disaster scenario was largely theoretical, but he pointed to some evidence that the West Antarctic ice sheet may, in fact, have melted at least once (120) before. Between about 110,000 and 130,000 years ago, when the last shared ancestors of all humans probably fanned out of Africa into Asia and Europe, the earth experienced a climatic history (125) strikingly similar to what has transpired in the past 20,000 years, warming abruptly from the chill of a great ice age.

31. The main purpose of the first two paragraphs of the passage (lines 1–26) is to:

A. Objectively recount the first example of the effects of global warming on sea level

B. Explain why the Dutch are more concerned than others about climatic change

C. Dramatically illustrate an occurrence that resulted from a rise in sea level

D. Create immediate sympathy for the victims of a catastrophic event

GO ON TO THE NEXT PAGE

Reading Test

32. It can reasonably be inferred from the passage that which of the following was most responsible for the 1953 disaster in the Netherlands?

    F. High winds and tides on the North Sea

    G. Meltwaters from mountain glaciers

    H. Substandard earthen dikes

    J. Inadequate warning systems

33. According to the passage, which of the following is most likely to be the root cause of a rise in sea level?

    A. Continued heating of the earth

    B. Heat expansion of the oceans

    C. Shrinkage of mountain glaciers

    D. Increased global precipitation

34. The gases most experts believe are responsible for global warming are called "greenhouse gases" because they:

    F. Filter out the sun

    G. Are created in a controlled environment

    H. Are given off by decayed plant materials

    J. Hold heat in

35. From information in the passage, with which of the following statements would the author be most likely to agree?

    A. The theory that global warming is caused by greenhouse gases is highly questionable.

    B. Warming of the earth's surface is a phenomenon of the twentieth century.

    C. There is some evidence that global warming will cause a continuing rise in sea level.

    D. Low-lying countries are doomed to disappear because of a rise in sea level caused by global warming.

36. The passage specifies that which of the following will be likely to cause increases in sea level?

    I. Thermal expansion of the ocean

    II. Meltwaters from mountain glaciers

    III. Melting of Antarctic ice

    F. I and II only

    G. II and III only

    H. III only

    J. I, II, and III

37. The most likely reason why scientists are drilling into the Antarctic ice cap and bouncing radar off the ocean is to:

    A. Stop the melting of the ice cap

    B. Slow the melting of the ice cap

    C. Help determine the exact causes of global warming

    D. Study past and current changes in sea level

38. According to the passage, some scientists believe that melting in the Antarctic may raise sea levels by:

    F. 5 or 6 meters

    G. 2 millimeters

    H. 30 centimeters

    J. 5 centimeters

39. According to J. H. Mercer's theory as it is described in the passage, global warming will cause catastrophic flooding because it will:

    F. Melt the world's largest glaciers, adding water to rivers and streams that flow into the sea

    G. Trigger disintegration of the Antarctic ice sheet by melting the ice shelves that currently stabilize it

    H. Change the proportion of land to water by increasing the total volume of global water

    J. Prevent the normal variations in sea level that have ensured the stability of coastlines since prehistoric times

40. Which of the following would most strongly support J. H. Mercer's theory as it is presented in the passage?

    A. A recurrence of the Dutch flooding of 1953

    B. Proof that the marine ice sheet melted previously and caused massive flooding

    C. A sudden cooling of the earth's surface followed by an ice age

    D. Proof that greenhouse gases are increasing in the earth's atmosphere

Reading Test

IF YOU FINISH BEFORE TIME IS CALLED, CHECK YOUR WORK ON THIS SECTION ONLY. DO NOT WORK ON ANY OTHER SECTION IN THE TEST.

Science Reasoning Test

Time: 35 Minutes

40 Questions

Directions: Each of the seven passages in this test is followed by several questions. Read each passage and then choose the best answer to each question that follows the passage. Refer to the passage as often as necessary to answer the questions. You may NOT use a calculator on this test.

Passage I

Puberty is the time of life when mature reproductive cells are first produced in the human body and when successful reproduction can begin. *Timing*, or the onset of puberty, depends upon several key variables. Figures 1 and 2 show two of these key variables for timing *menarche* (first menstruation) in human female populations from the 1830s to the 1950s in four nations representing Western society.

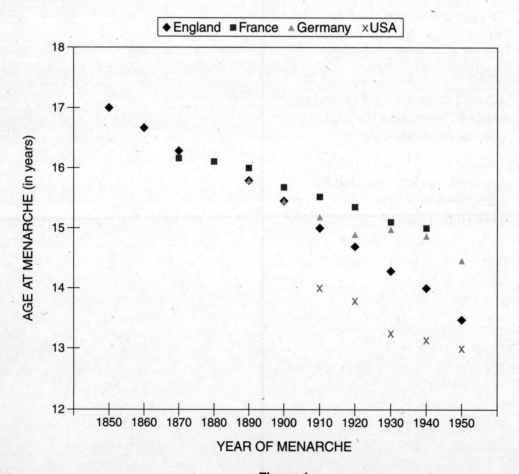

Figure 1

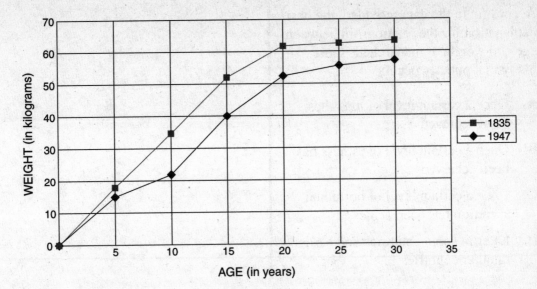

Figure 2

1. Based on the data provided, what can be concluded about age at menarche in Western society?

   A. It has been increasing over time.

   B. It has been decreasing over time.

   C. It has remained constant since the mid-nineteenth century.

   D. It has leveled off at approximately 14 years of age.

2. Based on the data provided, what can be concluded about body weight and puberty timing between 1835 and 1947?

   F. Body weight at the time of puberty increased.

   G. Body weight at the time of puberty decreased.

   H. Both body weight and age at puberty increased.

   J. Body weight remained unchanged while age decreased.

3. Based on the information provided in Figure 1, the reason the line representing the USA is shorter than the lines for England, France, and Germany is most likely because:

   A. The age at menarche in the USA is less than the age at menarche in the other countries.

   B. USA society was not considered a Western society until 1910.

   C. Data were not collected for the USA before 1910.

   D. Data were not collected for the USA after 1910.

4. According to the data provided, the weight range for menarche is between:

   F. 20 and 30 kilograms

   G. 30 and 40 kilograms

   H. 40 and 50 kilograms

   J. 50 and 60 kilograms

GO ON TO THE NEXT PAGE

5. According to the data provided, the best explanation for the relationship between age and weight at menarche is most likely that puberty occurs:

    A. Once a certain level of mass has been achieved

    B. Once a certain level of fatness has been achieved

    C. Once a certain level of hormonal secretion has been achieved

    D. Later in some countries and earlier in other countries

Passage II

In general, *matter* is anything that occupies space. *Solid* refers to a phase of matter that has definite shape and volume and that is not easily compressed (reduced). *Volume* refers to the measurement of matter in three dimensions. *Compressibility* refers to a reduction in volume due to an application of pressure. *Pressure* refers to force per unit area, where *force* is the reaction of matter to an increase in speed.

Table 1 presents data on the change of a specific volume of solid helium at −273°C resulting from the application of very high pressures. Table 2 presents volumes of various solids at 25°C. Table 3 presents volumes of salts and some other solids at 25°C.

TABLE 1		
Pressure (kg/cm^2)	Volume (ml/mole)	Compressibility $(1/v)(\partial v/\partial p)_r$
52	19.0	184×10^{-5}
91	18.0	135
141	17.0	100
???	16.0	73
305	15.0	52
475	14.0	37
718	13.0	25
1,105	12.0	16
1,715	11.0	12
2,240	10.5	10

TABLE 2						
Pressure (kg/cm^2)	Bakelite	Lucite	Nylon	Orthoclase	Potassium Alum	Potassium Phosphate
1	1.0000	1.0000	1.0000	1.0000	1.0000	1.0000
2,500	0.9633	0.9473				
5,000	0.9329	0.9153				0.9451
10,000	0.8903	0.8547	0.9829	0.9866	0.9929	0.9079
15,000	0.8613	0.8306				0.8806
20,000	0.8329	0.8125	0.9667	0.9275	0.9862	0.8586
30,000	0.8051	0.7857	0.9512	0.9113	0.9800	0.8241
40,000	0.7816	0.7661	0.9366	0.8981	0.9743	0.7966

GO ON TO THE NEXT PAGE

TABLE 3					
Pressure (kg/cm²)	C	Cs	Li	Rb	Sr
1	1.000	1.000	1.000	1.000	1.000
10,000		0.761	0.928	0.802	0.925
20,000		0.656	0.874	0.708	0.878
30,000	0.940	0.571	0.833	0.652	0.828
40,000	0.929	0.521	0.801	0.612	0.791
50,000	0.919	0.431	0.773	0.578	0.761
60,000	0.911	0.409	0.748	0.551	0.734
70,000	0.903	0.392	0.727	0.528	0.702
80,000	0.896	0.381	0.707	0.507	0.683
90,000	0.890	0.375	0.689	0.489	0.665
100,000	0.855	0.368	0.672	0.473	0.648

6. For a given volume of solid helium, the data in Table 1 indicate that volume decreases as pressure:

F. Increases

G. Decreases

H. Increases, then decreases

J. Decreases, then increases

7. According to Table 1, what is the most likely pressure (given in kg/cm²) that corresponds with 16 ml/mole of solid helium at −273°C?

A. 52

B. 207

C. 288

D. 349

8. Which of the following pairs of solids in Table 2 are the *least* compressible at 25°C?

   F. Bakelite and lucite

   G. Bakelite and potassium alum

   H. Nylon and lucite

   J. Nylon and potassium alum

9. Which of the solids listed in Table 3 is the *most* compressible at 25°C?

   A. Li

   B. Rb

   C. Cs

   D. Sr

10. Which of the following graphs best represents the relationship between volume and pressure for lithium (Li) at 25°C?

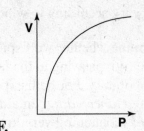

F.

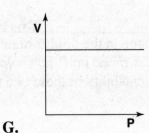

G.

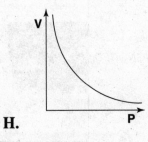

H.

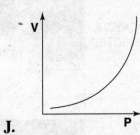

J.

GO ON TO THE NEXT PAGE

Passage III

Buckeye caterpillars take and store certain chemicals such as iridoid glycosides from their host plants. Wolf spiders prey upon buckeye caterpillars for food. Scientists have noted that these spiders prefer some buckeye caterpillars to others. They hypothesize that spiders have taste preferences that vary according to which plants the caterpillars eat.

In order to determine whether wolf spiders find buckeye caterpillars that store iridoid glycosides unpalatable (not pleasing to the taste), two experiments were conducted—one in the field and one in the laboratory. For both experiments, two types of caterpillars were used—those reared on *Plantago lanceolata* (containing very high levels of iridoid glycosides) and those raised on *P. major* (containing very low levels of iridoid glycosides).

Experiment 1 — In the Field

Spiders were located in the field at night by headlamp and were randomly offered either a buckeye caterpillar raised on *P. lanceolata* or a buckeye caterpillar raised on *P. major*. Figure 1 compares the acceptability of these two types of caterpillars to the spiders.

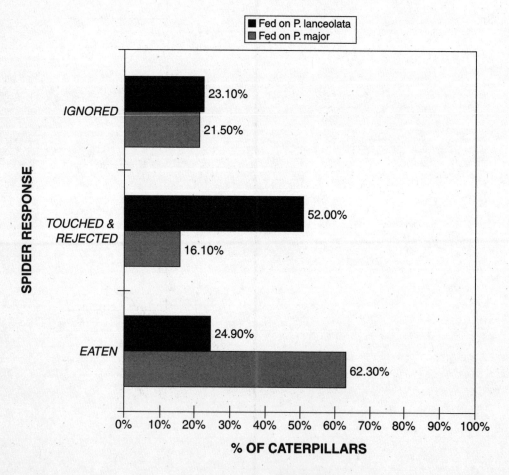

Figure 1

Experiment 2 — In the Lab

This experiment was conducted with 50 spiders collected in the field. Ten trials were conducted per spider. Every third day for approximately one month, two buckeye caterpillars were offered to each spider—one caterpillar raised on *P. lanceolata* and one raised on *P. major*—and spider responses were recorded. Figure 2 shows percentage of caterpillars eaten, and Figure 3 shows spider response, where higher values indicate greater acceptability of the caterpillar to the spider.

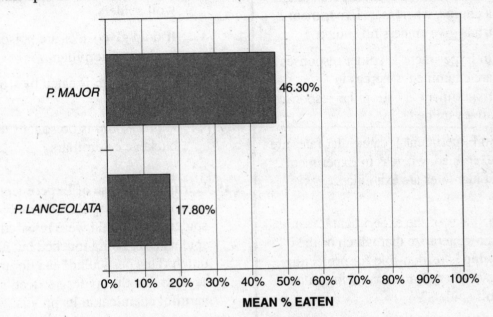

Figure 2

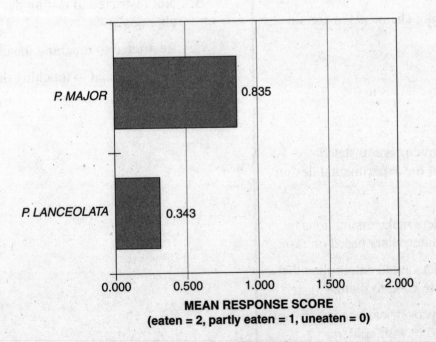

Figure 3

GO ON TO THE NEXT PAGE

11. How is the design of Experiment 1 different from the design of Experiment 2?

   A. In Experiment 1, trials give spiders no choice, whereas in Experiment 2, trials give spiders a choice.

   B. In Experiment 1, trials give spiders a choice, whereas in Experiment 2, trials give spiders no choice.

   C. In Experiment 1, spider responses are examined, whereas in Experiment 2, caterpillar responses are examined.

   D. In Experiment 1, caterpillar fates are examined, whereas in Experiment 2, spider fates are examined.

12. On the basis of the experimental results, one can generalize that which of the following is responsible for protecting buckeye caterpillars from being eaten by wolf spiders?

   F. Bitter-tasting chemicals in certain plants

   G. Sour-tasting chemicals in certain plants

   H. *P. major*

   J. Iridoid glycosides in the caterpillars

13. All of the following are unstated assumptions of the experimental design EXCEPT:

   A. Wolf spiders make distinctions between caterpillars based on taste.

   B. Wolf spiders avoid caterpillars that do not taste good to them.

   C. Iridoid glycosides are nontoxic (not poisonous) to wolf spiders.

   D. Iridoid glycosides are nontoxic (not poisonous) to buckeye caterpillars.

14. During the course of this study, four spiders died in the laboratory. All four of these spiders had eaten only caterpillars reared on *P. lanceolata*. This evidence may suggest that:

   F. Iridoid glycosides are poisonous to wolf spiders.

   G. Iridoid glycosides are poisonous to buckeye caterpillars.

   H. *P. lanceolata* is eaten by wolf spiders.

   J. *P. lanceolata* is poisonous to buckeye caterpillars.

15. During the course of Experiment 1, some of the caterpillars offered to spiders in the field were released by the spiders after being touched but not yet bitten. This particular behavior may suggest that the spider's detection of a harmful chemical in its prey is:

   A. Restricted to tasting the chemical

   B. Not restricted to tasting the chemical

   C. Restricted to touching the chemical

   D. Not restricted to touching the chemical

16. Which of the following conclusions about the relationship between caterpillar diet and caterpillar interactions with wolf spiders would be consistent with the results of the two experiments?

   F. Wolf spiders prefer buckeye caterpillars that have been raised on a diet of *P. lanceolata*.

   G. Wolf spiders prefer only large buckeye caterpillars that have been raised on a diet of *P. major*.

   H. Buckeye caterpillars fed on plants low in iridoid glycosides were preferred by wolf spiders to those fed on plants high in iridoid glycosides.

   J. Buckeye caterpillars fed on plants high in iridoid glycosides were preferred by wolf spiders to those fed on plants low in iridoid glycosides.

Passage IV

Some unstable radioactive chemicals like radon pass through a series of various chemical elements in the decay process before they reach a stable state. Scientists believe that the inhalation (breathing) of radioactive radon gas and its *progeny* (chemical products of decay) is the single greatest contributor to radiation doses found in human populations. ^{222}Rn is the dominant radon source, although it is believed that radiation doses from thoron (^{220}Rn) and its decay products also contribute to inhaled radiation. Atmospheric thoron (with a half-life of 55.6 seconds) originates primarily from gases released naturally from the top few centimeters of soil. One of its progeny is airborne ^{212}Pb. In contrast, radon gas (with a half-life of 3.8 days) originates from deeper soil depths.

Exhalation in the study refers to gas emissions from surface soils. *Half-life* refers to the time required for one-half of a given amount of radioactive material to undergo chemical change resulting from its decay.

GO ON TO THE NEXT PAGE

Study Site

Long-term changes in outdoor ground-level atmospheric doses of radon, thoron, and thoron progeny were established for a natural location in southern Germany. The environment consists mainly of grasses, though forests exist to the north. Soil depths average 10 to 20 centimeters of dry and compacted clay lying on top of a layer of gravel with an average depth of 8 to12 meters. In a typical year, the soil is frozen to a depth of about 2 to 50 cm from December through February. Generally, winds are from the west, and the climate is damp and foggy during autumn and winter.

Study Sampling, Data Collection Methods, and Results

Radon and thoron decay products were collected continuously on glass fiber filters located in an open field in the study site region. During collection of air samples, the filters were analyzed continuously by computerized gamma-spectrometry. The filters were changed every 24-hour period from 1 January 1991 to 31 December 1998.

Table 1 shows the results of the continuous measurements of thoron (^{220}Rn) and radon (^{222}Rn) at the site from 1991 to 1998. Figure 1 shows average monthly thoron concentrations in ground-level air at the site; Figure 2 shows average monthly radon concentrations.

TABLE 1				
	^{220}Rn (in Bq m^{-3})		^{222}Rn (in Bq m^{-3})	
Year	Mean	Range	Mean	Range
1991	0.083	0.062–0.120	8.700	6.000–12.000
1992	0.078	0.032–0.130	8.500	5.200–13.000
1993	0.075	0.043–0.140	8.900	4.600–13.000
1994	0.078	0.044–0.160	8.200	5.400–12.000
1995	0.086	0.055–0.120	7.800	6.000–12.000
1996	0.084	0.060–0.110	9.000	5.100–15.000
1997	0.082	0.047–0.130	8.000	4.800–16.000
1998	0.086	0.066–0.120	8.100	5.500–13.000
1991 – 1998	0.082	0.032–0.160	8.400	4.600–16.000

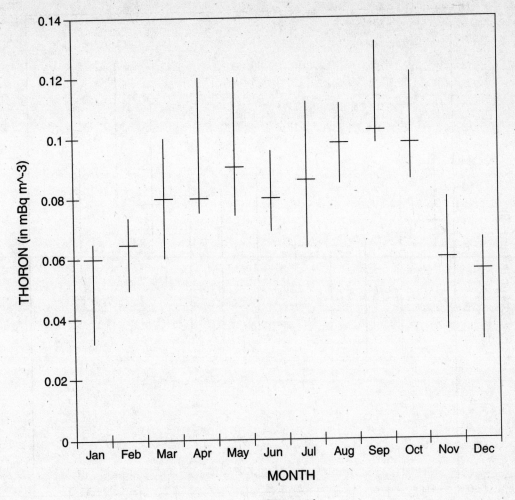

Figure 1

GO ON TO THE NEXT PAGE

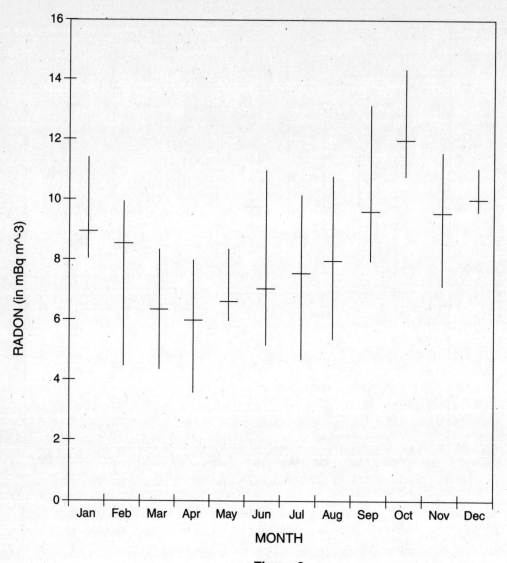

Figure 2

17. Based upon the results of the study, one can conclude that long-term average concentrations of radon are:

    A. Less than long-term average concentrations of thoron

    B. Greater than long-term average concentrations of thoron

    C. Equal to long-term average concentrations of thoron

    D. Equal to long-term average concentrations of thoron progeny

18. The study indicates that during the winter months (November through February):

    F. ^{222}Rn concentrations are high compared to concentrations of ^{220}Rn.

    G. ^{222}Rn concentrations are low compared to concentrations of ^{220}Rn.

    H. ^{222}Rn concentrations are related to ^{212}Pb activity concentrations.

    J. ^{220}Rn concentrations are related to ^{212}Pb activity concentrations.

19. What is the most probable reason for the difference between concentrations of ^{222}Rn and ^{220}Rn during the winter months?

- **A.** Radon source areas are much smaller than those for thoron, but the airflow is much larger.

- **B.** Thoron source areas are much smaller than those for radon, but the airflow is much larger.

- **C.** Short-lived thoron decays before it can pass through frozen or snow-covered soils, while longer-lived radon has time to move through winter soils to the air.

- **D.** Short-lived radon decays before it can pass through frozen or snow-covered soils, while longer-lived thoron has time to move through winter soils to the air.

20. Can the results of the study be applied to regions outside the study site?

- **F.** Probably, since the study did control for concentrations of soil decay gases.

- **G.** Probably, since the study did control for time of year and weather.

- **H.** Probably not, since the study did not control for soil or weather conditions.

- **J.** Probably not, since the study did not control for soil conditions or concentrations of soil decay gases.

21. In addition to the thoron progeny of ^{212}Pb (half-life 10.6 hr), the radioactive decay of ^{220}Rn (half-life 55.6 sec) also yields ^{216}Po (half-life 0.15 sec), ^{212}Bi (half-life 60.6 min), and, ultimately, ^{208}Pb (stable). Based on the design of the study, which of the following is the most likely reason researchers chose to measure concentrations of ^{212}Pb rather than concentrations of ^{216}Po or ^{212}Bi?

- **A.** ^{212}Pb has the longest half-life, thus increasing the likelihood of its detection.

- **B.** ^{212}Pb is closest in chemical composition to ^{208}Pb.

- **C.** ^{212}Pb is long lived compared to thoron.

- **D.** ^{212}Pb atoms are heavier than ^{216}Po and ^{212}Bi atoms.

22. In earlier studies, the dependence of ^{212}Pb concentration on wind direction was investigated at other locations in Germany, although the present study did not take wind direction into account. The best possible way to investigate the effects of wind direction on ^{212}Pb concentrations at the study site might be to record wind direction and ^{212}Pb concentration data:

- **F.** At the original study site location only

- **G.** At multiple selected locations within the original study site region only

- **H.** At selected sites located at distances outside of and away from the original study site

- **J.** At selected sites located at distances both inside and outside the original study site

GO ON TO THE NEXT PAGE

Passage V

By studying the oxygen content of dead sea animal skeletons in the sediments on the bottom of the ocean, geologists working in Australasia have been able to chart sea-level changes during the Quaternary period. Table 1 shows geological subdivisions of the Cenozoic era (which includes the Quaternary period). Figure 1 shows changes in sea level over the last 140,000 years.

Glaciation (or *glacial*) refers to periods during which ice-sheets, ice-caps, and glaciers grow. This term is used to describe periods of cold global climate that occurred at intervals during the Quaternary period. *Interglacial* refers to periods of warm climate, interspersed between the colder glacial periods. *Sea level* refers to long-term changes in the total volume of seawater held in the oceans of the earth, due to changes in the size of ice-sheets and thus in the volume of water locked up as ice.

TABLE 1			
GEOLOGICAL TIME UNITS			
Era	**Period**	**Epoch**	**Age**
Cenozoic	Quaternary	Holocene	Present Day 0.01 million years before present
		Pleistocene	2 million years before present
	Tertiary	Pliocene	7 million years before present
		Miocene	26 million years before present
		Oligocene	38 million years before present
		Eocene	54 million years before present
		Paleocene	65 million years before present

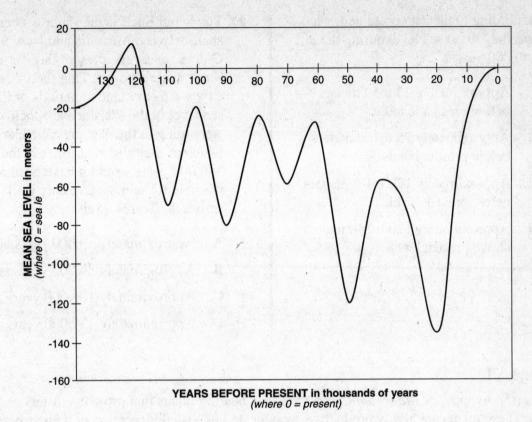

YEARS BEFORE PRESENT in thousands of years
(where 0 = present)

Figure 1

23. According to Table 1, what is the age range for the Quaternary period?

A. From 2 years to 10,000 years ago

B. From 2 million to 10,000 years ago

C. From 10,000 years ago to the present day

D. From approximately 2 million years ago to the present day

24. According to Figure 1, approximately how many years was the sea level at or above the present sea level?

F. Approximately 8,000 years

G. Approximately 15,000 years

H. Approximately 25,000 years

J. Approximately 30,000 years

25. According to the data presented, what can be concluded about sea levels during the last 100,000 years of the Pleistocene epoch?

A. They have remained constant over time.

B. They have generally been the same as sea levels today.

C. They have generally been lower than sea levels today.

D. They have generally been higher than sea levels today.

GO ON TO THE NEXT PAGE

26. According to the data presented, what was the lowest sea level during the last 140,000 years?

    F. Approximately 20 to50 meters below present levels

    G. Approximately 75 to100 meters below present levels

    H. Approximately 120 to140 meters below present levels

    J. Approximately 120 to140 meters above present levels

27. The Sahul Shelf is the shallow ocean shelf between Australia and New Guinea, under the present-day Torres Strait water passage. This shelf was exposed as dry land at periods of low sea level in the Pleistocene epoch. According to the data presented, at which of the following times in the past 140,000 years would it have been most possible for humans to easily walk across the Torres Strait?

    A. Approximately 50,000 years ago

    B. Approximately 80,000 years ago

    C. Approximately 100,000 years ago

    D. Approximately 120,000 years ago

Passage VI

Cycads (*Cycas* spp. and *Macrozamia* spp.) are seed bearing plants that grow in clusters or groves. These plants are highly productive, as indicated by visual inspection of their *strobuli* (seed cones). These cones typically contain a high seed count and high average seed weight. However, beyond this, botanists know very little about the cycad reproductive cycle, except that it may be characterized by *synchrony,* wherein plants in the same grove may reproduce at the same time.

Study 1 — Temperate Region #1

Researchers observed a grove of *Macrozamia* and found very small seed cones (weight = 0.6 g). Twice per month, they recorded observations on these plants and found that the seed cone reproductive cycle completed at the breaking up of the cones approximately 18 months after the beginning of seed production.

Study 2 — Tropical Region

A researcher collected a strobolus from an *M. moorei* that contained 226 mature seeds (mean seed weight = 25 g) and that produced over 5.5 kg of edible seeds in total. (Table 1 compares seed weights and other relevant data for three different cycad species.)

Study 3 — Temperate Region #2

During a field trip to find and collect some *M. communis* seeds, a researcher found a large grove that had just been burned by fire. The older, drier leaves of the cycads had been burned off, but the very young light green leaves seemed unaffected by the fire. Further, the fire had stopped burning at a paved road that bisected the grove, leaving one half of the grove burned and the other half unburned.

Six months later, the researcher returned to the burned site and recorded a considerable fresh growth of leaves and a remarkable production of seed cones. At this time, the researcher measured off two 50 by 50 m sample plots, one in the burned area and the other in an area which had not been burned but was otherwise equivalent in terms of soil nutrients, canopy, exposure, slope, and rainfall. Plants and seed cones were counted. Table 2 compares seed cone production in the two plots, and Table 3 compares the two plots as well as the tropical region.

TABLE 1								
	Seed Count			Seed Weight (in g)			Mean Seed Weight (in g)		
Species / Sample #	Number Mature (per plant)	Number Immature (per plant)	Total (per plant)	Mature Seeds (per plant)	Immature Seeds (per plant)	Total (per plant)	Mature (wt/count)	Immature (wt/count)	Total (wt/count)
Macrozamia communis									
S-1	106	29	135	770	55	825	7.26	1.9	6.11
S-2	102	34	136	520	60	580	5.10	1.8	4.26
S-3	58	120	128	465	145	610	8.02	1.2	3.43
S-4	116	5	121	965	15	980	8.32	3.0	8.10
S-5	98	---	98	880	---	880	8.98	---	8.98
S-6	135	10	145	1020	20	1040	7.56	2.0	7.17
S-7	153	2	155	1160	5	1165	7.58	2.5	7.52
S-8	148	---	148	1105	---	1105	7.47	---	7.47
Macrozamia moorei S-9	341	---	341	8016	---	8016	23.51	---	23.51
Cycas media S-10	20	---	20	130	---	130	6.50	---	6.50

TABLE 2		
	Burned Plot	Unburned Plot
Number of mature plants	142	151
Number of male cones	57	7
Number of female plants with *one* seed cone	6	7
Number of female plants with *two* seed cones	27	1
Number of female plants with *three* seed cones	3	0
Total number of seed cones	69	9

GO ON TO THE NEXT PAGE

		TABLE 3	
	Tropical Region	Temperature Region #2	
		Burned Plot	Unburned Plot
Sample area (in m²)	200	2500	2500
Total Plant Count	80	142	151
Area Per Plant (in m²)	2.5	16.5	17.6
Plants With Seed Cones	16	69	9
Average Seeds Per Plant	125	135	135
Average Weight Per Seed (in g)	6.5	7.5	7.5
Seeds Per Grounds (in g/m²)	64.9	28.0	3.65
Food Energy (in Kcal per m²)	131	56.1	7.2
Total Seed Weight In Plot (in kg)	13	69.8	9.1

28. The data presented indicate that the seed production of individual cycad plants is:

   F. Not highly variable

   G. Highly variable within a species only

   H. Highly variable between species only

   J. Highly variable both within and between species

29. Study 3 and Tables 2 and 3 suggest that researchers considered that cycad seed production should be thought of in terms of:

   A. The production of a single plant only

   B. The production of a whole grove of plants only

   C. Both single-plant and whole-grove production

   D. Potential food energy in Kcal per m²

30. Based on the data provided, which cycad species produces both the heaviest individual seeds and the greatest number of seeds per plant?

F. *M. communis*

G. *M. moorei*

H. *C. media*

J. One cannot determine this information from the data provided.

31. Which of the following is the best description of differences between the experimental designs of Studies 1 and 2 and the experimental design of Study 3?

A. Studies 1 and 2 examine natural reproduction; Study 3 examines fire-induced reproduction.

B. Studies 1 and 2 examine tropical-zone reproduction; Study 3 examines temperate-zone reproduction.

C. Studies 1 and 2 examine *Macrozamia* spp.; Study 3 examines *Cycas* spp.

D. Studies 1 and 2 are planned examinations of cycad reproduction in the same type of region; Study 3 examines cycad reproduction as a result of an accidental and unexpected event.

32. According to the data presented, all of the following can be considered benefits of fire to cycad productivity EXCEPT that fire appears to:

F. Increase cycad productivity in terms of number of seed cones per plant.

G. Increase cycad productivity in terms of number of seed cones per grove.

H. Synchronize seed production in groves.

J. Add nutrients to the soil, shortening the seed cone cycle from a normal seed production time of 18 months to a production time of approximately 6 months.

33. Other studies have revealed that consumption of raw cycad seeds is nearly always fatal, unless the toxins (poisons) in the seeds are removed first. Yet it is also known that cycad seeds have been widely consumed in human populations across Africa, Asia, and the Pacific for thousands of years. This fact suggests that cycads were likely:

A. synchronized by deliberate management of fire-burning in groves by humans

B. Not synchronized by deliberate management of fire-burning in groves by humans

C. Among the first plants detoxified by humans

D. Detoxified by humans

GO ON TO THE NEXT PAGE

Passage VII

In Australia during the Pleistocene epoch, several species of giant marsupial (pouch-bearing), plant-eating mammals became extinct, while numerous others continued to exist but dwarfed (became smaller) in size. There are two major hypotheses concerning these extinctions.

Environmental Hypothesis (A)

Some scientists believe that the extinctions and dwarfing of certain species can be attributed to known changes from a damp climate to a dry one between 30,000 and 10,000 years before present. Another subgroup of scientists favoring an environmental cause believe that the extinctions resulted directly from human-produced modifications to the environment by deliberate fire-burning of the landscape, an action that ultimately changed the plant communities that the giant marsupials depended upon for food. These human-produced modifications were believed to take place over many tens of thousands of years.

Predation Hypothesis (B)

Still other scientists believe that, within a relatively short period of time (that is, less than 10,000 years), hunting by humans caused the extinctions. Yet another group of scientists believes that the giant marsupial populations were reduced due to predation (preying upon and killing for food) by one of the few flesh-eating mammals on the island-continent—*Thylacoleo*, a small marsupial that today is extinct.

The Lanktown Swamp Site

At the Pleistocene-age site of Lanktown Swamp, the well-preserved remains of some 1,275 individual giant marsupials belonging to six extinct species were identified as having died 26,000 years before present. All were found to have been trapped in the ancient swampbed. Around 40% of the population also had evidence of "lumpy jaw"— a condition that is found in modern wild animals surviving under drought (dry) conditions. Fossil pollen samples from the site also indicate that at the time of the animal deaths, a treeless plain surrounded the area. Further, the nearest alternative watering hole was too far away for most of the large animals to travel to without dying first. Finally, three of the individuals showed evidence for being preyed upon by other mammals.

34. Scientists favoring the Predation Hypothesis divide into two subgroups. This hypothesis can be seen as comprising which two types of predation?

   F. Predation in moist climates, predation in dry climates

   G. Predation by humans, predation by other mammals

   H. Natural predation, predation by fire

   J. Predation by drought, predation by hunting

35. A scientist who supports the Environmental Hypothesis believes that the majority of the extinctions and dwarfing occurred during the documented period of major aridity (dryness) between 25,000 and 15,000 years before present. Which of the following statements, if true, would most seriously weaken support for this interpretation?

   A. Extinctions had already taken place by 37,000 years before present, when the environment was less arid.

   B. Extinctions had already taken place by 37,000 years before present, when the environment was more arid.

   C. Extinctions had not yet taken place by 37,000 years before present, when the environment was less arid.

   D. Extinctions had not yet taken place by 37,000 years before present, when the environment was more arid.

36. Geological evidence for southeastern Australia in particular suggests that humans and giant marsupials coexisted for many tens of thousands of years. This evidence is most inconsistent with which of the following hypotheses?

   F. Hypothesis A only

   G. Hypothesis B only

   H. Hypothesis A and Hypothesis B

   J. The evidence is not inconsistent with any hypothesis given.

37. The collective data from the Lanktown Swamp site best supports which of the following hypotheses?

   A. Hypothesis A only

   B. Hypothesis B only

   C. Hypothesis A and Hypothesis B

   D. Data from the Lanktown Swamp site supports none of the hypotheses.

38. At the Lanktown Swamp site, the data support all of the following hypotheses concerning the animal deaths EXCEPT that some of the animals:

   F. Became trapped and then died naturally

   G. Became trapped and then died by predation

   H. Could not travel to other water sources and so died from thirst

   J. Died due to drought

GO ON TO THE NEXT PAGE

39. All of the following are hypothetical site types that would most seriously *weaken* the arguments of a Predation Hypothesis scientist EXCEPT sites that contain:

A. Extinct marsupial remains with no indication of the presence of *Thylacoleo*

B. *Thylacoleo* remains in earlier (older) layers and extinct marsupial remains in later (younger) layers

C. Evidence of predation upon giant marsupials by *Thylacoleo*

D. No evidence of predation upon giant marsupials by *Thylacoleo* or humans

40. Which of the following hypothetical site types would lend the most support to arguments made by a Hypothesis-B scientist against Hypothesis A?

F. Sites older than 30,000 years with evidence for hunting of giant marsupials by humans that resulted in near elimination of the species

G. Sites older than 30,000 years with no evidence for hunting of giant marsupials by humans

H. Sites dated between 30,000 and 10,000 years before present with evidence for hunting of giant marsupials by humans

J. Sites dated between 30,000 and 10,000 years before present with no evidence for hunting of giant marsupials by humans

IF YOU FINISH BEFORE TIME IS CALLED, CHECK YOUR WORK ON THIS SECTION ONLY. DO NOT WORK ON ANY OTHER SECTION IN THE TEST.

Answer Key

English Test

1. B	20. H	39. C	58. F
2. F	21. D	40. G	59. A
3. A	22. H	41. A	60. F
4. J	23. D	42. J	61. D
5. B	24. J	43. B	62. F
6. H	25. C	44. J	63. B
7. D	26. H	45. D	64. G
8. G	27. A	46. H	65. A
9. D	28. G	47. A	66. G
10. G	29. D	48. H	67. C
11. C	30. F	49. C	68. J
12. F	31. B	50. J	69. B
13. C	32. G	51. B	70. H
14. G	33. D	52. J	71. A
15. D	34. H	53. D	72. G
16. G	35. A	54. F	73. C
17. D	36. G	55. B	74. H
18. H	37. B	56. J	75. C
19. B	38. H	57. C	

Mathematics Test

1. E	16. G	31. C	46. J
2. J	17. C	32. F	47. C
3. C	18. F	33. D	48. G
4. G	19. D	34. G	49. A
5. E	20. F	35. B	50. F
6. G	21. B	36. J	51. E
7. E	22. J	37. B	52. J
8. F	23. B	38. H	53. C
9. B	24. H	39. C	54. F
10. H	25. A	40. G	55. A
11. D	26. F	41. D	56. G
12. F	27. E	42. K	57. A
13. D	28. H	43. C	58. H
14. H	29. D	44. J	59. B
15. D	30. F	45. C	60. J

Reading Test

1. B	11. C	21. B	31. C
2. J	12. F	22. F	32. F
3. A	13. C	23. D	33. A
4. G	14. J	24. F	34. J
5. C	15. C	25. C	35. C
6. H	16. G	26. H	36. J
7. B	17. D	27. A	37. D
8. F	18. F	28. J	38. F
9. A	19. B	29. B	39. G
10. G	20. G	30. G	40. B

Science Reasoning Test

1. B	11. A	21. A	31. A
2. J	12. J	22. J	32. J
3. C	13. C	23. D	33. D
4. H	14. F	24. F	34. G
5. A	15. B	25. C	35. A
6. F	16. H	26. H	36. G
7. B	17. B	27. A	37. A
8. J	18. F	28. J	38. H
9. C	19. C	29. C	39. C
10. H	20. H	30. G	40. F

Scoring Your ACT Practice Test

To score your practice test, total the number of correct answers for each section. Don't subtract any points for questions attempted but missed, as there is no penalty for guessing. This score is then scaled from 1 to 36 for each section and then averaged for the all-important composite score. The average score is approximately 18.

For Your Own Benefit

To figure out your **percentage right** for each test, use the following formulas.

English Test

$$\frac{\text{Number right}}{75} \times 100 = \underline{\hspace{2cm}} \%$$

Mathematics Test

$$\frac{\text{Number right}}{60} \times 100 = \underline{\hspace{2cm}} \%$$

Reading Test

$$\frac{\text{Number right}}{40} \times 100 = \underline{\hspace{2cm}} \%$$

Science Reasoning Test

$$\frac{\text{Number right}}{40} \times 100 = \underline{\hspace{2cm}} \%$$

Practice Test 3 Analysis Sheet

	Possible	Completed	Right	Wrong
English Test	75			
Mathematics Test	60			
Reading Test	40			
Science Reasoning Test	40			
Overall Totals	215			

Analysis/Tally Sheet for Problems Missed

One of the most important parts of test preparation is analyzing **why** you missed a problem so that you can reduce the number of mistakes. Now that you've taken the practice test and checked your answers, carefully tally your mistakes by marking them in the proper column.

Reason for Mistake			
	Total Missed	Simple Mistake	Misread Problem	Lack of Knowledge
English Test				
Mathematics Test				
Reading Test				
Science Reasoning Test				
Total				

Reviewing the above data should help you determine **why** you're missing certain problems. Now that you've pinpointed the type of errors you made, take the next practice test, focusing on avoiding your most common types of errors.

COMPLETE ANSWERS AND EXPLANATIONS FOR PRACTICE TEST 3

Answers to English Test

Passage I

1. **B.** The quotation is a question, so it should end with a question mark. When the quoted words are a question, the question mark is placed inside the quotation marks and no period is needed.

2. **F.** The original version is the best of the four choices. The context calls for the present tense. Although both choices **H.** and **J.** are grammatical, they require four words, twice as many as **F.**

3. **A.** The idiom "other than" is correct. In choices **B.** and **C.**, the correct phrasing should be "from any perspective" and "different from." Choice **D.** can't be correct because the view from the earth is a "perspective in space."

4. **J.** The sentence opens with the participial phrase "Named after gods and goddesses." This phrase should be as near as possible to the word it modifies, "constellations." In the three other choices, the opening phrase seems to modify "inhabitants" or "myths" or "Hemisphere." Although the correct answer has the rather awkward repetition of "Named" and "names," it's the only version of the sentence here that avoids the misplaced modifier.

5. **B.** Because the sentence contrasts the names of the constellations of the Southern Hemisphere with those of the Northern, the conjunction that introduces the sentence should point to a contrast ("On the other hand") rather than a continuation ("Additionally," "And").

6. **H.** The passage has just cited the comic strip characters Calvin and Hobbes—names that are no more "silly" than Scooby Doo. Choices **F.** and **G.** are untrue; the sentence is related to the rest of the paragraph and it is grammatical.

7. **D.** The three wrong answers are redundant. "Turn of the century" and "the year 2000" mean the same; so do "approach" and "draw near."

8. **G.** The two adjectives should be separated by a comma. The semicolon and colon usually divide two independent clauses, but "meaningless in the natural world" is not a clause.

9. **D.** All of the other options are wordy, and since "complete" and "total" mean the same thing, using both of them is redundant.

10. **G.** This phrase should be introduced by the preposition "like." Choices **H.** and **J.** are grammatical, but wordier.

11. **C.** The connection of the paragraphs is that both names and numbers are created by humans and have no effect on the natural world. Although both choices **A.** and **B.** are true, they don't explain how the paragraphs are connected. Choice **D.** is simply wrong.

12. **F.** Because it's correct to say "did exist" and "will exist," choice **F.** is grammatical. But "will existed" in choices **G.** and **H.** isn't. Choice **J.** is wordy.

13. **C.** The context here calls for two commas, one before and one after the word "phlogistin."

14. **G.** The logical choice here is "However." The sentence before this one has a name given to something that turned out to be nonexistent, while this sentence deals with the opposite. In the phrase "In spite of this," there is no clear antecedent for "this."

15. **D.** Phrases like "the truth is," "the fact is," and "it is true that" are almost always wordy and expendable.

16. **G.** Only choice **G.** describes the content of the whole essay. Only the first two paragraphs deal with the names of the constellations (choice **F.**). The essay doesn't deal with "imaginary names" or the "development of scientific naming."

Passage II

17. **D.** Choice **C.** should read "that there are" rather than "there being." Choice **A.** isn't ungrammatical, but "the fact that" is a wordy and almost always superfluous expression. Choice **D.** is the best choice because it's the most concise and clearest phrase.

18. **H.** The answer here is the third element in a series that begins with two adjectives — "well-mannered," "thoughtful," and "xxx." To maintain the parallelism, the third term should also be an adjective ("sensitive"), not a verb and a noun (choices **F.** and **J.**) or a verb and an adjective (choice **G.**).

19. **B.** The best choice here is the shortest—the usual right answer so long as the brevity doesn't change the meaning. In this case, the use of "just" or "exact" isn't necessary with "same."

20. **H.** The context calls for an adjective to modify "relationship." "Reciprocal" is the adjective. You could use the noun "reciprocity" if the sentence read "should be one of reciprocity," although the expression is wordy.

21. **D.** Because the first sentence begins with the plural "Clients should" and this sentence continues the idea, it should also use the plural, "They should." The issue is the number of the verb, not the choice between "ought" and "should."

22. **H.** The best way to separate the parts of a series that doesn't have commas within its parts is with commas. Use the semicolon for a series with longer elements that have commas within them. Don't use the dash or the colon.

23. **D.** The proposed addition is not really connected to the subject of this paragraph, and it would interrupt its logical flow.

24. **J.** This is an indirect question. Consequently, it shouldn't have quotation marks and should be punctuated with a period. If it were a direct question (punctuated with quotation marks and a question mark), it would read "why is it," not "why it is."

25. **C.** The sentence has already introduced a subject and verb: "they don't order." We assume that this subject and the verb "don't" control the next verb ("don't send"). There's no need to repeat the pronoun.

26. H. The added phrase is parenthetical. It should be enclosed in parentheses. It could also be set off by a dash or by a comma but not by using a hyphen, colon, or semicolon.

27. A. The sentence before describes the customer's responsibility, and this sentence describes the waiter's. The transitional word here shouldn't suggest an opposition, as choices **B.** and **C.** do, or a conclusion (choice **D.**). "At the same time" is the best choice.

28. G. Keep adverbs as close as possible to the verbs they modify. By saying "have already said," you place this adverb nearest to both the verbs that it modifies.

29. D. An elliptical clause is one that implies but doesn't include its subject and its verb. Here you must imagine something like "they are" will follow the "Though." This sentence begins with two long elliptical clauses that describe waiters but don't include this implied subject. You must place the subject of these clauses as close to them as you can. In choices **A.**, **B.**, and **C.**, it seems to be "money" or "size" that is "willing to forgive" or "resentful." Only choice **D.** correctly begins the main clause of the sentence with "waiters," the noun that the two introductory clauses modify.

30. F. The correct word here is the preposition "except." The verb is "accept."

31. B. This sentence adds a logical, effective, and concluding step to the paragraph. Choice **A.** is unconvincing; the essay is so clearly personal that the point doesn't need reinforcement. Choices **C.** and **D.** are wrong; the addition isn't redundant, and it does support the point of the paragraph.

Passage III

32. G. The subject of the sentence is the singular "butterfly." The only one of the choices that's in agreement is the singular "is migratory." You could use the verb "to migrate," but the correct form would be the singular "migrates."

33. D. The best way to punctuate here is to use a period to make two sentences. There must be some punctuation between the two independent clauses, and the comma or the dash is inadequate. You could use a semicolon, although the period is a better choice.

34. H. The participial phrase "Covering as much as sixty miles a day" that opens the sentence should be followed by whatever it is that performs this action. It's not the "seasonal winds" or "wind" as in choices **F.** and **G.** The correct version (**H.**) places "the butterflies" immediately after the participial phrase. Although the active voice is normally to be preferred to the passive, there are times when you must use the passive to avoid a misplaced modifier. Choice **J.** can't be right, since it leaves the sentence without a main verb.

35. A. This is a direct question, correctly punctuated with a question mark. It isn't a quotation, so there's no reason to use quotation marks.

36. G. This phrase is the third in a series that begins with "by the position" and "by the magnetic field." To maintain the parallelism, this phrase should also use "by" with a noun: "by the scent."

37. B. "Consequently," "Also," and "At the same time" suggest a connection or similarity between what has gone before (birds and sea animals) and what is to follow (the butterflies). But the point is that the butterflies are different, unable to instruct their young, so the connective must mark a change of direction. Of the four choices, only "But" does this.

313

38. **H.** Although this sentence supplies interesting information, it isn't related to the main is-sue of the paragraph, how one generation does or does not teach another migration routes. Although the second and third sentences aren't about the butterfly, they are used to point out a difference between other migratory animals and the monarch. Although the sixth sen-tence doesn't answer the question the paragraph raises, the question is never answered in this essay.

39. **C.** The real problem here is the verb tense. The verb must indicate a past action (one per-formed by "ancestors"), so "made," not "make" or "making," is the right choice. The ear-lier phrase that parallels this one uses "that make" so the repetition of the pronoun "that" rather than "who" will maintain the parallel.

40. **G.** In this context you could say "Not a one" or "None" or "Not one" (choice **G.**) but none of the three other choices here.

41. **A.** Keep related words together. Since the prepositional phrase logically modifies "ecolo-gists," it's best placed as near as possible to this noun.

42. **J.** The wrong answers here aren't grammatical errors, but they're all much wordier than "is" with no change of meaning. In choice **A.**, the "maybe" is redundant, and so is the "theory theorizes" in choice **G.**

43. **B.** Despite its beginning with "How," this sentence isn't a question, but a statement of fact, and shouldn't have a question mark. Choices **C.** and **D.** are run-on sentences.

44. **J.** The sentence should be deleted. If, as the sentence before asserts, there is "still a mys-tery," obviously we "do not have an explanation." You could use one or the other of the two sentences, but there's no reason to use both.

45. **D.** The correct idiom here is "accidentally discovered," the adverb modifying the verb. Choice **B.** is grammatical but wordy.

46. **H.** There's no need for the comma here. The correct form is "safely," an adverb modify-ing the verb "arrived."

47. **A.** The original order of the paragraphs is a sensible one, and any change from the origi-nal order will present illogicalities.

48. **H.** The essay stresses our uncertainty about how the migrating insects find their way. Choice **F.** is true but the subject of only the first paragraph. The essay never makes a point as banal as **J.**

Passage IV

49. **C.** "Sundays" don't grow up in the Midwest; people do. The participle that begins this sentence should be followed as closely as possible by the noun or pronoun that it modifies, in this case, "I." Only choice **C.** places this pronoun first.

50. **J.** The briefest of the four choices here (**G.**) distorts the intended meaning. The best choice is **J.**, "had to be finished." Both choices **F.** and **H.** are grammatical, but also awk-ward and wordy.

51. **B.** Three of the answers begin with pronouns ("This" or "Which") with no specific an-tecedent; they're also wordier than choice **B.**

52. **J.** The best answer is the simplest here: "dull." You should reject the simile "dull as dishwater" as a cliche. "Dull and boring" is redundant, and "real dull" is a grammatical error, mistakenly using an adjective ("real") to modify another adjective.

53. **D.** Once again, the briefest expression is the best choice. The phrases "turned her off," "rubbed her the wrong way," and "was offputting" are slang and, since the sentence already includes the verb "disliked," redundant.

54. **F.** The paragraph has used subject and verbs like "I'd have to get," "I'd have to listen," and "I'd get." To maintain consistency, you should continue to use these forms, even if it requires repetition, as this choice does. In this paragraph, the repetition is part of the strategy to suggest the tediousness and sameness of the chores.

55. **B.** You could end the first sentence with a period and capitalize "On." Or you could use a semicolon after "grandfather." Since you don't have these choices here, the only correct alternative is to use a comma and the conjunction "and."

56. **J.** None of the three suggested changes improves the paragraph. In fact, they all weaken it. The strategy of the paragraph is to imitate the boring and repeated tasks with the repetition of phrases or the haircut references. The use of contractions is appropriate in an informal personal essay like this one.

57. **C.** You could say "along the same lines as" but not "along the same lines like." The best choice is the preposition "like" rather than the conjunction "as."

58. **F.** The dash is the correct choice here. If you end the sentence with a period or a semicolon after "car," the second sentence has only dependent clauses and is therefore a fragment.

59. **A.** The subject of the paragraph (and the essay) is the speaker's dislike of Sundays. The exact makeup of the Sunday meals is not nearly as important as the fact that the writer didn't enjoy them, and this long addition interrupts the listing of complaints.

60. **F.** The pronoun "who" is the subject of its clause ("who would go first"), and the whole clause, not solely the "who," is the object of the preposition. Choice **G.** confuses the contraction for "they are" ("they're") and "there."

61. **D.** The time sequence of the paragraph makes it clear that this sentence can come only after the fourth or fifth sentence. The addition is in keeping with the depressing tone of the essay so far.

62. **F.** The original version, which uses only a prepositional phrase without a subject and verb, is grammatical and to the point. There's no reason to expand it.

63. **B.** The antecedents of the pronoun are the plural "homework and Monday school days"; the plural "they" is correct. The rest of the paragraph uses the past tense, so the verb here should be "were" rather than "are."

Passage V

64. **G.** Because the phrase modifies the noun "application," you should use the adjective "rare" rather than the adverb "rarely." In choice **H.**, where the modified word is the verb "used," you need the adverb "rarely."

65. **A.** The original version correctly separates the first two parts of this series by commas and keeps the three elements parallel: three adverbs modified by "more."

66. **G.** If you begin the sentence with "Which" (choice **F.**) or "Saving" (choice **J.**), you don't have a complete sentence. The antecedent of the initial pronoun is the singular "page," so the correct choice is "It saves" rather than "They save."

67. **C.** "Conversely," "But," and "However" are used to introduce a contrast, not a continuation. The right choice here is "Also."

68. **J.** Both "on the cutting edge" and "ahead of its time" are cliches. To make matters worse, they say what has already been said by the adjective "advanced technologically." The sentence should end there.

69. **B.** "Perspective" is a noun meaning point of view. The right choice here is the adjective "prospective," which means expected, likely, or future.

70. **H.** The issue here isn't a difference in meaning, since all four choices are appropriate. But only "allow" is a plural and in agreement with the plural antecedent "programs."

71. **A.** This appositive is correctly punctuated with commas before and after.

72. **G.** Although the use of "twenty-three" suggests a plural, the subject of the first sentence is the singular collective noun "system." The pronoun that begins the next sentence refers to "system" and should be singular. Choice **J.** creates a sentence fragment.

73. **C.** In this context, you need "there will." Choice **B.** is a contraction for "they are," and choice **D.** is a possessive form.

74. **H.** The correct preposition in this idiom is "At."

75. **C.** In choices **A.**, **B.**, and **D.**, the "pen" is set to a "typewriter." By putting the phrase in parentheses and moving it ahead of the phrase "to paper," you solve this problem, and the sentence makes sense. The phrase recalls the mention of a typewriter at the beginning of the essay.

Answers to Mathematics Test

1. **E.** The following equation relates the information in the problem.

   $$16 = .25x$$

   where x represents the number of crackers in the box. Solving for x gives the answer of 64.

2. **J.** In the figure, $\angle y = 40°$, since it is a vertical angle to a 40° angle. Angles x and y and 40° must add up to 180°. Thus, $x = 100°$.

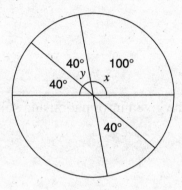

3. **C.** Each successive term is 3 more than the previous one. So the sequence is

   $-20, -17, -14, -11, -8, -5, -2, 1, 4, 7, 10$

4. **G.** Multiplying both sides of the proportion by 3 gives

   $(3)\,{}^x\!/_3 = (3)\,{}^4\!/_9$

   $\quad x = {}^{12}\!/_9$

   $\quad\ \ = {}^4\!/_3$

   $\quad\ \ = 1{}^1\!/_3$

   You could also cross multiply and then divide both sides of the equation by 9.

5. **E.** This figure represents the information in the problem.

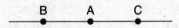

   From the figure, you can't determine if point A is closer to point B or point C. So the only possible answer is choice **E**.

6. **G.** If Dee buys 4 books at $7.60 each, she spends $30.40 on the books. Subtracting this amount from $42.00 gives $11.60.

7. E. Substitute the value of –5 for y and evaluate the expression.

$$y + 2(6 - y) = (-5) + 2(6 - (-5))$$
$$= (-5) + 2(11)$$
$$= (-5) + 22$$
$$= 17$$

8. F. Start with the innermost absolute value.

$$-\left|2 - \left|6 - (-2)\right|\right| = -\left|2 - |8|\right|$$
$$= -\left|2 - 8\right|$$
$$= -\left|-6\right|$$
$$= -6$$

9. B. Set up an equation using the given information and solve.

$$x = 4{,}500 - (.12)4{,}500$$
$$= 4{,}500 - 540$$
$$= 3{,}960$$

10. H. Although some students would try to solve this problem using algebra, probably the fastest approach is to simply substitute from the answers. Since

$$6^3 + 6^2 = 216 + 36$$
$$= 252$$

the best answer is 6.

11. D. Solve for y.

$$-24 = -8 - y$$
$$-24 + 8 = -y$$
$$-16 = -y$$
$$16 = y$$

12. F. First set up the variables. Make sure you start with $R = x$.

$$R = x$$
$$S = x + 8$$
$$S = 3T$$
$$3T = x + 8$$
$$T = (\tfrac{1}{3})(x + 8)$$

13. D. First find the coordinates of the corner opposite the corner given. Using the midpoint formula gives the following.

$$x_m = \frac{x_1 + x_2}{2} \qquad y_m = \frac{y_1 + y_2}{2}$$

$$1 = \frac{4 + x_2}{2} \qquad 3 = \frac{-2 + y_2}{2}$$

$$2 = 4 + x_2 \qquad 6 = -2 + y_2$$

$$-2 = x_2 \qquad 8 = y_2$$

Using this point $(-2,8)$ and the other given corner $(4,-2)$, you can determine the length and width of the rectangle. The length is 10 and the width is 6. So the area is 60 square units. (As an alternative method, determine the horizontal and vertical distance between the given corner and the center, double each, and multiply.)

14. H. Multiply and collect similar terms.

$$2(x + y) - (x - y) = 2x + 2y - x + y$$

$$= x + 3y$$

15. D. From the figure, you see that $\angle BDC = 140°$. So $\angle DBC = 20°$. These facts imply that $\triangle BCD$ is isosceles.

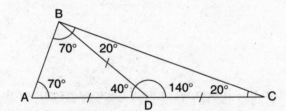

So $BD = AD$ and $\angle BAC = \angle ABD$. Therefore, these angles are each 70°. So the size of $\angle ABC$ is the sum of 70° and 20°, or 90°.

16. G. First determine the slope of the given line. Put the equation into slope-intercept form $y = mx + b$.

$$5x - 2y = -2$$

$$-2y = -5x - 2$$

$$y = \tfrac{5}{2}x + 1$$

From this equation, you see that the slope of this line is $\tfrac{5}{2}$. Perpendicular lines have slopes that are negative reciprocals of each other. So the slope of line m, which is perpendicular to the given line, is $-\tfrac{2}{5}$.

17. C. Solve the equation for x.

$$3x^2 - 10x = 8$$
$$3x^2 - 10x - 8 = 0$$
$$(3x + 2)(x - 4) = 0$$
$$3x + 2 = 0 \quad \text{or} \quad x - 4 = 0$$
$$x = -\tfrac{2}{3} \quad \text{or} \quad x = 4$$
$$x = -\tfrac{2}{3}$$

So $x = 4$.

The negative value for x doesn't make sense, since x is the length of a pencil.

18. F. The ratio of the areas of similar figures is the square of the ratio of the lengths of corresponding sides. Therefore, since the areas are in a 4 to 1 ratio, the sides must be in a 2 to 1 ratio. Since the shorter side of the smaller rectangle is 4 inches, the shorter side of the larger rectangle must be 8 inches.

19. D. Set up an equation using the given data and solve.

$$x = 32.75 + (.30)(32.75)$$
$$= 32.75 + 9.825$$
$$= 42.575$$

This rounds up to $43.

20. F. The common factor in this binomial is $9ac$. Factor this out of the expression and the result is choice **F**.

21. B. This problem asks for the value of q. Multiply the second equation by -3 and add to the first equation, which allows you to solve for q directly.

$$3p + 2q = 8$$
$$p - 4q = 5$$

$$3p + 2q = 8$$
$$-3p + 12q = -15$$
$$14q = -7$$
$$q = -1/2$$

22. J. Watch out for the change of units. One approach is to solve in terms of kilograms first. Then convert to pounds.

$$\tfrac{1}{800} = \tfrac{x}{1{,}200}$$

Solving this proportion gives $x = 1.5$, but this is in kilograms. Since there are 2.2 pounds in a kilogram, multiply by 2.2, which gives the answer of 3.3.

23. B. The key to this problem is noting that each small rectangle is twice as long as it is wide. The 2 shaded rectangles, taken together, form a square. Since the area of the square is 25, each edge of the square must be 5. Therefore, it's easy to calculate the dimensions of the overall rectangle. The length of each small rectangle is 5, and the width is 2.5. The length of the overall rectangle is 15, and the width is 10. So the perimeter is 50.

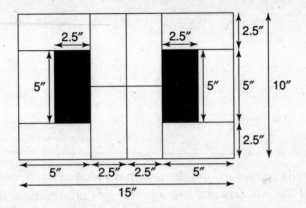

24. H. This problem involves the sum of 2 products. The total cost is made up of the daily service fee and the water usage charge.

$$c = (31)(.20) + (42)(.95)$$

$$= 6.20 + 39.90$$

$$= \$46.10$$

25. A. This problem can be solved by either an additive or subtractive process. In this case, the subtractive process is probably easier and faster. First, draw a line to complete the large rectangle. Calculate the missing sides. Determine the area of the 3 small rectangles and subtract their areas from the area of the large rectangle.

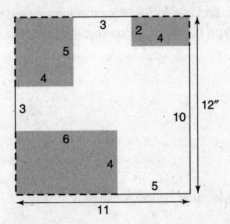

$$A = (11)(12) - (4)(5) - (6)(4) - (2)(4)$$

$$= 132 - 20 - 24 - 8$$

$$= 80$$

26. F. Solve for y by subtracting 4 from both sides of the inequality and then multiply both sides by -1 which reverses the direction of the inequality symbol.

$$4 - y > 2$$

$$4 - 4 - y > -2 - 4$$

$$-y > -6$$

$$y < 6$$

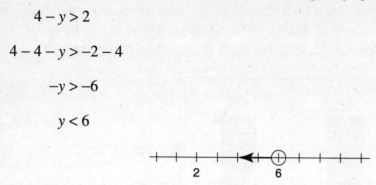

So the correct answer is **F.**

27. E. Although you could divide to find the decimal value of each, or you could form a proportion with pairs of the answers and use a process of elimination, there is a more direct method. Since the numerator of each fraction is the largest integer less than half of the denominator, the fraction that is closest to .5 in value will be the one with the largest denominator.

28. H. These 3 numbers form a Pythagorean triple, since the sum of the squares of the smaller two is the same as the square of the largest. Therefore, this triangle is a right triangle and the height and base are 10 and 24. The area is half their product.

29. D. The minimum will be 1 more than the lowest common multiple of these 3 numbers. Since the lowest common multiple is 120, the minimum must be 121. You also could try dividing each of the answers by 6, 8, and 10 to see which answer gives a remainder of 1 in each case.

30. F. First, calculate the lengths of the longer sides in terms of the shortest side. The 3 sides could be listed as a, $a + 2$, and $a + 5$. Because the longest side must be shorter than the sum of the other 2 sides, you have the following inequality.

$$(a) + (a + 2) > a + 5$$

$$2a + 2 > a + 5$$

$$2a - a > 5 - 2$$

$$a > 3$$

Since $a > 3$, the longest side must be longer than 8.

31. C. The facts that $a > 0$ and $b < 0$ are not important; only that they are not equal to 0 is important. Add by finding the lowest common multiple.

$$\frac{2b}{a} + \frac{a}{b} = \frac{2b^2}{ab} + \frac{a^2}{ab}$$
$$= \frac{2b^2 + a^2}{ab}$$
$$= \frac{a^2 + 2b^2}{ab}$$

32. F. Because the figure is made up of 2 right triangles, use the Pythagorean theorem to establish 2 equations using h.

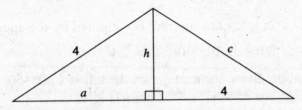

$$h^2 + a^2 = 4^2 \qquad\qquad h^2 + 4^2 = c^2$$
$$h^2 = 16 - a^2 \qquad\qquad h^2 = c^2 - 16$$

Set the two equations equal to each other and solve for c.

$$c^2 - 16 = 16 - a^2$$
$$c^2 = 16 + 16 - a^2$$
$$c^2 = 32 - a^2$$

33. D. Let x be the width of the original rectangle. Calculate the difference in areas.

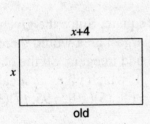 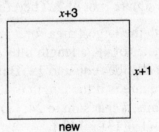

$$(x)(x + 4) = x^2 + 4x \qquad\qquad (x + 1)(x + 3) = x^2 + 4x + 3$$

The area of the new rectangle is 3 more than the original.

34. G. Since
$$\tan\theta = \frac{\sin\theta}{\cos\theta}$$
and
$$\sin\theta > \cos\theta > 0$$
then $\tan\theta > 1$

35. B. This inequality involves an absolute value. Therefore, there are two inequalities to solve.

$$-(x-2) < 3 \qquad x - 2 < 3$$
$$-x + 2 < 3 \qquad x < 3 + 2$$
$$-x < 3 - 2 \qquad x < 5$$
$$-x < 1$$
$$x > -1$$

So x is greater than -1 and less than 5.

36. J. This is a weighted average. Each number is weighted by the appropriate percentage.

$$a = 4(.25) + 3(.30) + 2(.20) + 1(.10) + 0(.15) = 2.4$$

37. B. From the information given, the triangle on the left is a 30°–60°–90° right triangle, and the triangle on the right is a 45°–45°–90° right triangle.

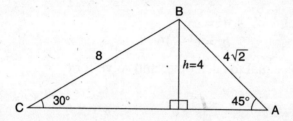

In the triangle on the left, the side opposite the 30° angle is half the length of the hypotenuse. So $h = 4$. To find the hypotenuse of a 45°–45°–90° right triangle, multiply a leg by the square root of 2. Therefore, $AB = 4\sqrt{2}$.

38. H. The rectangle with the largest area for a given perimeter is a square. Since the given rectangle has a perimeter of 48, a length plus a width is 24. The largest area would therefore be a square with all sides equal to 12. But the sides must be odd integers. So the closest you can get to a square is if the length is 13 and the width is 11, which gives an area of 143. [Try pairs of numbers that sum to 24: $(1)(23) = 23$, $(3)(21) = 65$, $(5)(19) = 95$, $(7)(17) = 119$, $(9)(15) = 135$, $(11)(13) = 143$.]

39. C. Since opposite sides of a parallelogram are parallel, EF is also parallel to AB. So $\angle EFD = \angle BAD = 60°$. Since the sum of the interior angles of a triangle is 180°,

$$y = 180 - 60 - 40$$
$$= 80°$$

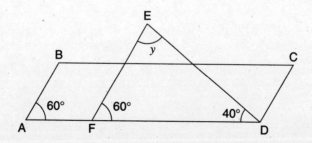

40. **G.** The y-coordinate of the x-intercept is equal to 0. Therefore, set $y = 0$ in the equation and solve for x.

$$2x + 3y = -12$$
$$2x + 3(0) = -12$$
$$2x = -12$$
$$x = -6$$

41. **D.** A good technique for comparing these square roots is to rewrite the square root by bringing the number on the outside of the root back under the root. The one closest to the square root of 49 is the answer.

$$6\sqrt{2} = \sqrt{72}$$
$$2\sqrt{6} = \sqrt{24}$$
$$5\sqrt{3} = \sqrt{75}$$
$$3\sqrt{5} = \sqrt{45}$$
$$4\sqrt{4} = \sqrt{64}$$

You can see that $3\sqrt{5}$ is the closest to the value of 7.

42. **K.** In order to be perpendicular, the slopes of the lines must be negative reciprocals of each other. Therefore, solve each equation for y to determine the slope.

$$2x + 4y = -3 \qquad\qquad kx - 2y = 6$$
$$4y = -2x - 3 \qquad\qquad -2 = -kx + 6$$
$$y = -\tfrac{1}{2}x - \tfrac{3}{4} \qquad\qquad y = \tfrac{k}{2}x - 3$$

Since the slopes must be negative reciprocals,

$\tfrac{k}{2} = 2$, or $k = 4$

43. **C.** Two supplementary angles add up to 180°. Two complementary angles add up to 90°. Therefore, if θ represents an angle, then $180 - \theta$ could represent the supplement of the angle, and $90 - \theta$ could represent the complement of the angle. So you can write the following equation.

$$180° - \theta = 4\left(90° - \theta\right)$$
$$180° - \theta = 360° - 4\theta$$
$$3\theta = 180°$$
$$\theta = 60°$$

44. **J.** This is a difference of two squares problem.

$$a^2 - b^2 = (a + b)(a - b)$$

Since $a + b = -6$, you get

$$-12 = (-6)(a - b)$$

Dividing by -6 leaves

$$2 = a - b$$

45. C. The maximum area will occur when the triangle is a right triangle. Therefore, the side of length 9 and the side of length 12 are the height and base of the triangle. So

$$c^2 = a^2 + b^2$$
$$= 9^2 + 12^2$$
$$= 81 + 144$$
$$c^2 = 225$$
$$c = 15$$

46. J. Use the formula for slope.

$$m = \frac{y_2 - y_1}{x_2 - x_1}$$
$$-3 = \frac{a - (-4)}{(-4) - 2}$$
$$-3 = \frac{a + 4}{-6}$$
$$18 = a + 4$$
$$18 - 4 = a$$
$$14 = a$$

47. C. The height of the tree (h) is the side opposite the angle of elevation. The distance from the tree (62) is the side adjacent to the angle.

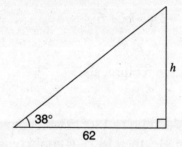

The tangent of an angle is defined as the opposite side divided by the adjacent side. Therefore, you have the following equation. (Distance measurements are in feet.)

$$\tan 38° = \frac{h}{62}$$
$$h = 62 \tan 38°$$

48. G.

4 and 30

6 and 15

8 and 22

9 and 24

12 and 40

From this list, you see that the numbers could be 6 and 15.

49. A. This is a composition of functions.

$$f(g(x)) = (2x - 1)^2 - (2x - 1) - 2$$
$$= 4x^2 - 4x + 1 - 2x + 1 - 2$$
$$= 4x^2 - 6x$$

50. F. If $\overline{AB} = x$, then

$$\overline{BC} = \frac{x\sqrt{2}}{2}$$

since it is half the length of the diagonal of a square face of the cube. Using the Pythagorean theorem gives

$$\overline{AC} = \sqrt{x^2 + \left(\frac{x\sqrt{2}}{2}\right)^2}$$

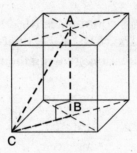

$$= \sqrt{x^2 + \frac{x^2}{2}}$$

$$= x\sqrt{1 + \frac{1}{2}}$$

$$= x\sqrt{\frac{3}{2}}$$

$$= \frac{x\sqrt{6}}{2}$$

$$\cos \angle ABC = \frac{\text{adjacent}}{\text{hypotenuse}}$$

$$= \frac{\dfrac{x\sqrt{2}}{2}}{\dfrac{x\sqrt{6}}{2}}$$

$$= \left(\frac{x\sqrt{2}}{2}\right)\left(\frac{2}{x\sqrt{6}}\right)$$

$$= \frac{\sqrt{2}}{\sqrt{6}}$$

$$= \sqrt{\frac{1}{3}}$$

$$= \frac{\sqrt{3}}{3}$$

51. E. The ratio of the areas of similar figures is the square of the ratio of the lengths of corresponding sides. If the ratio of the areas of 2 circles is 9 to 4, then the ratio of the radii is 3 to 2. Since the sum of the radii is 20π, then

$$3x + 2x = 20\pi$$

$$5x = 20\pi$$

$$x = 4\pi$$

Therefore, the radii are $2x$ and $3x$. So the radius of the larger circle is 12π. You can now calculate the area.

$$A = \pi r^2$$

$$\pi \left(12\pi\right)^2$$

$$x = 144\pi^3$$

52. J. The y-intercept for all 3 lines has coordinates $(0, -b)$. The x-intercepts for the 3 lines have coordinates of $(-4, 0)$, $(6, 0)$, and $(k, 0)$, respectively. Use the slope formula to calculate the slope of each line. Set up an equation showing their sum equal to 0 and solve for k.

$$m = \frac{y_2 - y_1}{x_2 - x_1} \qquad m = \frac{y_2 - y_1}{x_2 - x_1} \qquad m = \frac{y_2 - y_1}{x_2 - x_1}$$

$$= \frac{0 - (-b)}{(-4) - 0} \qquad = \frac{0 - (-b)}{(6) - 0} \qquad = \frac{0 - (-b)}{x_2 - x_1}$$

$$= \frac{b}{-4} \qquad\qquad = \frac{b}{6} \qquad\qquad = \frac{0 - (-b)}{(k) - 0}$$

$$\qquad\qquad\qquad\qquad\qquad\qquad\qquad = \frac{b}{k}$$

$$\frac{b}{-4} + \frac{b}{6} + \frac{b}{k} = 0$$

$$\frac{1}{b}\left(\frac{b}{-4} + \frac{b}{6} + \frac{b}{k}\right) = 0\left(\frac{1}{b}\right)$$

$$\frac{1}{-4} + \frac{1}{6} + \frac{1}{k} = 0$$

$$\frac{1}{k} = \frac{1}{4} - \frac{1}{6}$$

$$\frac{1}{k} = \frac{1}{12}$$

$$k = 12$$

53. C. If the roots of this parabola sum to 0, the roots must be an equal distance from the origin. Therefore, the line of symmetry for the parabola must be the y-axis. Using the equation for the line of symmetry, solve for k.

$$x = {-b}/{2a}$$

$$0 = {-k}/{2}$$

$$0 = -k$$

$$0 = k$$

54. F. First, find the slope of the given lines.

$$-3y = -x - 2 \qquad ky = -2x + a$$

$$y = \tfrac{1}{3}x + \tfrac{2}{3} \qquad y = -\tfrac{2}{k}x + \tfrac{a}{k}$$

Since the lines are parallel, their slopes are equal.

$$\tfrac{1}{3} = -\tfrac{2}{k}$$

$$k = -6$$

Now substitute the value of k and the coordinates of the point $(-3,4)$ into the equation and solve for a.

$$2x + ky = a$$

$$2(-3) + (-6)(4) = a$$

$$-6 + (-24) = a$$

$$-30 = a$$

55. A. Simplifying,

$$\left|\left(\frac{1}{x+y}\right)(x-y)\right| = \left|\frac{x-y}{x+y}\right|$$

If

$$\left|\frac{x-y}{x+y}\right| > 1$$

then

$$\frac{x-y}{x+y} > 1 \quad \text{or} \quad \frac{x-y}{x+y} < -1$$

For each of these last 2 inequalities, if $x > 0$, then $y < 0$. Also, if $x < 0$, then $y > 0$. So x and y must be of opposite signs. Therefore, $xy < 0$.

56. G. Let x be the length of the lawn. Use the following diagram to set up an equation to express the area of the walkway.

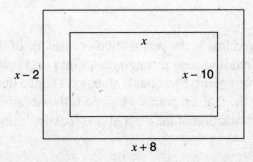

$$A = [(x+8)(x-2)] - [(x)(x-10)]$$

$$= (x^2 + 6x - 16) - (x^2 - 10x)$$

$$= x^2 + 6x - 16 - x^2 + 10x$$

$$= 16x - 16 \text{ feet}$$

57. A. The first 4 answers are first-quadrant angles. Since

$$\sin 30° = \frac{1}{2} \text{ and } 30° = \frac{\pi}{6} \text{ radians}$$

then

$$\sin 3x = \frac{1}{2} \Rightarrow 3x = \frac{\pi}{6} \text{ and } x = \frac{\pi}{18}$$

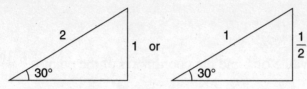

58. H. First, find the coordinates of the midpoint of the segment connecting the 2 given points. Then find the slope of that line segment.

$$x_m = \frac{x_1 - x_2}{2} \qquad\qquad y_m = \frac{y_1 - y_2}{2}$$

$$x_m = \frac{2 + (-4)}{2} \qquad\qquad y_m = \frac{y_1 - y_2}{2}$$

$$= \frac{-2}{2} \qquad\qquad\qquad y_m = \frac{4 + 6}{2}$$

$$= -1 \qquad\qquad\qquad\qquad = \frac{10}{2}$$

$$= 5$$

$$m = \frac{y_2 - y_1}{x_2 - x_1}$$

$$= \frac{6 - 4}{(-4) - 2}$$

$$= \frac{2}{-6}$$

$$= \frac{-1}{3}$$

The equation of the desired line is the perpendicular bisector of the segment joining the 2 given points. So the desired line goes through the point (−1,5) (which is the midpoint of the segment joining the 2 given points) and has a slope of 3 (since the desired line is perpendicular to the segment joining the 2 given points, its slope is the negative reciprocal of that segment's slope). Writing the equation of the desired line [passing through (−1,5) and slope of 3],

$$y - y_1 = m(x - x_1)$$

$$y - 5 = 3[x - (-1)]$$

$$y - 5 = 3x + 3$$

$$-5 - 3 = 3x - y$$

$$-8 = 3x - y$$

$$3x - y = -8$$

59. **B.** The first bag contains 2 red marbles and 1 white marble. The probability that a red marble is selected from the first bag is ⅔. Think of this marble as being ⅔ red and ⅓ white. If this marble is dropped into a bag with 2 red and 2 white marbles, think of the bag as now containing 5 marbles with 2 ⅔ of them being red. Therefore, the probability of picking a red marble out of the second bag is

$$\frac{2\frac{2}{3}}{5} = \frac{\frac{8}{3}}{5} = \frac{8}{15}$$

60. **J.** To solve this inequality, you can't cross multiply or multiply both sides by x. Since this is an inequality, you would have to change the direction of the inequality if you multiply by a negative number. Since you don't know if x is positive or negative, you must use another method. Subtract the quantity on the right from both sides, combine the left side into a single fraction, and determine for what values of x the left side is negative.

$$\frac{8}{x} < \frac{2-x}{x}$$

$$\frac{8}{x} - \frac{2-x}{x} < 0$$

$$\frac{8-(2-x)}{x} < 0$$

$$\frac{6+x}{x} < 0$$

Because the numerator and denominator must be of opposite signs, and the numerator is greater than the denominator, the numerator must be positive and the denominator must be negative. The integer values for which the numerator is positive and the denominator is negative are $-1, -2, -3, -4$, and -5. Therefore, there are 5 values of x.

Answers to Reading Test

Passage I

1. **B.** The Salazars live on the American side of the Mexican Texas border, which means choice **D.** is incorrect. Chihuahua, choice **A.**, is the "wild country" in Mexico where Sancho Salazar goes to hunt and fish, and the passage implies that San Elizario, choice **C.**, is a place where Indians live.

2. **J.** Nothing in the passage implies that the girls intrude on Eduviges' life or relationship with her family, choice **F.**; in fact, Eduviges sees to it that they spend time with her family. The passage also doesn't suggest that she scoffs at their feelings for Sancho or that she insults him directly, choice **G.**, although it does imply that she feels superior to him. Choice **H.** is incorrect; Eduviges wants her daughters to be "Spanish ladies," not American girls.

3. **A.** See lines 28–35 and 52–53. Ofelia behaves as her mother wants her to. There is no evidence that she is envious of Josie, choice **B.** Ofelia is not a peacemaker, choice **C.**; Serena fills that role (lines 90–104). And although Ofelia ignores her father's talk about Mexico and, according to her grandmother, isn't his favorite, nothing suggests that he ignores her, choice **D.**

4. **G.** See lines 10–2 and 14–16. Sancho feels that his Indian blood makes him at home with the land and the sky, but Eduviges doesn't make this positive connection, choice **F.**, and although perhaps she might believe poverty, choice **H.**, and laziness, choice **J.**, are the result of Indian blood, these aren't mentioned in the passage.

5. **C.** Obviously Josie isn't afraid of her mother's reaction, choice **A.**; she often disobeys Eduviges or ignores her criticism. Also, she doesn't disapprove of her father, choice **B.**, and, when he went into the mountains, "her spirit went with Sancho." Nothing indicates that she doesn't like being thought of as his favorite, choice **D.**

6. **H.** Eduviges sees to it that the girls are around her family more, choice **F.**, but Serena and Josie themselves "sensed that their blood was closer to the earth than an Angel's ought to be." We don't learn whether the Angels have any Indian blood (although the passage implies that they don't), choice **G.**, but it's Eduviges' indoctrination, not the absence of Indian blood, that makes the girls believe Angels are more important than Salazars. There is no evidence to support choice **J.**

7. **B.** In lines 23–27, Josie longs to be free of her mother, and she wonders what life with the Indians would be like. She also responds to her father's description of his hunting and fishing trips. Nothing in the passage suggests that she associates being Indian with creativity, choice **A.**, or determination, choice **C.** Choice **D.** might seem a possible answer, but she thinks of freedom, not loss, when she considers what it would be like to live like an Indian.

8. **F.** Upset that she couldn't go with her father, Josie probably resents her aunt's solicitude. She isn't pointing out that her aunts have a spiritual connection with lizards, choice **G.** Her aunt might believe she has a fever, choice **H.**, but this isn't the case, nor is her mother's typical response, choice **J.**, an accurate description of Josie's motives.

9. **A.** Although it may appear his wife controls him, choice **B.** (for example, he doesn't want the girls to tell her about his feelings for the wild country), Sancho actually does what he wants (lines 57–65). He is devoted to his family (lines 41–44) and nothing indicates that he despises his wife, choice **C.**; "tolerates" would be a better description of his feelings. Although he doesn't want to be part of her "phony family exercises," it isn't because he's ashamed, choice **D.**; it's because he has "more important things to do," such as fishing.

10. **G.** Josie isn't scornful or cynical (choices **F.** and **H.**), and although she may secretly want to be free from her mother's advice, she doesn't turn it into a joke, choice **J.**

Passage II

11. **C.** Adams's words support the author's description of the campaign as "boisterous." Although he may have been disgusted with tactics, nothing suggests this represents the people's attitude, choice **B.**, or that Adams rejected either or both candidates, choice **A.** His comment about civil war has nothing to do with the American Civil War, choice **D.**, but rather with the heat of the campaign.

12. **F.** See lines 23–33. Choice **J.** may be a tempting answer because the Whigs did have a strong desire to win, but nothing indicates that this desire didn't exist in previous elections as well. Choice **G.** isn't supported by the passage. Although the press played a role in the election, choice **H.**, nothing suggests that it hadn't in previous elections also.

13. **C.** Jackson is making a bid for the support of the masses, which indicates a place where he delivers speeches, not a barn, choice **A.**, a receptacle for ballots, choice **B.**, or a voting booth, choice **D.**, where such a bid would be too late.

14. **J.** See lines 29–35. The passage doesn't support choice **F.**; although Adams notes "inflammatory harangues" against Van Buren in the first paragraph, nothing suggests that the violent feelings made more people vote. Also, choice **H.** is incorrect. Nothing indicates that Harrison had "long been a popular favorite," and in fact, the passage suggests Harrison's image was created during the campaign. No evidence supports choice **G.**

15. **C.** The *Democratic Review* admits "with chagrin" that "we" have taught the Whigs the tactics that successfully elected Andrew Jackson, suggesting the paper supported Jackson. The "chagrin" indicates that the paper didn't present Harrison as a military hero or support his candidacy (choices **A.** and **B.**). Although choice **D.** may be true, nothing in the passage clearly supports the inference.

16. **G.** See lines 76–78. In spite of the Whigs' portrayal of Harrison, he didn't have a career like Jackson's, choice **F.** (lines 59–61). Choice **H.** might be tempting, but while the Whigs inflated Harrison's military achievements, they didn't fabricate his career. Also, "disaster" in choice **J.** is too strong a word to describe his lackluster record (lines 61 and 68).

17. **D.** See lines 71–73. A comparison is made with "Old Hickory," choice **A.**, who is therefore obviously someone else (Andrew Jackson, in fact). Choice **B.** also refers to Jackson; calling Harrison "the Hero of Tippecanoe" was an effort to elevate him to Jackson's status as "the Hero of New Orleans." "Hard cider," choice **C.**, became a symbol of the campaign but wasn't Harrison's nickname.

18. **F.** Ironically, these words were from a negative description of Harrison by a fellow Whig and friend of Henry Clay, the man passed over as the party's candidate. They weren't meant as a compliment, choice **G.** A newspaper reporter only reported the words, choice **H.**; Clay's friend, not Clay himself, choice **J.**, was responsible for them.

19. **B.** According to the passage, "slogans, mottos, nicknames, and catchwords" abounded in Harrison's campaign. The nickname "Tippecanoe" related to Harrison's military career, not his humble background, choice **A.** No prejudices are exploited in this slogan, choice **C.** Neither "Tippecanoe" nor "Tyler" is related to Andrew Jackson's career, choice **D.**; Tyler was Harrison's running mate.

20. **G.** The main point of the passage is that the Whigs created a successful "people's candidate" persona for Harrison, modeled on Andrew Jackson's image, and that their electioneering was energetic. Van Buren may have been viewed as an elitist, but nothing indicates that the entire press supported Harrison as a result, choice **F.** Also, the finances of the Whigs' campaign, choice **H.**, aren't alluded to in the passage, and the author explicitly states that Harrison wasn't from as humble a background as the party leaders suggested, choice **J.**

Passage III

21. **B.** The first paragraph says the large French population in the late 1700s is what made New Orleans unique. Choice **D.** is irrelevant; proximity to Haiti isn't mentioned in the passage.

22. **F.** See lines 18–20. The passage doesn't say that New Orleans was located between slave and free states (choices **H.** and **J.**), only that it was convenient to several slave states. New Orleans was an important seaport, choice **G.**, but it was the availability of work that drew African-Americans.

23. **D.** An alderman wanted to limit prostitution to a certain area, which indicates that prostitution itself was legal. Choice **A.** assumes too much. Nothing suggests the French were irreverent or that they "encouraged" loose morality—only that they enjoyed pleasures such as music and dancing. Although musicians benefited from "the district," choice **B.** isn't supported by the passage. Choice **C.** is simply incorrect; class distinctions aren't mentioned in the passage.

24. **F.** See lines 53–56. Choices **H.** and **J.** are misleading; nightclubs and publishers adopted the name "because" it was associated with jazz history. Choice **G.** is incorrect, although the district was important to musicians.

25. **C.** See lines 61–64. Choices **A.** and **B.** are tempting choices and may be the reasons Storyville is important to jazz history. However, its importance to the musicians was that it provided jobs. Choice **D.** isn't mentioned in the passage.

26. **H.** The fifth paragraph (lines 82–129) makes this clear with several details—for example, they spoke French, embraced European music, sent their children to Paris, and owned slaves. Although they were successful, nothing suggests that Creoles were the ruling class, choice **G.**, or that they were descended from runaway slaves, choice **F.** Also, the passage doesn't imply that Creoles were rejected by either whites or African-Americans, choice **J.**

27. **A.** See lines 111–113. Some uptown musicians were trained (lines 113–114), choice **B.**, although their music was rougher. Uptown music may have included influences of band and church music, choice **C.**, but this answer is incorrect because nothing suggests that these influences weren't also in Creole music. Although the passage indicates that evidence regarding improvisation is sketchy, "some reports" suggest that little improvisation was used, choice **D.** (lines 121–124).

28. **J.** Choice **F.** isn't supported in the passage; the paragraph doesn't concern Creole music. Choice **G.** is a possible answer, but this isn't the chief purpose of the paragraph. Also, this paragraph doesn't emphasize either the European, choice **H.**, or the African tradition; it stresses the variety of music in New Orleans, from opera to the musical cries of street vendors.

29. **B.** See lines 105–107. It is the downtown area where Creoles lived. Storyville is more likely to be considered the birthplace of jazz, choice **D.**, and the center of musical activity, choice **A.** Choice **C.** could be true, but it isn't indicated in the passage.

30. **G.** See line 124, where improvisation is linked to "totally fresh melodic invention." No evidence supports choices **F.** and **H.** Today, improvisation is sometimes associated with instrumental solos in the middle of a piece, choice **J.**, but this isn't part of the definition.

Passage IV

31. **C.** This opening dramatically introduces the reader to the problems caused by a rise in sea level. It doesn't specify global warming, choice **A.**, as the cause of the disaster. Although the author does say that the flooding explains the Dutch interest in future sea level increases, that statement isn't the main purpose of the paragraphs. Also, the passage doesn't say the Dutch are more concerned than others, choice **B.** Choice **D.** is irrelevant to the purpose of the paragraphs and the main idea of the passage.

32. **F.** See lines 8 and 11. Nothing in the passage implies that meltwaters caused the high tides, choice **G.**, and although it's possible the dikes and warning systems were inadequate, they weren't most responsible for the disaster (choices **H.** and **J.**).

33. **A.** According to the passage, increases in sea level could occur for several reasons (choices **B.** and **C.** among them), all tied to the heating of the earth. Choice **D.** is irrelevant to the passage; precipitation isn't mentioned.

34. **J.** Like a greenhouse, these gases hold heat in. Notice the description of "heat-trapping" in lines 38–39. The gases clearly don't filter out the sun, choice **F.** Although greenhouses may create a "controlled environment" for plants, gases like carbon dioxide aren't produced in a controlled environment, and therefore this wouldn't account for the name, choice **G.** Also, don't mistakenly choose **H.** because greenhouses have something to do with plants; that fact is irrelevant here.

35. **C.** The author doesn't question the theory of global warming (choice **A.**, lines 34–39), although he does indicate that it hasn't been proven that such warming will change sea level and cause flooding (choice **D.**, lines 69–72). In lines 116–129 he describes a time over 100,000 years ago when the earth underwent a period of warming, and therefore choice **B.** is incorrect.

36. J. All three of these are cited as causing an increase in sea level. See lines 45–48, 55–60, and 63–69.

37. D. See lines 79–83. Nothing suggests that these actions have an effect on the ice cap itself (choices **A.** and **B.**). Also, the scientists aren't studying the reasons for global warming, choice **C.**, but more accurately the possible results of global warming on sea level.

38. F. See lines 68–69. It's the melting in the Antarctic that represents the biggest threat to sea level. Choice **G.** is the amount scientists believe the ocean has been creeping upward each year. Choice **H.** is the amount thermal expansion might raise sea level in 100 years, and choice **J.** is the amount that glacial meltwaters may have boosted the ocean in the past 100 years.

39. G. This loss of stability and subsequent disintegration is described in lines 103–115. Mercer's theory isn't concerned with other glacial melting, choice **F.** Choice **H.** isn't covered in the passage, and choice **J.** is both irrelevant and incorrect.

40. B. If positive proof were available that West Antarctic ice melted previously because of a period of global warming, this would lend force to the author's argument that current global warming poses a similar threat. Choice **C.** is irrelevant; Mercer's theory is based on global warming, not a cooling of the earth's surface. Choice **A.**, while it may seem tempting, is incorrect; the 1953 flooding had nothing to do with melting Antarctic ice. Since Mercer's theory doesn't concern greenhouse gases, choice **D.** would neither support it nor call it into question.

Answers to Science Reasoning Test

Passage I

1. **B.** This is a straightforward question that relies on information found in Figure 1 only. Figure 1 shows the age at menarche for a period of approximately one hundred years. For each of the four countries, the trend lines change over time. For example, in England between 1850 and 1950, age at menarche decreases from 17 to between 13 and 14. In the USA between 1910 and 1950, age at menarche decreases from 14 to 13.

2. **J.** This difficult question requires using information from both figures. Figure 1 shows that age at puberty timing has decreased over time from age 17 in 1850 to age 13 in 1950 (approximately). Figure 2 shows weight at various ages. The weight (*y*-axis) where age 17 (*x*-axis) intersects with the line for 1835 is approximately 45 kg. Similarly, the weight where age 13 (*x*-axis) intersects with the line for 1947 is also approximately 45 kg. So, while age at menarche has been decreasing, size at menarche (based on body weight in kilograms) has remained unchanged.

3. **C.** This question is best solved by process of elimination. Choice **A.** is true, but doesn't relate directly to the question. Choice **B.** requires knowledge of the definition of *Western*, which isn't provided in the passage. Choice **D.** is incorrect because Figure 1 clearly shows data for the USA for years after 1910.

4. **H.** This question is similar to question 2, except that it uses the term *menarche* instead of *timing*. As explained above, over the last century, body weight at menarche has remained unchanged at approximately 45 kilograms.

5. **A.** This question is best solved by process of elimination. *Fatness* and *hormonal secretion* are variables that aren't directly identified in the data provided; therefore choices **B.** and **C.** can't be correct. Choice **D.** is true, but it doesn't relate directly to the question. *Mass* refers to weight, a variable that is directly identified in the data provided.

Passage II

6. **F.** The values in the volume column decrease from 19.0 to 10.5. The values in the pressure column increase from 52 to 2,240.

7. **B.** Volume decreases as pressure increases. Since the corresponding pressure for a volume of 17ml/mole is 141, and the corresponding pressure for a volume of 15ml/mole is 305, a number between 141 and 305 is needed to correspond to a volume of 16ml/mole. This eliminates choices **A.** and **D.**, which fall outside the range. Choice **C.** is too close to 305 to represent the trend of increase in pressure.

8. **J.** Solids that are *least* compressible will have volumes at the highest pressures that are closest to their volumes at a pressure of 1 kg/cm^2. If you scan the volumes at a pressure of 40,000 kg/cm^2, in the bottom row of the table, you'll see that the volumes for nylon (at 0.9366) and potassium alum (at 0.9743) represent those closest to a volume of 1.

9. **C.** Solids that are *most* compressible will have volumes at the highest pressures that are farthest from their volume at a pressure of 1 kg/cm². If you scan the volumes at a pressure of 100,000 kg/cm², in the bottom row of the table, you'll see that the volume for Cs (at 0.368) represents the volume with the greatest change from a volume of 1.

10. **H.** This question is best solved by process of elimination. Volume (*y*-axis) decreases as pressure (*x*-axis) increases. You can eliminate graphs **F.** and **J.**, since these slopes show volume increasing. You can eliminate graph **G.**, since it shows a volume slope that doesn't change in response to increasing pressure.

Passage III

11. **A.** In Experiment 1, field spiders weren't given a choice when presented with caterpillars for food. In Experiment 2, lab spiders were presented with a choice between caterpillars fed on *P. major* and caterpillars fed on *P. lanceolata*.

12. **J.** Three of the answer choices are very similar, so you should take care to choose the answer that is the most specific and directly related to material in the passage. Since the data indicate that spiders ate significantly more *P. major*-reared caterpillars, choice **H.** is incorrect. Of the remaining three possible answers, choice **J.** is the only one that is supported by information in the passage and is therefore the correct answer.

13. **C.** The experimental design does *not* assume that iridoid glycosides are nontoxic to wolf spiders, choice **C.** If it were so assumed, then the scientists would not have expected that spiders would consistently reject caterpillars raised on plants high in this chemical (which was the case).

14. **F.** Wolf spiders don't directly eat *P. lanceolata* (choice **H.**). Instead, they eat caterpillars that store chemicals that are found in this plant. Four spiders that were fed *only* caterpillars high in iridoid glycosides died, which suggests that this chemical may be harmful, and even fatal, to wolf spiders.

15. **B.** Notice how Figure 1 displays the information. This information (and the information in this question) indicates that spiders may, using the sense of touch, be sensitive to the presence of harmful chemicals in their prey (touch-and-reject). Spider responses of taste-and-reject (indicated by partly eaten caterpillars, as shown in Figure 3) may indicate detection of a harmful chemical by taste. So choices **A.** and **C.** are incorrect. While both choices **B.** and **D.** are suggested by the experiments, of the choices given, this *particular behavior* (caterpillars released after being touched but not yet bitten) suggests only choice **B.**

16. **H.** For this question, arriving at a logical conclusion based on the data may be best accomplished by a process of elimination. The data clearly indicate that spiders don't prefer caterpillars that have been raised on plants high in iridoid glycosides. So choices **F.** and **J.** are incorrect. There are two problems with choice **G.** The word *only* is too broad. It could not be determined from these experiments that the spiders have no *other* food preferences (in normal circumstances in the wild, for example). Also, nothing in the data concerns the size of the caterpillars preferred, and this choice indicates a preference for *large* caterpillars. Be careful you don't assume things not based on information given.

Passage IV

17. **B.** Table 1 shows, for the period from 1991 to 1998, that the mean average of radon concentrations (8.4 Bq m^{-3}) is significantly higher than the mean average of thoron concentrations (0.082 Bq m^{-3}).

18. **F.** To answer this question, you must compare the horizontal lines in Figures 1 and 2 for the winter months. In Figure 1 (thoron), the values corresponding with winter horizontal lines are the lowest in the entire figure; in Figure 2 (radon), the values corresponding with the winter horizontal lines are among the highest in the entire figure. Neither of these figures details monthly concentrations for ^{212}Pb.

19. **C.** Both thoron and radon gas originate from soil exhalations. During the winter months, there is usually snow and/or ice cover on the ground. Since the half-life of thoron is only 55.6 seconds, during months with a heavy winter ground cover, thoron is likely to decay well before it reaches the air. However, since radon has such a long half-life relative to thoron (3.8 days), it has time to move through the winter ground cover and reach the atmosphere. During the winter months, then, atmospheric concentrations of radon are likely to be much higher than atmospheric concentrations of thoron.

20. **H.** This study was performed in a single region. The control variables for this study were concentrations of particular soil decay product only. The study didn't control for soil conditions or meteorological conditions, which vary significantly between regions.

21. **A.** Of the variables considered in the list of answer choices (that is, half-life, chemical composition, and atomic weight), half-life is the only variable that is discussed in the passage text. Choices **B.** and **D.** are therefore incorrect. Additionally, ^{212}Pb has the longest half-life of any of the progeny of thoron listed in the question, meaning it is the most likely progeny to be detected in the study. This fact would be important to researchers, since the very short half-life of thoron directly affects its ability to be detected, especially during the winter months. Although choice **C.** is true, it doesn't directly relate to the question.

22. **J.** Wind direction is most likely to diffuse or move atmospheric concentrations of ^{212}Pb across distance, as well as to disperse or diminish concentrations relative to distance traveled. The best investigation of the effects of wind on ^{212}Pb concentrations would consequently include a comparison of data at the site, within the site, and beyond the site region.

Passage V

23. **D.** This is a straightforward question. According to Table 1, the bottom range of the Quaternary period (at the beginning of the Pleistocene epoch), or earliest date, is approximately 2 million years before the present. The top range, or most recent date, is the present.

24. **F.** The period between approximately 118,000 years ago and 126,000 years ago is 8,000 years.

25. **C.** This question requires first looking at Table 1 to get the age range for the Pleistocene epoch. According to the table, the Pleistocene epoch spans from approximately 2 million years before present to approximately 10,000 years before present. If you look at Figure 1 for the period between 140,000 years before present to 10,000 years before present, you'll see that it's apparent that sea levels during this time have generally been lower than sea levels today.

26. **H.** According to Figure 1, the two lowest recorded sea levels occurred approximately 20,000 years ago and 50,000 years ago—between 120 and 140 meters below present levels.

27. **A.** During this period, the seas were lowest approximately 20,000 years ago and 50,000 years ago.

Passage VI

28. **J.** Table 1 shows that seed weight in grams per plant varied widely *within* collected samples of *M. communis*—from 580 grams in sample 2 to 1,165 grams in sample 7 (nearly twice the weight of sample 2). Mean seed weight also varied widely *between* species—from 3.43 grams in sample 3 (*M. communis*) to 23.51 grams in sample 9 (*M. moorei*). Also, total seed count varied widely *between* species as well—from 20 seeds per plant in sample 10 (*C. media*) to 341 seeds per plant in sample 9 (*M. moorei*).

29. **C.** Table 2 shows that in Study 3, fire-burning increased the number of seed cones per female plant, apparently enhancing the productivity of a single plant. Fire-burning also increased the total number of seed cones per plot from 9 to 69.

30. **G.** According to Study 2 and Table 1, *M. moorei* yields both the heaviest seeds and the highest number of seeds per plant.

31. **A.** This question is straightforward and best solved by process of elimination. Choices **B.** and **C.** are inaccurate according to the text of the passage. Choice **D.** suggests that Study 1 and Study 2 are conducted in the same type of region, which is incorrect. Study 3 differs from the other two studies in its examination of the variable of fire-induced cycad productivity.

32. **J.** In the passage text and accompanying tables, number of seed cones per plant, number of seed cones per grove, and cone cycle synchrony are all mentioned. Soil nutrients are mentioned, but not as a benefit of fire.

33. **D.** It is reasonable to assume that if cycad seeds are toxic but that they have been consumed for thousands of years without harm, they must have been detoxified at some point in time.

Passage VII

34. **G.** Predation Hypothesis scientists divide along the type of predator—humans versus *Thylacoleo*.

35. **A.** Hypothesis A states a direct cause between an arid environment and the extinctions, which implies the notion that the animals thrived in a wetter environment. Since the period before the documented period of aridity (25,000 to 15,000 years before present) is one that is characterized by the passage text as "damp" or wet, any extinctions that occurred prior to this period would refute the scientist's interpretation. At 37,000 years before present, the environment was not arid.

36. **G.** Some advocates of Hypothesis A suggest that human-produced changes to the environment by fire-burning took place over many tens of thousands of years. Yet Hypothesis B states that killing of the giant marsupials by humans occurred in less than 10,000 years.

37. A. Of the animals at the site, 510 (40%) show evidence of "lumpy jaw," a condition associated with drought. Further, the fossil pollen samples indicate that the region lacked large trees, which require water for growth and maintenance. This information best supports the hypothesis that environmental factors influenced the extinctions.

38. H. The passage text indicates that all of the animals were found to have been trapped in the swamp ($n = 1,275$); that some of the animals may have died from predation ($n = 3$); and that some of the animals may have died due to drought ($n = 510$). The passage text also indicates travel distance to alternate watering sources but doesn't mention any evidence for death by thirst or dehydration. Drought could lead to death from conditions other than thirst—from starvation, for example, if the drought has produced a lack of food.

39. C. Some advocates of Hypothesis B suggest that the extinctions were caused by predation by *Thylacoleo* (note the EXCEPT).

40. F. Some advocates of Hypothesis B suggest that human hunting caused the extinctions, while Hypothesis A suggests that the extinctions were caused by environmental changes due to increasing aridity between 30,000 and 10,000 years before present. A scientist favoring Hypothesis B and disproving Hypothesis A would consequently look for sites that are older than 30,000 years (when the environment was wetter) that also showed evidence for human hunting and near extinction of the giant animals.

ANSWER SHEETS FOR PRACTICE TEST 4

ENGLISH TEST

1 (A) (B) (C) (D)	26 (F) (G) (H) (J)	51 (A) (B) (C) (D)
2 (F) (G) (H) (J)	27 (A) (B) (C) (D)	52 (F) (G) (H) (J)
3 (A) (B) (C) (D)	28 (F) (G) (H) (J)	53 (A) (B) (C) (D)
4 (F) (G) (H) (J)	29 (A) (B) (C) (D)	54 (F) (G) (H) (J)
5 (A) (B) (C) (D)	30 (F) (G) (H) (J)	55 (A) (B) (C) (D)
6 (F) (G) (H) (J)	31 (A) (B) (C) (D)	56 (F) (G) (H) (J)
7 (A) (B) (C) (D)	32 (F) (G) (H) (J)	57 (A) (B) (C) (D)
8 (F) (G) (H) (J)	33 (A) (B) (C) (D)	58 (F) (G) (H) (J)
9 (A) (B) (C) (D)	34 (F) (G) (H) (J)	59 (A) (B) (C) (D)
10 (F) (G) (H) (J)	35 (A) (B) (C) (D)	60 (F) (G) (H) (J)
11 (A) (B) (C) (D)	36 (F) (G) (H) (J)	61 (A) (B) (C) (D)
12 (F) (G) (H) (J)	37 (A) (B) (C) (D)	62 (F) (G) (H) (J)
13 (A) (B) (C) (D)	38 (F) (G) (H) (J)	63 (A) (B) (C) (D)
14 (F) (G) (H) (J)	39 (A) (B) (C) (D)	64 (F) (G) (H) (J)
15 (A) (B) (C) (D)	40 (F) (G) (H) (J)	65 (A) (B) (C) (D)
16 (F) (G) (H) (J)	41 (A) (B) (C) (D)	66 (F) (G) (H) (J)
17 (A) (B) (C) (D)	42 (F) (G) (H) (J)	67 (A) (B) (C) (D)
18 (F) (G) (H) (J)	43 (A) (B) (C) (D)	68 (F) (G) (H) (J)
19 (A) (B) (C) (D)	44 (F) (G) (H) (J)	69 (A) (B) (C) (D)
20 (F) (G) (H) (J)	45 (A) (B) (C) (D)	70 (F) (G) (H) (J)
21 (A) (B) (C) (D)	46 (F) (G) (H) (J)	71 (A) (B) (C) (D)
22 (F) (G) (H) (J)	47 (A) (B) (C) (D)	72 (F) (G) (H) (J)
23 (A) (B) (C) (D)	48 (F) (G) (H) (J)	73 (A) (B) (C) (D)
24 (F) (G) (H) (J)	49 (A) (B) (C) (D)	74 (F) (G) (H) (J)
25 (A) (B) (C) (D)	50 (F) (G) (H) (J)	75 (A) (B) (C) (D)

MATHEMATICS TEST

1 (A) (B) (C) (D) (E)	26 (F) (G) (H) (J) (K)	51 (A) (B) (C) (D) (E)
2 (F) (G) (H) (J) (K)	27 (A) (B) (C) (D) (E)	52 (F) (G) (H) (J) (K)
3 (A) (B) (C) (D) (E)	28 (F) (G) (H) (J) (K)	53 (A) (B) (C) (D) (E)
4 (F) (G) (H) (J) (K)	29 (A) (B) (C) (D) (E)	54 (F) (G) (H) (J) (K)
5 (A) (B) (C) (D) (E)	30 (F) (G) (H) (J) (K)	55 (A) (B) (C) (D) (E)
6 (F) (G) (H) (J) (K)	31 (A) (B) (C) (D) (E)	56 (F) (G) (H) (J) (K)
7 (A) (B) (C) (D) (E)	32 (F) (G) (H) (J) (K)	57 (A) (B) (C) (D) (E)
8 (F) (G) (H) (J) (K)	33 (A) (B) (C) (D) (E)	58 (F) (G) (H) (J) (K)
9 (A) (B) (C) (D) (E)	34 (F) (G) (H) (J) (K)	59 (A) (B) (C) (D) (E)
10 (F) (G) (H) (J) (K)	35 (A) (B) (C) (D) (E)	60 (F) (G) (H) (J) (K)
11 (A) (B) (C) (D) (E)	36 (F) (G) (H) (J) (K)	
12 (F) (G) (H) (J) (K)	37 (A) (B) (C) (D) (E)	
13 (A) (B) (C) (D) (E)	38 (F) (G) (H) (J) (K)	
14 (F) (G) (H) (J) (K)	39 (A) (B) (C) (D) (E)	
15 (A) (B) (C) (D) (E)	40 (F) (G) (H) (J) (K)	
16 (F) (G) (H) (J) (K)	41 (A) (B) (C) (D) (E)	
17 (A) (B) (C) (D) (E)	42 (F) (G) (H) (J) (K)	
18 (F) (G) (H) (J) (K)	43 (A) (B) (C) (D) (E)	
19 (A) (B) (C) (D) (E)	44 (F) (G) (H) (J) (K)	
20 (F) (G) (H) (J) (K)	45 (A) (B) (C) (D) (E)	
21 (A) (B) (C) (D) (E)	46 (F) (G) (H) (J) (K)	
22 (F) (G) (H) (J) (K)	47 (A) (B) (C) (D) (E)	
23 (A) (B) (C) (D) (E)	48 (F) (G) (H) (J) (K)	
24 (F) (G) (H) (J) (K)	49 (A) (B) (C) (D) (E)	
25 (A) (B) (C) (D) (E)	50 (F) (G) (H) (J) (K)	

CUT HERE

READING TEST

1 Ⓐ Ⓑ Ⓒ Ⓓ		26 Ⓕ Ⓖ Ⓗ Ⓙ	
2 Ⓕ Ⓖ Ⓗ Ⓙ		27 Ⓐ Ⓑ Ⓒ Ⓓ	
3 Ⓐ Ⓑ Ⓒ Ⓓ		28 Ⓕ Ⓖ Ⓗ Ⓙ	
4 Ⓕ Ⓖ Ⓗ Ⓙ		29 Ⓐ Ⓑ Ⓒ Ⓓ	
5 Ⓐ Ⓑ Ⓒ Ⓓ		30 Ⓕ Ⓖ Ⓗ Ⓙ	
6 Ⓕ Ⓖ Ⓗ Ⓙ		31 Ⓐ Ⓑ Ⓒ Ⓓ	
7 Ⓐ Ⓑ Ⓒ Ⓓ		32 Ⓕ Ⓖ Ⓗ Ⓙ	
8 Ⓕ Ⓖ Ⓗ Ⓙ		33 Ⓐ Ⓑ Ⓒ Ⓓ	
9 Ⓐ Ⓑ Ⓒ Ⓓ		34 Ⓕ Ⓖ Ⓗ Ⓙ	
10 Ⓕ Ⓖ Ⓗ Ⓙ		35 Ⓐ Ⓑ Ⓒ Ⓓ	
11 Ⓐ Ⓑ Ⓒ Ⓓ		36 Ⓕ Ⓖ Ⓗ Ⓙ	
12 Ⓕ Ⓖ Ⓗ Ⓙ		37 Ⓐ Ⓑ Ⓒ Ⓓ	
13 Ⓐ Ⓑ Ⓒ Ⓓ		38 Ⓕ Ⓖ Ⓗ Ⓙ	
14 Ⓕ Ⓖ Ⓗ Ⓙ		39 Ⓐ Ⓑ Ⓒ Ⓓ	
15 Ⓐ Ⓑ Ⓒ Ⓓ		40 Ⓕ Ⓖ Ⓗ Ⓙ	
16 Ⓕ Ⓖ Ⓗ Ⓙ			
17 Ⓐ Ⓑ Ⓒ Ⓓ			
18 Ⓕ Ⓖ Ⓗ Ⓙ			
19 Ⓐ Ⓑ Ⓒ Ⓓ			
20 Ⓕ Ⓖ Ⓗ Ⓙ			
21 Ⓐ Ⓑ Ⓒ Ⓓ			
22 Ⓕ Ⓖ Ⓗ Ⓙ			
23 Ⓐ Ⓑ Ⓒ Ⓓ			
24 Ⓕ Ⓖ Ⓗ Ⓙ			
25 Ⓐ Ⓑ Ⓒ Ⓓ			

SCIENCE REASONING TEST

1 Ⓐ Ⓑ Ⓒ Ⓓ		26 Ⓕ Ⓖ Ⓗ Ⓙ	
2 Ⓕ Ⓖ Ⓗ Ⓙ		27 Ⓐ Ⓑ Ⓒ Ⓓ	
3 Ⓐ Ⓑ Ⓒ Ⓓ		28 Ⓕ Ⓖ Ⓗ Ⓙ	
4 Ⓕ Ⓖ Ⓗ Ⓙ		29 Ⓐ Ⓑ Ⓒ Ⓓ	
5 Ⓐ Ⓑ Ⓒ Ⓓ		30 Ⓕ Ⓖ Ⓗ Ⓙ	
6 Ⓕ Ⓖ Ⓗ Ⓙ		31 Ⓐ Ⓑ Ⓒ Ⓓ	
7 Ⓐ Ⓑ Ⓒ Ⓓ		32 Ⓕ Ⓖ Ⓗ Ⓙ	
8 Ⓕ Ⓖ Ⓗ Ⓙ		33 Ⓐ Ⓑ Ⓒ Ⓓ	
9 Ⓐ Ⓑ Ⓒ Ⓓ		34 Ⓕ Ⓖ Ⓗ Ⓙ	
10 Ⓕ Ⓖ Ⓗ Ⓙ		35 Ⓐ Ⓑ Ⓒ Ⓓ	
11 Ⓐ Ⓑ Ⓒ Ⓓ		36 Ⓕ Ⓖ Ⓗ Ⓙ	
12 Ⓕ Ⓖ Ⓗ Ⓙ		37 Ⓐ Ⓑ Ⓒ Ⓓ	
13 Ⓐ Ⓑ Ⓒ Ⓓ		38 Ⓕ Ⓖ Ⓗ Ⓙ	
14 Ⓕ Ⓖ Ⓗ Ⓙ		39 Ⓐ Ⓑ Ⓒ Ⓓ	
15 Ⓐ Ⓑ Ⓒ Ⓓ		40 Ⓕ Ⓖ Ⓗ Ⓙ	
16 Ⓕ Ⓖ Ⓗ Ⓙ			
17 Ⓐ Ⓑ Ⓒ Ⓓ			
18 Ⓕ Ⓖ Ⓗ Ⓙ			
19 Ⓐ Ⓑ Ⓒ Ⓓ			
20 Ⓕ Ⓖ Ⓗ Ⓙ			
21 Ⓐ Ⓑ Ⓒ Ⓓ			
22 Ⓕ Ⓖ Ⓗ Ⓙ			
23 Ⓐ Ⓑ Ⓒ Ⓓ			
24 Ⓕ Ⓖ Ⓗ Ⓙ			
25 Ⓐ Ⓑ Ⓒ Ⓓ			

CUT HERE

English Test

Time: 45 Minutes

75 Questions

Directions: In the left-hand column, you will find passages in a "spread out" format with various words and phrases underlined and numbered. In the right-hand column, you will find a set of responses corresponding to each underlined portion. If the underlined portion is correct standard written English, is most appropriate to the style and feeling of the passage, or best makes the intended statement, mark the letter indicating "NO CHANGE." If the underlined portion is not the best choice given, choose the one that is. For these questions, consider only the underlined portions; assume that the rest of the passage is correct as written. You will also see questions concerning parts of the passage or the whole passage. Choose the response you feel is best for these questions.

Passage I

> *The following paragraphs are given a number in brackets above each one.*

Saving the Lynx

[1]

[1] Environmental groups are working to preserve some of the few remaining regions of wilderness without roads. [2] <u>They hope to save</u> the Loomis State Forest in Washington

1. A. NO CHANGE

    B. Hoping to save

    C. It is hoped they may save

    D. Hopefully saving

from <u>logging. [3] Because the</u> forest is one of
₂

the last habitats of the <u>lynx a sleek cousin of the</u>
₃

<u>bobcat</u> which was nearly made extinct by fur
₃

traders. [4] Only a small number of this rare

cat <u>survive in</u> the northern Cascades. [5]
₄

[2]

The state is thinking about building roads

<u>for logger's</u> in this area, <u>and this</u> would be a
₆   ₇

2. **F.** NO CHANGE
   G. logging; because the
   H. logging. The
   J. logging. Since the

3. **A.** NO CHANGE
   B. lynx, a sleek cousin of the bobcat,
   C. lynx, a sleek cousin of the bobcat
   D. lynx, a sleek, cousin of the bobcat,

4. **F.** NO CHANGE
   G. survives in
   H. having survived in
   J. surviving in

5. The writer wishes to add the following
   sentence to the first paragraph:

   *Several lumber companies, however, have
   expressed an interest in leasing lands in
   this area for cutting.*

   Which sentence would this addition most
   logically follow?

   A. Sentence 1
   B. Sentence 2
   C. Sentence 3
   D. Sentence 4

6. **F.** NO CHANGE
   G. for loggers'
   H. for loggers
   J. for the loggers'

7. **A.** NO CHANGE
   B. and that
   C. which
   D. a step that

threat for the lynx, and also to the wolverines
8

and grizzly bears of the region. Even more en-
9

dangered are the pine marten, a weasel-like
9

animal with nice fur. The fisher, another rare
10

member of the marten family, is also
11

threatened.
11

[3]

[1] Conservation groups are hoping to pur-
chase land in the Loomis Forest to prevent logging and roads. [2] The cost is over thirteen
million dollars, or $550 an acre. [3] So far
about three million dollars has been raised. [4]
A fund-raising drive is now underway. [12]

---

8. F. NO CHANGE
  G. threat to
  H. threatening for
  J. threatful for

9. A. NO CHANGE
  B. in greater danger are
  C. more endangered is
  D. in greater danger was

10. F. NO CHANGE
  G. fine fur.
  H. neat fur.
  J. rad fur.

11. A. NO CHANGE
  B. as also threatened.
  C. had also been threatened.
  D. will also be threatened.

12. The author wishes to add the following information to this essay:

The price represents the estimated income the state will lose if logging is not permitted in the Loomis Forest.

This sentence would most logically be placed in the third paragraph AFTER

  F. Sentence 1
  G. Sentence 2
  H. Sentence 3
  J. Sentence 4

GO ON TO THE NEXT PAGE

[4]

A lot of the money has come from high-tech workers at companies in the Seattle area. These donors who are wealthy, but young enough to still hike in wilderness areas. They went to college when the environmental movement was at its height, and one reason they came to Washington is because of its unspoiled natural beauty. Fund-raisers are visiting the rich Seattle companies and show films of the beautiful and elusive lynx, hoping to raise the balance that is needed to buy the lands and save the forest and its rare and endangered animals. 16

13. A. NO CHANGE

    B. who are wealthy and young enough

    C. are wealthy, but young enough

    D. who are wealthy but are young enough

14. F. NO CHANGE

    G. they came to Washington because

    H. coming to Washington on account

    J. one reason for their coming to Washington is because

15. A. NO CHANGE

    B. and they show

    C. and showing

    D. and they are showing

16. Suppose the writer had been asked to write a short essay on the habitat and habits of an endangered animal. Would this essay successfully fulfill the assignment?

    F. Yes, because the essay deals with the threat to the habitat of the lynx, a highly endangered animal.

    G. Yes, because the essay refers to several endangered animals, including the lynx and two kinds of marten.

    H. No, because the focus of the essay is the effort to preserve a habitat, not on the animals that live there.

    J. No, because the essay does not reveal whether or not the campaign to save the forest has been successful.

Passage II

> *The following paragraphs are given a number in brackets above each one.*

Coronation Day

[1]

I was born in <u>California and my mother</u> and
₁₇

father were born in <u>Thailand. Which</u> used to
₁₈
be called Siam. In the twentieth century it
came to be called Thailand. The family of the
present king became rulers in 1782, over two
hundred years ago. During World War II,
Thailand <u>being occupied</u> by Japan, but after
₁₉
the war the real political power was in the
hands of the military, even though there still
was a king.

17. A. NO CHANGE
  B. California, my mother
  C. California, but my mother
  D. California: my mother

18. F. NO CHANGE
  G. Thailand which
  H. Thailand; which
  J. Thailand, which

19. A. NO CHANGE
  B. was occupied
  C. occupied
  D. having been occupied

GO ON TO THE NEXT PAGE

[2]

A few years ago, my mother went to Thailand to visit my grandparents at the time when a new king was being crowned. My grandparents lived in a small town not far from the capital city, which is called Bangkok. 20

21

20. The author wishes to combine the second paragraph with the third. Which of the following is the best version of the two sentences that now make up the second paragraph?

   F. NO CHANGE

   G. A few years ago, when a new king was being crowned, my mother went to Thailand to visit my grandparents, who lived in a small town near the capital, Bangkok.

   H. A few years ago, my mother went to Thailand to visit my grandparents at the time when a new king was being crowned. They lived in a small town near the capital which is called Bangkok.

   J. A few years ago, my mother went to Thailand to visit my grandparents. At the time, a new king was being crowned. They live in a small town near the capital, Bangkok.

21. Which of the following sentences, if added at the end of the second paragraph, makes the best transition to the third?

   A. For centuries, the coronation of the Thai king has taken place in Bangkok.

   B. Bangkok is a city built on rivers with a population of over six million.

   C. Bangkok has been the Thai capital for more than three hundred years.

   D. The Southeast Asia Treaty Organization has its headquarters in Bangkok.

[3]

<u>As it happens,</u> the coronation ceremony
22

of a Thai king <u>are somewhat ancient.</u>
23

<u>It has a long history that has been passed</u>
24
<u>down from olden times.</u> On coronation day,
24

<u>a Brahmin poured holy water on the king's</u>
25
<u>hands, a Brahmin being a member of the</u>
25
<u>priestly caste.</u> Then, after the ceremony, the
25
king could issue royal commands with
the blessing of the gods Siva, Vishnu, and
Brahma. Later, Buddhist monks also

participate <u>with</u> the coronation. In modern
26
times, the Representatives and Senators will

22. **F.** NO CHANGE
  G. In fact,
  H. However,
  J. OMIT the underlined phrase.

23. **A.** NO CHANGE
  B. is somewhat ancient.
  C. are ancient.
  D. is ancient.

24. **F.** NO CHANGE
  G. Passed down from olden times, and
    having a long history.
  H. Its ancient history has been passed
    down from olden times.
  J. OMIT the underlined sentence.

25. **A.** NO CHANGE
  B. a Brahmin, a man of the priestly
    caste, pours holy water on the king's
    hands.
  C. a Brahmin pours holy water on the
    king's hands, being a member of the
    priestly caste.
  D. being a member of the priestly caste,
    a Brahmin pours holy water on the
    king's hands.

26. **F.** NO CHANGE
  G. to
  H. in
  J. OMIT the underlined word.

GO ON TO THE NEXT PAGE

also offer holy water to <u>the king. Thus combin-</u>

<u>ing</u> the religious and the political. 28
₂₇

[4]

<u>Unlike the musical "The King and I,"</u>
₂₉
Thailand today is a democracy, but it still has a

king. <u>England is also a democracy with a king.</u>
₃₀
The coronation of the king combines the new

democratic people with religion and ancient

<u>ceremony. Thus Thailand honors</u> the past and
₃₁
marches into the future.

27. **A.** NO CHANGE
   B. king, combining
   C. king, and this combines
   D. king and thus they combine

28. Which of the following is a recurring grammatical problem throughout this paragraph?

   F. inconsistency in the verb tenses
   G. pronoun case errors
   H. confusion of adverb and adjective
   J. parallelism errors

29. **A.** NO CHANGE
   B. Unlike "The King and I,"
   C. Different from "The King and I,"
   D. Unlike the country in "The King and I,"

30. Which of the following is the best version of this sentence?

   F. NO CHANGE
   G. As England is also a democracy with a king.
   H. Reduce the sentence to the phrase "Like England" to be placed at the beginning of the preceding sentence.
   J. Reduce the sentence to the phrase "like the English" to be placed at the end of the preceding sentence.

31. **A.** NO CHANGE
   B. ceremony. Thus, Thailand honoring
   C. ceremony, thus Thailand honors
   D. ceremony, thus honoring

Passage III

The following paragraphs are given a number in brackets above each one.

Becoming a French Chef

[1]

Why is French cooking so <u>famous? Some</u> answers are that they have a long history of

<u>eating good</u> and eaters who are fussy. They also have wonderful fresh fruits, vegetables,

meats and fish. <u>And the key</u> is the way chefs in France are trained. In France, a chef is looked

up to and respected <u>like a doctor or lawyers are</u> in the U.S.A. Some Americans who want to become chefs go to France to learn. But a far

32. F. NO CHANGE
  G. famous! Some
  H. famous, some
  J. famous. Some

33. A. NO CHANGE
  B. good eating
  C. well eating
  D. good eats

34. F. NO CHANGE
  G. But the key
  H. While the key
  J. So the key

35. A. NO CHANGE
  B. like a doctor is or lawyers are
  C. like a doctor or lawyer
  D. as a doctor or a lawyer

GO ON TO THE NEXT PAGE

larger number of American cooks are trained in the United States. 36

36. Which of the following versions of the last sentence in the first paragraph would most improve the transition to the second paragraph?

   F. Change the word "But" to "However."

   G. Add the clause "but a far larger number of American cooks are trained at home." at the end of the preceding sentence.

   H. Place the clause "Though a far larger number of American cooks are trained at home," at the beginning of the preceding sentence.

   J. Change the word "cooks" to "chefs."

[2]

[1] There they start training at a young age.
                            37

37. A. NO CHANGE

   B. In France training begins

   C. They start their training there

   D. In France, they start training

[2] They begin with two or three years of
            38
technical study and apprentice work. [3] An

38. F. NO CHANGE

   G. Beginning with

   H. There are, to begin,

   J. To begin, there is

apprenticeship in France is not like being an
                                  39
intern in the U.S. [4] Apprenticeships descend
39
from a system that dates back to the middle ages. [5] The work is very hard and boring, like peeling huge piles of vegetables or they
                                     40
wash pots and pans and kitchen utensils. [6]
40
The pay is small, and the hours are long, but

39. A. NO CHANGE

   B. having an internship

   C. working as an intern

   D. an internship

40. F. NO CHANGE

   G. you wash

   H. having to wash

   J. washing

the chance to watch a master chef at work is worth it. [41]

41. Suppose the author wished to add the following sentence to this paragraph:

An apprentice in a French kitchen usually works eleven hours each day.

It would most logically come AFTER

   A. Sentence 2

   B. Sentence 3

   C. Sentence 4

   D. Sentence 5

[3]

Chefs in training work long hours, <u>and this requires</u> great physical strength. This is the <u>reason perhaps,</u> far more chefs are men than women in France. A next step after apprenticeship might be learning a specialty, like making pastries or desserts. French chefs can qualify for five different certificates, <u>which are like degrees from American colleges.</u> There is a competition every third year, like the Olympics, and the winner may use the letters M.O.F. after his name and (maybe) becomes famous.

42. F. NO CHANGE

   G. which requires

   H. and it requires

   J. requiring

43. A. NO CHANGE

   B. reason perhaps

   C. reason, perhaps

   D. reason, perhaps,

44. F. NO CHANGE

   G. and these are like degrees in American colleges.

   H. being similar to degrees in American colleges.

   J. like American colleges.

[4]

The most respected cooking schools in France are in the <u>capital Paris.</u> They have been in operation for more than fifty years. But

45. A. NO CHANGE

   B. capital city Paris.

   C. capital which is Paris.

   D. capital, Paris.

GO ON TO THE NEXT PAGE

most American students go to schools like the Cordon Blue where they speak English. [46]

Passage IV

Lee Falk who died in 1999, was the author of two successful comic strips, "Mandrake the Magician" and "The Phantom." First published in 1935 and 1937 respectfully, they were the oldest comic strips written continuously by the original author. Some strips are older, but they

have not been written by their first author, who has died or retired.

Falk's first success was "Mandrake the Magician." It is the story of a magician and escape artist, like the great Houdini of early in the twentieth century, who has adventures here and abroad and all over the world. It is still carried by many newspapers.

[1] An even greater hit was "The Phantom."
[2] The Phantom wears a sort of purple

46. The author wishes to reduce this essay to three paragraphs and to include the information now in the last paragraph elsewhere. Where is the best place for these three sentences?

- **F.** At the beginning of the first paragraph
- **G.** At the end of the first paragraph
- **H.** At the end of the second paragraph
- **J.** At the beginning of the third paragraph

47. A. NO CHANGE
- **B.** Lee Falk who died in 1999
- **C.** Lee Falk, who died in 1999
- **D.** Lee Falk, who died in 1999,

48. F. NO CHANGE
- **G.** retrospectively
- **H.** respectively
- **J.** respectably

49. A. NO CHANGE
- **B.** were not written
- **C.** are unwritten
- **D.** are no longer written

50. F. NO CHANGE
- **G.** here, abroad, and all over the world.
- **H.** abroad and over the whole wide world.
- **J.** all over the world.

body-stocking and a black mask. [3] <u>He rode</u> a white horse and is accompanied by his faithful wolf-dog. [4] <u>Appearing not only in news-papers, Falk made his purple-clad hero</u> a star in cartoons and <u>the serials that used to show on Saturday mornings for kids</u>. [5] <u>It became</u> a full-length movie in the 1990s, but because it didn't have expensive special effects and car chases, it was not a big hit. 55

51. A. NO CHANGE

B. He rides

C. Riding

D. He rode on

52. F. NO CHANGE

G. Appearing not only in newspapers, Falk made the Phantom

H. Appearing not only in newspapers, Falk's purple-clad hero became

J. Falk made his purple-clad hero who was appearing not only in newspapers

53. A. NO CHANGE

B. serials shown for kids on Saturday mornings.

C. Saturday morning serials that were shown then for kids.

D. serials that used to be shown on Saturday mornings for kids.

54. F. NO CHANGE

G. Becoming

H. "The Phantom" became

J. "The Phantom" was made into

55. The author wishes to add the following sentence to this paragraph:

The Phantom lives in a jungle kingdom which he rules from a skull-shaped throne.

The sentence will fit best AFTER

A. Sentence 1

B. Sentence 3

C. Sentence 4

D. Sentence 5

GO ON TO THE NEXT PAGE

During the Second World War, the Phantom fought against the enemies of democracy, like the Fascists. <u>It was banned in Italy by</u>₅₆ <u>Mussolini; in Spain it was also banned by the</u>₅₆ <u>dictator Franco.</u>₅₆ Especially popular in Scandinavia, the Phantom was a symbol of the

Resistance during <u>the time when Germany oc-</u>₅₇ <u>cupied Norway.</u>₅₇ The popularity of the figure has not declined. In Sweden, there is a Phantom theme park today.

Unlike the superheroes like Superman, Batman, or <u>Spiderman who came later</u>₅₈ the Phantom does not have supernatural power. He

cannot see through buildings, or fly, <u>and is un-</u>₅₉ <u>able to stick to the ceiling.</u>₅₉ He still has managed to fight crime and stomp out evil for over sixty years without getting himself killed. And he still <u>looks fit</u>₆₀ in his purple suit.

56. **F.** NO CHANGE
   G. The dictators Mussolini, in Italy, and Franco, in Spain, banned the comic.
   H. In Italy, it was banned by Mussolini, and also by the dictator Franco in Spain.
   J. Banned by Mussolini in Italy, it was also banned by the Spanish dictator Franco.

57. **A.** NO CHANGE
   B. the time of Germany's occupying Norway.
   C. the German occupation of Norway.
   D. when Norway was occupied by the Germans.

58. **F.** NO CHANGE
   G. Spiderman who came later,
   H. Spiderman, who came later,
   J. Spiderman, who came later

59. **A.** NO CHANGE
   B. and he cannot stick to ceilings.
   C. and stick to the ceiling.
   D. or stick to the ceiling.

60. **F.** NO CHANGE
   G. looks fitfully
   H. fits good
   J. looks to fit

61

Passage V

[1] We all think that the first men to reach the top of Mount Everest are Edmund Hillary and Tenzing <u>Norgay who made their</u> historic
62
climb in 1953. [2] It is possible that two British climbers reached the summit almost thirty years earlier. [3] George Mallory and Andrew Irvine, members of an assault on the world's highest mountain in 1924, were last seen just one thousand feet below the summit <u>and climbing toward</u> the top. [4] Then they dis-
63
appeared. [5] We don't know if they reached the top and died on the way down or if they never reached the summit.

61. The writer is considering adding the following sentence at the beginning of the last paragraph:

Like Bruce Wayne or Clark Kent, the alter-egos of Batman and Superman, the Phantom also has a dual identity.

The writer should (or should not) make this addition because

A. The addition will distort the meaning of the paragraph by revealing a human aspect of the Phantom.

B. The addition of this sentence will mislead the reader into expecting a fully developed account of the Phantom's human characteristics.

C. The sentence adds an additional specific detail to describe the Phantom, which readers who do not know the comic may appreciate.

D. The addition will explain why the Phantom is especially popular in the Scandinavian countries.

62. F. NO CHANGE
G. Norgay, who made his
H. Norgay who made the
J. Norgay, who made their

63. A. NO CHANGE
B. and they were climbing toward
C. having climbed toward
D. and they climbed to

GO ON TO THE NEXT PAGE

64

64. The author is considering adding several sentences to the paragraph describing the successful Hillary and Tenzing expedition of 1953. Would such an addition improve the paragraph and the essay as a whole?

   F. No, because the Hillary and Tenzing climb was fifty years ago, and the essay is concerned only with the present.

   G. No, because the focus of the essay is on Mallory and Irvine and the mystery of what happened to them.

   H. Yes, because most readers are familiar with their names, but Mallory and Irvine are obscure.

   J. Yes, because the addition will give the reader a fuller sense of the dangers of mountain climbing.

65

65. The author wishes to add the following detail about Mallory:

Today Mallory is known, if at all, for replying to the question why he wanted to climb a mountain, "Because it is there."

The best place for this sentence is AFTER

   A. Sentence 1

   B. Sentence 2

   C. Sentence 3

   D. Sentence 5

[1] Later climbers which have reached the

summit have found no sign of the two

66. F. NO CHANGE

   G. who have reached

   H. who having reached

   J. who upon reaching

Englishmen, and this is not surprising since the

67. A. NO CHANGE

   B. which is not surprising

top of Everest is swept by high winds almost

   C. not a surprise,

   D. and this is no surprise

without stop. [2] Mallory and Irvine are said to carry small Kodak cameras. [3] A new expedition is planning to make a search for those cameras and answer the question of what

happened. [4] The odds are against them finding the Kodaks because the windstorms, avalanches, and moving glaciers have probably hidden them forever. [5] And even if they are found, the chance that the film could still be developed after thirty years of exposure to the winds or the fierce solar rays of that high elevation are remote.

[1] The expedition searching for signs of Mallory and Irvine will follow a route similar to the early climbers. [2] They will approach the mountain from the Chinese side. [3] Their purpose is not to reach the top themselves but

they hope a discovery of whatever they can about the climbers who disappeared so many years ago. [4] If it turns out that Mallory and Irvine reached the top before Hillary and

68. F. NO CHANGE
  G. to have carried
  H. to be carrying
  J. that they carried

69. A. NO CHANGE
  B. finding
  C. that they will find
  D. that they may find

70. F. NO CHANGE
  G. is remote.
  H. are remotely.
  J. were remote.

71. A. NO CHANGE
  B. to that of the early climbers.
  C. to the route that was taken by the early climbers.
  D. to the early climber's.

72. F. NO CHANGE
  G. hopefully they will discover
  H. to discover
  J. discovering

GO ON TO THE NEXT PAGE

Tenzing, <u>that does not lessen or diminish their</u>
₇₃
<u>achievement.</u> [5] The successful mountaineer
₇₃
has to do more that just get to the top of a
mountain. He also has to get down.

74

75

73. A. NO CHANGE

B. it will not lessen or diminsh their achievement.

C. this feat does not diminish their achievement.

D. the accomplishments of Hillary and Tenzing is neither lessened nor diminished.

74. The author wishes to add the following detail to the final paragraph:

Since many of these climbers have reached the summit on an earlier expedition, they can concentrate on the search.

The best position for the sentence is after:

F. Sentence 1

G. Sentence 3

H. Sentence 4

J. Sentence 5

75. Which of the following is the most appropriate title for this essay?

A. The Conquest of Everest

B. A Mount Everest Mystery

C. The Missing Kodak

D. The First at the Top

IF YOU FINISH BEFORE TIME IS CALLED, CHECK YOUR WORK ON THIS
SECTION ONLY. DO NOT WORK ON ANY OTHER SECTION IN THE TEST.

STOP

Mathematics Test

Time: 60 Minutes

60 Questions

Directions: In the Mathematics Test, each of the problems includes five choices (A, B, C, D, E or F, G, H, J, K). You are to solve each problem and choose the correct answer.

Note:

Unless it is otherwise stated, you can assume all of the following.

1. Figures are NOT necessarily drawn to scale.

2. Geometric figures lie in a plane.

3. The word "line" means a straight line.

4. The word "average" refers to the arithmetic mean.

1. A runner is training for a long distance race. During a practice session, she runs 31 miles at an easy pace. If 1 kilometer is equivalent to 0.62 miles, approximately how many kilometers did she run during the practice session?

A. 19

B. 20

C. 31

D. 50

E. 53

2. Beka's dad's only income is his Social Security check. He is currently receiving $940 per month in benefits. He has been informed that this amount will increase 5.5% next year. How much will his benefits be next year?

F. $945.17

G. $945.50

H. $991.70

J. $995.00

K. $1,457.00

3. Twelve students took a writing proficiency exam. The results of the exam are shown in the following chart. What was the approximate average score earned by these twelve students?

Score	0	1	2	3	4	5	6
# of students	1	0	2	2	1	4	2

A. 3.0

B. 3.6

C. 3.8

D. 4.0

E. 5.0

GO ON TO THE NEXT PAGE

4. Bus X travels 360 miles in 10 hours. Bus Y travels 240 miles in 6 hours. What is the difference, in miles per hour, between the average speed of bus X and the average speed of bus Y?

F. 2

G. 4

H. 6

J. 8

K. 10

5. There are two values of x such that $(2 - x)(x + 5) = 0$ What is the sum of those two values?

A. −10

B. −7

C. −3

D. 3

E. 7

6. The perimeter of parallelogram $WXYZ$ is three times as long as the length of $\overline{WX}$. If the length of $\overline{XY}$ is 4 inches, how many inches long is $\overline{WX}$?

F. 4

G. 8

H. 12

J. 15

K. 16

7. The total measure of all the interior angles in a polygon is 900°. How many sides does the polygon have?

A. 4

B. 5

C. 6

D. 7

E. 8

8. If $wxyz \neq 0$, which of the following is equivalent to $\dfrac{w^2 x}{yz^2}$

F. $\dfrac{xw^4 y^3 z}{w^2 z^3 x^2 y^4}$

G. $\dfrac{w^3 z^2 x^5 y}{wz^4 x^4 y^2}$

H. $\dfrac{z^6 x^3 y^3 w^3}{w^5 z^4 x^4 y^2}$

J. $\dfrac{yz^2}{w^2 x}$

K. $\dfrac{(wx)^2}{(yz)^2}$

9. In the figure below, $\overline{AB}$ is parallel to $\overline{CD}$. What is the measure of $\angle B$?

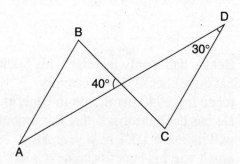

A. 70°

B. 80°

C. 90°

D. 100°

E. 110°

10. If $x = -4$ and $y = -6$, then $\left| \dfrac{x+y}{x-y} \right| = ?$

   F. 1

   G. 2

   H. 4

   J. 5

   K. 12

11. Forty-eight students took a test. Eight received a grade of A. Ten received a grade of B. Ten received a grade of D. Two received a grade of F. The rest received a grade of C. What percent of the students received a grade of C?

   A. 20%

   B. 25%

   C. 30%

   D. 33⅓%

   E. 37½%

12. If two positive whole numbers, a and b, have a greatest common factor of x and a least common multiple of y, which of the following must be true?

   F. $x > y$

   G. $x < y$

   H. $x/a = b/y$

   J. $y = xa$ or $y = xb$

   K. $x = ya$ or $x = yb$

13. If $a = -3$ and $b = -1$ and $c = 3$, then $ab^2c - a^2b^3c + abc = ?$

   A. -27

   B. -9

   C. 9

   D. 27

   E. 45

14. The perimeter of a rectangle is $(2x - 2)$ inches. If the width of the rectangle is decreased by 4 inches and the length of the rectangle is increased by $(x + 2)$ inches, what is the new perimeter (in terms of x), in inches?

   F. $4x - 6$

   G. $3x - 2$

   H. 2

   J. $4x + 10$

   K. $3x + 6$

15. If $(x - a)^2 = x^2 + 40x + a^2$ for all real values of x, then $a = ?$

   A. -40

   B. -20

   C. -10

   D. 10

   E. 20

16. Zena bought four gifts for her mother: a pen for $10, a book for $15, a sweater for $30, and a ring for $60. Alice bought the same four items during a sale. She saved 20% each on the pen and book, and she saved 30% each on the sweater and ring. What was the total amount Alice saved on her purchases?

   F. $23.00

   G. $28.75

   H. $31.50

   J. $32.00

   K. $33.00

GO ON TO THE NEXT PAGE

Mathematics Test

365

17. In the standard rectangular coordinate system, what is the slope of a line that contains the points $(-6, 4)$ and $(2, -2)$?

A. $-\frac{3}{4}$

B. $-\frac{2}{3}$

C. $-\frac{1}{2}$

D. $\frac{4}{3}$

E. 2

18. In the standard rectangular coordinate system, how many distinct zeros does $y = (x + 4)(x - 1)(x - 1)(x - 3)$ have?

F. 0

G. 1

H. 2

J. 3

K. 4

19. The expression $\dfrac{\left(\dfrac{1}{x} + \dfrac{1}{y}\right)}{2}$ is equivalent to which of the following?

A. $\dfrac{2xy}{x + y}$

B. $\dfrac{x + y}{2xy}$

C. $\dfrac{2x + 2y}{xy}$

D. $\dfrac{xy}{2x + 2y}$

E. $2xy$

20. Pencils can be purchased for $0.39 each or 12 for $4.20. How much do you save per pencil by purchasing the pencils by the dozen?

F. $0.03

G. $0.04

H. $0.12

J. $0.24

K. $0.48

21. What is the product of the polynomials $(2x^2 y^2 + xy^2)$ and $(-x^2 y + xy^2)$?

A. $-2x^4 y^3 + x^2 y^4$

B. $2x^2 y^2 - x^2 y + 2xy^2$

C. $2x^2 y^2 - x^2 y$

D. $-2x^4 y^3 + 2x^3 y^4 - x^3 y^3 + x^2 y^4$

E. $-2x^6 y^7$

22. Given $\triangle ABC$ with $\angle ACB = 90°$ (see figure), what is the value of $\dfrac{\tan \theta}{\sin \theta}$?

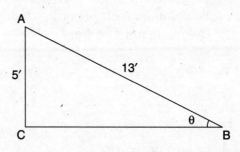

F. $\frac{5}{12}$

G. $\frac{12}{5}$

H. $\frac{12}{13}$

J. $\frac{13}{12}$

K. $\frac{13}{5}$

23. Amy is 8 years younger than Sean. If Amy will be x years old 12 years from now, how old was Sean 6 years ago?

    A. $x - 12 + 8 - 6$

    B. $x + 12 - 8 + 6$

    C. $x - 12 - 8 + 6$

    D. $x + 12 + 8 - 6$

    E. $x - 12 + 8 + 6$

24. If $(x - 3)$ is a factor of $x^2 - kx - 15$, then $k = ?$

    F. -5

    G. -2

    H. 2

    J. 3

    K. 5

25. What is the length of the side of a square in inches, if the length of the diagonal is 16 inches?

    A. 4

    B. $4\sqrt{2}$

    C. $4\sqrt{3}$

    D. $8\sqrt{2}$

    E. $8\sqrt{3}$

26. Simplify $(-2x^2)^4$.

    F. $8x^8$

    G. $16x^6$

    H. $-16x^6$

    J. $16x^8$

    K. $-16x^8$

27. Some engines require that oil be mixed with gasoline to help lubricate the engine. If one gallon is equivalent to 128 ounces, and 16 ounces of oil are mixed with 8 gallons of gasoline, what is the ratio of gasoline to oil in the mixture?

    A. ½

    B. ²⁄₁

    C. ¹⁄₆₄

    D. ⁶⁴⁄₁

    E. ¹⁄₂₅₆

28. If $x^2 - 13 = -4$, then what is the least possible value of $2x - 5$?

    F. -11

    G. -4

    H. -1

    J. 1

    K. 4

29. What is the graph of the solution set of $-2 - y > -4$?

    A.

    B.

    C.

    D.

    E.

GO ON TO THE NEXT PAGE

30. If x varies inversely as the square of y, and y varies directly as the square root of z, then which of the following shows the correct relationship between x and z?

F. x varies inversely as the square of z

G. x varies inversely as z

H. x varies directly as z

J. x varies directly as the square of z

K. x varies directly as the square root of z

31. In the standard rectangular coordinate system, if $(-6,2)$ and $(-4,2)$ are the endpoints of $\overline{AB}$ and if $(6,2)$ and $(4,-2)$ are the endpoints of $\overline{CD}$, what is the midpoint of the segment joining the midpoints of $\overline{AB}$ and $\overline{CD}$?

A. $(0,1)$

B. $(1,0)$

C. $(0,2)$

D. $(2,0)$

E. $(1,1)$

32. In the standard rectangular coordinate system, if the graphs of the lines $y = \frac{2}{3}x - 4$ and $2y = ax + 3$ are perpendicular, then $a = ?$

F. -3

G. $-\frac{3}{2}$

H. $-\frac{2}{3}$

J. $\frac{2}{3}$

K. $\frac{3}{2}$

33. What is the graph of the solution set of $|3 - x| < 2$?

A.

B.

C.

D.

E.

34. If the price of m cups is equal to the price of n plates, and 4 cups cost \$8.00, how much will 6 plates cost, in dollars?

F. $\frac{3m}{n}$

G. $\frac{6m}{n}$

H. $\frac{12m}{n}$

J. $\frac{3n}{m}$

K. $\frac{12n}{m}$

35. In the standard rectangular coordinate system, which of the following points does not satisfy the inequality $x - y > -2$?

A. $(-3,-4)$

B. $(2,3)$

C. $(4,-2)$

D. $(2,-4)$

E. $(-2,1)$

36. Given the triangle below, what is the sine of angle *B*?

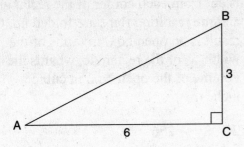

F. −½

G. $\dfrac{\sqrt{5}}{3}$

H. 2

J. $\dfrac{2\sqrt{5}}{5}$

K. $\dfrac{5\sqrt{5}}{2}$

37. The following are the equations of two lines drawn in the standard rectangular coordinate system. What is their point of intersection?

$4x - 3y = 12$
$2x + 2y = -15$

A. (6,4)

B. (−4.5,−10)

C. (1.5,−2)

D. (0.5,−8)

E. (−1.5,−6)

38. A rectangle is four times as long as it is wide. If the area of the rectangle is 48 square inches, what is the length of the rectangle, in inches?

F. $2\sqrt{3}$

G. 8

H. $4\sqrt{6}$

J. $8\sqrt{3}$

K. 12

39. The sum of twice a number and nine times the reciprocal of the number is −9. One solution for the number is −3. What is another solution?

A. −3

B. −³⁄₂

C. −²⁄₃

D. ²⁄₃

E. ³⁄₂

40. If the diagonal of a square is $2\sqrt{3}$ inches long, what is the perimeter of the square?

F. 4

G. 8

H. $4\sqrt{6}$

J. $8\sqrt{3}$

K. 36

GO ON TO THE NEXT PAGE

41. The outside dimensions of a rectangular picture frame are 12 inches by 15 inches. The frame is 2 inches wide all around the picture. What is the perimeter, in inches, of the picture?

    A. 38

    B. 42

    C. 46

    D. 54

    E. 88

42. If $\triangle ABC$ is inscribed in a circle with center O such that the center of the circle lies in the interior of the triangle and if $\angle BAO = 55°$, then what is the measure of $\angle ACB$?

    F. 25°

    G. 30°

    H. 35°

    J. 40°

    K. 45°

43. If a circle of radius 5 inches is inscribed in a square, what is the difference between the area of the square and the area of the circle, in square inches?

    A. $100 - 25\pi$

    B. $100 - 10\pi$

    C. $50 - 10\pi$

    D. $50 - 5\pi$

    E. $25 - 5\pi$

44. A rectangle is twice as long as it is wide. If a square, 4 inches on each side, is cut from each corner of the rectangle and the resulting flaps are folded up, the result is an open box. In terms of the width, x, of the rectangle, what is the volume of the open box, in cubic inches?

    F. $8x^2 - 256$

    G. $4x^2 - 64x + 256$

    H. $x^2 - 16x + 64$

    J. $x^2 - 12x + 32$

    K. $8x^2 - 96x + 256$

45. The difference of two positive numbers is 4. Their product is 4 less than 4 times their sum. Find the smaller number.

    A. −4

    B. −2

    C. 2

    D. 4

    E. 6

46. Circle A has an area of 40π. Circle B has an area of 80π. What is the ratio of the radius of circle A to the radius of circle B?

    F. $\dfrac{\sqrt{2}}{8}$

    G. $\frac{1}{4}$

    H. $\frac{1}{2}$

    J. $\dfrac{\sqrt{2}}{4}$

    K. $\dfrac{\sqrt{2}}{2}$

47. Which of the following is equivalent to $y = e^{2x}$?

   A. $x = ln2y$

   B. $x = 2lny$

   C. $x = lny/2$

   D. $x = e^{2y}$

   E. $x = ½ e^{y}$

48. If $X = \begin{bmatrix} -2 \\ 4 \end{bmatrix}$ and $Y = \begin{bmatrix} -6 \\ -4 \end{bmatrix}$ then $2X - ½Y = ?$

   F. $\begin{bmatrix} -7 \\ 6 \end{bmatrix}$

   G. $\begin{bmatrix} -1 \\ 10 \end{bmatrix}$

   H. $\begin{bmatrix} 4 \\ 8 \end{bmatrix}$

   J. $\begin{bmatrix} 2 \\ 12 \end{bmatrix}$

   K. $\begin{bmatrix} 8 \\ 16 \end{bmatrix}$

49. If $2a - b > 0$ and $ab < 0$, then which of the following must be true?

   A. $a < 0$

   B. $a < 1$

   C. $b < 0$

   D. $b > a$

   E. $b > 0$

50. If $\angle A$ is the smallest angle in $\triangle ABC$, $\angle C = 90°$, and $\sin A = x$, then $\sin B = ?$

   F. $\sqrt{x-1}$

   G. $1 - x$

   H. $\sqrt{x^2 - 1}$

   J. $1/x$

   K. $\sqrt{1 - x^2}$

51. Which of the following is equivalent to $y = \sin\left(x + \dfrac{\pi}{4}\right)$?

   A. $\cos\left(x + \dfrac{\pi}{4}\right)$

   B. $\cos\left(x - \dfrac{\pi}{4}\right)$

   C. $\cos\left(x + \dfrac{\pi}{2}\right)$

   D. $\cos\left(x - \dfrac{\pi}{2}\right)$

   E. $\cos\left(x\right)$

52. A cube has a total surface area of 384 square meters. What is the length of the main diagonal of the cube, in meters?

   F. $8\sqrt{2}$

   G. $8\sqrt{3}$

   H. $16\sqrt{2}$

   J. $16\sqrt{3}$

   K. $24\sqrt{2}$

GO ON TO THE NEXT PAGE

Mathematics Test

53. In a scalene triangle, the measure of the smallest angle is 8° less than one-third the measure of a second angle, and the measure of the third angle is 8° less than four times the measure of the smallest angle. What is the measure of the largest angle in the triangle?

   A.   74°

   B.   79.5°

   C.   84°

   D.   85.5°

   E.   88°

54. A rug maker charges $8.00 per square yard of rug plus $2.00 per yard for binding the perimeter on all his rectangular rugs. What would be the total cost for the following 6 rectangular rugs?

Quantity	Length (yards)	Width (yards)
2	5	4
1	8	5
3	10	8

   F. $880

   G. $1,280

   H. $2,560

   J. $2,900

   K. $3,660

55. Twenty-four identical, individual cubes have a total surface area of 576 square feet. If these 24 cubes are stacked to form a rectangular solid 4 cubes long, 3 cubes wide, and 2 cubes high, what is the total surface area of the resulting solid?

   A.   52 square feet

   B.   104 square feet

   C.   208 square feet

   D.   312 square feet

   E.   576 square feet

56. Tony has taken 6 out of 8 tests in a mathematics class. If each test is worth the same number of points and Tony's average on the first 6 tests was 78, what would his average have to be on the next two tests so that his overall average on all 8 tests would increase to 80?

   F.   82

   G.   84

   H.   86

   J.   88

   K.   164

57. What is the difference in length between the major axis and the minor axis of the ellipse $4(x - 4)^2 + 25(y - 2)^2 = 100$?

   A.   3 units

   B.   6 units

   C.   7 units

   D.   21 units

   E.   29 units

58. Which of the following equations could be represented by this graph?

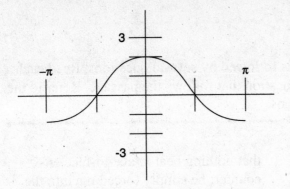

F. $\sin 2\theta$

G. $2 \sin \theta$

H. $\cos 2\theta$

J. $2 \cos \theta$

K. $\frac{1}{2} \cos \theta$

59. In the standard rectangular coordinate system, what is the maximum value of k for which these two lines will be perpendicular?

$4x - ky = 6$

$6x + ky = 8$

A. $3\sqrt{2}$

B. $2\sqrt{6}$

C. $4\sqrt{2}$

D. $4\sqrt{3}$

E. $3\sqrt{6}$

60. If four coins are dropped on a table, and the probability that any one coin will land heads up is $\frac{1}{2}$, what is the probability that exactly 2 of the 4 coins will land heads up?

F. $\frac{1}{4}$

G. $\frac{5}{16}$

H. $\frac{3}{8}$

J. $\frac{7}{16}$

K. $\frac{1}{2}$

IF YOU FINISH BEFORE TIME IS CALLED, CHECK YOUR WORK ON THIS SECTION ONLY. DO NOT WORK ON ANY OTHER SECTION IN THE TEST.

STOP

Reading Test

Time: 35 Minutes

40 Questions

Directions: Each of the four passages in this test is followed by several questions. Read each passage and then choose the best answer to each question that follows the passage. Refer to the passage as often as necessary to answer the questions.

Passage I

Prose Fiction: This passage is from Sheila Ballantyne's Imaginary Crimes (©1982 by Sheila Ballantyne).

Marian Linden taught piano in a small, immaculate studio apartment on 9th Avenue North. For some reason that I will never understand, she agreed to
(5) take me as a pupil at a reduced rate the summer I turned twelve. I had fought with Daddy for months over my lessons with Hazel. Even when I told him that she hit my fingers with a ruler when I
(10) made mistakes, he was curiously undisturbed; I guess the price was right. He continued sending Greta to her, free of charge, but I finally refused. After a standoff of many months, he started to
(15) throw Marian Linden's name around as though he'd known her all his life. Some prodigy who lived in the north end of town had given a recital that was covered by the local papers, and Miss
(20) Linden's picture had been featured as his teacher. Maybe she reminded Daddy of his sister, Mabel. Maybe he was just desperate to find someone more impressive than Hazel who could keep me at
(25) the keyboard with a minimum of strife, and thus fulfill another one of Mother's dreams. By the time he'd begun alluding to my Carnegie Hall debut, he must have realized it would help to start with
(30) lessons. He didn't phone Miss Linden because he had learned from experience

that nothing beat a face-to-face encounter; he simply forced me into the car one Saturday and brazened it out at
(35) her door five miles later.

I was too awed by her to sulk. She was very gracious, inviting us into her living room and even offering tea. I sat stiffly in a straight-backed chair and listened as
(40) Daddy calmly cited Mother's death, my nonexistent talent, his great dreams for me and, incidentally, the multimillion-dollar property in his name, the timber rights to which at this very moment no
(45) less than five major lumber companies were turning purple competing for. Marian Linden listened politely, drew in her breath at the appropriate moments, and said, "I see." It was hard to interpret
(50) her reactions; she had an innate dignity that made her seem very well-contained. She was not an old woman, but she carried herself with a certain respect and treated others that way, too. Her amber
(55) hair was thick, and just beginning to gray. She wore it in an upswept style, held in place with a large tortoise-shell comb.

As Daddy's voice droned on, I let my
(60) eyes wander around the apartment. The walls were a stark white and the Steinway glistened richly at the far end of the room, by the window. There was a small Oriental rug in the middle of the

(65) room, and well-chosen prints hung at balanced intervals along the white walls. By the end of our visit, she had agreed to take me on provisionally, at the reduced fee. I don't know whether it was
(70) kindness or pity that motivated her and I have trouble making that distinction even to this day. The interview felt no different from renting the homes, or being enrolled in the Edgemont School:
(75) After watching him operate, I always felt I had gained admission by fraudulent means. I would argue this point with myself, saying: Well, most of what he said was true, wasn't it? And I'd an-
(80) swer, yes, it was true, but there are certain uses to which the truth can be put, certain ways of manipulating it, that come dangerously close to lying. The gold mines and properties weren't true;
(85) those were just figments of his imagination. But then I'd get confused; because if those weren't true, then how would we survive? I ended up believing in them, while at the same time retaining
(90) my skepticism about them—which amounted to a form of nonbelief, without the risk.

Once a week I took the bus after school to the dark brick building with the
(95) leaded windows and climbed the stairs to Miss Linden's apartment. She had no delusions about my future, only a steady belief in the perfectibility of present skills. It took her about three weeks to
(100) see that something was standing in my way of achieving that goal. She tried, in a gentle and respectful way, to find out what was wrong. I was torn between the wish to confess the chaos at home and
(105) its effects on my concentration, and the fear of more Police Department matrons if I did. Investigating a second complaint, they would be sure to notice Daddy's growing disintegration and
(110) remove us from the home. I couldn't

explain that, for me, the lessons had become less a goal than an emotional oasis. I was terrified that she would terminate them because of my lack of
(115) progress, yet could think of no way to overcome the turmoil inside that kept me from progressing. It was enough just to be in her presence each week, to slide onto the piano bench and feel her there
(120) at my side, concerned, and knowing what she was doing. It was enough to see the evidence of art and truth and civilization there on her walls, and in her gestures. I groped for some way to get
(125) this across to her, but failed.

1. According to the passage, the narrator refuses to take piano lessons from Hazel because she

   A. Is scornful of Hazel's musical talents.

   B. Resents her father.

   C. Doesn't like Hazel or her teaching methods.

   D. Is envious of her sister Greta's talents.

2. Which of the following is the most likely reason that the narrator's father wants Marian Linden to be his daughter's piano teacher?

   F. He saw her picture in the newspaper with one of her prodigies.

   G. She is less expensive than Hazel.

   H. He trusts her because he feels he has known her all his life.

   J. She reminds him of his wife Mabel.

GO ON TO THE NEXT PAGE

3. Which of the following best describes the narrator's feelings upon first meeting Marian Linden?

    A. She is petulant and resentful because of her father's bullying.

    B. Although nervous, she is excited by the idea of working with Marian Linden.

    C. She is impressed by Marian Linden and her surroundings.

    D. Although suspicious of Marian Linden, she likes being in the apartment.

4. From lines 30-35, it is reasonable to infer that the narrator's father

    F. Has confidence in his powers of persuasion.

    G. Feels guilty about his behavior as a father.

    H. Wants to be a pianist himself.

    J. Wants to help build his daughter's self-confidence.

5. The description of Marian Linden in the second paragraph emphasizes her

    A. Wealth.

    B. Dignity.

    C. Beauty.

    D. Intelligence.

6. To the narrator, Marian Linden's response (line 49, "I see.") indicates that the piano teacher

    F. Doesn't believe what the narrator's father is saying.

    G. Thinks that the narrator's father is more interested in money than in his daughter.

    H. Is polite but does not reveal what she is thinking.

    J. Recognizes the father's mental instability.

7. When the narrator says in lines 76–77 that she feels she has often gained admission by "fraudulent means," she means that

    A. Her father believes in her even though there is no foundation for that belief.

    B. She is able to make others accept her out of pity.

    C. She doesn't allow herself to reveal her true feelings.

    D. Her father twists the truth to achieve his goals.

8. Which of the following is the best interpretation of the narrator's "nonbelief, without the risk" (lines 91–92)?

    F. In spite of the fact that he has let her down many times, she has to believe in her father because she loves him.

    G. For the sake of survival, she has to believe what her father says, even though on some level she knows many of his claims are untrue.

    H. She respects her father while at the same time knowing he is deluded.

    J. She does not want to accuse her father of lying because to do so she would risk losing him.

9. It is reasonable to infer from lines 107–110 that

 A. The narrator has been in trouble with the law.

 B. Someone has lodged a previous complaint with the police about the narrator's father.

 C. The narrator's family has been running from the law because of the father's criminal past.

 D. The narrator is the victim of a custody battle.

10. The main reason that the piano lessons with Marian Linden are important to the narrator is that

 F. The piano teacher is the first person who has treated her with respect.

 G. Unlike the narrator's father, Marian Linden has no illusions about her but accepts her anyway.

 H. Marian Linden represents the success that can come with developing your talent.

 J. Marian Linden represents the success that can come with never giving up on your dreams.

Passage II

Social Science: *This passage is from* Wilderness and the American Mind *by Roderick Nash (©1967 by Yale University).*

The concept of a wilderness system marked an innovation in the history of the American preservation movement. It expressed, in the first place, a determi-
(5) nation to take the offensive. Previous friends of the wilderness had been largely concerned with *defending* it against various forms of development.

But the post-Echo Park mood was confi-
(10) dent, encouraging a bold, positive gesture. Second, the system meant support of a wilderness in general rather than of a particular wild region. As a result, debate focused on the theoretical value of
(15) wilderness in the abstract, not on a local economic situation. Finally, a national wilderness preservation system would give an unprecedented degree of protection to wild country. Previously, preser-
(20) vation policy in the National Forests had been only an administrative decision subject to change at any time by Forest Service personnel. Even the laws creating National Parks and Monuments
(25) deliberately left the way open for the construction of roads and tourist accommodations. The intention of the wilderness bill, however, was to make any alteration of wilderness conditions
(30) within the system illegal.

Congress lavished more time and effort on the wilderness bill than on any other measure in American conservation history. From June 1957 until May 1964
(35) there were nine separate hearings on the proposal collecting over six thousand pages of testimony. The bill itself was modified and rewritten numerous times. One reason for the extraordinary delay
(40) in reaching a decision was the vigorous opposition to the permanent preservation of wilderness from wood-using industries, oil, grazing and mining interests, most professional foresters, some
(45) government bureaus, and proponents of mass recreation with plans for mechanized access to outdoor areas. At the root of their dissent was the feeling that a wilderness preservation system would
(50) be too rigid and inflexible. Adhering to the multiple-use conception of the function of the public domain, they contended that the bill locked up millions of acres in the interests of a small number

GO ON TO THE NEXT PAGE

(55) of campers. It was not that the critics of the system opposed wilderness preservation on principle. They agreed for the most part with W. D. Hagenstein, Executive Vice President of the

(60) Industrial Forestry Association, that wilderness had its place. "The only question," he asserted, "is where and how much. To dedicate, willy-nilly, millions of acres of land to wilderness

(65) before they are adequately studied to determine their highest uses to society, cannot be justified under either multiple- or single-use concepts." The ambivalence such a statement reflects is

(70) understandable in the light of the history of the American attitude toward wilderness: Appreciation is so relatively new that it is difficult to deny the claims of civilization—especially with the finality

(75) of the wilderness system.

In defense of the bill, preservationists hastened to assure men like Hagenstein that it did not consist of "willy-nilly" removal of land from productive purposes

(80) but only gave legal sanction to areas already administered as wilderness. They pointed out that the most land the system would ever include was about fifty million acres or roughly two percent of

(85) the nation. And they added, in David Brower's words, that "the wilderness we now have is all . . . men will ever have." A century had brought greatly changed conditions. "If the year were 1857 in-

(90) stead of 1957," one supporter of the legislation wrote, "I'd definitely say no." But given the almost total dominance of civilization, he was compelled to work for saving the remnants of undeveloped

(95) land. Repeatedly, preservationists explained that they were endeavoring to protect the right of future generations to experience wilderness. Answering the argument that only a tiny minority

(100) actually went into wild country for recreation, they declared that for many just *knowing* wilderness existed was immensely important. As for the objection on multiple-use grounds, wilderness ad-

(105) vocates exposed as fallacious the assumption that this doctrine must apply to every acre. True multiple use, they contended, made sense only for the public domain as a whole, providing for

(110) economic uses on some portions and wilderness recreation on others.

11. According to the passage, one of the reasons the idea of a wilderness system represented a change in thinking was that it

   A. Was based on realistic economic goals rather than idealistic hopes.

   B. Would give more decision-making power to the Forest Service and provide more national parks and monuments.

   C. Would not allow the construction of highways and recreational facilities in national parks.

   D. Was based on preserving wilderness in general rather than on preserving particular local wilderness areas.

12. It is reasonable to infer from the first paragraph that the preservation movement

   F. Had become a major political force.

   G. Had recently enjoyed a victory for its cause.

   H. Was becoming progressively more alienated.

   J. Was finally able to make effective compromises.

13. It would be reasonable to infer from the passage that opponents of the wilderness bill would agree with all of the following EXCEPT

   A. Commercial interests should be considered in any preservation legislation.

   B. A legislated wilderness system wouldn't benefit most of the population.

   C. There is no need to preserve wilderness in an industrial nation.

   D. Land considered for wilderness preservation should be studied to determine its best social use.

14. Preservationists argued that a wilderness system would include at the most

   F. Two percent of the land in the nation

   G. Ten percent of the land in the nation

   H. Two percent of the land in the nation in addition to those areas already sanctioned as wilderness areas

   J. Fifteen million acres of land

15. From the third paragraph of the passage it would be reasonable to infer that the wilderness bill had more appeal in the 1950s than it would have had in the 1850s because

   A. The economic incentives for developing land were weaker in the 1950s than in the 1850s.

   B. By the 1950s, industrial civilization was well established and undeveloped land was becoming scarcer.

   C. People in the 1950s were subject to greater stress than people in the 1850s and therefore needed the escape that wilderness would provide.

   D. People in the 1850s were more opposed to government regulation than were people in the 1950s.

16. According to the passage, which of the following best describes the attitude toward wilderness of those who opposed wilderness legislation in the 1950s?

   F. Hostility

   G. Ambivalence

   H. Fearfulness

   J. Indifference

17. According to the passage, arguments against a wilderness preservation system were most likely based on

   A. The belief that the system was a stop-gap measure in preventing development.

   B. The idea that government involvement in regulating the environment was inappropriate.

   C. The belief that such a rigid system would forbid any commercial use of wilderness land.

   D. The awareness that wood-using industries would find ways to circumvent any preservation system.

GO ON TO THE NEXT PAGE

Reading Test

18. From the passage, it is reasonable to infer that the "multiple-use conception of the function of the public domain" (lines 51–52) refers to the idea that

F. Land appropriated by the government should be used for many purposes to benefit many citizens.

G. If the government designates by law that certain wilderness areas must be preserved, then many people will be able to "experience wilderness."

H. Mechanized access to outdoor areas should be provided by the government to help more people have access to wilderness.

J. Private industry should be allowed to manage public lands so that more people will benefit from them.

19. Opposition to the wilderness system was particularly strong because it

A. Threatened an end to free enterprise

B. Would prevent too many citizens from enjoying the outdoors

C. Made wilderness areas off limits to any alterations

D. Was supported by a group of fanatical businessmen

20. According to the passage, which of the following best summarizes the preservationist's basic view of the wilderness?

F. It provides important recreational benefits for many people in an industrial society.

G. It is of value in and of itself.

H. It represents innocence and beauty.

J. It should be preserved because of its historical importance.

Passage III

Humanities: *The following passage is from* The Great Illusion, 1900-1914 *by Oron J. Hale (©1971 by Oron J. Hale).*

Concurrently with revolutionary developments in science, new styles and forms in the arts made their appearance and clamored for contemporary recogni-
(5) tion. Doubtless there was some interreaction between the revolutionary developments in art and those in science. Wassily Kandinsky, the first twentieth-century painter to plunge into abstrac-
(10) tionism, has recorded how the discovery that there were bodies smaller than atoms caused him to rethink the whole problem of reality in nature and art. Franz Marc, an associate of
(15) Kandinksy's, declared: "The art of tomorrow will give form to our scientific convictions." Guillaume Apollinaire, poet and press agent for Cubism, related the multiple perspective style of the
(20) Cubist artists to the newest mathematics and introduced the term "fourth dimensional" into the vocabulary of modern aesthetics. The principal styles in painting of the prewar period—Fauvism,
(25) Cubism, Abstraction, and Futurism—paralleled on the time scale the momentous achievements of Röntgen, Curie, Planck, Einstein, Rutherford, Correns, De Vries, and Morgan. However, the as-
(30) sumption of cross-fertilization should not be pushed too far. No cultural group was more isolated and estranged from science than the avant-garde artists. At most, through popular media of commu-
(35) nication, they were made aware of the revolutionary changes in the scientists' conception of nature. We must also assume that changes in the concept of "reality," which the scientist developed and
(40) the philosopher sensed, also affected the

artist. Artist, scientist, philosopher, all experienced a sharp displacement of their conceptions of "reality."

Change was in the air, and the sensitive
(45) artist felt the pulse of the new century. In the 1890s, and increasingly as we approach 1900, the word "new" appears so frequently and in so many connections as to attract the historian's attention—
(50) the "new humor," the "new realism," the "new woman," the "new drama," and the "new art." It crept into title pages and appeared on mastheads—*The New Review, New Ages, New Statesman*, and
(55) *Nouvelle Revue*. Furthermore, technology with its geometric patterns and the optical effects that came with speed— the train, the motorcar, the airplane— were not without suggestive influence
(60) on the artists. More directly, the camera was taking out of the artist's hand the actual task of making records and providing "visual aids," thus requiring reconsideration of his social and
(65) intellectual function. From published remarks and writings we know that young artists felt that a new age required a new art. The generation of avant-garde artists that now began to gain attention wanted
(70) to escape from bondage to the nineteenth century; they felt that traditional modes and canons were antiquated if not hypocritical; they were skeptical and wanted to arouse strong feeling in their
(75) audience, to destroy lethargy, to participate in a cultural revolution.

21. The main idea of the first paragraph is that in the early 20th century

    A. Artists and scientists joined forces against tradition.

    B. Scientific discoveries led to an artistic backlash that glorified imagination.

    C. Mathematics led to the Cubist's new perspective on the world.

    D. New developments in science affected the main artistic movements of the period.

22. It can reasonably be inferred from the first paragraph that

    F. Cubism was the most important movement in the early 20th century.

    G. Avant-garde artists had more in common with scientists than they did with philosophers.

    H. Röntgen and Correns were important prewar scientists.

    J. Apollinaire was the most important spokesman for modern art.

23. The first artist to embrace abstract painting was

    A. Kandinsky.

    B. Marc.

    C. De Vries.

    D. Apollinaire.

24. "Cross-fertilization," in line 30, most probably refers to

    F. The influence that artists exerted on scientists.

    G. The influence science had on art.

    H. Scientists influencing artists and artists influencing scientists.

    J. The negative effect of science on the artistic version.

GO ON TO THE NEXT PAGE

25. In line 32, "estranged" most nearly means

  A. Foreign.

  B. Misunderstood.

  C. Alienated.

  D. Unusual.

26. In lines 44–55, the author uses examples to show that during this period there was

  F. Widespread interest in change.

  G. Bitterness toward traditional manners and morals.

  H. Complete faith in science and technology.

  J. Great superficiality in people's view of the world.

27. According to the passage, the prewar period was characterized by

  A. A growing friction between scientists and avant-garde artists.

  B. The dominance of "fourth-dimensional" art.

  C. Public acceptance of artistic styles such as Fauvism.

  D. A change in the artist's view of physical reality.

28. According to the passage, forms of modern transportation influenced artists because of the

  F. Visual effects of their speed.

  G. Innovative use of traditional materials.

  H. Clean, geometrical lines of their designs.

  J. Psychological effects of the freedom they offered.

29. In the author's view, which of the following best describes the camera's effect on artists in the early 20th century?

  A. It made them reconsider their function as recorders of people and events.

  B. It brought them innovative techniques.

  C. It rendered them virtually obsolete in the eyes of society.

  D. It pushed them to a rejection of all forms of realistic painting.

30. According to the passage, all of the following statements might fairly characterize artists of this period EXCEPT

  F. They looked at familiar things with a new eye.

  G. They saw art as inferior to science.

  H. They believed that the modern age demanded a new kind of art.

  J. They didn't mind shocking their audiences.

Passage IV

Natural Science: This passage is from Why Aren't Black Holes Black? *by Robert M. Hazen with Maxine Singer (©1997 by Robert M. Hazen and Maxine Singer).*

In an effort to reduce a difficult and complex question to its essence, scientists at times tend to oversimplify nature. Such has been the case more
(5)   than once in studies of the history of the Earth. Two centuries ago a debate raged between catastrophists and uniformitarianists, who asked, "What is the

dominant mechanism of geological
(10) change?" The former claimed that epic
events such as the biblical deluge shape
the planet, while the latter argued for
gradual and steady change over unimag-
inable eons. Similarly, neptunists and
(15) plutonists reduced the complex issue of
rock genesis to a question of the action
of water versus the action of heat. In
each case, the models that seem closest
to the mark combine these extremes.

(20) A similarly polarized debate has en-
livened recent studies of evolution.
Darwin's original thesis, and the point
of view supported by evolutionary
"gradualists," is that change occurs
(25) slowly and in small increments. Such
changes are all but invisible over the
short time span of modern observations,
and, it is argued, they are usually ob-
scured by innumerable gaps in the
(30) imperfect fossil record. Gradualism is a
comforting, steady state model, repeated
over and over again in generations of
textbooks. By the early twentieth century the question about evolution rate
(35) had been answered in favor of gradualism to most biologists' satisfaction.

Sometimes a closed question must be
reopened as new evidence, or new arguments based on old evidence come to
(40) light. In 1972, paleontologists Stephen
Jay Gould and Niles Eldredge chal-
lenged conventional wisdom with a
dramatic variation on natural selection.
This opposing viewpoint, called punctu-
(45) ated equilibrium, posits that species
change one to another in relatively
sudden bursts, without a leisurely transition period. These episodes of rapid
speciation are separated by relatively
(50) long static spans during which a species
may change hardly at all.

The punctuated equilibrium hypothesis
attempts to explain a curious feature of
the fossil record —one that has been
(55) familiar to all paleontologists for more
than a century, but has usually been
ignored. Many distinctive fossil species
appear to remain unchanged for millions
of years—a condition of stasis at odds
(60) with Darwin's model of continuous
change. Numerous distinctive marker or
"index" fossils, for example, are abundant throughout the world's rocks, and
prove useful in dating sediments.
(65) Intermediate fossil forms predicted by
Darwin's gradualism, however, are for the
most part lacking. In most localities, a
given species of clam or coral persists
essentially unchanged throughout a thick
(70) formation of rock, only to be replaced
suddenly by a new and different species.
Furthermore, similar discontinuous sequences of distinctive organisms are
commonly found in several widely
(75) separated localities.

The evolution of North American
horses, which was once presented as
a classic textbook and museum example
of gradual evolution, is now providing
(80) equally compelling evidence for
punctuated equilibrium. A convincing
fifty-million-year sequence of modern
horse ancestors, each slightly larger,
with more complex teeth, a longer face,
(85) and more prominent central toe, seemed
to prove Darwin's contention. But close
examination of those fossil deposits now
reveals a somewhat different story, one
that is wonderfully displayed in the
(90) recently rearranged exhibit of horse
evolution at New York's American
Museum of Natural History. Horses
evolved in discrete steps, each of which
persisted almost unchanged for millions
(95) of years and was eventually replaced by

GO ON TO THE NEXT PAGE

Reading Test

a distinctive newer model. The four-toed *Eohippus* preceded the three-toed *Miohippus*, for example, but North American fossil evidence suggests a (100) jerky transition of distinct species between the two genera. If evolution has been a continuous, gradational process, one might expect that almost every fossil specimen would be slightly different (105) from every other.

If it seems difficult to imagine how major changes could occur rapidly, consider this: An alteration of a single gene in flies is enough to turn a normal fly (110) with a single pair of wings into one that has two pairs of wings.

The question of evolution rate must now be turned around: Does evolution ever proceed gradually, or does it always (115) occur in short bursts? Detailed field studies of continuous sequences of fossiliferous rocks provide the best potential tests of gradualism versus punctuated equilibrium. Occasionally, a sequence of (120) fossil-rich strata permits a comprehensive look at one type of organism over long time spans.

Peter Sheldon's trilobite localities in central Wales, for example, offer a de- (125) tailed glimpse into three million years of one marine environment. In that study, each of eight different trilobite species was observed to undergo a gradual change in the number of segments— (130) typically an increase of one or two segments over the whole time interval. No significant discontinuities were observed, leading Sheldon to conclude that environmental conditions were quite (135) stable during that period.

Similar exhaustive studies are required for many different kinds of organisms from many different time intervals.

Most researchers expect to find that (140) both modes of speciation are correct: Slow, continuous change may be the norm during periods of environmental stability, while rapid speciation occurs during periods of environmental stress. (145) But a lot more studies like that of Peter Sheldon are needed before we can say for sure.

31. The main idea of paragraph one is that

   A. Scientists frequently disagree strongly about the causes of natural phenomena.

   B. Scientific theories sometimes oversimplify complex natural processes.

   C. Extremists such as catastrophists and uniformitarianists do a disservice to science by failing to compromise.

   D. Ultimately, scientific truth is impossible to attain.

32. "Polarized," as it is used in line 20, most nearly means

   F. At two extremes.

   G. Negative and positive.

   H. Intensified.

   J. Factual and hypothetical.

33. Based on evidence in the passage, the gradualist's approach to evolution could be seen as most similar to

    A. The catastrophist's view of geological change.

    B. The neptunist's view of rock genesis.

    C. The plutonist's view of rock genesis.

    D. The uniformitarianist's view of geological change.

34. Which of the following would be most likely to support the gradualist's approach to evolution?

    F. Evidence of the emergence of a new species after a major geological event

    G. Evidence of a species rapidly adapting to a change in the environment

    H. Evidence of small, incremental changes in a species over a long period of time

    J. Evidence of the parallel development of two distinct species

35. The hypothesis of punctuated equilibrium

    A. Attempts to refute the theory of natural selection.

    B. Resulted from the discovery of new fossils.

    C. Helps explain the innumerable gaps in the existing fossil record.

    D. Addresses aspects of the existing fossil record previously ignored.

36. According to the passage, which of the following could be expected if the hypothesis of punctuated equilibrium is correct?

    F. A significant number of marker or "index" fossils

    G. Rapid speciation

    H. Fossils showing continuous change over millions of years

    J. Balanced speciation

37. According to the passage, the example of the evolution of North American horses (lines 76–105) can be used to support

    A. Only the punctuated equilibrium hypothesis.

    B. Only the gradualist viewpoint.

    C. Neither the gradualist nor the punctuated equilibrium point of view.

    D. Both the gradualist and punctuated equilibrium viewpoints.

38. The author uses the example of the dramatic change in a fly to illustrate that

    F. Even today the effects of gene alteration are uncertain.

    G. Species continue to evolve.

    H. Long periods of time are not required for major changes in a species.

    J. Natural selection operates through genetic alteration.

GO ON TO THE NEXT PAGE

Reading Test

39. Peter Sheldon's findings (lines 123–135) are most significant to evolutionary theories because they indicate

   A. Small changes in a species over a long period of time.

   B. A stable marine environment.

   C. Significant changes in some trilobites.

   D. The simultaneous development of different forms of trilobites.

40. It is reasonable to infer from the passage that the author believes that

   F. Although there is conflicting evidence, most research supports the punctuated equilibrium hypothesis.

   G. The decision by the American Museum of Natural History to rearrange the horse evolution exhibit proves that the gradualist argument is the stronger view.

   H. Environmental stress is more common than environmental stability.

   J. More studies of species over a long period of time are needed before any theory can be advanced with confidence.

IF YOU FINISH BEFORE TIME IS CALLED, CHECK YOUR WORK ON THIS SECTION ONLY. DO NOT WORK ON ANY OTHER SECTION IN THE TEST.

Science Reasoning Test

Time: 35 Minutes

40 Questions

Directions: Each passage in this test is followed by several questions. After you read each passage, select the correct choice for each of the questions that follow the passage. Refer back to the passage as often as necessary to answer the questions.

Passage I

Table 1 presents physical data for the nine planets in the solar system. Table 2 provides some miscellaneous astronomical constants (values that do not change). In Table 1, average distances, masses, diameters, and gravities are given *relative* to the Earth, where Earth = 1 and values for all other planets are proportional to the Earth data. To find *absolute* (or actual) values for these data, use the appropriate astronomical constant provided in Table 2.

TABLE 1					
PLANETS *(alphabetized)*	**MEAN DISTANCE TO SUN, relative to Earth** *(Earth= 1)*	**MASS, relative to Earth** *(Earth= 1)*	**MEAN DIAMETER, relative to Earth** *(Earth= 1)*	**MEAN DENSITY** *(g/cm^2)*	**SURFACE GRAVITY, relative to Earth** *(Earth= 1)*
Earth	1.000000	1.000	1.00	5.52	1.00
Jupiter	5.202803	318.350	10.97	1.33	2.65
Mars	1.523691	0.107	0.52	4.12	0.39
Mercury	0.387099	0.054	0.38	5.46	0.38
Neptune	30.057767	17.26	3.38	2.47	1.23
Pluto	39.517740	<0.100	0.45	<5.50	<0.50
Saturn	9.538843	95.300	9.03	0.71	1.17
Uranus	19.181945	14.580	3.72	1.56	1.05
Venus	0.723332	0.814	0.97	4.96	0.87

GO ON TO THE NEXT PAGE

387

TABLE 2	
CONSTANT	**VALUE**
Mass of Earth	5.97×10^{27} g
Mass of Earth's Moon	1.987×10^{33} g
Mass of Sun	7.343×10^{25} g
Moon's Mean Distance from Earth	384,400 km
Sun's Diameter	864,408 miles
Sun's Mean Density	1.41 g/cm³
Sun's Radius	6.965×10^{10} cm

1. Table 1 lists the planets in alphabetical order. If, instead, the planets were listed in order of distance to the sun (closest to farthest), which four planets would be at the end of the list?

   A. Mercury, Venus, Earth, Mars

   B. Mars, Earth, Venus, Mercury

   C. Saturn, Uranus, Neptune, Pluto

   D. Pluto, Neptune, Uranus, Saturn

2. According to the data provided, which two planets are closest to the Earth?

   F. Venus and Mars

   G. Jupiter and Mars

   H. Mercury and Venus

   J. Venus and Jupiter

3. According to the data provided, which planet has a surface gravity that is most similar (closest) to the surface gravity of Earth?

   A. Neptune

   B. Saturn

   C. Uranus

   D. Venus

4. According to the data provided, which planet is the smallest?

   F. Earth

   G. Mars

   H. Mercury

   J. Venus

5. According to the data provided, what is the approximate absolute (actual) mass of Mars?

   A. 6×10^{26} g

   B. 6×10^{27} g

   C. $6 \times 10 \times 26$ g

   D. 0.107 g

Passage II

In July 1986, an accident occurred at the Chernobyl Nuclear Power Plant that discharged radionuclides (radioactive particles) into the atmosphere, producing widespread airborne contamination. Seven years later, scientists conducted a series of experiments on soils at a site 30 km from the plant to investigate the influence of different types of agricultural and transportation activities on secondary contamination by release into the atmosphere of radionuclides buried in soils after the disaster.

During the experimental trials, soil and meteorological parameters were measured. Some of the trials were performed during neutral weather conditions, with the remainder of the experiments performed during slightly and moderately unstable weather conditions. Table 1 details the findings of these experimental trials of six different types of activities, and compares these with trials for a control situation of no performed activities and resuspension of particles by wind transport only.

TABLE 1							
ACTIVITY	DATE OF TRIAL	TIME OF TRIAL	AVERAGE WIND VELOCITY $(m\,s^{-1})$	AVERAGE FRICTION VELOCITY $(m\,s^{-1})$	SOIL HUMIDITY (DAMPNESS) (% moisture)	^{137}Cs ACTIVITY CONCENTRATION $(mBq\,m^{-3})$	^{137}Cs MEAN DIAMETER (μm)
Resuspending of particles by wind	05/14/93 to 05/20/93	12:00 - 10:00	2.2	0.20	5.7 7.0 7.1	0.54	5.6
Assembling of study equipment	05/07/93	10:00 - 15:20	4.3	0.40	---	0.81	13.8
	05/08/93	10:00 - 15:20	4.3	0.40	---	0.81	13.8
Cutting grass	05/08/93	10:00 - 17:00	5.6	0.55	6.2	1.7	5.5
Plowing with small tractor	05/11/93	12:20 - 14:10	3.5	0.31	6.1	4.6	7.7
	05/11/93	16:15 - 17:25	3.5	0.32	7.4	4.6	7.7
	05/12/93	11:45 - 13:45	4.6	0.42	5.2	6.7	5.6
	05/12/93	16:30 - 18:30	5.0	0.44	4.9	6.7	5.6
	05/23/93	10:40 - 12:50	4.7	0.47	1.9	41.7	7.1
	05/25/93	11:15 - 13:05	5.0	0.48	3.5	28.1	8.7
Plowing with big tractor	05/13/93	11:30 - 16:30	6.7	0.60	---	68.1	6.8
	05/13/93	17:15 - 18:40	6.8	0.61	3.7	68.1	6.8
Driving of one (1) large truck	05/21/93	15:00 - 16:40	3.1	0.30	4.0	39.3	8.1
	05/22/93	10:50 - 12:15	4.6	0.45	2.6	78.1	8.2
	05/22/93	15:06 - 16:06	4.8	0.46	2.1	78.1	8.2
	05/25/93	16:00 - 17:10	4.7	0.42	3.5	169.0	6.5
Driving of two (2) large trucks	05/24/93	15:30 - 18:30	3.1	0.31	1.4	96.7	6.6

GO ON TO THE NEXT PAGE

6. According to the information provided, how many experimental trials were conducted for the study during the month of May 1993?

    F. 15

    G. 16

    H. 17 total; 1 control and 16 experimental

    J. 23 total; 7 control and 16 experimental

7. Overall, results of the measurements of the study indicate that during simulated agricultural and transport activities, airborne radionuclide concentrations of ^{137}Cs

    A. decreased considerably.

    B. increased considerably.

    C. remained constant throughout the activities.

    D. were not impacted by the activities.

8. According to the data presented, airborne radionuclide concentrations that were resuspended into the atmosphere due to agricultural and transport activities were most impacted by which of the following experimental conditions?

    F. wind velocity

    G. friction velocity

    H. date

    J. time of day

9. Which of the following statements about the relationship between agricultural/transport activities and airborne contamination would be most consistent with the results of the study?

    A. Activities in contaminated areas increase the velocity and friction of wind.

    B. Activities in contaminated areas increase the wind transport of radionuclides.

    C. Activities in contaminated areas increase the particle size of radionuclides.

    D. Activities in contaminated areas increase the resuspension of radionuclides.

10. Based on the findings of the study, which of the following groups of people are in the most danger from secondary contamination by inhalation of resuspended aerosol?

    F. employees at nuclear power plants

    G. scientists studying the effects of resuspended radioactive particles

    H. people involved in agricultural or transport activities at nuclear power plants

    J. people involved in agricultural or transport activities in or near a radiation-contaminated zone

11. In general, the size of ^{137}Cs radionuclide particles during simulated agricultural and transport activities remained fairly constant for all activities EXCEPT

   A. resuspending of particulate by wind.

   B. assembling of equipment for the study.

   C. cutting grass.

   D. plowing with small tractor.

Passage III

Menopause refers to the ending of a woman's menstrual cycle. Physiologically, as the ovaries age, they are unable to respond to follicle-stimulating hormone (FSH) and luteinizing hormone (LH) stimulation. As a result, estrogen production decreases, as does the production of progesterone. Some symptoms of menopause include: irregular periods, hot flashes, memory loss, irritability, depression, anxiety, water retention, change in sleep patterns, low sex drive, night sweats, insomnia, incontinence, and weight gain.

There are two schools of thought about whether or not the decreasing natural supplies of estrogen and progesterone should be replaced by synthetic versions of these hormones. *Hormone replacement therapy (HRT)* is synthetic hormonal replacement of estrogen and sometimes progesterone for purposes of delaying menopause.

PRO - HRT Position

Scientists who defend HRT say that even though estrogen raises the risk for endometrial cancer, the benefits of HRT to postmenopausal women far outweigh the risks. Some of these benefits include decrease in menopausal symptoms (see above) and a decreased risk for coronary heart disease and osteoporosis.

CON - HRT Position

Scientists arguing against the use of synthetic hormones to treat menopausal symptoms cite significant increases in deaths from breast cancer directly credited to HRT. Some of these scientists also believe that uses of synthetic progesterone produce numerous unpleasant side effects because synthetic progesterone does not adequately mimic or imitate naturally-produced progesterone.

12. On which of the following points do the two positions seem to be in agreement?

   F. Use of postmenopausal estrogens is correlated with healthy female body function.

   G. Use of postmenopausal estrogens is correlated with some forms of cancer.

   H. Natural female hormones should be replaced with synthetic hormones at menopause.

   J. Synthetic female hormones should be replaced with natural hormones at menopause.

GO ON TO THE NEXT PAGE

13. A con-HRT scientist would most likely make which of the following statements to a pro-HRT scientist?

    A. Even if synthetic estrogen does decrease risk for heart disease, it increases breast cancer so much that its use should not even be considered.

    B. Even if synthetic estrogen does decrease risk for breast cancer, it increases heart disease so much that its use should not even be considered.

    C. Even if synthetic estrogen does decrease risk for endometrial cancer, it increases breast cancer so much that its use should not even be considered.

    D. Even if synthetic estrogen does decrease risk for heart disease, it increases endometrial cancer so much that its use should not even be considered.

14. Pesticides contain *xenoestrogens,* a chemical substance that mimics estrogen. These xenoestrogens are known to interfere with the normal process of hormonal regulation in women's bodies and are therefore being blamed for a range of disorders—from infertility and endometriosis to ovarian and breast cancer. This research is most likely to be cited by which group of scientists in support of their position on HRT use?

    F. Pro-HRT only

    G. Con-HRT only

    H. Both Pro-HRT and Con-HRT

    J. Neither Pro-HRT nor Con-HRT

15. Which of the following statements is most likely to be made by a female patient whose decision to use HRT is directly influenced by her pro-HRT medical practitioner?

    A. "Since breast cancer runs in my family, I want to do whatever I can to reduce my chances of getting it. Plus, I would like to get rid of my hot flashes."

    B. "Since heart disease runs in my family, I want to do whatever I can to reduce my chances of getting it. Plus, I would like to get rid of my hot flashes."

    C. "I would rather let nature take its course and not put anything synthetic into my body."

    D. "I would rather let nature take its course and so I definitely plan to use synthetic hormones."

16. Natural progesterone is a term for the progesterone found in plant sources like wild yam that mimics the structure of progesterone in the body. Its consumption has been found to decrease the risk for breast cancer, to help reverse osteoporosis, and to treat certain symptoms of menopause. This data would most likely be useful to which group of scientists and their patients?

    F. Pro-HRT only

    G. Con-HRT only

    H. Both Pro-HRT and Con-HRT

    J. Neither Pro-HRT nor Con-HRT

17. Which of the following statements, if true, would most seriously weaken support for the menopause-without-medicine position?

A. Natural progesterone ingestion has been linked to decreases in cancers of the female reproductive system in post-menopausal patients.

B. Natural progesterone ingestion has been linked to increases in cancers of the female reproductive system in post-menopausal patients.

C. Research shows that using hormones from natural sources has the same benefits as synthetics, but with fewer side effects.

D. After menopause, the female body continues to naturally produce estrogens (female hormones), though at much lowered and more consistent levels.

18. Some recent studies show that the synthetic estrogens contained in birth control pills are associated with increased risk of clotting and salt retention, which can lead to high blood pressure, heart attacks, and stroke. If true, these studies may seriously weaken arguments made by which group of scientists?

F. Pro-HRT only

G. Con-HRT only

H. Both Pro-HRT and Con-HRT

J. Neither Pro-HRT nor Con-HRT

Passage IV

Oriental hornets (*Vespa orientalis*) are insects that live in colonies and build one nest a year during the hot summer months. The silk spun by the pupating larva of these hornets can receive, store, and discharge energy in the forms of electricity and heat for use by the entire nest. In one study, silk removed from a nest was electrically charged in the laboratory for time periods ranging from 5 minutes to 18 hours. The pupal silk was then allowed to discharge the stored energy naturally, in order to determine the most efficient charging time for this particular hornet species. The measurements for each time period were duplicated on average between four to six times under similar conditions—a temperature of 30° and a relative humidity of 90%, in total darkness. These conditions duplicate conditions found inside an Oriental hornet nest found in nature.

Current is the flow of electrical charge over time, measured in amperes or amps. *Charging time* refers to the amount of time (in minutes) that current (in amperes) was allowed to accumulate in the spun silk. *Relaxation time* refers to the amount of time (in minutes) for the accumulated current to decrease. This is also referred to as *discharge time*.

GO ON TO THE NEXT PAGE

Results of the study are presented in Figures 1 and 2.

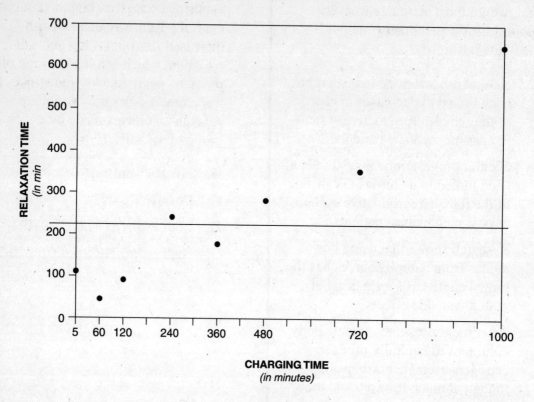

Figure 1

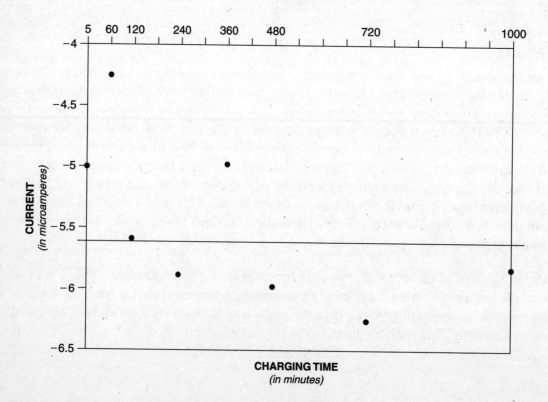

Figure 2

19. According to the design of the study, two experimental variables were tested to determine their dependence on one control variable. These two variables are

    A. current and charging time, as a function of discharge time.

    B. current and discharge time, as a function of charging time.

    C. charging time and discharge time, as a function of current.

    D. charge over time, measured in amps.

20. A central hypothesis implied in the design of the study is that the method of charging pupal silk in the laboratory is

    F. not important to understanding the phenomenon of charging silk with electricity.

    G. important to understanding the phenomenon of charging silk with electricity.

    H. dissimilar to the method of charging that occurs in nature.

    J. similar to the method of charging in nature.

21. According to the data presented, approximately how many hours does it take to discharge a current that has accumulated in the pupal silk overnight (specifically, a period of 18 hours)?

    A. < 4 hours

    B. 6 hours

    C. 8 hours

    D. > 10 hours

22. Based on the data provided, for the period between four and six hours of charging time, the relationship between discharge time and current is that

    F. discharge time increases while current decreases.

    G. discharge time increases while current increases.

    H. discharge time decreases while current increases.

    J. discharge time decreases while current decreases.

23. An unexpected finding of the study was that charge durations of 4-6 hours were particularly efficient. One possible hypothetical explanation for this finding might be that this is the time period in nature during which pupal silk

    A. absorbs excess energy for later use.

    B. absorbs excess energy for immediate use.

    C. releases excess energy for later use.

    D. releases excess energy for immediate use.

GO ON TO THE NEXT PAGE

24. Based upon the study, which of the following represents the best hypothesis about the uses of stored and released energy by the Oriental hornet in the regulation of temperature in the nest?

   F. Heat from winter days is converted to electricity, stored, and released during the summer.

   G. Heat from winter days is converted to electricity, stored, and released during colder nights.

   H. Heat from summer days is converted to electricity, stored, and released during the winter.

   J. Heat from summer days is converted to electricity, stored, and released during cooler nights.

Passage V

After a sound has been produced in an enclosed space (or room), it will be reflected by the boundaries (walls, ceilings, floors) of that enclosure. Although some energy is lost upon each reflection, several seconds may pass before the sound falls to a level that is not detectable to the human ear.

Reverberation refers to this continuation of sound after its initial production. Some reverberation adds a pleasant quality to the *acoustics* (sound design) of a room, while too much reverberation can destroy acoustics. *Reverberation time,* an important standard in architectural acoustics, refers to the time required for a specific sound to fall to one-thousandth of its initial pressure.

Using data on the sound preferences of large groups of people, acoustical engineers have come up with curves for optimum reverberation time. Figure 1 shows optimum reverberation time as a function of sound frequency in cycles per second (cps). Figure 2 shows optimum reverberation time for different types of rooms and performance spaces as a function of room volume.

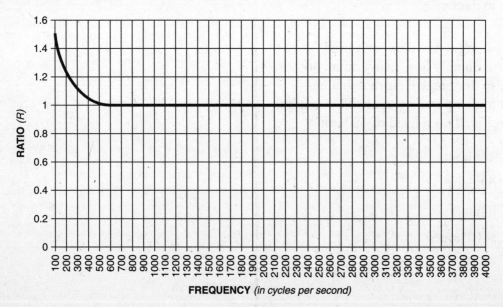

FREQUENCY *(in cycles per second)*

Figure 1

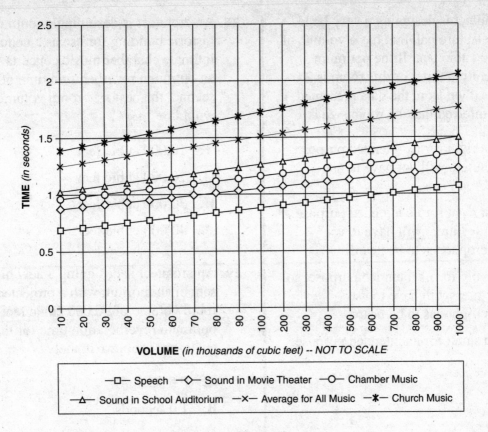

VOLUME *(in thousands of cubic feet) -- NOT TO SCALE*

—□— Speech   —◇— Sound in Movie Theater   —○— Chamber Music
—△— Sound in School Auditorium   —✕— Average for All Music   —✱— Church Music

Figure 2

25. Figure 1 is a chart for computing optimum reverberation time based on sound frequency. The time at any frequency is given in terms of a ratio (R), which is then multiplied by the optimum reverberation time. If one assumes that a ratio of 1 indicates the optimum, what is the minimum frequency at which the optimum can be computed?

A. 100 cps

B. 300 cps

C. 500 cps

D. 700 cps

26. According to the data presented in Figure 2, all of the following statements about optimum reverberation times (ORT) for different sounds/enclosures are true EXCEPT

F. the ORT for speech is shorter than the ORT for movie theaters.

G. the ORT for church music is longer than the ORT for chamber music.

H. the ORT for school auditoriums is shorter than the ORT for movie theaters.

J. the ORT for school auditoriums is longer than the ORT for speech.

GO ON TO THE NEXT PAGE

27. An architect is designing a very large college lecture hall that has a volume of 100,000 cubic feet. If the optimum reverberation time for this room is 2.0 seconds, then from the data presented, it can be inferred that the room size is

  A. just right for its intended purpose; lecturers will not have to use microphones.

  B. just right for its intended purpose, but lecturers will have to use microphones to be heard.

  C. too big for its intended purpose, so lecturers will have to use microphones to be heard.

  D. too small for its intended purpose.

28. An architect is designing a room in a historic building for use as a venue for intimate chamber music concerts. For an optimum reverberation time of 1 second, the best size room volume would be

  F. 10,000 cubic feet.

  G. 20,000 cubic feet.

  H. 30,000 cubic feet.

  J. 40,000 cubic feet.

29. An architect is designing a new high school auditorium with a projected room volume of 90,000 cubic feet. The optimum reverberation time for this enclosure is approximately

  A. 0.5 seconds.

  B. 1.0 seconds.

  C. 1.5 seconds.

  D. 2.0 seconds.

Passage VI

The Earth's crust has three classes of rock based on their origin and position in the process geologists refer to as the rock cycle:

Igneous rocks form from the eventual cooling of liquid *magma* (hot molten or partially molten material) during events like volcanic eruptions. They are categorized by the composition of their minerals and by texture. Common descriptors of texture include coarse-grained, fine-grained, and glassy.

Sedimentary rocks form when existing igneous, sedimentary, and metamorphic rocks are altered by weathering or erosion. They are categorized as having an origin that is either *detrital* (formed when particles of different sizes and shapes are naturally cemented together) or *chemical* (formed by precipitation, or the emergence of mineral matter from solution).

Metamorphic rocks form when existing rocks are altered by heat and pressure, as in cases of volcanic eruptions and in the buckling or uplifting of some mountain ranges. They are categorized as having textures that are either *foliated* (with cleavage) or *nonfoliated* (with no cleavage). *Cleavage* refers to the specific property of a mineral that allows it to break along a smooth plane surface.

Figure 1 depicts all these processes in the rock cycle.

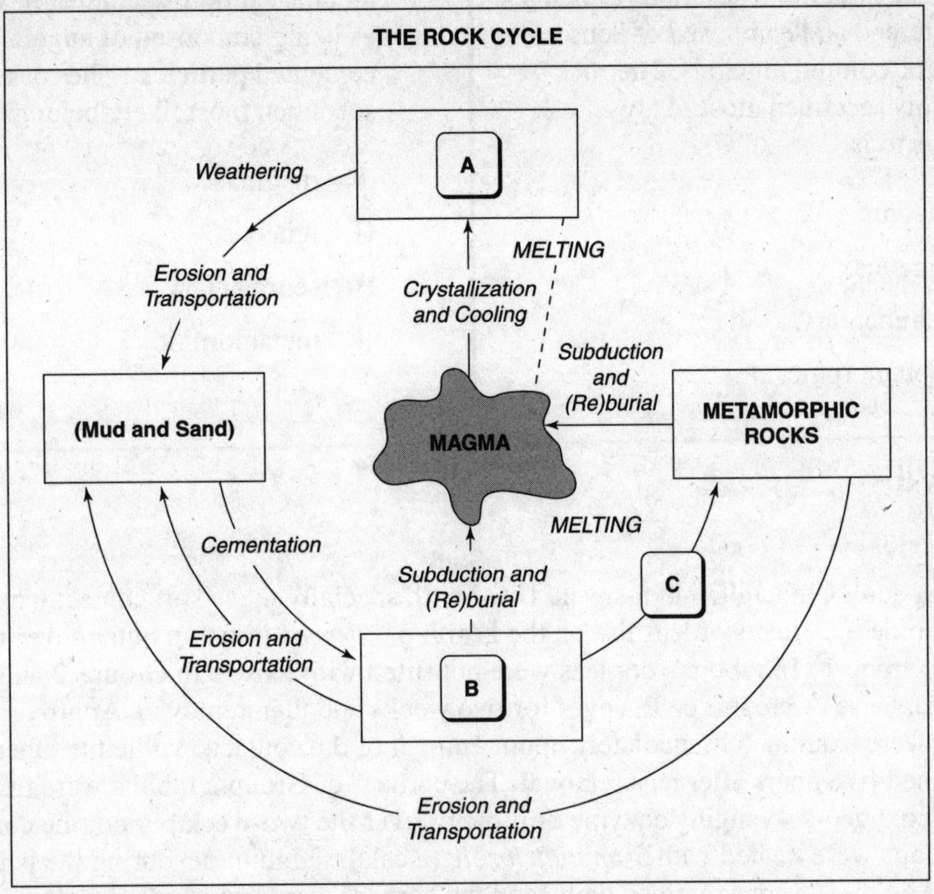

Figure 1

30. Based on the information provided, what type of rock corresponds with the box labeled "A" in Figure 1?

   F. magma

   G. igneous

   H. sedimentary

   J. metamorphic

31. Based on the information provided, what type of rock corresponds with the box labeled "B" in Figure 1?

   A. magma

   B. igneous

   C. sedimentary

   D. metamorphic

32. Based on the information provided, what geologic process corresponds with the arrow labeled "C" in Figure 1?

   F. weathering

   G. erosion and transportation

   H. compaction and cementation

   J. heat and pressure

GO ON TO THE NEXT PAGE

33. While in the field, a geologist discovers a rock specimen she describes as being fine-grained and composed of dense and dark-colored minerals. The rock class this specimen most likely belongs to is

    A. magma.

    B. igneous.

    C. sedimentary.

    D. metamorphic.

34. While in the field, a geologist discovers an unusual rock specimen he describes as being composed of angular, cemented particles. The rock class this specimen most likely belongs to is

    F. magma.

    G. igneous.

    H. sedimentary.

    J. metamorphic.

Passage VII

The Study

In this study, adult Chinchilla rabbits were fitted with specially made soft contact lenses in order to determine the effects of lens use on the health of *corneas* (the thin outer covering of the eyeball). In Group 1 (15 rabbits), corneas were not fitted with lenses. In Groups 2 and 3 (15 rabbits each), lenses were left on the eyes for two weeks and then removed. Approximately half the corneas were examined immediately upon removal of the contacts, while the other half were examined five hours after lens removal. The corneas of Group 2 rabbits were treated with *catalase* (an oxygen-scavenging enzyme or protein) over the two-week period; the corneas of Group 3 rabbits were treated with *3-aminotriazole* (a catalase inhibitor) during the period of lens use. All animals were examined daily, and the corneas were documented photographically. Additionally, enzyme activity in the corneas was examined at three stages of the study: at the beginning of the two-week period; upon lens removal; and, in some cases, five hours after lens removal.

The Results

In rabbit corneas not fitted with contact lenses, the activity of *xanthine oxidase* (an oxygen-generating enzyme or protein) and catalase were balanced and present in high levels—both before and after the study. In rabbit corneas fitted with lenses, xanthine oxidase activity was high and comparable to levels found in the control group. In general, though, catalase activity was found to be significantly reduced upon removal of the lenses. But when corneas were treated with catalase during lens use, this decrease in catalase activity was prevented. In contrast, after treatment with the catalase inhibitor 3-aminotriazole, the activity of the catalase enzyme was nearly absent, and rabbits in this group suffered extreme inflammation of the eye. Further, for those rabbits whose corneas were examined 5 hours after lens removal, imbalances were also found to exist between the enzymes lactate dehydrogenase and lysosomal hydrolase.

35. According to the design of the study, which group of rabbits constitutes the control group?

    A. rabbits in Group 1

    B. rabbits in Group 2

    C. rabbits in Group 3

    D. adult Chinchilla rabbits found in nature

36. According to the design of the study, the most likely reason for examining some corneas immediately upon removal of contact lenses and some corneas five hours later is to determine

    F. the activity levels of xanthine oxidase and catalase.

    G. the activity levels of lactate dehydrogenase and lysosomal hydrolase.

    H. whether additional disturbances appear after lens removal.

    J. whether additional disturbances appear before lens removal.

37. The results of this study suggest that prolonged use of contact lenses can damage the cornea, primarily resulting from imbalances in the activity levels of which pair of enzymes?

    A. catalase and 3-aminotriazole

    B. xanthine oxidase and catalase

    C. xanthine oxidase and 3-aminotriazole

    D. dehydrogenase and lysosomal hydrolase

38. From the results of the study, it can be hypothesized that supplementing contact lens use with drops of catalase

    F. is insignificant.

    G. can damage the corneas.

    H. can prevent some damage to the corneas.

    J. can inhibit production of 3-aminotriazole.

39. From the results of the study, which of the following statements holds true for the relationship between catalase and inflammation of the eye?

    A. There is no relationship between catalase and inflammation.

    B. Excessive amounts of catalase can lead to inflammation.

    C. Presence of catalase can lead to inflammation.

    D. Absence of catalase can lead to inflammation.

40. The study suggests that in the corneas of non-contact lens wearers, the enzyme activity of corneal catalase is present in

    F. high levels comparable to levels of 3-aminotriazole.

    G. low levels comparable to levels of 3-aminotriazole.

    H. high levels comparable to levels of xanthine oxidase.

    J. low levels comparable to levels of xanthine oxidase.

IF YOU FINISH BEFORE TIME IS CALLED, CHECK YOUR WORK ON THIS SECTION ONLY. DO NOT WORK ON ANY OTHER SECTION IN THE TEST.

Answer Key

English Test

1. A	20. G	39. D	58. H
2. H	21. A	40. J	59. D
3. B	22. J	41. D	60. F
4. F	23. D	42. J	61. C
5. B	24. J	43. D	62. J
6. H	25. B	44. F	63. A
7. D	26. H	45. D	64. G
8. G	27. B	46. G	65. D
9. C	28. F	47. D	66. G
10. G	29. D	48. H	67. C
11. A	30. H	49. D	68. G
12. G	31. A	50. J	69. B
13. C	32. F	51. B	70. G
14. G	33. B	52. H	71. B
15. C	34. G	53. B	72. H
16. H	35. C	54. H	73. C
17. C	36. H	55. B	74. G
18. J	37. B	56. G	75. B
19. B	38. H	57. C	

Mathematics Test

1. D	16. J	31. A	46. K
2. H	17. A	32. F	47. C
3. C	18. J	33. C	48. G
4. G	19. B	34. H	49. C
5. C	20. G	35. E	50. K
6. G	21. D	36. J	51. B
7. D	22. J	37. E	52. G
8. G	23. A	38. J	53. D
9. E	24. G	39. B	54. J
10. J	25. D	40. H	55. C
11. E	26. J	41. A	56. H
12. H	27. D	42. H	57. B
13. D	28. F	43. A	58. J
14. F	29. B	44. K	59. B
15. B	30. G	45. E	60. H

Reading Test

1. C	11. D	21. D	31. B
2. F	12. G	22. H	32. F
3. C	13. C	23. A	33. D
4. F	14. F	24. G	34. H
5. B	15. B	25. C	35. D
6. H	16. G	26. F	36. G
7. D	17. C	27. D	37. D
8. G	18. F	28. F	38. H
9. B	19. C	29. A	39. A
10. J.	20. G	30. G	40. J

Science Reasoning Test

1. C	11. B	21. D	31. C
2. F	12. G	22. H	32. J
3. C	13. A	23. A	33. B
4. H	14. G	24. J	34. H
5. A	15. B	25. C	35. A
6. G	16. H	26. H	36. H
7. B	17. B	27. C	37. B
8. F	18. F	28. G	38. H
9. D	19. B	29. C	39. D
10. J	20. J	30. G	40. H

Scoring Your ACT Practice Test

To score your practice test, total the number of correct answers for each section. Don't subtract any points for questions attempted but missed, as there is no penalty for guessing. This score is then scaled from 1 to 36 for each section and then averaged for the all-important composite score. The average score is approximately 18.

For Your Own Benefit

To figure out your **percentage right** for each test, use the following formulas.

English Test

$$\frac{\text{Number right}}{75} \times 100 = \underline{\hspace{2cm}} \%$$

Mathematics Test

$$\frac{\text{Number right}}{60} \times 100 = \underline{\hspace{2cm}} \%$$

Reading Test

$$\frac{\text{Number right}}{40} \times 100 = \underline{\hspace{2cm}} \%$$

Science Reasoning Test

$$\frac{\text{Number right}}{40} \times 100 = \underline{\hspace{2cm}} \%$$

Practice Test 4 Analysis Sheet

	Possible	Completed	Right	Wrong
English Test	75			
Mathematics Test	60			
Reading Test	40			
Science Reasoning Test	40			
Overall Totals	215			

Analysis/Tally Sheet for Problems Missed

One of the most important parts of test preparation is analyzing **why** you missed a problem so that you can reduce the number of mistakes. Now that you've taken the practice test and checked your answers, carefully tally your mistakes by marking them in the proper column.

	Reason for Mistake			
	Total Missed	Simple Mistake	Misread Problem	Lack of Knowledge
English Test				
Mathematics Test				
Reading Test				
Science Reasoning Test				
Total				

Reviewing the above data should help you determine **why** you're missing certain problems. Now that you've pinpointed the type of errors you made, take the next practice test, focusing on avoiding your most common types of errors.

Answers to English Test

Passage I

1. **A.** The correct phrase contains the subject and main verb of this sentence. Options **B.** and **D.** are participles, not verbs, while **C.** is wordy, passive, and a distortion of the original meaning.

2. **H.** If a period or a semicolon appears after "logging" and the third sentence begins with "because" or "since," the third sentence is a dependent clause and an incomplete sentence. Only in **H.** is the sentence complete.

3. **B.** The phrase "a sleek cousin of the bobcat" is a non-restrictive appositive defining the noun "lynx." It should be set off with commas on both sides.

4. **F.** The number (singular or plural) of the word "number" is tricky. "The number" is normally singular, while "a number" may be singular or plural. Here, since "number" means more than one, the verb should be plural to agree with the noun.

5. **B.** Because the sentence refers to "this area," it should follow a sentence that refers to an area in which the logging company is interested. The best choice is the second sentence, which refers to the Loomis State Forest.

6. **H.** In this context, there is no need for the apostrophe to indicate a possessive.

7. **D.** The problem in this sentence is that the pronoun "this" has no specific antecedent (a word that another word refers back to), but refers to the whole clause that begins the sentence. The problem is not solved by changing the pronoun ("this" or "that" or "which"). The best version adds a noun ("step") to which the pronoun ("that") refers.

8. **G.** The idiom is "threat to," rather than "threat for." To say "a threatening for" is very awkward, and "threatful" is an invented word.

9. **C.** The subject of this sentence, though it comes after the verb, is the singular "the pine marten." The correct phrase has the singular verb "is."

10. **G.** Though "nice" is not a grammatical error, it is slipshod diction, and less effective in this context than "fine." Both "rad" and "neat" are slang.

11. **A.** The paragraph is written in the present tense, and there is no reason to change here to a verb in a past or a future tense.

12. **G.** The most appropriate place for this addition is after the first mention of a "price." The second sentence refers to a specific "cost" for the land.

13. **C.** If the verb "are" is part of a relative clause introduced by "who," the sentence has no main verb. Only **C.** makes a complete sentence.

14. **G.** The phrase "the reason is . . . because" is a phrase to avoid. The "because" is unnecessary in **F.** and **J.** In **H.**, there is no main verb.

15. **C.** To maintain the parallel with the first verb ("are visiting"), the best choice is "and showing."

16. **H.** Although the essay is concerned with an endangered habitat and mentions a few animals, it says nothing of their habits, and concentrates on the human effort to preserve the forests.

Passage II

17. **C.** The compound sentence with an "and" needs a comma; though "and" is not wrong, "but," which points out the contrast of the two places, is better.

18. **J.** If the first sentence ends with "Thailand" and a period or a semicolon, the second sentence is a fragment. The comma is needed because the clause with "which" is non-restrictive.

19. **B.** The participles ("being occupied," and "having been occupied") cannot take the place of a main verb in the first half of this sentence. The required construction here is the passive "was occupied."

20. **G.** The original version, **F.**, **H.**, and **J.** are all wordy. The most concise version is **G.**

21. **A.** Because the subject of the third paragraph is the coronation, the sentence that mentions both Bangkok and the coronation is the best transition.

22. **J.** All of the three suggested phrases add nothing. The best version begins with the subject of the sentence.

23. **D.** The subject is the singular "ceremony," so the verb must be the singular "is." As a rule, there is no reason to qualify the adjective "ancient" with a word like "somewhat."

24. **J.** The preceding sentence has already called the "ceremony" "ancient." To repeat this information two more times is a waste of time.

25. **B.** There are two problems here: The modifying phrase ("a man of the priestly caste") must be placed as close to Brahmin as possible. The verb should be in the present tense to be consistent with the rest of the paragraph. Here, the word "being" is an unneeded word.

26. **H.** The idiomatic preposition with the verb "participate" is "in."

27. **B.** The original version is a sentence fragment. The comma should replace the period. The "this" is unnecessary and is a pronoun without a specific antecedent.

28. **F.** The verb tenses here jump around from the present to the past to the present to the future. None of the other errors is present.

29. **D.** The three incorrect versions compare Thailand (a country) and a musical, while the intention is to compare Thailand with the Siam in the musical. The comparison makes sense when a word like "country" or "place" is added.

30. **H.** The best solution is the most concise: Reduce the sentence to a two-word phrase and avoid the redundancy.

31. **A.** The original phrasing is grammatical. **B.** is a fragment, **C.** is a run-on, and **D.** is a parallelism error ("honoring" and "marches").

Passage III

32. **F.** The sentence is a question and needs a question mark.

33. **B.** Either "good eating" or "eating well" will do here, but "good eats" is slang.

34. **G.** The best conjunction here is "but," which points to a contrast between the answers of the preceding sentence and the different one in this.

35. **C.** With the preposition ("like"), there should be no verb; while with the conjunction, ("as") a verb is necessary.

36. **H.** Because the next paragraph is about training in France, by moving the sentence about training in America to precede the reference to Americans who go to France, the first paragraph leads much more logically into the second.

37. **B.** Without the change in the last sentence of the preceding paragraph, the reference of the "There" is unclear (France or the United States?). The gerund "training" is clearer than the ambiguous pronoun "they."

38. **H.** The pronoun "They" is still ambiguous. **G.** results in a sentence fragment, while **J.** is an agreement error (the subject is the plural "years"). **H.** avoids these errors.

39. **D.** To preserve the comparison with "an apprenticeship," the best choice is another noun, "an internship."

40. **J.** Again, to keep the parallelism, the construction should be like that of "peeling." The best choice is the simplest, the gerund "washing."

41. **D.** Because the fifth sentence tells about the apprentice's hard work, the sentence fits best after the fifth sentence and leads logically to the sixth.

42. **J.** None of the three pronouns ('this," "which," "it") has a specific antecedent; the solution is to avoid the pronoun altogether.

43. **D.** The "perhaps" is parenthetical and should be set off with commas before and after.

44. **F.** The original version is correct. **G.** and **H.** are wordy, and though brief, **J.** makes an illogical comparison.

45. **D.** The best version is the briefest and correctly separates the word in apposition (Paris) by using a comma.

46. **G.** Of these choices, the best fit is at the end of the first paragraph, before the more detailed descriptions of a chef's training.

Passage IV

47. **D.** Because this is a non-restrictive clause (if it were left out, the sentence would still make sense), it should have commas at the beginning and at the end.

48. **H.** The right word here is "respectively." "Respectfully" means "with respect," "retrospectively" means "looking back," and "respectably" means "worthily."

49. **D.** Only "are no longer written" will fit here. The phrases "were not written," "are unwritten," and "have not been written" make no sense in this context since the strips were once written by the original authors.

50. **J.** Three of the four choices are wordy. The single phrase "all over the world" includes "here" and "abroad."

51. **B.** The verbs of this paragraph are in the present tense ("wears"). The participle "riding" leaves the sentence without a subject.

52. **H.** Options **F.**, **G.**, and **J.** are all dangling participles suggesting that the author, not the comics, appeared in newspapers. The revision of **H.** avoids the dangling participle.

53. **B.** None of these versions is ideal, but **B.** is the shortest and keeps the related words as close together as possible.

54. **H.** The reference of the "It" is not immediately clear, and the participle "Becoming" leaves the sentence without a subject. **H.** is preferable to **J.** because it is active, not passive, and has two fewer words.

55. **B.** Because it describes the comic book character, the addition must go in the first part of the paragraph. Placing it after the third rather than the first sentence will avoid the awkward repetition of the same first two words in two sentences in a row.

56. **G.** Option **G.** is better than **H.**, since it has an active verb. Both **F.** and **J.** are wordier.

57. **C.** Here, the briefest is the best choice.

58. **H.** This non-restrictive relative clause should have commas on both sides.

59. **D.** The sentence has begun a series ("cannot see . . . or fly") that is logically concluded with "or stick."

60. **F.** The idiomatic phrase is "looks fit." The three other choices have quite different meanings.

61. **C.** Because the paragraph begins with a comparison of the Phantom and other comic book heroes, this addition is not out of place. The sentence does not explain the popularity in Scandinavia, but it does add a detail that is consistent with the tone and content of the paragraph. Since the paragraph presents the Phantom as mortal, option **A.** is untrue.

Passage V

62. **J.** The restrictive clause should have a comma before the "who"; the pronoun should be the plural "their" to agree with the plural mountaineers.

63. **A.** The original version is correct, describing in the present tense the last sight of the missing climbers. There is no need for the pronoun "they."

64. **G.** The subject of the essay is the search for traces of the missing climbers, not other mountaineers. Both the paragraph and the essay as a whole are better without additional irrelevant information about Hillary and Tenzing.

65. **D.** Though not ideal, after the fifth sentence is the better choice. "Mallory" makes no sense unless the sentence comes after the third, which introduces the name. The trouble with placing the sentence after the third is its interruption of the progression from the third ("climbing toward the top") to the fourth ("disappeared") to the fifth ("we don't know"). Placing the added sentence at the end will avoid the interruption.

66. **G.** The pronoun to refer to human "climbers" is "who" rather than "that." The perfect tense ("have reached") is correct in this context.

67. **C.** The phrase "not a surprise" is idiomatic (the verb and subject are understood), and avoids the vague pronouns in the other three choices.

68. **G.** Because the carrying was done many years ago and is, we presume, no longer the case, the correct verb tense is "to have carried," rather than a present tense like "to carry" or "to be carrying."

69. **B.** The objective "them" is incorrect before the gerund "finding." By using only "finding," words are saved and the problem of pronoun case does not arise. The clauses in **C.** and **D.** are wordier, but not more expressive.

70. **G.** The antecedent of the underlined phrase is "the chance," much earlier in the sentence. The singular noun calls for a singular verb ("is") and an adjective ("remote").

71. **B.** The phrase "a route similar to" calls for a second term that is parallel to a "route." "To the climbers" cannot be right. To "that" (that is, a route) of the early climbers will work as will "to the early climbers'," but, unlike **D.**, the apostrophe must come after the "s."

72. **H.** With correlatives like "not . . . but," the words following each of the two terms should be parallel in structure. Here, the "not" is followed by the infinitive "to reach," so the "but" should be followed by another infinitive, such as "to discover."

73. **C.** The pronouns ("that," "it") have no specific antecedents. The use of a noun like "feat" solves this problem. Another difficulty here is the redundancy of "lessen" and "diminish," which **C.** avoids.

74. **G.** The best place for this addition is after the comment on the intentions of the searchers in the third sentence.

75. **B.** Of the four choices, "A Mount Everest Mystery" is the best. The essay is not about the conquest of Everest. It raises the question of who was first at the top, but it does not answer it. The missing Kodak is only a part of the mystery. The unknown fate of the early climbers and modern efforts to discover what happened is best summarized by "A Mount Everest Mystery."

Answers to Mathematics Test

1. **D.** The following procedure can be used to change units of measure. If you multiply by a fraction that has a value of 1, no change in value occurs. Thus

$$\left(\frac{31\,\text{miles}}{1}\right)\left(\frac{1\,\text{kilometer}}{0.62\,\text{miles}}\right) = 50\,\text{kilometers}$$

Therefore, **D.** is the correct choice.

2. **H.** Next year's benefits can be calculated by multiplying the current benefit by 1.055. This gives the correct result of $991.70 directly. (If you prefer a two-step process, first multiply the original benefit of 0.055, which gives the increase in benefits. Then add this increase to the original benefits to get the benefits for next year.) This also gives the correct answer.

3. **C.** The average can be calculated by multiplying each score by the number of students receiving that score, and then adding the products. Then divide this answer by the total number of students.

$$A = \frac{(0)(1)+(1)(0)+(2)(2)+(3)(2)+(4)(1)+(5)(4)+(6)(2)}{12} = 3.8$$

4. **G.** The average speed (rate) follows from the formula $d = rt$. If both sides of this equation are divided by the time (t), we get $r = d/t$. Therefore, the average speed of bus X is $r = d/t = {}^{360}/_{10} = 36$ miles per hour, and the average speed of bus Y is $r = d/t = {}^{240}/_{t} = 40$ miles per hour. The difference is therefore 4 miles per hour.

5. **C.** If a product of two factors is equal to zero, then one, or both, of the factors must have a value of zero. Therefore, $(2 - x) = 0$, and hence $x = 2$, or $(x + 5) = 0$ and hence $x = -5$. Adding these two answers gives the required result, or $-5 + 2 = -3$.

6. **G.** The diagram below helps organize the given data. Let x represent the length of $\overline{WX}$ and P represent the perimeter of the parallelogram. Since $P = 2x + 8$ and $P = 3x$, $2x + 8 = 3x$, and therefore, $x = 8$.

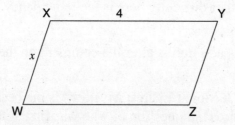

7. **D.** The formula that relates the number of sides (n) of a polygon and the sum of the interior angles (x) is $x = (n - 2)(180°)$. Substituting 900° for x gives the following:

$$(n - 2)(180°) = x$$

$$(n - 2)(180°) = 900°$$

$$n - 2 = {}^{900°}/_{180°}$$

$$n - 2 = 5$$

$$n = 7$$

8. **G.** When dividing variables of the same base, subtract the exponents. Thus,
$$\frac{w^3 z^2 x^5 y}{wz^4 x^4 y^2} = \frac{w^2 x}{yz^2}$$

9. **E.** Since $\overline{AB}$ is parallel to $\overline{CD}$, $\angle A \cong \angle D$ (alternate interior angles), and therefore $\angle A = 30°$. The sum of the measures of the interior angles in a triangle is $180°$. Therefore,
$$\angle B = 180° - 40° - 30° = 110°.$$

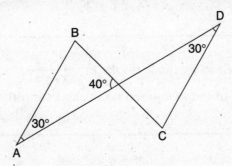

10. **J.** Substitute the given values in the expression and simplify.
$$\left|\frac{x+y}{x-y}\right| = \left|\frac{(-4)+(-6)}{(-4)-(-6)}\right| = \left|\frac{-10}{2}\right| = 5$$

11. **E.** The total number of students is 48. Subtract from 48 the number of students earning an A, B, D, or F. This leaves the number that earned a C: $x = 48 - 8 - 10 - 10 - 2 = 18$. We can use a proportion to solve:
$$\frac{part}{whole} = \frac{\%}{100} \Rightarrow \frac{18}{48} = \frac{x}{100} \Rightarrow x = 37.5$$

12. **H.** The product of two positive whole numbers is equal to the product of their least common multiple and their greatest common factor. Therefore, $ab = xy$ or $x/a = b/y$.

13. **D.** This is a substitution problem, as follows.
$$ab^2c - a^2 b^3 c + abc$$
$$= (-3)(-1)^2(3) - (-3)^2(-1)^3(3) + (-3)(-1)(3)$$
$$= -9 - (-27) + 9$$
$$= 27$$

14. **F.** If the width of a rectangle is decreased by 4 inches, the perimeter will decrease by 8 inches. If the length of a rectangle is increased by $(x + 2)$ inches, the perimeter will increase by $2(x + 2)$. Therefore, the new perimeter will be $(2x - 2) - 8 + 2(x + 2) = 4x - 6$ inches.

15. **B.** First square the left side of the equation. Then solve for a.
$$(x - a)^2 = x^2 + 40x + a^2$$
$$x^2 - 2xa + a^2 = x^2 + 40x + a^2$$
$$-2xa = 40x$$
$$-2a = 40$$
$$a = -20$$

16. J. Calculate the amount of savings on each item and then add to find the total amount of savings.

$(.20)(\$10.00) = \$2.00$

$(.20)(\$15.00) = \$3.00$

$(.30)(\$30) = \$9.00$

$(.30)(\$60) = \$18.00$

Total $= \$32.00$

17. A. The slope of a line is given by the formula $m = \dfrac{y_2 - y_1}{x_2 - x_1}$

Substitute the coordinates of the two given points and simplify.

$$m = \frac{y_2 - y_1}{x_2 - x_1}$$
$$m = \frac{4 - (-2)}{(-6) - 2}$$
$$m = \frac{6}{-8}$$
$$m = -\frac{3}{4}$$

18. J. The zeros, or roots, occur where the value of the function is zero. This occurs at -4, 1, and 3. Therefore, there are three distinct zeros. At $x = 1$ there is a double root.

19. B. To simplify this complex fraction, multiply both the numerator and denominator by the least common multiple of all the denominators. In this case, that is xy.

$$\frac{\left(\dfrac{1}{x} + \dfrac{1}{y}\right)}{2}$$
$$\frac{(xy)}{(xy)} \cdot \frac{\left(\dfrac{1}{x} + \dfrac{1}{y}\right)}{2}$$
$$\frac{y + x}{2xy}$$
$$\frac{x + y}{2xy}$$

20. G. Dividing $\$4.20$ by 12 gives $\$0.35$. This means when purchasing by the dozen, each pencil costs $\$0.35$. This is a savings of $\$0.04$ per pencil.

21. D. To find the product of these two binomials, we can use the FOIL method. This gives four products. None of the terms are similar.

$(2x^2 y^2 + xy^2)(-x^2 y + xy^2)$

$-2x^4 y^3 + 2x^3 y^4 - x^3 y^3 + x^2 y^4$

22. J. Calculate the length of the missing side of the triangle using the Pythagorean theorem. Find the values of $\sin\theta$ and $\tan\theta$, substitute, and divide.

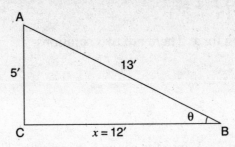

$$x^2 + 5^2 = 13^2$$

$$x^2 + 25 = 169$$

$$x^2 = 144$$

$$x = 12$$

$$\frac{\tan\theta}{\sin\theta} = \frac{\frac{5}{12}}{\frac{5}{13}} = \left(\frac{5}{12}\right)\left(\frac{13}{5}\right) = \frac{13}{12}$$

23. A. Subtracting 12 years from x gives Amy's age now $(x - 12)$. Adding 8 years to Amy's age now will give Sean's age now $(x - 12 + 8)$. Subtracting 6 years from Sean's age now gives Sean's age 6 years ago $(x - 12 + 8 - 6)$.

24. G. This trinomial will factor into two binomials. Since the product of the constants must be (-15) the other factor must be $(x + 5)$. Now we can solve for k.

$$(x - 3)(x + 5) = x^2 - kx - 15$$

$$x^2 + 2x - 15 = x^2 - kx - 15$$

$$2x = -kx$$

$$-2 = k$$

25. D. This problem can best be solved using the Pythagorean theorem.

$$x^2 + x^2 = 16^2$$

$$2x^2 = 256$$

$$x^2 = 128$$

$$x = \sqrt{128}$$

$$x = \sqrt{(64)(2)}$$

$$x = 8\sqrt{2} \text{ inches}$$

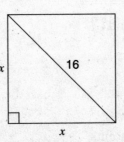

26. J. When you raise a power to a power, you multiply the powers.

$$(-2x^2)^4 = (-2)^4 (x^2)^4 = 16x^8$$

27. **D.** Set up the ratio and reduce.

$$\frac{\text{ounces of gasoline}}{\text{ounces of oil}} = \frac{(8)(128)}{16} = \frac{64}{1}$$

28. **F.** First solve the equation for x. There are two solutions.

$$x^2 - 13 = -4$$

$$x^2 = 9$$

$$x = \pm 3$$

Substitute each value, 3 and -3, into the second expression. The value of -3 gives the smaller result.

$2x - 5$	$2x - 5$
$2(3) - 5$	$2(-3) - 5$
1	-11

29. **B.** First solve the inequality.

$$-2 - y > -4$$

$$-y > -2$$

$$y < 2$$

The solution set is all numbers less than 2.

30. **G.** First set up the equations from the given information.

$$x = \frac{k}{y^2} \qquad y = c\sqrt{z}$$

Substitute the value of y in the second equation into the first equation, eliminating y.

$$x = \frac{k}{y^2} = \frac{k}{\left(c\sqrt{z}\right)^2} = \frac{k}{c^2 z} = \frac{m}{z}$$

($c, k,$ and m are constants and $m = \frac{k}{c^2}$)

Therefore, x varies inversely as z.

31. **A.** First, calculate the midpoints of $\overline{AB}$ and $\overline{CD}$

$$(x, y) = \left(\frac{(-6) + (-4)}{2}, \frac{2 + 2}{2}\right) = (-5, 2)$$

$$(x, y) = \left(\frac{(6) + (4)}{2}, \frac{2 + (-2)}{2}\right) = (5, 0)$$

Now find the midpoint of these two midpoints.

$$(x, y) = \left(\frac{(-5) + 5}{2}, \frac{2 + 0}{2}\right) = (0, 1)$$

32. F. The slopes of perpendicular lines are negative reciprocals of each other. Since the slope of the line $y = \frac{2}{3}x - 4$ is $\frac{2}{3}$, the slope of any line perpendicular to that line must be $-\frac{3}{2}$. Find the slope of the second line.

$$2y = ax + 3$$

$$y = \frac{a}{2}x + \frac{3}{2}$$

The slope is $\frac{a}{2}$

Then $\frac{a}{2} = -\frac{3}{2}$, $a = -3$

33. C. This inequality involves an absolute value. Therefore, we have two equations to solve.

$$3 - x < 2 \qquad\qquad -(3 - x) < 2$$

$$-x < -1 \qquad\qquad -3 + x < 2$$

$$x > 1 \qquad\qquad\qquad x < 5$$

The value of x must lie between 1 and 5.

34. H. If we let p = cost of a plate and c = cost of a cup ($\$\frac{8}{4} = \$2$), then

$$np = mc$$

$$6np = 6mc$$

$$6p = \frac{6m(2)}{n}$$

$$6p = \frac{12m}{n}$$

35. E. In this problem, we could try each answer choice in the inequality, but if we solve the inequality for one of the variables, we can more easily see the correct answer.

$$x - y > -2$$

$$x > y - 2$$

Checking the answer choices now is easier. We see that all the choices work except **E**.

36. J. First find the third side of the right triangle using the Pythagorean theorem.

$$3^2 + 6^2 = x^2$$

$$45 = x^2$$

$$\sqrt{45} = x$$

$$3\sqrt{5} = x$$

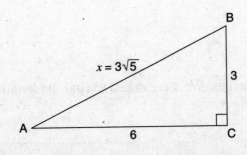

The sine of an angle is defined as the side opposite the angle divided by the hypotenuse. Thus

$$\sin B = \frac{6}{3\sqrt{5}} = \frac{6\sqrt{5}}{3\sqrt{5}\sqrt{5}} = \frac{2\sqrt{5}}{5}$$

37. E. One method to solve this problem is to work from the answers. Try each pair of values in both equations and find the pair that works. Another method is to solve the system of equations, as follows.

$4x - 3y = 12$

$2x + 2y = -15$

Multiply the first equation by 2 and the second equation by 3.

$8x - 6y = 24$

$6x + 6y = -45$

Now add and solve for x.

$14x = -21$

$x = -1.5$

Now substitute back in one of the original equations and solve for y.

$4x - 3y = 12$

$4(-1.5) - 3y = 12$

$-6 - 3y = 12$

$-3y = 18$

$y = -6$

Thus, the point of intersection is $(-1.5, -6)$.

38. J. The area of a rectangle is the product of its length and width. The length of the rectangle is four times the width. The area is 48 square inches. Substitute in the area formula and solve.

$A = lw$

$48 = (4w)(w)$

$48 = 4w^2$

$12 = w^2$

$\sqrt{12} = w$

$2\sqrt{3} = w$

Thus, the width is $2\sqrt{3}$ inches. We were asked to find the length. Multiplying the width by 4 gives the length as $8\sqrt{3}$.

39. B. One method is to work from the answers. Since we are adding twice a number and nine times the reciprocal of the number and end up with a negative answer, the number must be negative. This observation limits us to the first three choices. We could now test each of these answers, as follows. Since (-3) is given as an answer, start by trying choice **B.**

$2(-\frac{3}{2}) + 9(-\frac{2}{3}) = (-3) + (-6) = -9$

Since this answer choice works, stop. You found the correct choice. You could try the other choices, but they would not work. Another method is to set up an equation and solve.

$$2x + 9(\frac{1}{x}) = -9$$
$$2x^2 + 9 = -9x$$
$$2x^2 + 9x + 9 = 0$$
$$(2x + 3)(x + 3) = 0$$
$$x = -3, -\frac{3}{2}$$

This method gives the result directly.

40. H. Use the Pythagorean theorem to determine the length of the side of the square.

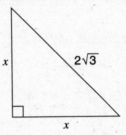

$$x^2 + x^2 = \left(2\sqrt{3}\right)^2$$
$$2x^2 = 12$$
$$x^2 = 6$$
$$x = \sqrt{6}$$

Therefore, the perimeter is $4\sqrt{6}$.

41. A. If the overall width of the frame is 12 inches, and there is a two-inch border of frame around the picture, then the picture must be $12 - 2 - 2$ or 8 inches wide. If the overall length of the frame is 15 inches and there is a two-inch border of frame around the picture, then the picture must be $15 - 2 - 2$ or 11 inches long. Therefore, the perimeter of the picture is $11 + 11 + 8 + 8 = 38$ inches.

42. H. Draw a figure such as the one below. Since $\overline{AO} = \overline{BO}$, $\angle ABO = 55°$ because base angles of an isosceles triangle are congruent. Now subtract these two base angles from 180° to obtain $\angle AOB = 70°$. Since inscribed $\angle ACB$ cuts off the same arc as $\angle AOB$, its angle measure is one half as large as that of $\angle AOB$. Thus, $\angle ACB = 35°$

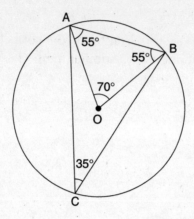

43. A. Use the formula $A = \pi r^2$ to calculate the area of the circle.

$A = \pi r^2$

$A = 25\pi$ square inches

Since the radius of the circle is 5 inches, the diameter must be 10 inches. Thus, the area of the square is 100 square inches. Therefore, the difference between the area of the square and the area of the circle is $100 - 25\pi$ square inches.

44. K. Using the figures below, the volume of the open box is

$v = lwh = (4)(2x - 8)(x - 8) = 8x^2 - 96x + 256$ cubic inches

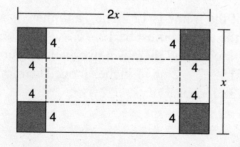

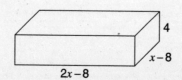

45. E. If two numbers differ by 4, then they can be represented by x and $x + 4$. The following equation shows the relationships given in the problem:

$$(x)(x + 4) = (4)(x + x + 4) - 4$$

$$x^2 + 4x = 8x + 16 - 4$$

$$x^2 - 4x - 12 = 0$$

$$(x - 6)(x + 2) = 0$$

Thus, the possible values for x are 6 and -2. If we use 6, we get 6 and 10 as the numbers. If we use -2, we get -2 and 2. Since the problem asked for positive numbers, we must use 6 and 10, making **E.** the correct choice.

46. K. The ratio of the areas of these circles is 1 to 2. Since the ratio of the areas of similar figures is the square of the ratio of corresponding linear measures, the ratio of the linear measures is 1 to $\sqrt{2}$. This simplifies as follows:

$$\left(\frac{r_1}{r_2}\right)^2 = \frac{A_1}{A_2} = \frac{1}{2} \Rightarrow \frac{r_1}{r_2} = \sqrt{\frac{1}{2}} = \frac{1}{\sqrt{2}} = \frac{\sqrt{2}}{2}$$

47. C. Take the natural log of both sides of the equation.

$$y = e^{2x}$$

$$ln\, y = ln(e^{2x})$$

$$ln\, y = 2x$$

$$^{ln\, y}\!/_2 = x$$

48. G. This problem involves scaler multiplication and subtraction of matrices. To multiply a matrix by a scaler, multiply each element in the matrix by the scaler. To subtract the results, subtract corresponding elements in the matrices.

$$2x - \frac{1}{2}y = 2\begin{bmatrix} -2 \\ 4 \end{bmatrix} - \frac{1}{2}\begin{bmatrix} -6 \\ -4 \end{bmatrix}$$

$$= \begin{bmatrix} -4 \\ 8 \end{bmatrix} - \begin{bmatrix} -3 \\ -2 \end{bmatrix}$$

$$= \begin{bmatrix} -1 \\ 10 \end{bmatrix}$$

49. C. Since $ab < 0$, a and b must be of opposite sign. Also, $2a - b > 0 \Rightarrow a > \frac{b}{2}$. If b is positive, then a would also be positive, giving both a and b the same sign. Thus, b must be negative, or $b < 0$.

50. K. Since $\sin A = \frac{x}{1} = \frac{opposite}{hypotenuse}$, let $\overline{BC} = x$ and $\overline{AB} = 1$. The missing side of the triangle is calculated using the Pythagorean theorem. Therefore,

$$\sin B = \frac{adjacent}{hypotenuse} = \frac{\sqrt{1 - x^2}}{1} = \sqrt{1 - x^2}$$

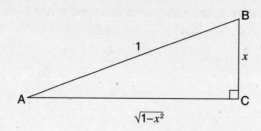

51. B. The graph of the cosine is the same as the graph of the sine, except that it is shifted $\frac{1}{2}\pi$ to the left. Thus, $\sin x = \cos\left(x - \frac{\pi}{2}\right)$. Therefore, $\sin\left(x + \frac{\pi}{4}\right) = \cos\left(x + \frac{\pi}{4} - \frac{\pi}{2}\right) = \cos\left(x - \frac{\pi}{4}\right)$

52. G. If a cube has a total surface area of 384 square meters, then each of the six square faces has an area of 64 square meters. Each edge is therefore 8 meters long. Using the Pythagorean theorem, we can find the length of a diagonal of one of the faces.

$d^2 = 8^2 + 8^2$

$d^2 = 128$

$d = \sqrt{128} = 8\sqrt{2}$

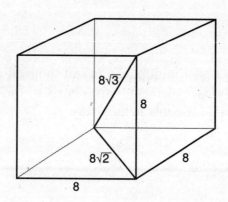

The main diagonal of the cube is the hypotenuse of a right triangle where one leg in an edge of the cube (8 meters) and the other leg is the diagonal of a face of the cube ($8\sqrt{2}$ meters). Using the Pythagorean theorem again, we can calculate the main diagonal.

$d^2 = 8^2 + \left(8\sqrt{2}\right)^2$

$d^2 = 64 + 128$

$d = \sqrt{192} = 8\sqrt{3}$ meters

53. D. First set up variables for each angle of the triangle.

smallest angle	=	$\frac{1}{3}x - 8$
second angle	=	x
third angle	=	$4(\frac{1}{3}x - 8) - 8$
	=	$\frac{4}{3}x - 40$

These three angles must add up to 180°.

$$(\tfrac{1}{3}x - 8) + (x) + (\tfrac{4}{3}x - 40) = 180$$
$$\tfrac{8}{3}x - 48 = 180$$
$$\tfrac{8}{3}x = 228$$
$$x = 85.5°$$

54. **J.** The total cost is made up of $8.00 per square yard for the carpet plus $2.00 per yard of perimeter. First find the total square yards in all the carpets.

$a = 2(5)(4) + 1(8)(5) + 3(10)(8) = 320$ square yards.

Then calculate the total perimeter of all the carpets.

$p = 2(18) + 1(26) + 3(36) = 170$ yards.

Then calculate the total cost.

$c = \$8.00(320) + \$2.00(170) = \$2,900.00$

55. **C.** First divide the total surface area by the number of cubes to determine the total surface area per cube.

$^{576}/_{24} = 24$

Since each cube has a total surface area of 24 square feet, each of its six faces must have an area of 4 square feet. Therefore, each cube is 2 feet on an edge. The rectangular solid is therefore 8 feet long, 6 feet wide, and 4 feet high. The total surface area of the rectangular solid is

$a = 2(8)(6) + 2(6)(4) + 2(8)(4) = 208$ square feet.

56. **H.** A single equation can be used to calculate the required amount.

$$80 = \frac{\big((6)(78) + 2(x)\big)}{8}$$
$$640 = (6)(78) + 2(x)$$
$$640 = 468 + 2x$$
$$172 = 2x$$
$$86 = x$$

57. **B.** First divide both sides of the equation by 100.

$$\frac{(x-4)^2}{5^2} + \frac{(y-2)^2}{2^2} = 11$$

From this form of the equation, we see that distance from the center of the ellipse to the end of the major axis is 5 units, and the distance from the center of the ellipse to the end of the minor axis is 2 units. Therefore, the difference in length between the major and minor axes is $10 - 4 = 6$ units.

58. **J.** This is a graph of the cosine function. It has an amplitude of 2 and a period of 2π. Therefore, answer choice **J.** is correct.

59. B. Calculate the slope of each line.

$$4x - ky = 6 \qquad\qquad 6x + ky = 8$$
$$-ky = -4x + 6 \qquad\qquad ky = -6x + 8$$
$$y = \tfrac{4}{k}x - \tfrac{6}{k} \qquad\qquad y = -\tfrac{6}{k}x + \tfrac{8}{k}$$

In order for these two lines to be perpendicular, their slopes must be negative reciprocals of each other. Thus

$$\tfrac{4}{k} = \tfrac{k}{6}$$
$$k^2 = 24$$
$$k = \sqrt{24}$$
$$k = \pm 2\sqrt{6}$$

Because we are looking for the maximum value for k, choice **B.** is correct.

60. H. A total of $2^4 = 16$ different combinations of outcomes are possible. The number of times exactly 2 heads appear can simply be counted. They could be coins 1 and 2, 1 and 3, 1 and 4, 2 and 3, 2 and 4, or 3 and 4. Thus, there are 6 different ways exactly 2 heads could appear. Therefore, the probability of having exactly 2 heads up when 4 coins are dropped (flipped) is $\tfrac{6}{16} = \tfrac{3}{8}$.

Answers to Reading Test

Passage I

1. **C.** **A.** and **D.** could be true, but nothing in the passage indicates that they are, whereas the narrator does mention that she had fought for months with her father about taking the lessons and also that Hazel hit her with a ruler. When choosing answers, be sure to base them on what the passage directly states or implies, not on what might simply seem plausible. **B.** is perhaps the second-best answer, but resentment of her father doesn't seem to be behind her rejection of Hazel, since she does agree to take lessons from Marian.

2. **F.** From what we learn about the narrator's father, this is the most likely reason. He is impressed by Marian Linden. **G.** is incorrect; Greta takes lessons from Hazel "free of charge." **H.** is also wrong; he throws her name around "as if he has known her all his life," but this happens even before he meets her. Finally, Mabel is his sister, not his wife, making **J.** incorrect.

3. **C.** See line 36. The suggestion is that she might normally sulk in this situation **A.**, but is "too awed" to do so. She shows no signs of excitement **B.** but rather sits stiffly in her chair. Although she does like Marian Linden's apartment, nothing indicates that she is suspicious of the woman **D.**

4. **F.** Notice the choice of the word "brazened." Also note that he has learned that face-to-face interviews are better than phone calls, indicating his confidence. Nothing in the passage suggests that he feels guilt **G.**; when the narrator tells him about Hazel, he is "curiously undisturbed." There is also no indication that he wants to be a pianist **H. J.** might seem a reasonable choice, but neither in these lines nor in the rest of the passage is there a suggestion that he is concerned about his daughter's self-confidence. He is wrapped up in his own self-image.

5. **B.** See lines 49–51. Although it appears Marian Linden is financially comfortable **A.** and intelligent **D.**, neither of these is as central to the description of her. The description of her appearance suggests that she is attractive, not beautiful **C.**, and, more importantly, her appearance is secondary to the dignity she projects.

6. **H.** The narrator says that it was hard to interpret Marian Linden's reactions; therefore, **F.**, **G.**, and **J.**, while theoretically plausible, are not indicated in the passage.

7. **D.** Notice the phrase "after watching him operate" (line 75). Also, see lines 79–83. The narrator mentions that perhaps she is accepted out of pity, but it is not because *she* has used it to manipulate people **B. C.** may be true but is not what the narrator means by "fraudulent means." **A.** is also perhaps tempting but again does not refer to the means by which the narrator gains admission.

8. **G.** See lines 86–88. The narrator "knows" her father is less than honest, but to admit that his gold mines and properties are "figments of his imagination" is to admit the family's life is based on illusions. **F.** and **H.** are not good answers because throughout the passage the narrator's feelings about her father are more complex than love and don't suggest respect. She is by turns insecure, confused, doubtful, and scornful. **J.** is not indicated anywhere in the passage.

9. **B.** There is no evidence for **C.** or **D.**, and **B.** is more likely than **A.**, based on the picture of the father in the passage.

10. **J.** Notice in lines 112–113 that she refers to the lessons as an "emotional oasis." Also see lines 117–125. While it is true that Marian Linden treats everyone with respect and that she has "no delusions" about the narrator's future, neither **F.** nor **G.** is as pertinent as **J. H.** is incorrect; it is a cliché that describes a situation typical of some television movies and is not indicated by anything in this passage.

Passage II

11. **D.** See lines 11–13. **C.** might appear correct, but the bill addressed wilderness areas, not specifically national parks. **A.** is clearly wrong; economic goals were irrelevant to the preservationists' view. **B.** is incorrect because the Forest Service already had the power to change policy, and the legislation would change that.

12. **G.** The reference to the post-Echo Park mood (confidence) suggests that Echo Park has been a victory for the cause. **F.** is the second-best choice, but "major political force" is too strong based on this passage. Whether or not **H.** and **J.** might be true is irrelevant; neither can reasonably be inferred from the passage.

13. **C.** It may appear at first that opponents would agree with all of these statements, but see lines 56–61. On the other hand, **A.**, **B.**, and **D.** are all either stated or implied in the passage.

14. **F.** This is a simple question of fact. See lines 82–85. **H.** is contradicted in lines 76–81.

15. **B.** See the comment by one of the legislation's supporters (lines 86–87). The passage doesn't imply that economic incentives have decreased **A.** — quite the contrary. Although **D.** might seem plausible, there is no evidence to support it. The passage doesn't suggest different levels of stress **C.** (and the people of the 1850s might well disagree with the statement).

16. **G.** One point in paragraph two is that opponents of the legislation reflected what the author calls ambivalence; appreciation of wilderness was "relatively new" in a country that prided itself on industrial progress. **F.** and **J.** are too strongly negative, and **H.** is unlikely.

17. **C.** The rigidity of the proposed system bothered opponents the most (lines 47–57). They were on the side of development, not against it **A.**, nor were they concerned with industries circumventing the law **D.** (They might, in fact, have been among those who would circumvent it if they could.) Although some opponents might agree with **B.**, this is not a point made in the passage.

18. **F.** The idea is that if land is taken over by the government, it should serve many purposes; it should not, as the opponents suggested this bill would do, preserve land for a small number of campers. The other answers do not address the issue of multiple-use of public lands.

19. **C.** Opponents of the bill felt it went too far, according to the passage. **A.** is far too extreme an answer, while **B.** was not the concern of most opponents. Although perhaps some preservationists would agree with **D.**, this is not suggested or implied in the passage.

20. **G.** The last paragraph suggests this answer. Preservationists talk about the right of future generations to "experience" wilderness, and perhaps more significantly, the importance of simply knowing that wilderness exists. This indicates that they are not thinking in terms of its usefulness in the sense implied by **F.** Also, the passage doesn't suggest that those supporting the wilderness system attached any abstract or symbolic qualities to it **H.**, or that its "historical significance" was their reason for wanting to preserve it.

Passage III

21. **D.** Science influenced art, but scientists and artists didn't "join forces" **A.** See lines 31–33. Neither was there an artistic backlash **B.**, according to the passage. **C.** might seem correct, but in addition to being overstated, it is also a secondary point.

22. **H.** Of the inferences represented here, it is the only one that can be clearly drawn from the passage. These men are listed with other important scientists of the period (lines 27–29). **F.** and **J.** are both incorrect; the use of "most important" is a clue. **G.** is not implied by information in the passage.

23. **A.** This is a question of fact (lines 8–10). The other artists are mentioned in the first paragraph, but Kandinsky is specifically linked to Abstractionism.

24. **G.** Both the dictionary definition of "cross-fertilize" and the information in the passage support this answer. "Cross-fertilize" does not refer to mutual influence **H.**, though the word may sound as if it would. **F.** and **J.** are not indicated in the passage.

25. **C.** Although "estranged" includes the word "strange," neither "foreign" **A.** nor "unusual" **D.** is a correct definition, nor does either fit the context effectively. **B.** is also inappropriate in context.

26. **F.** All the examples are of the use of the word "new." In lines 66–76, **G.** might be implied, but the examples chosen do not pertain to that point. **H.** is overstated, and **J.** is not a point made in the passage.

27. **D.** See lines 8–14 and lines 37–43. **A.** is contradicted, and **B.** is both too specific and an overstatement. Public reaction to any of the artistic movements is not covered in this passage **C.**

28. **F.** Geometric patterns **H.** are mentioned, but not in connection to modes of transportation, whereas the optical effects of speed are specifically cited. **G.** and **J.** are both irrelevant to the passage, even though they may seem true.

29. **A.** See lines 60–65. **B.** is irrelevant to the passage, and both **C.** and **D.** are overstatements.

30. **G.** Nothing implies that artists saw art as "inferior" to science. **F.**, **H.**, and **J.** are all stated or implied in the passage.

Passage IV

31. **B.** Although **A.** is suggested by the first paragraph, it is not the main idea. Nothing indicates that the author believes **C.**, and **D.** is an issue that isn't addressed.

32. **F.** A polarized debate is one between opposite positions. **G.**, which relates to batteries, doesn't fit the context here. **H.** and **J.** are not correct definitions of the word.

33. **D.** According to the passage, both uniformitarianists and gradualists view development as slow and steady, one in reference to geological development, the other in reference to evolutionary development. **A.** represents the opposite view of geological change. Although it is possible to see similarity between **B.** and the gradualists, the connection with **D.** is stronger.

34. **H.** See lines 20–25. **F.** and **G.** would both tend to support the punctuated equilibrium view. **J.** is irrelevant to the two theories; it is not covered in the passage.

35. **D.** This new hypothesis addressed the fact that many fossil species didn't change over millions of years, something that was previously recognized but ignored. **A.** is not a good choice; punctuated equilibrium is a "dramatic variation" of natural selection, not a refutation. **B.** and **C.** are simply incorrect.

36. **G.** "Equilibrium" may suggest balance **J.**, but that meaning is irrelevant here. **H.** supports the opposing theory, and **F.** doesn't apply to this issue.

37. **D.** **A.** might be tempting, but notice the use of the phrase "equally compelling evidence" (line 80).

38. **H.** The author specifically addresses his reason for using this example in lines 106–107. **G.** and **J.** might be true statements, but they are not the reason the author uses the example. **F.** is irrelevant to the passage.

39. **A.** See lines 126–131. **B.** is true, but not as significant to the evolutionary theory. Neither **C.** nor **D.** is supported in the passage.

40. **J.** See the last sentence of the passage. The author may seem to lean towards **F.**, but this is not the final point. **H.** isn't implied in the passage, and **G.** is inaccurate and, even if accurate, would not "prove" a theory.

Answers to Science Reasoning Test

Passage I

1. C. This question requires *first* determining which of the planets is farthest from the sun (relative to the Earth's distance from the sun), and *then* placing these planets in distance order from closest to farthest. In terms of Earth's distance to the sun, mean distances for Saturn, Uranus, Neptune, and Pluto are approximately 9.5, 19, 30, and 39.5, respectively. Therefore, **C.** is the correct answer.

2. F. This question requires careful reading. Note the question asks about distance from Earth, not distance from the sun. The relative distance from Earth of Venus is 1.0 minus 0.7 or 0.3, while the relative distance from Earth of Mars is 1.5 minus 1.0 or 0.5. Therefore, **F.** is the correct answer.

3. C. The relative surface gravity of Earth is 1.0. Relative to Earth's gravity, the surface gravity of Uranus is 1.05. Therefore, **C.** is the correct answer.

4. H. The smallest planet has the smallest mass. Relative to Earth's mass, the mass of Mercury is 0.054. The relative masses of all other planets are larger than this. Therefore, **H.** is the correct answer.

5. A. According to Table 2, the mass of the Earth is approximately 6×10^{27} grams. According to Table 1, the mass of Mars is approximately one-tenth that of Earth's mass. The mass of Mars is therefore 6×10^{26} grams. **A.** is the correct answer.

Passage II

6. G. This question requires careful reading. Note the question asks about experimental (not control) trials only. Between May 7 and 25, 1993, for the six activities measured, sixteen separate trials were conducted. Therefore, **F.** is the correct answer.

7. B. According to Table 1, ^{137}Cs concentration during resuspension by wind (control) is 0.54 mBq m^{-3}. Concentrations during the experimental trials ranged from 0.81 to 169.0 mBq m^{-3}. Therefore, **B.** is the correct answer.

8. F. The best approach to this question is to look at the data for activities that were tested more than once (for example, "plowing with small tractor" and "driving of one large truck"). Since date and time are descriptive rather than experimental variables, answers **H.** and **J.** can be eliminated. Of the remaining two experimental variables, values for friction velocity do not vary significantly within an activity. Wind velocity fluctuates the most, with higher wind speeds causing correspondingly higher concentrations of ^{137}Cs. Therefore, **F.** is the correct answer.

9. D. Results of the study suggest a direct relationship between soil-disturbing activities and an increase in atmospheric concentrations of resuspended radionuclides, especially ^{137}Cs. Wind speed data is provided, but transportation distances are not, so answer **B.** is incorrect. Similarly, answer **C.** is incorrect because the data clearly show that particle size of ^{137}Cs remains fairly constant across all activities (with the exception of outlier data for equipment assembly). Therefore, **D.** is the correct answer.

10. **J.** This study was conducted in a radiation-contaminated zone after a serious nuclear power plant accident. Specifically, it examined the relationship between atmospheric secondary contamination resulting from certain soil-management and transportation activities. Therefore, **J.** is the correct answer.

11. **B.** The mean diameters of ^{137}Cs for particulate resuspension, grass cutting, and small-tractor plowing are 5.6, 5.5, and 5.6–8.7, respectively. The mean diameter of ^{137}Cs for equipment assembly lies well outside this mean range at 13.8. Therefore, **B.** is the correct answer.

Passage III

12. **G.** Pro-HRT scientists admit that estrogen is involved in endometrial cancer. Con-HRT scientists admit that synthetic estrogen is involved in deaths by breast cancer. Both positions acknowledge estrogen is linked to some forms of cancer. Therefore, **G.** is the correct answer.

13. **A.** Pro-HRT scientists cite decreases in heart disease as a benefit of HRT. Con-HRT scientists cite significant increases in deaths by breast cancer as a cost of HRT. Therefore, **A.** is the correct answer.

14. **G.** In support of their arguments, Con-HRT scientists cite the high correlation between synthetic estrogens and breast cancer incidence. Xenoestrogen-containing pesticides are also involved in a range of medical conditions (including breast cancer). This research directly supports the Con-HRT position. Therefore, **G.** is the correct answer.

15. **B.** The Pro-HRT position acknowledges that two benefits of synthetic hormone use include a decrease in heart disease and a decrease in menopausal symptoms such as hot flashes. Therefore, **B.** is the correct answer.

16. **H.** The Pro-HRT position highlights decreases in osteoporosis and certain menopausal symptoms like hot flashes. The Con-HRT position highlights decreases in breast cancer incidence. Scientists from both positions would consequently be interested in uses of natural progesterone. Therefore, **H.** is the correct answer.

17. **B.** The Con-HRT position is interested in menopause without medicine, and would therefore be the position most interested in research on hormones produced from natural sources. If natural hormones were found to be linked directly to increases in female-reproductive system cancers, this would seriously weaken support for menopause without medicine. Therefore, **B.** is the correct answer.

18. **F.** The Pro-HRT position highlights that synthetic estrogens are linked to lowered risks associated with heart disease. If synthetic estrogens in birth control pills were found to be linked directly to increases in heart disease incidence, this would seriously weaken support for the Pro-HRT position. Therefore, **F.** is the correct answer.

Passage IV

19. **B.** According to the two figures, fluctuations in relaxation time (or discharge time) and current are measured for given periods of charging. Therefore, **B.** is the correct answer.

20. **J.** The passage text indicates that temperature, humidity, and relative darkness/lightness were kept constant to duplicate conditions inside an Oriental hornet nest found in nature. Therefore, **J.** is the correct answer.

21. **D.** Figure 1 shows relaxation time as a function of specific charging times. Eighteen hours of charging time corresponds with 1,080 minutes along the *x*-axis. The corresponding value on the *y*-axis is between 600 and 700 minutes, or greater than 10 hours. Therefore, **D.** is the correct answer.

22. **H.** Figure 1 shows a decrease in relaxation time for a charging time of between 240 and 360 minutes. Figure 2 shows an increase in current for a charging time of between 240 and 360 minutes. Therefore, **H.** is the correct answer.

23. **A.** From the passage text, one can infer that charging takes place in nature when the dark nest is exposed to ambient heat during summer days. Electrical discharge in the form of heat would be required, then, from sunset until dawn—when ambient temperatures are presumably below those found in the nest. Pupal silk, then, conducts energy beyond its immediate needs during the day for use later at night. Therefore, **A.** is the correct answer.

24. **J.** The passage text indicates that the Oriental hornet only builds its nest once per year during the hot summer months. Since these insects are not active during the winter, answers **F.**, **G.**, and **H.** can be eliminated. The study implies that the hornets are taking energy in the form of ambient summer air temperatures, converting it into stored electricity, and releasing it as heat when ambient air temperatures fall below the 30°C temperature range that is considered ideal in the nest—at night. Therefore, **J.** is the correct answer.

Passage V

25. **C.** According to Figure 1, the ratio (*R*) falls as frequency rises up to a frequency of 500 cps, which has a corresponding ratio of 1. Frequencies higher than 500 cps share the same ratio (*R*) of 1. The minimum frequency, then, is 500 cps. Therefore, **C.** is the correct answer.

26. **H.** None of the optimum reverberation time curves for the six different sounds/enclosures overlaps. And since the slope of all the curves is positive (where values along the *x*-axis and the *y*-axis both increase), it is apparent that the sound with the shortest ORT is speech while the sound with the longest ORT is church music. The ORT for movie theaters is actually shorter than the ORT for school auditoriums. Therefore, **H.** is the correct answer. (Note the EXCEPT.)

27. **C.** According to Figure 2, a room that is 100,000 cubic feet in volume with an optimum reverberation time of 2.0 seconds would be better suited for church music. Speech without a microphone will not be heard in such a room, for it will be too large for its intended purpose as a lecture hall. Therefore, **C.** is the correct answer.

28. **G.** The point on the curve for chamber music that corresponds with a *y*-axis value of 1.0 seconds is an *x*-axis value of 20,000 cubic feet. Therefore, **G.** is the correct answer.

29. **C.** The point on the curve for auditorium sounds that corresponds with an *x*-axis value of 90,000 cubic feet is a *y*-axis value of approximately 1.5 seconds. Therefore, **C.** is the correct answer.

Passage VI

30. **G.** The passage text clearly states that igneous rocks are formed from the cooling of magma. Therefore, following the corresponding direction of the arrows in the rock cycle diagram, **G.** is the correct answer.

31. **C.** The passage text clearly states that sedimentary rocks are formed first by the weathering and transport of existing igneous rocks, and second by the process of cementation. Therefore, following the corresponding direction of the arrows in the rock cycle diagram, **C.** is the correct answer.

32. **J.** The passage text clearly states that metamorphic rocks are formed by the application of heat or pressure to pre-existing rocks. Therefore, **J.** is the correct answer.

33. **B.** The passage text clearly states that igneous rocks are classified by mineral composition and grain (or texture). Therefore, **B.** is the correct answer.

34. **H.** The passage text clearly states that detrital sedimentary rocks have particles of differing size and shape that are cemented together. Therefore, **H.** is the correct answer.

35. **A.** Rabbits in Group 1 were not fitted with contact lenses, though corneal enzyme activity was documented for this group of rabbits. Therefore, **A.** is the correct answer.

36. **H.** Scientists recorded enzyme activity levels immediately upon removal of the contact lenses and five hours later in order to determine whether or not additional disturbances appear after lens removal. Therefore, **H.** is the correct answer.

37. **B.** In healthy corneas without contact lenses, activity levels of xanthine oxidase and catalase are present and high. Wearing contact lenses reduces the levels of catalase, resulting in an imbalance in the cornea between these two enzymes. Therefore, **B.** is the correct answer.

38 **H.** Treating eyes with catalase during lens use prevented the catalase activity levels from dropping. Treating eyes with 3-aminotriazole during lens use caused the activity levels to drop. Corneas treated with 3-aminotriazole were found upon the conclusion of the study to be inflamed. It can therefore be hypothesized that catalase can prevent some damage to the corneas. Therefore, **H.** is the correct answer.

39. **D.** Treating eyes with 3-aminotriazole during lens wear caused the activity levels of catalase to drop. These eyes were later found to be suffering from inflammation. It can therefore be hypothesized that the absence of catalase leads to the inflammation. Therefore, **D.** is the correct answer.

40. **H.** In corneas of the control group of rabbits, the enzymatic activity levels of catalase and xanthine oxidase were present and high. Therefore, **H.** is the correct answer.

The Final Touches

- Make sure that you are familiar with the testing center location and nearby parking facilities.

- The last week of preparation should be spent primarily on reviewing strategies, techniques, and directions for each area.

- Don't *cram* the night before the exam. It's a waste of time!

- Remember to bring the proper materials to the test — identification, admission ticket, three or four sharpened Number 2 pencils, a watch, a calculator, and a good eraser.

- Start off crisply, concentrating first on the items that you can do most easily, and then coming back and trying the others.

- If necessary, try to eliminate one or more of the choices, and then guess. There is no penalty for guessing, so answer every question.

- Mark in reading passages, underline key words, write out information, make notations on diagrams, take advantage of being permitted to write in the test booklet.

- Make sure that you are answering "what is being asked" and that your answer is reasonable.

- Using the "Four Successful Overall Approaches to Taking the ACT" (see the Introduction) is the key to getting the ones right that you should get right — resulting in a good score on the ACT.

CliffsNotes

LITERATURE NOTES

Absalom, Absalom!
The Aeneid
Agamemnon
Alice in Wonderland
All the King's Men
All the Pretty Horses
All Quiet on the Western Front
All's Well & Merry Wives
American Poets of the 20th Century
American Tragedy
Animal Farm
Anna Karenina
Anthem
Antony and Cleopatra
Aristotle's Ethics
As I Lay Dying
The Assistant
As You Like It
Atlas Shrugged
Autobiography of Ben Franklin
Autobiography of Malcolm X
The Awakening
Babbit
Bartleby & Benito Cereno
The Bean Trees
The Bear
The Bell Jar
Beloved
Beowulf
The Bible
Billy Budd & Typee
Black Boy
Black Like Me
Bleak House
Bless Me, Ultima
The Bluest Eye & Sula
Brave New World
The Brothers Karamazov
Call of the Wild & White Fang
Candide
The Canterbury Tales
Catch-22
Catcher in the Rye
The Chosen
The Color Purple
Comedy of Errors...
Connecticut Yankee
The Contender
The Count of Monte Cristo
Crime and Punishment
The Crucible
Cry, the Beloved Country
Cyrano de Bergerac
Daisy Miller & Turn...Screw
David Copperfield
Death of a Salesman
The Deerslayer
Diary of Anne Frank
Divine Comedy-I. Inferno
Divine Comedy-II. Purgatorio
Divine Comedy-III. Paradiso
Doctor Faustus

Dr. Jekyll and Mr. Hyde
Don Juan
Don Quixote
Dracula
Electra & Medea
Emerson's Essays
Emily Dickinson Poems
Emma
Ethan Frome
The Faerie Queene
Fahrenheit 451
Far from Madding Crowd
A Farewell to Arms
Farewell to Manzanar
Fathers and Sons
Faulkner's Short Stories
Faust Pt. I & Pt. II
The Federalist
Flowers for Algernon
For Whom the Bell Tolls
The Fountainhead
Frankenstein
The French Lieutenant's Woman
The Giver
Glass Menagerie & Streetcar
Go Down, Moses
The Good Earth
Grapes of Wrath
Great Expectations
The Great Gatsby
Greek Classics
Gulliver's Travels
Hamlet
The Handmaid's Tale
Hard Times
Heart of Darkness & Secret Sharer
Hemingway's Short Stories
Henry IV Part 1
Henry IV Part 2
Henry V
House Made of Dawn
The House of the Seven Gables
Huckleberry Finn
I Know Why the Caged Bird Sings
Ibsen's Plays I
Ibsen's Plays II
The Idiot
Idylls of the King
The Iliad
Incidents in the Life of a Slave Girl
Inherit the Wind
Invisible Man
Ivanhoe
Jane Eyre
Joseph Andrews
The Joy Luck Club
Jude the Obscure
Julius Caesar
The Jungle
Kafka's Short Stories
Keats & Shelley
The Killer Angels
King Lear
The Kitchen God's Wife
The Last of the Mohicans

Le Morte Darthur
Leaves of Grass
Les Miserables
A Lesson Before Dying
Light in August
The Light in the Forest
Lord Jim
Lord of the Flies
Lord of the Rings
Lost Horizon
Lysistrata & Other Comedies
Macbeth
Madame Bovary
Main Street
The Mayor of Casterbridge
Measure for Measure
The Merchant of Venice
Middlemarch
A Midsummer-Night's Dream
The Mill on the Floss
Moby-Dick
Moll Flanders
Mrs. Dalloway
Much Ado About Nothing
My Ántonia
Mythology
Narr. ...Frederick Douglass
Native Son
New Testament
Night
1984
Notes from Underground
The Odyssey
Oedipus Trilogy
Of Human Bondage
Of Mice and Men
The Old Man and the Sea
Old Testament
Oliver Twist
The Once and Future King
One Day in the Life of Ivan Denisovich
One Flew Over the Cuckoo's Nest
100 Years of Solitude
O'Neill's Plays
Othello
Our Town
The Outsiders
The Ox-Bow Incident
Paradise Lost
A Passage to India
The Pearl
The Pickwick Papers
The Picture of Dorian Gray
Pilgrim's Progress
The Plague
Plato's Euthyphro...
Plato's The Republic
Poe's Short Stories
A Portrait of the Artist...
The Portrait of a Lady
The Power and the Glory
Pride and Prejudice
The Prince
The Prince and the Pauper
A Raisin in the Sun

The Red Badge of Courage
The Red Pony
The Return of the Native
Richard II
Richard III
The Rise of Silas Lapham
Robinson Crusoe
Roman Classics
Romeo and Juliet
The Scarlet Letter
A Separate Peace
Shakespeare's Comedies
Shakespeare's Histories
Shakespeare's Minor Plays
Shakespeare's Sonnets
Shakespeare's Tragedies
Shaw's Pygmalion & Arms...
Silas Marner
Sir Gawain...Green Knight
Sister Carrie
Slaughterhouse-Five
Snow Falling on Cedars
Song of Solomon
Sons and Lovers
The Sound and the Fury
Steppenwolf & Siddhartha
The Stranger
The Sun Also Rises
T.S. Eliot's Poems & Plays
A Tale of Two Cities
The Taming of the Shrew
Tartuffe, Misanthrope...
The Tempest
Tender Is the Night
Tess of the D'Urbervilles
Their Eyes Were Watching God
Things Fall Apart
The Three Musketeers
To Kill a Mockingbird
Tom Jones
Tom Sawyer
Treasure Island & Kidnapped
The Trial
Tristram Shandy
Troilus and Cressida
Twelfth Night
Ulysses
Uncle Tom's Cabin
The Unvanquished
Utopia
Vanity Fair
Vonnegut's Works
Waiting for Godot
Walden
Walden Two
War and Peace
Who's Afraid of Virginia...
Winesburg, Ohio
The Winter's Tale
The Woman Warrior
Worldly Philosophers
Wuthering Heights
A Yellow Raft in Blue Water